T0372678

THE CAMBRIDGE HANDBOOK OF COMMONS RESEARCH INNOVATIONS

The commons theory, first articulated by Elinor Ostrom, is increasingly used as a framework to understand and rethink the management and governance of many kinds of shared resources. These resources can include natural and digital properties, cultural goods, knowledge and intellectual property, and housing and urban infrastructure, among many others. In a world of increasing scarcity and demand—from individuals, states, and markets—it is imperative to understand how best to induce cooperation among users of these resources in ways that advance sustainability, affordability, equity, and justice. This volume reflects this multifaceted and multidisciplinary field from a variety of perspectives, offering new applications and extensions of the commons theory, which is as diverse as the scholars who study it and is still developing in exciting ways.

SHEILA R. FOSTER is a Professor of Law and Public Policy at Georgetown University and is an award-winning authority on environmental and climate justice, urban governance, and racial inequality. Foster has served as the co-director LabGov, chair of the Global Parliament of Mayors advisory committee, and a member of the New York City's Mayors Panel on Climate Change.

CHRYSTIE F. SWINEY is an attorney, legal scholar, and political scientist with an expertise in international and human rights law. She holds graduate degrees from Harvard Law, Oxford, and Georgetown, and has worked in international development for over a decade. Chrystie is a widely published author, with works including a book on the global spread of restrictive NGO laws.

The Cambridge Handbook of Commons Research Innovations

Edited by

SHEILA R. FOSTER

Georgetown University School of Law

CHRYSTIE F. SWINEY

Georgetown University School of Law

Shaftesbury Road, Cambridge CB2 8EA, United Kingdom

One Liberty Plaza, 20th Floor, New York, NY 10006, USA

477 Williamstown Road, Port Melbourne, VIC 3207, Australia

314–321, 3rd Floor, Plot 3, Splendor Forum, Jasola District Centre, New Delhi – 110025, India

103 Penang Road, #05–06/07, Visioncrest Commercial, Singapore 238467

Cambridge University Press is part of Cambridge University Press & Assessment,
a department of the University of Cambridge.

We share the University's mission to contribute to society through the pursuit of
education, learning and research at the highest international levels of excellence.

www.cambridge.org
Information on this title: www.cambridge.org/9781009295710

DOI: 10.1017/9781108938617

First published 2022
First paperback edition 2023

A catalogue record for this publication is available from the British Library

Library of Congress Cataloging-in-Publication data
NAMES: Celebrating Commons Scholarship (Conference) (2018 : Georgetown University School of Law) | Foster, Sheila
R., 1963– editor. | Swiney, Chrystie Flournoy, 1979– editor.
TITLE: The Cambridge handbook of commons research innovations / edited by Sheila R. Foster, Georgetown University
School of Law; Chrystie F. Swiney, Georgetown University School of Law.
DESCRIPTION: Cambridge, United Kingdom ; New York, NY : Cambridge University Press, 2021. | Series: Cambridge
law handbooks | "This book grew out of a conference organized in 2018 to mark the fiftieth anniversary of Garrett
Hardin's The Tragedy of the Commons, one of the the most cited articles of the 20th century. The conference was less a
celebration of the substance of Hardin's essay than an acknowledgment of how it has shaped a half decade of research
and theory. The conference, held at Georgetown University's Law Center in Washington D.C"–ECIP
acknowledgement. | Includes bibliographical references and index.
IDENTIFIERS: LCCN 2021006931 (print) | LCCN 2021006932 (ebook) | ISBN 9781108837217 (hardback) | ISBN
9781108938617 (epub)
SUBJECTS: LCSH: Commons–Congresses. | Natural resources, Communal–Congresses. | Common heritage of
mankind (International law)–Congresses. | Sociological jurisprudence–Congresses. | Hardin, Garrett, 1915-2003. The
tragedy of the commons–Congresses.
CLASSIFICATION: LCC K756.A6 C45 2021 (print) | LCC K756.A6 (ebook) | DDC 333.2–dc23
LC record available at https://lccn.loc.gov/2021006931
LC ebook record available at https://lccn.loc.gov/2021006932s

ISBN   978-1-108-83721-7   Hardback
ISBN   978-1-009-29571-0   Paperback

Cambridge University Press & Assessment has no responsibility for the persistence
or accuracy of URLs for external or third-party internet websites referred to in this
publication and does not guarantee that any content on such websites is, or will
remain, accurate or appropriate.

Contents

Figures

Tables

Contributors

Robert Haskell Abrams

Hope M. Babcock

Barbara L. Bezdek

William Blomquist

Greg Bloom

Rebecca Bratspies

Bryan Bruns

Brigham Daniels

Anthony J. DeMattee

Alexandra Flynn

Andrew P. Follet

David M. Forman

Sheila Foster

Maija Halonen-Akatwijuka

Blake Hudson

Christian Iaione

Itzchak E. Kornfeld

Sheldon Bernard Lyke

Herbert Toledo Martins

Sofia Croso Mazzuco

Andrea McArdle

Pradeep Kumar Mishra

Elena De Nictolis

Erik Nordman

Daniel Ogbaharya

Evagelos Pafilis

Taylor Petersen

John Powell

Angie Raymond

Michelle Reddy

Haim Sandberg

Scott J. Shackelford

Fernando Rios de Souza

Chrystie Swiney

Introduction

Commons Research in the Twenty-Frist Century and Beyond

Sheila R. Foster & Chrystie F. Swiney

This book grew out of a conference organized in 2018 to mark the fiftieth anniversary of Garrett Hardin's *The Tragedy of the Commons*, one of the the most cited articles of the twentieth century. The conference was less a celebration of the substance of Hardin's essay than an acknowledgment of how it has shaped half a decade of research and theory. The conference, held at Georgetown University's Law Center in Washington, DC, brought together nearly fifty researchers from over twenty different nations to present their research on a wide variety of interdisciplinary and transdisciplinary perspectives on the "commons." The scope and depth of research presented at this conference could hardly have been imagined by Garrett Hardin when he published his essay in 1968. Nor could he have imagined that the first woman to win the Nobel Prize in Economic Science, Elinor Ostrom, would debunk the central assumption underlying his famous essay – that shared resources must be either privatized or heavily regulated in order to prevent their depletion. In many ways, however, Ostrom revived what might have been a waning theory and field by setting in motion a whole new line of inquiry and research empirically demonstrating the variety of ways that resource users and communities come together to cooperatively utilize and sustainably manage shared resources.

As this eclectic volume illustrates, the concept of the "commons" has dramatically expanded to include many kinds of shared resources, both physical and virtual, in addition to a variety of other topics, including the global atmosphere, cities and urban infrastructure, neighborhoods and community gardens, technology and software, knowledge sharing and data networks, civil society organizations and humanitarian aid, among others. The body of research that now broadly falls under the category of "commons literature" is, needless to say, both vast and diverse, defying traditional categories and even Ostrom's original conceptualization of the parameters of her research agenda.

For much of the latter half of the twentieth century, Hardin's *Tragedy* was the starting point for many researchers thinking about the social dilemmas characterizing depletable, open access resources. Hardin's stylized tale of tragedy unfolds in the context of a "pasture open to all" on which each individual herdsman is motivated by self-interest to continue adding cattle until the combined actions of all the herdsman result in overgrazing, eventually depleting the resource. While Hardin was not the first to note that self-interest can result in collective failure, he provided a memorable parable that elegantly illustrated how individualistic-minded motivations can destroy or deplete shared resources. As Hardin summed up his core insight, "freedom in the commons" – or unregulated and open access too a shared resource – "brings ruin to all." Absent a system of private enterprise or government control (i.e., allocation of use and other rights), it would be difficult, if not impossible, to avert this tragic result. Individual users of a commons will always fully exploit their access to shared resources to their advantage, according to Hardin, while absorbing only a small fraction of the marginal cost of that use.

Since its publication, Hardin's article has gained impressive traction with a broad range of scholars from across the globe in diverse fields of study. For many years after its publication, the concept of the "commons" was consonant with Hardin's open pasture where everyone had rights of inclusion and no one had rights of exclusion. These "common pool resources," as they came to be known, are characterized by the difficulty of excluding users from them ("nonexcludability") and the potential for overconsumption ("rivalrousness"), meaning that one user's share or consumption of the good diminishes the availability of that good to others. Many scholars, and this is particularly true of legal scholars, have tended to hew very closely to these neo classical economic assumptions when analyzing resource dilemmas or problems through the lens of the commons. These scholars start from the idea that the commons, or common pool resource, is an unrestricted and unregulated open access resource that allows uncoordinated actors to overconsume or over exploit a resource. They then proceed to analyze the collective action problems that beset these resources and propose solutions to avoid "tragic" outcomes.

The year 2020 marks the thirtieth anniversary of Elinor Ostrom's seminal book, *Governing the Commons: The Evolution of Institutions for Collective Action.* In this influential work, Ostrom challenged the core assumption underlying Hardin's *Tragedy* by refuting the view that individuals cannot collectively come together and manage common pool resources sustainably without resorting to either a system of public regulation or private property rights. Ostrom's research revealed that many social groups and communities around the world, in entirely different contexts and focused on entirely different resources, have successfully averted the Hardinian curse pertaining to shared resources by developing and maintaining self-governing institutions. She identified a number of these self-organized resource governance regimes, including common lands governed by local village communities in Switzerland and Japan, irrigation communities in Spain and the Philippines, as well as other examples of fisheries and irrigation projects managed communally in Turkey, California, and Sri Lanka. Many of these have survived for multiple generations and involved the investment of significant resources by the participants involved, who together designed basic rules to structure their interactions and usage of the shared resource, created organizations to manage and oversee the resource, held each other accountable through collective monitoring, and enforced collectively agreed-upon norms to reduce the probability of free-riding.

Ostrom's groundbreaking work spawned an explosion of research and a dedicated community of "commons" scholars following in her methodological footsteps. These scholars continue to test and extend Ostrom's "design principles," originally applied to successful commons institutions, to a range of new geographical and resource settings. They also utilize Ostrom's Institutional Analysis and Development (IAD) framework, which predated her work on common pool resources, to analyze collective action situations with a focus on institutions involving multiple actors. The IAD framework includes both "endogenous" (internal) and "exogenous" (external) variables that can influence how well individuals cooperate together, and act collectively, to achieve shared goals for both themselves and their communities in light of social dilemmas and biophysical constraints. The IAD framework was later expanded into Ostrom's social-ecological system (SES) framework, a fuller elaboration of the relevant contextual variables that contribute to collective action situations involving multiple actors. The IAD and SES frameworks continue to be used by scholars to examine case studies of lobster fisheries, forests, irrigation systems, grazing pastures, and other scarce, congestible, and nonrenewable natural resources.

The literature on collectively governed natural "common pool" resources has spawned, over time, further refinements of Ostrom's methodological frameworks as scholars have sought to apply her insights to other communities and new situations across the world. Ostrom and others are credited with opening up a healthy cross-disciplinary conversation and embrace of multiple research methods, including the case and field studies used by Ostrom, in addition to laboratory and field experiments, game theory and agent-based models to test and understand the conditions under which cooperation between different actors is possible and can be sustained. There is now a robust literature on the commons building on the incredible legacy left by Ostrom, and her many collaborators, pushing the boundaries of old and "new" common pool resources and the challenges they face in terms of conceptual clarity, institutional design, technological advancements, and various kinds of new governance dilemmas. The emerging literature on the knowledge commons and urban commons, for instance, not only explore the ways that Ostrom's design principles and IAD framework apply to different kinds of resources, but they expand and redefine our very understanding of "resources" anew. These newer interpretations and forms of commons challenge the characteristics of traditional CPRs. They can, for example, more closely resemble traditional non scarce, non rivalrous public goods (e.g., highways, transportation systems, public schools) than potentially endangered natural resources.

Applying commons theory to new and different contexts opens up a whole new range of theoretical and applied questions, in addition to highlighting new social dilemmas and institutional questions that give rise to new normative implications not previously considered or even imagined. Conceptualizing urban assets, neighborhood institutions, or civil society organizations as a commons, for example, raises important questions about the state's role in incentivizing the production and governance of shared goods and services, and the nature and size of the community that engages in collective action. Thinking about data and information as pooled resources opens up a new set of questions about the role of producers of goods that are not naturally existing, and the interplay between open access resources and the role of property rights in designing well-functioning innovation systems.

Given the robust literature on the increasing heterogeneity of the commons, and the various ways in which researchers continue to expand Ostrom's work beyond natural resources, one might wonder whether the conceptual boundaries of the commons have been stretched to their full potential, and perhaps even beyond the point of a coherent definition or methodological approach. We think not. This volume illustrates that the field continues to change and evolve without losing the core research questions that decades of commons scholars have wrestled with. At the same time, while the new and evolving contexts to which commons theory is applied and adapted may not stretch the original concept past its breaking point, they do enlarge the empirical and normative space in which researchers and practitioners locate new social dilemmas and identify new responses and solutions to those dilemmas. As such, we can now distinguish between two kinds of evolution, or innovations, in commons research, both of which are represented in this book. The first kind of innovation, as mentioned, involves the extension of existing commons definitions and methodological frameworks to different kinds of goods and resources, which involves adapting the original frameworks and principles to new challenges and dilemmas. The second kind of innovation, which is potentially more disruptive to the existing conceptions and frameworks, attempts to apply the original concepts to new social, political, and economic contexts that yield new dimensions to our understanding of the term "commons."

Consider two examples in contemporary commons literature that illustrate the latter kind of evolution or innovation. The first example is the normative valence that the term "commons" is associated with in certain academic disciplines and by some scholars and activists. The language of the commons has been taken up by activists, progressive thinkers, and scholars around the world to intervene in what many consider the excessive commodification and privatization of resources and goods. The language of the "commons" is deployed to bring under scrutiny the ways that modern capitalism has resulted in the enclosure by elites of many shared resources – i.e., public water or utility systems, vacant land, housing, information and data – that should be left in the public domain, accessible to the public, and not privatized. For example, the Italian movement known as "benicomunismo," which roughly translates as "commonism," was centered initially around a national referendum on "water as a commons." This movement was triggered by a national government measure that would allow local public services and utilities (including the integrated water system) to be auctioned off on the market, where private corporations could bid on them. After the proposal's defeat, the movement took further root throughout Italy through occupation by activists of abandoned and underutilized cultural structures, such as theaters. These structures, most famously the Teatro Valle in Rome, were inhabited and revived in an effort to retain these spaces for communal or public use. The occupations were in response to the state's threat to privatizate them; occupation of the structures by activists, academics, and others was intended to "recover people's possession" of these public structures and "open up" these spaces for the flourishing of common goods like culture.

This more normative strain of the commons literature is particularly present in the burgeoning literature on the urban commons. Thinking of the city as a commons, argues architect Stavros Stavrides, supports the idea that urban dwellers should appropriate or reclaim public space as a commons through "collective inventiveness," which requires resistance to the idea that cities are sites of capital production and surplus. The commons, according to these scholars, must be "wrenched" from the capitalist landscape of cities out of fear that collective resources are always susceptible to being co-opted by the market. The roots of progressive reformers' commons analysis is traceable in part to the work of Michael Hardt and Anthony Negri (2009), who refer to the "common," rejecting the term "commons" as a reference to "pre-capitalist shared spaces that were destroyed by the advent of private property." Cities are "to the multitude what the factory was to the industrial working class," they argue. In other words, it is the "factory for the production of the common," a means of producing common wealth." The commons thus becomes a collective claim to property in neighborhoods and communities as a response to the appropriation and enclosure of those places through private property rights. The poor have a right "not to be excluded" from the property of the city, argue property scholars who embrace this vision of cities as composed of common property. As such, they should be able to claim streets, parks, and buildings, among other resources, over which they have a legitimate interest.

The second example illustrating evolution of the term "commons" is the transformation of the word from a noun into a verb – "commoning" – to mark a turn away from the IAD and SES frameworks that Ostrom and many of her academic followers applied. Here we see a shift from a focus on studying collective forms of governance toward a focus on community and communal social development. For some scholars like Peter Linebaugh, "commoning" is a process – i.e., the social process of users in the course of managing shared resources and reclaiming to understand commons as socially produced. That is, commons are created, used, preserved, and managed by some collection of people in community with each other. In his words, "there is no commons without commoning." Commons theorists David Bollier and Silke Helfrich further build out the idea of commoning to argue that the commons is an ongoing social process and practice involving human interaction and social relations within communities – whether they be physical or digital communities. They understand commons as a blend or co-mingling of a physical (or digital or natural) resource with "social practice and diverse forms of institutionalization." Commoning thus describes the bottom-up practice of collectively creating or constructing resources and begins with the internal work that a community of users must do to create new common goods. This conceptualization then expands to develop the capacity for collective management of existing resources based on strong cooperative norms and shared goals. In this sense, commoning is highly pragmatic, involving the establishment of rules and conditions, and in some cases institutions, for collectively sharing resources among a defined social group or group of users.

Amanda Hurons' rich account of tenant organizing in Washington, DC to create limited equity, cooperatively owned housing, in response to displacement from their neighborhood as land values rise and landlords' attempt to extract higher rent, is the first book length account to focus on "commoning" dynamics in thick social and economic contexts. For years, tenants across the city worked together to pool their money to purchase their apartment buildings so that they could remain in place and exercise control over the increasingly scarce resource of affordable housing. To create and sustain this collectively owned and controlled resource, however, residents who were often strangers to each other (and did not even speak the same language in some cases) had to create their own governing structures, negotiate with city officials, locate financing, work collaboratively to repair and remodel their aging buildings, write bylaws for making decisions, and decide on rules of access and exclusion (i.e., who is and is not allowed to buy into the coops). Huron describes the creation of these urban commons as "unintentional" in the sense that the residents involved were not seeking to create common interest communities nor to create a new institution to democratically govern themselves and their shared resource. These were essentially strangers coming together – tenants who happened to live in the same community – united by the shared pressure and challenge of a housing crisis. Commoning is one option among a limited array of options, she argues, for people without access to capital and where pure economic self-interest is not driving the creation of the commons. Constructed commons, like those the housing coops described above, can create and support new kinds of collaborative economies that promote community stability, control, and affordability over the long term.

These two examples of the kinds of innovation in commons research and theory demonstrate the wide lane available for scholars who find new arenas, and new dimensions, to collective action and shared resource challenges that could benefit from the insights of the rich literature on the commons. This book demonstrates that innovation in commons scholarship need not mean stretching the concept of the commons beyond the core research questions that traditionally defined it, and fueled Ostrom's own work. The authors in this volume instead represent the kind of influence that both Hardin and Ostrom continue to have on understanding the variety of resource dilemmas that exist in different contexts, and the conditions for effective collective action to overcome those dilemmas through social norms, rules, and institutional arrangements. In other words, while the research questions remain much the same, the contexts in which scholars and researchers are asking them, as this book illustrates, continue to evolve.

In Part I of the book, *Revisiting the Origins and Evolution of Commons Thought*, the contributing authors offer unique perspectives on Hardin, Ostrom and their contributions over time and as applied and understood today. William Blomquist argues that innovations in commons research and extensions of the commons framework have moved far beyond the archetypal village grazing pasture. The dynamism of the field may therefore prompt some reflection on what "commons theory" or "the commons framework" means in non-territorially bounded commons. Fortunately, the origins of Elinor Ostrom's framework are compatible with such innovations and extensions; indeed, reexamining the line of inquiry that gave rise to the Ostrom framework may benefit those working now on the field's research frontiers. A political scientist, Ostrom was principally concerned throughout her career – and acutely in the period leading to Governing the Commons – with how people manage (and sometimes fail) to organize the governance of anything by creating and modifying institutional arrangements for coordinating their behavior and pursuing shared goals. In this chapter, those original questions that animated Ostrom's work are reconsidered for the insights they can provide for current innovations in commons research.

Andrew P. Follet, Brigham Daniels, Taylor Petersen unpacks Garrett Hardin's Tragedy of the Commons by explaining how the controversial views of its complicated author and the explosive time in which Garrett Hardin wrote his landmark essay. They note that Hardin is a complicated figure. His core argument in The Tragedy of the Commons, often excerpted out of many anthologies, is an argument for population control. While others advocated for population control, Hardin's particular views veered from the mainstream, and incorporated aspects that both at his time and today would be considered racist and xenophobic. Given the controversial author taking on a challenging subject, it is quite surprising that the essay got the reception it did. In addition to the essay's merits, it had great timing, launched precisely when the environmental movement neared its tipping point and just before his most controversial idea – population control – was about to enter the public realm as a serious matter of debate.

Haim Sandberg challenges a key precondition for sustaining commons institutions – tight-knit communities. This is the kind of "kinship" that seems to be present in so many of Ostrom's examples of successful commons institutions. The chapter explores kinship and the Commons through the lens of Israel's Bedouin Experience. Sandberg argues that the gradual transformation of traditional nomadic societies into modern urban societies reflects a major change that has weakened the ability of kinship relations to serve as a social incentive to support sustainable common property regimes resulting in the fostering of a modern urban tragedy of the commons. The scholarly debate between Hardin and Ostrom on the most effective form of regulation of common property, he argues, is an effort both to identify and to influence the path of human evolution. The chapter illuminates this debate by analyzing both theories of social evolution and examining closely the urbanization processes undergone by Bedouin society in Israel. It highlights the link between strong tribal kinship relations and sustainable management of the commons, showing how the weakening of blood ties reduces the incentive to cooperate. It raises the question whether societies in which kinship ties have become less powerful can still produce strong enough incentives for collaboration.

Part II of the book, *Averting New Tragedies*, considers previously unexplored or particularly vexing common pool resource dilemmas that could lead to tragic outcomes, and novel ways to potentially avoid those tragedies. Greg Bloom explores the way that community resource directory data comprises information about the accessibility of health, human, and social services that are available to people in need. Such services are provided by a disjointed landscape of governments, non profit organizations, contractors, and other civic institutions. A market of "infomediaries" aggregate this information manually, for private use in their proprietary channels, making it available for other uses only as a commodity to be sold. The result is a digital anti-commons, in which resource data is simultaneously overproduced and underutilized. This tragedy causes various kinds of systemic dysfunction across the so-called safety net. He outlines strategic interventions pursued through the Open Referral Initiative – including development of data exchange standards, open source infrastructural tools, a community of practice, and sustainable business models and associated methods of pre-competitive cooperation that can effectively provision community resource directory information as open data.

Blake Hudson argues that the resource management complications posed by "Temporal Commons" – the common pool of time shared by present and future generations when making resource management decisions – are understudied in the literature. The chapter describes their nature, before detailing how the typical solutions to the tragedy of the commons – private property, government regulation, and Elinor Ostrom's successful collective action model – fail to adequately account for temporal commons. The chapter also explores some factors that distinguish temporal commons from traditionally studied commons, making them subject to a potentially more inevitable form of tragedy. The chapter concludes with initial thoughts on avenues for better addressing the dilemmas created by temporal commons.

Bryan Burns analyzes the transformation of climate dilemmas from tragedy to cooperation through application of the prisoner's dilemma game, which provides an elementary two-person model of the social dilemma situation at the heart of the tragedy of the commons, where incentives discourage cooperation that could be better for everyone. The chapter explores solutions for "changing the game," turning a social dilemma into a win-win situation, and the implications for crafting cooperation in commons. He proposes that solutions to commons problems can work by changing a Prisoner's Dilemma incentive structure into a Stag Hunt where cooperation is a win-win equilibrium. However, Stag Hunt is still a social dilemma with an assurance problem where choosing the cooperative option risks getting the worst outcome, if the other person does not also cooperate. So, distrust and a desire to avoid the worst outcome (maximizing the minimum payoff) could lead to an inferior equilibrium where everyone is worse off than they might have been. Changes that switch the rank of the two lowest-ranked outcomes turn Stag Hunt into a harmonious game of Concord, also known as No Conflict, where all the incentives align to encourage cooperation.

In Part III, *New Forms of Contested Commons*, the authors probe new social and economic dilemmas attendant to some forms of shared but contested resources. In each of the chapters, the authors utilize insights from the commons to intervene in tensions between private and public roles, and individual and community interests, in managing shared resources. Andrea McArdle applies commons theory to public housing in the United States, which, despite decades of disinvestment and mismanagement, remains a significant community asset serving affordable housing needs. Using New York City's embattled Housing Authority (NYCHA), the nation's largest public housing agency, as a case study, the chapter argues that public housing, though not a classic common pool resource, serves a broad swath of vulnerable urban residents and can be reimagined under an urban commons framework. Doing so ensures that, in a time of transitioning uses of public housing assets, residents have meaningful input concerning disposition of space within public housing campuses. The democratizing implications of commons theory respond to NYCHA residents' essential exclusion (despite requirements in federal law) from revenue-driven decisions increasing private developers' control over NYCHA properties through long-term leases and public–private partnerships. Grounded in residents' urban knowledge, experience, and need, and informed by the social function of property theory, applying commons principles adds normative and theoretical heft to residents' equitable stake in decisions concerning public housing's increasingly threatened spaces.

Michelle Reddy extends the concept of the commons to humanitarian aid as a shared and contested common resource. Acknowledging that much of the commons literature focuses on collaborative governance of environmental resources, she argues that due to the pressures of climate change, the number of natural disasters will only increase, and humanitarian crises are already on an uptake. She cites as an example the 2013–2016 West Africa Ebola Epidemic, which occurred along the border of three countries with different institutional histories. Drawing on interviews with 100 civil society organizations and domestic NGOs, Reddy illustrates how top-down management of the 2013–2016 Ebola Response by governmental and international organizations led to policy failure, only until local organizations were involved. Ebola unveils the inefficiency of neglecting local actors, typical in international humanitarian response. In addition, contestation of humanitarian aid resources viewed as "commons" by recipients and "private" by international aid organizations fuels tensions in the aid relationship, and particularly during a crisis where local buy-in is essential.

John Powell explores the economic system as a "co-created" commons. He argues that while we all share the institutional arrangements that generate economic benefits, neither the wealth generated by the system, nor the negative impacts, are shared equally. The result is an economic system focused on the privatisation of shared resources that generates inequalities around the globe. His chapter brings together two broad strands of literature on commons: one arising from the public trust doctrine, and the other based on the economic characteristics of a good or service in terms of its access ("excludability") and consumption ("subtractability"). Powell links these concepts with more recent work on "productive commons," where shared resources are generated through collaborative activity, and ideas from evolutionary economics, which explore the economic system as a process and structure of rules, rather than as a series of transactions based on the allocation of property rights. Evidence is provided to support the argument that commons are an integral element of the economic system, and as a result account for some of its efficiencies and, where rule structures fail, for negative impacts on socio economic and ecological systems.

Part IV, *Urban Landscape and Infrastructure as a Commons*, is dedicated to exploring an emerging and robust literature on the urban commons and the idea of the city as a commons. Can we conceptualize some urban assets and shared resources in cities differently and, if so, how might it change the management and governance of those resources and the democratic character of cities themselves? Rebecca Bratspies embraces the urban forest as an urban commons – a site of public contestation, agency and public management. While forests are among the most classic common resources, urban forests are generally not thought of as forests or even as collective goods. Instead, street trees are typically perceived as individual trees, separate and atomized from each other. She notes, however, that some urban policymakers manage their trees as a publicly owned, publicly designed forest and that the value of trees in the urban context support this view. Urban trees are increasingly viewed as mitigating some of the most negative environmental impacts of urbanization, in addition to their positive aesthetic, psychological, sociological, and spiritual impacts. Bratspies concludes that it is past time to think of the urban forest as a commons. This chapter begins that task by laying out the case for rethinking the urban forest, treating it as a unified public commons, and involving citizens in managing that commons.

Elena De Nictolis and Christian Iaione offer an empirical assessment of the City of Bologna's groundbreaking regulatory experiment on enabling urban commons throughout the city. The "Regulation on public collaboration for the Urban Commons" proposed the creation of "pacts of collaboration" between the local government and different actors and sectors in the city for the care and regeneration of a variety of urban resources. The regulation produced more than 400 signed pacts of collaboration and spurred a regulatory race to adopt its framework by, to date, more than 180 Italian cities. The chapter presents an empirical assessment of 280 pacts signed between 2014 and 2016. The authors' analytical approach to this investigation is rooted in the literature on political economy and the literature on the quality of democracy. Their analytic approach is designed to assess whether a model of co-governance of urban assets as commons impacts on the democratic qualities of equality and rule of law at the urban level. In their final analysis of the historic regulation, they suggest that Bologna may have missed an opportunity to create multi stakeholder partnerships and collective economic institutions, at the neighborhood level and throughout the city, aimed at promoting sustainable and inclusive economic development in distressed areas of the city. They conclude that legal recognition of the urban commons is not sufficient if not coupled with an integrated policy program and more political and financial investment in urban commons as neighborhood collective economic units

Sofia Croso Mazzuco investigates how the urban commons "scene" has been developing in different parts of Brazil, through a systemic analysis of three distinct urban design and architectural projects. Mazzuco outlines challenges and opportunities from the perspectives of stakeholders' and the outcomes achieved in each project. The first project analyzed is an innovative school that was co-designed and will be co-built with, and for, an outskirts community in Sergipe, northeast of Brazil. The second project is a public space collective regeneration in a shantytown in Santos, Brazil's biggest harbor city. The third project, a network of ten public spaces for children, was co-designed and co-built with primary and nursery schools in its hosting community in Campinas (a country town of São Paulo). All projects are contextualized before, during, and after their common interventions, illuminating strategies to strengthen urban commons capacity in Brazilian and similar cities.

In Part V, *Reassessing Old and New Institutions for Collective Action*, the chapter authors focus on the kinds of institutions and organizations that could be viewed as sites of collective action around governance of shared, common governance. They assess, or reassess, these institutions using the analytical tools of commons researchers, including but not limited to Ostrom's IAD framework. Alexandra Flynn's Chapter focuses on Business Improvement Districts (BIDs), a hybrid public/private entity, that some consider to be an example of a CPR institution. Flynn reviews the scholarly treatment of BIDs in relation to the urban commons, both in regard to the property that they govern, and in the multifarious governance networks that result among them and other bodies. Her chapter lays out squarely the tensions raised by property law and legal geography scholars who question whether BIDs are examples of or in conflict with the urban commons. In the final analysis, Flynn advances a typology that focuses on decision-making, representation and accountability as normative measures of the urban commons. Using this typology, she inquires whether the language of the urban commons can be used to understand BIDs, or whether this characterization embeds, legitimates, and privileges these bodies within city decision-making to the detriment of other claims.

Barbara Bezdek queries whether a community land trust (CLT) is a commons, either metaphorically or in actuality. This inquiry is motivated by the ubiquity of CLTs in equitable development movements: reclaiming commons for the commoners in contexts of vacant disinvested housing held away from people needing it for housing by its private and State 'stewards.' CLTs are part of nearly every progressive response to today's affordable housing crisis because they decommodify housing, taking it out of the speculative market, and securing land for permanently affordable housing. Although the CLT offers an intermediate form of land ownership and control between the speculative market and the State, Bezdek argues that its distinct tenure and shared equity legal structure is not sufficient, alone, to merit a commons analysis. The chapter considers emerging CLTs as a form of urban commons and contributes to the contemporary turn of commons literature beyond its origins regarding natural common pool resources, toward the influence of commons models in additional areas of policy making and forms of resource management that avoid overly individuated ownership and control by the speculative market and the State. The author concludes that the legal form of community land trust recognized in American law maps onto the common property spectrum, in weak and robust degrees, within the commons frame of the pioneering work of Elinor Ostrom and her colleagues. The CLT-as-Commons analysis here emphasizes two characteristics of enduring commons: self-governance and the transgenerational resource preservation inherent in the concept of commons "management."

Anthony DeMattee and Chrystie Swiney apply Ostrom's Institutional Analysis and Development (IAD) Framework to the institutional arrangements that structure and organize the operating environments for civil society organizations (CSOs). They begin by defining what is meant by "civil society" and "CSOs," and highlight their essential attributes. DeMattee and Swiney then discuss the importance of the legal and regulatory frameworks that underlie the existence and operations of CSOs. They assess the role of CSOs in preventing commons tragedies from emerging. After presenting the types of rules that inform every IAD action situation and applying them to the existing research on CSO laws, the authors conclude by reconceptualizing CSO regulatory regimes through the lens of Ostrom's IAD framework and analysis.

Erik Nordman considers through the lens of polycentric governance the 2030 District Energy Program, which twenty cities across North America have joined. To join the 2030 District resource conservation program, building owners in participating cities voluntarily pledge to reduce CO_2 emissions from building energy use and transportation, as well as water use, by 50% by 2030. The 2030 Districts range in size and climate. In the absence of robust climate change regulations, the 2030 Districts' voluntary, non regulatory approach is a novel way to reduce resource use. However, it is unclear whether participating buildings are reducing resource use and what methods are most useful in holding the participants accountable for meeting their voluntary goals. Therefore, Nordman uses the Institutional Analysis and Development (IAD) framework to build a conceptual model of the 2030 District program. Using Grand Rapids, Michigan, as a case study, his analysis finds that the IAD framework is an appropriate tool to understand the complex relationships among a 2030 District's biophysical attributes, network of actors, and energy systems. The analysis suggests that the 2030 Districts may be able to achieve their goals if they meet certain conditions, such as having strong participation incentives, clear performance standards, compliance monitoring, and reduced free-riders.

Part VI, *Managing and Restoring the Commons*, explores the ways that communities and individuals work together, often with government entities, to manage traditional natural resource "commons" to avoid tragedies and even to restore degraded common pool resources. Pradeep Kumar Mishra explores the way that traditional common pool resources (CPR) in India, on which rural communities depend for their livelihoods, have degraded significantly in the past few decades. Considering that a number of funded projects have been implemented for their revival, Mishar notes the important role that facilitating government agencies play an important role. However, he argues, the extant literature on CPR institutions does not put much emphasis on facilitated institutions where an external agency plays critical roles. His chapter tries to fulfil this gap by understanding how facilitating organisations have engaged with local dynamics and influenced the outcomes. Based on a qualitative study of CPRs in 19 villages facilitated by 11 agencies in India, the study found that CPR development interventions are context specific and often go through iterative processes. The facilitating organization does not play the role of a catalyst, rather it actively influences the decision making process through a set of complex interactions at community level. In doing this, the priorities and preferences of the facilitating organization (which need not be compatible with the community's priorities) comes to the forefront.

Fernando Rios Fe Souza and Herbert Martins investigate the Peruíbe, Itanhém, and Jucuruçu River Basin Committee (CBHPIJ), located at the Southern end of the state of Bahia, Brazil, to understand the factors and conditions that impede effective operation of the Committee. Theoretically, the study follows the Institutional Analysis Development – Social Ecological System framework (IAD-SES) built by Ostrom (1990, 2009), which presents eight design principles representing an ideal type of analysis of relations between society, economy, and environment. Such a model allows the comparison between reality and the ideal-type and, thus, the comprehension of difficulties faced by the Committee. To explore the function, and functioning, of the committee the authors interviewed fourteen members of the management system and ten water users. The research findings reveal that the Committee lacks recognition from users, and that everyone needs to recognize limits and biophysical conditions, enforce rules with equity, and respect the heterogeneity of the community involved according to their various narratives.

Daniel Ogbaharya examines – based on comparative analysis of co-management schemes from Eastern and Southern Africa – how informal institutions (mainly customary authorities) contribute to intra-communal trust in the context of community-based wildlife management in Namibia and Tanzania. More specifically, this chapter considers how the integration of informal institutions in the form of customary authorities – de facto institutions governing historical claims to collective rights and adjudicating "tradeoff conflicts" over wildlife – is crucial to the success of collaborative management. Recent studies in collaborative management identify social and communal trust as a key determinant of positive socio ecological outcomes. While many recent studies have provided in-depth cases on how formally constituted rules and procedures mediate social trust in the governance of natural resources, the author notes a need for more research on the role of informal institutions – social norms that are enforceable but not fully codified – in enhancing or derailing inter-communal trust, thereby crucially determining ecological and social outcome.

Itzchak Kornfeld argues that one contemporary tragedy of the commons is that common pool resources are shrinking in urban areas. This phenomenon is coupled with the fact that runoff from paved areas is increasing as more and more land is being built upon. This chapter discusses two examples of how the construction or reconstruction of new commons in and around urban areas, increases individual well-being and social interactions, while also expanding natural areas. The first example is the rehabilitation of the Alexander Stream situated north of Tel Aviv, Israel. Until recently the stream was a catchment for raw sewage flowing from both the Palestinian territories and areas in Israel. The watercourse and its banks were derelict and ignored. The subsequent restoration included the planting of trees mentioned in the Bible, building of a series of parks and reestablishing the habitat of the semi-extinct Nile soft Shell Turtle. The second example is Orlando, Florida's Easterly Wetlands (Artificially) Constructed Wetlands Reclamation Project. The 1,220-acre wetland was built in lieu of a wastewater treatment plant and contains wetland varietal plants, including cattails, water hyacinth and duckweed. These absorb the wastewater's nutrients. Likewise, hardwood trees were planted and bike and hiking paths were built. These attract people and wildlife alike.

Part VII, *Law, Legal Theory and the Commons*, engages the often overlooked influence that commons theory has on legal scholars, legal doctrines, and jurisprudential frameworks. Robert Abrams assesses the prior Appropriation doctrine as a response to the Tragedy of the Commons.

Even though watercourses are a quintessential common pool resource, in arid regions of the United States, use of the available water is privatized by the adoption of prior appropriation. Abrams argues that the prior appropriation doctrine has admirably done its job in eliminating unauthorized, illegal, self-help redistributions of the commons that threatened a tragic free-for-all competition. However, over time, prior appropriation proved inadequate at solving other commons problems. Prior appropriation creates strong incentives to over-rapid development of water-dependent uses and wastefully excessive uses designed to obtain the right to use (in perpetuity) larger than needed amounts of water. As such, checks in prior appropriation have failed to do their job and a major environmental problem looms in the form of ever-increasing instances of total stream dewatering. Abrams concludes that prior appropriation could, in theory, address de-watering, but has consistently failed to do so. Additional coercive law is needed, the most effective and direct of which is rigorous implementation and enforcement of minimum flow and level regimes.

Hope Babcock's chapter focuses on how to manage the impending development of outer space and its resources in the absence of regulation. She invokes the public trust doctrine to bridge the gap between managing outer space resources and commons theory and to suggest a hybrid management approach that melds commons theory with private property incentives contributes to commons scholarship. Developed nations and commercial interest favor a system based private property rights to offset the risks and costs of space development. Developing countries, fearing monopolization and inequitable distribution of space development's benefits, favor a commons model. Babcock argues that the commons approach is a better fit with the animating principles of international space law, which ban appropriation of space resources and promote their equitable distribution. Among the various property tools for managing activities in outer space, she suggests application of the public trust doctrine because of its consistency with international space law, its anti-monopolistic features, and cost effectiveness. The doctrine would also prevent over consumption and a slide into hostilities and inequities. However, since the doctrine may not encourage space development, Babcock recommends its modification to allow the use of private property management tools, like tradable development rights.

David Forman reflects on what he calls a biotechnology "regulatory commons" problem. He focuses on a series of federal court decisions invalidating Hawain ordinances that sought to address perceived environmental and human health risks associated with genetically engineered (GE) seed crops or genetically modified organisms (GMOs). Disparate local efforts in three counties were all rooted in constitutional amendments, adopted in 1978, that established self-executing environmental rights and public trust responsibilities consistent with Native Hawaiian cultural values – i.e., recognizing rights and responsibilities in the management of natural resources for the benefit of present and future generations. The federal courts ignored these provisions and relevant Hawaiian case law applying a normative framework rooted in intergenerational equity and the precautionary principle. The federal courts instead applied preemption principles, despite significant gaps in federal and state regulation of GE/GMO seed crops under the Coordinated Framework for Regulation of Biotechnology. Forman argues that private enterprise continues to be privileged under a centralized management scheme that relies on scientifically indefensible regulatory assumptions of "substantial equivalence" that are essentially appeals to ignorance – based on policy choices made decades ago assigning risks associated with scientific uncertainty to future generations. He concludes by suggesting rulemaking petitions reviewable in state courts as a potential legal tool for addressing this regulatory commons tragedy.

Sheldon Bernard Lyke argues that race-based affirmative action in higher education is an intangible commons where the shared resource is diversity, the members are universities and students, and the individuals who seek to end affirmative action are agents of enclosure. The diversity commons provides insight into the conservation vulnerabilities of other commons resources. When affirmative action faces hostile litigation – universities (i.e., the protectors of the diversity commons) focus solely on diversity arguments. Universities' interests diverge from minority students when they fail to offer equality based defenses (i.e., that admissions are racially discriminatory). While many members of the commons have overlapping interests, a commons is vulnerable to the extent that commons managers have divergent interests from other members. In the diversity commons, a possible solution is to grant minority students intervenor status so they can advance equality arguments. This solution, if applied abstractly to other commons, would mean introducing gridlock as a conservation tool. One manifestation of gridlock could be to give all commons members with use rights the power to defend against development and enclosure.

Part VIII, *Technology, the Internet and the Future of Commons Governance*, offers unique insights on the role of technology on both traditional and contemporary kinds of resources – ranging from irrigation systems to data. Maija Halonen-Akatwijuka and Evagelos Pafilis examine the effect of technological change on the incentives to cooperate in the provision of traditional CPRs. Their analysis focuses on CPRs that require investments in improvement and maintenance, such as irrigation systems. The authors find that major technological improvements, such as replacing a primitive irrigation system with a modern system, risk compromising cooperation as the temptation to freeride on other farmers' investments is increased. By contrast, minor technological improvements within an existing irrigation system, such as strengthening water diversion devices, do not hinder incentives to cooperate. In their analysis, an irrigation system can be well managed for a long period of time during technological progress when changes are minor. When technology changes are major, cooperation can be maintained if the community is patient and initially their discount factor is well above the critical level for cooperation. However, when the threshold is reached, any further major technological improvement will lead to a breakdown of cooperation and collapse of investments in the irrigation system.

Scott Shackelford and Angie Raymond's chapter frames Internet and data governance using the literature developed by Elinor Ostrom and her collaborators, including the idea of polycentricity, to analyze the future of data governance. Their starting point is that data is an increasingly central component of not only ongoing trade negotiations, but also is integral to the evolution of cyberspace as seen in the rollout of 5G technologies powering the Internet of Things. Ongoing security concerns involving the Chinese firm Huawei are only one aspect of this larger debate about the role of the State in Internet governance, and how to govern data transfers across borders and sectors. Shackelford and Raymond argue that the Internet balkanization that would occur in a true digital Cold War would dramatically disrupt the knowledge commons along with the potential benefits of the Internet of Everything. However, polycentricity offers useful insights into governing an increasingly fractured cyberspace.

PART I

Revisiting the Origins and Evolution of Commons Thought

Linking the Origins and Extensions of Commons Theory

William Blomquist

The idea of the commons and commons theory have been applied, extended, and reshaped through a rapidly expanding body of work especially in the last twenty years or so. This handbook plus a volume published last year[1] collect several of these contributions, and many others can be found in programs and proceedings of conferences such as the recent biennial meetings of the International Association for the Study of the Commons and the Sixth Workshop on the Ostrom Workshop. To say the least, commons theory and the study of the commons constitute an active and lively field.

Some extensions of the commons concept are to situations that are not natural resources but are nonetheless territorially defined or bounded (e.g., in this volume the chapters by Bezdek, De Nictolis et al., De Visscher, and, McArdle). Most of these examples address common spaces and facilities in urban environments. Other extensions involve situations not territorially defined or bounded, at least not in familiar or conventional ways (e.g., in this volume the chapters by Babcock, Bloom, Lyke, Powell, Shackelford, and DeMattee/Swiney).[2] Work on the commons is thus proceeding along a variety of directions.

In a recent article in *Human Ecology*, Vaccaro and Beltran lament the "conceptual blurring" perceived in these extensions.[3] They are wary, to say the least, of characterizations of the commons and commons theory as applying to cases and settings beyond natural resources per se, and of confusing common pool resources with open access, the latter of which is associated

---

[1] Hudson B, Rosenbloom J, and Cole D (eds.) (2019). *Routledge Handbook of the Study of the Commons*. Abingdon, UK: Routledge.

[2] See also: Evans BJ (2019) Ethical standards for unconsented data access to build genomic and other medical information commons. In Hudson B, Rosenbloom J and Cole D (eds.) *Routledge Handbook of the Study of the Commons*. New York: Routledge, pp. 294–207; Frischmann, B (2019) Infrastructure and its governance: the British Broadcasting Corporation case study. In Hudson B, Rosenbloom J and Cole D (eds) *Routledge Handbook of the Study of the Commons*. New York: Routledge, pp. 256–280; Frischmann B, Madison M and Strandberg K (eds) (2017) *Governing Medical Commons*. Cambridge: Cambridge University Press; Madison MJ, Frischmann BM and Strandberg KJ (2019) Knowledge commons. In Hudson B, Rosenbloom J and Cole D (eds) *Routledge Handbook of the Study of the Commons*. New York: Routledge, pp. 76–90; Majumdar MA, Zuk PD and McGuire AL (2019) Medical information commons. In Hudson B, Rosenbloom J and Cole D (eds) *Routledge Handbook of the Study of the Commons*. Abingdon, UK: Routledge, pp. 281–293; Wormbs N (2019) Technology dependent commons. In Hudson B, Rosenbloom J and Cole D (eds) *Routledge Handbook of the Study of the Commons*. New York: Routledge, pp. 308–318.

[3] Vaccaro I and Beltran O (2019) What do we mean by 'the commons?' An examination of conceptual blurring over time. *Human Ecology* 47(3), 331–340.

with earlier "tragedy of the commons" forecasts.[4] Much of what this volume presents as "innovations" in commons research, they might be expected to regard instead as departures from it. They would prefer a restoration of the terminology of "the commons" and of "commons theory" to their earlier and more limited understandings.

I proceed nevertheless, believing that despite Vaccaro and Beltran's advice, those horses are unlikely to return willingly to the barn. Their critique, however, contains an insightful and useful point of departure for this essay. They write – quite correctly, in my view – that from the publication of *Governing the Commons*[5] onward, two intellectual pursuits have been merged: the study of natural resources and the study of collective action. They go on to make several valuable points about how the structures and practices human beings devise for managing resources are quite different from the resources themselves, which is plainly true. This provides an opportunity, for which I am grateful, to use this essay to discuss linkages between the origins of commons theory (as it is attributed to the work of Elinor Ostrom and others) and its current extensions.

ELINOR OSTROM, THE STUDY OF COLLECTIVE ACTION AND INSTITUTIONS, AND THE COMMONS

Understandably, Ostrom is closely and extensively associated with both the study of the commons and the management of common pool resources. The commons, however, became an intriguing and exciting field for the application of the research that she was already doing on collective action and institutions. Her most renowned book, *Governing the Commons*, was published in 1990 and readers might sensibly infer that this was the topic that absorbed most of her time and attention during the 1980s (or even earlier). That was not the case.[6]

Ostrom's primary focus during the 1980s was the development of her Institutional Analysis and Development (IAD) framework. In 1982, she returned from a sabbatical at the Center for Interdisciplinary Research in Bielefeld, Germany, where she had spent a great deal of time in dialogue with colleagues in game theory, policy analysis, and political economy.[7] Upon returning to Indiana University in 1982, she embarked on a sustained endeavor to develop theoretical and analytical tools for understanding the conditions under which boundedly rational individuals may coordinate their behavior to achieve collective action (for the provision of public goods and services, the mitigation and resolution of shared problems, or both) through the creation, maintenance, and reform of institutional arrangements. Inspired by game theory, she hoped to develop a framework for understanding institutions and human actions that would

---

[4] The conflation of "common pool resource" and "common property resource" earns some of their most sharply worded dismissal. Of the idea of a common property resource, they write: "There is no such a thing" (Vaccaro and Beltran 2019, 332). Of common pool resources, they add, "CPRs are an intellectual fiction," and refer to "the common pool resource artifice [as] one of the sources of the conceptual murkiness that is currently apparent in commons research" (333).

[5] Ostrom E (1990) *Governing the Commons: The Evolution of Institutions for Collective Action*. Cambridge: Cambridge University Press.

[6] What follows in this section of the chapter is partly a firsthand account, although I will provide some documentary resources to which a reader may refer for confirmation and further examination. As a doctoral student I was assigned as Elinor Ostrom's research assistant in August 1982 and became part of a team of researchers who worked together for the next several years. That was followed by other conversations and collaborations from time to time in the subsequent decades.

[7] Ostrom reflected on the significance of this sabbatical experience in Margaret Levi's 2010 "An Interview with Elinor Ostrom," www.annualreviews.org/userimages/ContentEditor/1326999553977/ElinorOstromTranscript.pdf

consist of a few basic elements that could be combined in varied configurations to generate and analyze a multiplicity of situations.

At the core of her inquiry during this period were three topics: rules as mechanisms for interpersonal coordination, the "action situation" as a fundamental unit of social interaction and decision-making, and the concept of "levels of action" to capture the interrelation of embeddedness and agency (i.e., people not only create institutions but also live and operate within institutions). Common pool resources – a topic that had held her interest as a PhD student in the early 1960s when she wrote a dissertation on the development of management arrangements for arresting the overuse and degradation of groundwater basins underlying the Los Angeles coastal plain[8] – represented a type of action situation that might be captured and illuminated through the application of this approach to institutional analysis. Thus, her primary endeavor in the 1980s was the development of the IAD framework, and the commons was an interesting potential application.

This assertion is readily confirmed by a look at the work she produced between her return from Bielefeld in 1982 and the publication of *Governing the Commons* in 1990.[9] A review of her CV.[10] and the online archives of the Ostrom Workshop at Indiana University[11] disclose the following. Of the fifty working papers, conference papers, journal articles, books, and chapters in edited volumes she produced from 1982 through 1990 (including *Governing the Commons* itself), eighteen or just over one-third were about the commons, and all of those appear from 1985 through 1990. More frequently appearing – and starting earlier – are works bearing titles such as, "Coproduction of Public Services," "The Elements of an Action Situation," "Analytical Tools for Institutional Design," "Actions and Rules," "Reflections on the Elements of Institutional Analysis," and many more. During the 1980s, her principal pursuit was building the IAD framework and explaining how people devise, live with, and modify institutional arrangements for collective action. The application of these developments in institutional analysis to the commons appears in smaller numbers, all in the latter half of the decade. *Governing the Commons* itself bears the subtitle "The Evolution of Institutions for Collective Action."

This process of development is echoed in her other best-known book, *Understanding Institutional Diversity*, published in 2005 after several years of prodigious output on the commons and the management of common pool resources. Given the notoriety of Ostrom's work on the commons and the fact that a few years later she would be awarded the Nobel Prize largely on the basis of it, the layout and content of the 2005 book is instructive – nine chapters, with the commons featured in Chapters 8 and 9. Chapters 1–7 contain occasional references to the commons as a type of action situation, but the focus is on where the IAD framework came from, its component elements, and its overall logic. When the commons emerges as the focus of Chapters 8 and 9, it appears explicitly as a field for the application of the IAD framework. In other words, *Understanding Institutional Diversity* unfolds largely as Ostrom's research did in the 1980s – first crafting and assembling tools for understanding institutions and collective action and then applying them to the management of common pool resources.

---

[8] See Ostrom (1990), pp. xiii–xiv.

[9] Prior to her sabbatical during 1981–1982, Ostrom's empirical research had been primarily on metropolitan organization and the provision and production of public services. This included large-scale comparative analyses of policing, street maintenance and lighting, and both public perceptions of service delivery and quality as well as performance measures. All of this fed, and was fed by, her interest in institutional arrangements and reform, but it was not oriented toward work on the commons or on natural resources.

[10] Available at https://ostromworkshop.indiana.edu/pdf/CVs/eostrom_vitae.pdf.

[11] Available at https://ostromworkshop.indiana.edu/library/.

None of the preceding observations should be read as suggesting that Ostrom was anything less than fascinated by the commons and devoted to understanding how human beings can successfully and sustainably solve commons problems, or as suggesting that the commons was some sort of afterthought. Far from it – she spent decades researching, theorizing about, and trying to understand the commons and people's efforts to (as she often put it) "cope with the commons." The point, rather, is that as deeply interested in the commons as Ostrom was, it was part of a larger intellectual endeavor for her – the quest to understand how people can overcome social dilemmas and create, maintain, and adapt ways of living and working together even in challenging circumstances. For Ostrom, the commons is "among the core social dilemmas facing all peoples."[12]

A CLOSER LOOK AT THE ORIGINS: ELEMENTS OF INSTITUTIONAL ANALYSIS

The task that remains is to link these observations with the extensions and innovations that are captured in this handbook and appearing in so many other outlets these days. Doing so requires a closer look at the approach to institutional analysis Ostrom constructed before and while she was building her explanation of commons governance. This will not be a full recitation of the IAD framework – for that, see *Understanding Institutional Diversity* among other works. Here, we will zero in on some connections between elements of the IAD framework and Ostrom's analysis of common pool resource situations.

Action situations are structured by configurations of rules.[13] The rules structuring an action situation can be classified into seven types – boundary, position, scope, choice, information, aggregation, and payoff rules. We will not examine each, but it is worthwhile to consider a few.

"Boundary rules" define who is "in" and who is "out" of a situation – who enters and how and whether and how one exits. For Ostrom, these kinds of rules were essential to understanding any action situation, especially common pool resource situations. They go to the heart of whether and how anyone can be excluded from access to a resource as well as who can have access. The existence of clear boundary rules consequently appears as one of the design principles of the long-enduring common pool resource management system that Ostrom identifies in *Governing the Commons*.

"Choice rules" define what actions may, must, or must not be taken by individuals participating in an action situation. These too are essential, first to understanding a common pool resource situation and then to thinking about how it might be changed. Can anyone extract and use whatever and however much they wish, by any means and at any time? Welcome to the tragedy of the commons. Avoiding the tragedy usually necessitates the adoption and maintenance of choice rules limiting what participants can do, whether those limitations come in the form of quantity limits, restrictions on harvesting technologies, or specifications of where and when use of the commons may occur.

"Information rules" may be less obvious, but they are no less significant. What participants in an action situation know about the situation and each other, who must disclose what information to whom and under what conditions, whether there are accessible and transparent data or other knowledge resources available to the participants, and more, shape participants' strategies, choices, and actions. In the collective use of a shared resource – that is, in the commons – what people understand about the resource they share, what they must report about their use, to whom,

---

[12] Ostrom E (2005) *Understanding Institutional Diversity.* Princeton, NJ: Princeton University Press, p. 219.
[13] Ostrom E (1986) An agenda for the study of institutions. *Public Choice* 48(1), 3–25; also, Ostrom E (2005).

how often, how transparently, and more, appeared both analytically and in empirical studies to be crucially related to the prospects for successful collective action to sustain it.

"Aggregation rules" identify how individual choices are converted into collective decisions. Most of Ostrom's work transcended disciplinary boundaries, but she was a political scientist after all, and in politics the most important questions are who gets to make the decisions and how those decisions are made. The aggregation rules that structure an action situation include those essential questions – how collective decisions and results are obtained. In the context of a common pool resource, this distills to such consequential matters as whether our collective outcome will simply be whatever results from each individual's own choices and actions (in isolation), whether some individuals make decisions for others, or whether there are mechanisms for collective decision-making and conflict resolution. The presence of such mechanisms does not guarantee that commons tragedies will be averted, but analytical logic and empirical evidence suggests that their absence can be expected to make tragedies more likely.

Moving away from the rules and the rule typology so important to the IAD framework – and thus to Ostrom's work on the commons – we turn to another component of the framework: the biophysical attributes of the resource. The action situations we populate and the potential opportunities and risks we encounter within them are bounded in important ways by the possibilities and limits the world contains and provides. For Ostrom, this was true not only of natural resources and their management – the research she and her students and colleagues performed during the 1970s on public services provided by local governments took into account such factors as the diffusion and brightness of street lighting and the materials of street surfacing. Certainly, in trying to understand and manage natural resources, however, people ignore the biophysical attributes of the resource at their peril and do well to closely tailor their management arrangements to those attributes. Long after *Governing the Commons*, Ostrom continued to criticize simplistic commons models that treated resources as relatively homogeneous.[14] Her development with other colleagues of the Social-Ecological Systems (SES) framework during the 2000s was, in many respects, an expansion of the IAD framework's attention to biophysical attributes and their influence on action situations and their outcomes.

Ostrom's work on institutions and the commons in the late 1980s and early 1990s included theorizing about property rights and the management of natural resources. Schlager and Ostrom (1992) established a complementary conceptual framework for understanding natural resource governance and management in terms of rules defining and assigning different bundles of rights.[15] The rules governing rights to a natural resource were more than on-off, can-cannot, or in-or-out dichotomies. Instead, there could be (and usually were, according to empirical studies) layers of rules defining rights of access to the resource, rights to exclude others, rights to withdraw/harvest/use units extracted from the resource, rights to alienate (transfer) either the units withdrawn or one's right to withdraw, and rights to participate in management decisions about the resource. Whether and to what extent a resource bore characteristics of a commons, and whether and to what extent a commons was at risk of overuse and degradation, would depend on the configuration of these rules defining varying kinds of rights of participants in that resource situation. Here again, the analysis and theorizing is more general, and its application to a natural resource situation brings it into potential dialogue with the commons.

---

[14] *See*, e.g., Ostrom (2005), pp. 236–237.
[15] E. Schlager and E. Ostrom (1992) Property-rights regimes and natural resources: a conceptual analysis. *Land Economics* 68(3), 249–262.

Although many more observations could be made about the IAD framework and the commons, an additional one can be added before concluding this section of the essay. One of the earliest components of the IAD framework was the concept of "levels of action."[16] As noted before, the "levels of action" concept provided a means for recognizing and incorporating the issue of embeddedness and agency in the relationship of human beings with institutions. Our choices and actions are taken within sets of rules but rules are also human creations, which means that it is not only possible but normal for human beings to occasionally shift from acting as rule followers to acting as rule makers. This observation holds in any action situation, but it became especially important to Ostrom's subsequent work on the commons. Although opportunities to change the rules vary significantly from one setting to another, the fact that human beings can and do operate and interact at different levels of action raises the prospect that people are not "doomed" or locked into tragic conditions. One of Ostrom's early conference papers on the commons, given in 1986, was titled "How Inexorable Is the 'Tragedy of the Commons'? Institutional Arrangements for Changing the Structure of Social Dilemmas." Having developed the concept of "levels of action" early during the construction of the IAD framework, Ostrom subsequently put it to use in her consideration of the commons in order to add a crucial element that allowed for change: people are capable (again, with greater or lesser difficulty depending on particular circumstances) of changing institutional arrangements that encourage destructive behaviors. In Ostrom's view, paraphrasing Hardin, ruin does *not* have to be the destination toward which we all rush. Neither success nor failure is guaranteed – outcomes in collective action situations are always contingent.

EXTENSIONS AND INNOVATIONS IN COMMONS RESEARCH: THE LINK

How does this excursion through the intellectual archives of Ostrom's theorizing about institutions and the commons in the 1980s and 1990s relate to the contemporary work featured in this handbook and elsewhere? In my view, the linkage is substantial and (I hope) useful.

Elinor Ostrom was known as a scholar of the commons and probably always will be. There is nothing wrong with that; she obviously was a scholar of the commons, arguably the finest one we have had thus far, and clearly the most influential. She was not, however, first and foremost a scholar of natural resources, nor did her interest in problems of the commons start there. Her interest in problems of the commons grew out of her interest in how human beings in interdependent social situations find ways to solve problems, coordinate their behavior, and establish and sustain mutually beneficial relationships. She intended the IAD framework that she constructed in the 1980s to be a means for understanding "the tools that individuals use in creating structure in the multiple action situations they face in life."[17] Shared use of natural resources was *a* kind of "action situation" – an important one, to be sure, and the one to which she applied the IAD framework most often for the rest of her career. Nevertheless, she did not seek to understand natural resource management and then build a theoretical framework for doing so; she built a theoretical framework for understanding institutions and collective action and then applied it to many cases involving natural resources and, more specifically, commons dilemmas in the use of natural resources.

---

[16] Kiser LL and Ostrom E (1982) The three worlds of action: A meta-theoretical synthesis of institutional approaches. In Ostrom E (ed) *Strategies of Political Inquiry*. Beverly Hills: Sage, pp. 179–222.

[17] Ostrom (2005), p. 219.

Among other things, this means that Vaccaro and Beltran are correct in my view for sharply drawing the distinction between the task of theorizing about and understanding institutional arrangements such as various property regimes and the task of studying natural resources. What we understand today as "commons theory" – to whatever extent we trace it to Ostrom and her work – is indeed properly understood as theorizing about institutional arrangements and the challenges and opportunities of governance and collective action. Therefore, unlike Vaccaro and Beltran and perhaps other scholars concerned about conceptual blurring or drift, I view the extension of commons theory to situations other than natural resources as entirely predictable.

For Ostrom and others who collaborated with her over the years on the IAD framework, the challenges of and the opportunities for successful, sustained, and productive collective action were never bound to the context of natural resources.[18] Rather, the analytical tools for understanding institutions and collective action could be beneficially applied to natural resource situations, but potentially to many other circumstances as well – conceivably to all "the multiple action situations [we] face in life."[19] From this perspective, decoupling what has come to be known as commons theory from natural resources is not a sign of intellectual entropy, and may even signal intellectual vitality.

How then to proceed? As scholars extend commons theory beyond natural resource applications, and beyond territorially defined and bounded resources, what are the touchstones of commons theory that are to be kept in mind and put to use? From my reading, a lot of the contemporary work starts with the design principles from *Governing the Commons*, perceiving those as some sort of distilled essence of Ostromian commons theory. This does not necessarily do any harm, but it misses out on the full utility of Ostrom's work as it can be applied to commons situations.

For one thing, we should recall what the design principles were about: they were the commonly observed features found in the comparative study of *long-enduring* common pool resource management cases. That is to say, they were characteristics that had tended to emerge over time as users of a resource had created and modified institutional arrangements and adapted them to their particular circumstances of place, use and community. They are not a blueprint for managing a commons or even for governing a commons. One sure way to get Ostrom to raise her voice in quick and firm disagreement was to hint or suggest that they were – "no panaceas!" she would swiftly retort.[20] She came to second-guess naming them "design principles" at all because the term had so often been understood to suggest that one could somehow deliberately design a successful commons regime by implementing (worse still, imposing) them. What she had intended was something more like patterns – the recurring similarities found across the successful cases she had studied. But the words had already suffused through the literature (today, we would say, already gone viral), and those horses too were long gone and beyond corralling.

Instead of starting with the design principles, it may be more productive to start with the elements of inquiry that started the body of commons research that led subsequently to the design principles. That is to say, start with what Ostrom called "the elements of institutional

[18] This is clear in Ostrom's own work in collaboration with Charlotte Hess. *See* Hess C and Ostrom E (2003) Ideas, artifacts, and facilities: information as a common-pool resource. *Law and Contemporary Problems* 66:111–145; Hess C and Ostrom E (2007) A framework for analyzing the microbiological commons. *International Social Science Journal* 188: 335–348; C. Hess and E. Ostrom, eds. (2007) *Understanding Knowledge as a Commons* (Cambridge: MIT Press).
[19] Ostrom (2005), p. 219.
[20] See, for example, "Elinor Ostrom, defender of the commons, died on June 12th, aged 78." *The Economist*, June 30 2012, p. 94.

analysis" in the title of one of her papers from 1985, the same year her first papers about common pool resources appeared. What are the attributes of the community of people involved in a situation? What are the attributes of the physical resource(s) with which they are interacting? (This may include non material resources such as data, which may lack material substance but still have properties by which it is more and less readily stored, transmitted, and modified.)

Proceed then to the rule typology. "Boundary rules" – who is in and who is out, and how do they get there? What positions do people in the situation hold and by what means are those positions defined and changed? What choices do the rules currently in use authorize or oblige people to take; what do they know about their situation and about each other; how are their individual preferences and actions aggregated into collective decisions and courses of action; how are the benefits and burdens of effort and outcomes distributed, and so on? More particularly in the context of shared resources, Schlager's and Ostrom's questions are applicable, too – how are rights of access and exclusion, rights of use, rights of transfer, and rights of management defined, and how and by whom? By acquainting oneself with the rule typology, one can peer into the design principles and see them differently – not as a starting point or as a set of prescriptions, but as the possible results of entire configurations of boundary, position, scope, choice, information, aggregation, and payoff rules. The challenge and the opportunity for people in the kind of action situation we may characterize as a commons is how to adjust the rules in use in their current situation in ways that would produce a pattern more nearly like the ones Ostrom saw in sustained and sustainable commons situations.

That last part – adjusting the rules in ways that might promote a more sustainable result – means thinking in terms of levels of action. Here there may be monsters. Many of us see "levels of action" but instead read "levels of government." They are not the same – really, not even close. The levels of action concept that informs Ostromian commons theory pertains to the people in the commons action situation themselves. As stated earlier, it is premised on the observation that people can be both rule followers and rule makers. People in a deteriorating and destructive commons situation that is created or reinforced by the rules in use do not necessarily have to throw themselves on the mercy of some higher authority. They may be able to modify at least some of the rules governing their situation themselves. Depending on the circumstances, it may often be the case that either assistance or forbearance of other authorities can be helpful, but shifting levels of action does not have to mean turning to some other level of government.

An important element of the enduring attraction of commons theory as developed by Elinor Ostrom has been her emphasis on the prospects of self-organized action by people within a situation to alter their situation. That insight, reinforced by evidence from multiple cases, added significantly to the contrast between Ostrom's commons theory and the theory of inevitable tragedy that had prevailed before. As scholars extend commons theory into new realms through innovative research and fresh rounds of theorizing, remembering the importance of the levels of action concept and putting it to use will remain essential. Are there any guarantees that people will be able to change rules effectively? No. Does the world provide many examples of people making things worse instead of better? Of course. Again, alas, no panaceas, but no inexorable tragedies either – outcomes will depend on what people do, and that is both the good news and the bad.

The fact that many scholars from all over the world and across many disciplines are extending commons theory beyond the context of natural resources, even beyond territorially bound resources, is exciting. Some applications of the idea of the commons will work out well, and others will disappoint – it's the nature of doing research. Knowing that commons theory did not originate in the study of natural resources and is not bound to that may be usefully reassuring at least to some degree – if we fail, it will not be because we should never have tried in the first place. And understanding the origins of commons theory in the study of collective action, and how people succeed and fail in resolving the whole array of social dilemmas that arise in all the action situations of our lives, may help fortify us a bit for the intellectual journeys ahead.

2

The Tragedy of Garrett Hardin's Commons

Andrew P. Follett, Brigham Daniels, and Taylor Petersen

Garrett Hardin's 1968 article *The Tragedy of the Commons*[1] has become a central environmental fable. Hardin was not the first to conceive of the commons or the tragedy,[2] yet he very often gets credit for both, perhaps because of the article's simple parable and catchy title.[3] It is among the most cited pieces of environmental scholarship, and an excerpted version of the paper has become a staple of introductory textbooks and anthologies on topics ranging from economics to environmental sociology.[4]

When introducing Hardin's article or the concept of "the tragedy of the commons" more broadly, such a description is generally offered: individual actors rationally seek to maximize personal gain and, in so doing, contribute to collective problems which degrade commonly managed resources to the detriment of all users.[5]

However, while this point certainly makes an appearance in Hardin's article, we argue that such a framing of his primary objective is incorrect. Hardin's main point (and the subject of the bulk of his article) is that, because the world is becoming overcrowded, controlling the human population requires a reexamination of individual liberties.[6] This is not an interpretive reach – it is his stated

---

[1] Garrett Hardin, "The Tragedy of the Commons," *Science*, 162, No. 3859 (1968): 1243–1248.

[2] Elinor Ostrom, *Governing the Commons: The Evolution of Institutions for Collective Action* (Cambridge University Press, 1990): 2; H. D. P. Lee, "Aristotle's Politics – Sir Ernest Baker: The Politics of Aristotle," *The Classical Review*, 63, no. 3 (1949): 100–101 (citing Aristotle: "What is common to the greatest number has the least care bestowed upon it. Everyone thinks chiefly of his own, hardly at all of the common interest.").

[3] Barton H. Thompson Jr., "Tragically Difficult: The Obstacles to Governing the Commons," *Environmental Law* 30, no. 2 (January 2000): 241–278. *See also* Robert Stephen Hawkshaw, Sarah Hawkshaw & U. Rashid Sumaila, "The Tragedy of 'The Tragedy of the Commons': Why Coining Too Good a Phrase Can Be Dangerous," *Sustainability*, 4, no. 1 (2012): 3141–3150 ("[Hardin] is the frequent victim of drive-by-citation. The tragedy of the commons is invoked because it sounds good, not for what Hardin was actually advocating.").

[4] Siegfried Von Ciriacy-Wantrip, "The Economics of Environmental Policy," *Land Economics*, 47, no. 1 (1971): 35–45; Robyn Eckersley, *Environmentalism and Political Theory: Toward an Ecocentric Approach* (State University of New York Press, 1992); Ian Burton, *The Environment as Hazard* (The Guilford Press, 1993): 124. Examples are legion; the paper has been cited over 40,000 times per Google Scholar.

[5] *See, e.g.*, Daniel J. Rankin, Katja Bargum & Hanna Kokko, "The tragedy of the commons in evolutionary biology," *TRENDS in Ecology and Evolution*, 22, no. 12 (2007): 644; David Grossman & Ruth Kark, "Communal Holdings and the Economic Impact of Land Privatization," in *Policies and Strategies in Marginal Regions* (W. Leimgruber, R. Majoral & C-W. Lee eds., 2003): 23.

[6] Hardin, "The Tragedy of the Commons," 1243.

thesis.[7] Hardin suggests coercive,[8] illiberal means of population control,[9] merely using the idea of the commons as a thought experiment, a sort of stepping-stone to introduce issues of social morality, human rights, and the nature of the state. A read through of the full article would no doubt surprise or even offend most readers, even those generally familiar with commons scholarship.

Rather than an exploration of natural resource management, *The Tragedy of the Commons* should be remembered at its core as controversial social commentary aimed first and foremost at denying "categorically" individual reproductive rights (called the right or the freedom to breed[10]), challenging classical liberalism, and questioning rights-oriented institutions.[11] In this light, it seems all the more surprising to a contemporary audience that Hardin has managed to take credit for what might otherwise be considered a relatively well-understood principle among social scientists, even before his time.[12]

In this chapter, we seek to put *The Tragedy* in context – both within Hardin's larger body of scholarship and within the historical moment in which it originated – to illuminate its meaning and criticize its value to a modern audience, and we show that, because of the unique political circumstances of the time period in which it was written, it is likely that Hardin's thinking caught on at least at first *because* of his focus on population control, not in spite of it. While we join in the chorus of scholars repudiating Hardin's historically and empirically under informed thinking, we also wish to center our criticism more broadly on the radical, illiberal, and anti-egalitarian premises that underlie *The Tragedy of the Commons*.

After benignly discussing the proposition that some issues are beyond technical solution, Hardin's Trojan horse bursts: because of the growing human population, certain freedoms must be abolished.[13] In particular, it is the "intolerable" "freedom to breed," in Hardin's own austere words, coupled with "the belief that everyone born has an equal right to the commons,"[14] which fuels the unfolding tragedy of environmental breakdown and resource degradation.[15]

Such a proposal is in and of itself deeply flawed. However, Hardin was not concerned merely with reproductive rights in a universal sense – he ties overpopulation and access to the commons specifically to race, religion, and class. How can a welfare state that is committed to the right to breed, he asks, "deal with the family, the religion, the race, or the class ... that adopts overbreeding as a policy to secure its own aggrandizement?"[16] To Hardin, reproduction is a sort of competition between demographic groups,[17] and he is certainly not indifferent about which groups win and which lose.[18]

---

[7] *Id. See also id.* 1244. *See also* Craig Straub, "Living in a World of Limits – An interview with noted Biologist Garrett Hardin," *The Social Contract* (Fall 1997).

[8] Hardin, "The Tragedy of the Commons," 1247. Elsewhere, Hardin suggests a model of population control based on the contemporary, command-and-control Chinese methods. Garrett Hardin, "There is no Global Population Problem," *The Social Contract*, (Fall 2001): 20.

[9] Hardin, "The Tragedy of the Commons," 1247; *id.* 1246.

[10] *Id.* 1246.

[11] *Id.*

[12] Ostrom, *Governing the Commons*, 2; Thompson, "Tragically Difficult," 242; Beryl L. Crowe, "The Tragedy of the Commons Revisited," *Science*, 166, no. 3909 (1969): 1103–1107.

[13] *Id.* 1245–1246.

[14] *Id.* 1246. *See also* Garrett Hardin, *Limits of Altruism* (Indiana University Press, 1977) ("coupling the concept of freedom to breed with the belief that everyone born has an equal right to the commons 'locks' the world into a tragic course of action.").

[15] Hardin, "The Tragedy of the Commons," 1246.

[16] *Id.*

[17] *See* Garrett Hardin, "A Second Sermon on the Mount," *Perspectives in Biology and Medicine*, 6, no. 3 (1963): 366–371. *See also* John Cairns, Jr., "Garrett Hardin," Proceedings of the American Philosophical Society 149, no. 3 (2005): 418.

[18] Hardin, "The Tragedy of the Commons," 1246. *See also* Hardin, "Limited World, Limited Rights," *Society*, 17, no. 4 (1980): 5–8.

While *The Tragedy of the Commons* makes little effort to conceal Hardin's arguments, any remaining ambiguities can be put to rest by consulting Hardin himself – identifying themes and central ideas underpinning the body of his work to construct a more coherent, rigorous, and intellectually honest interpretation of *The Tragedy*.[19] Throughout Hardin's work,[20] we find consistent appeals to values and ideologies best described as nativist, far-right, and illiberal. Celebrating Hardin's life and academic career not long after Hardin's death, John Cairns, Jr. explained that Hardin's work emphasized several "unifying themes," focusing generally on a need for immigration control, reduced multiculturalism, and punitive state action (a consequence of larger populations).[21]

In fact, Cairns's characterization of Hardin's themes largely blunts their radical nature. In an essay titled "Conspicuous Benevolence and the Population Bomb," for example, Hardin leverages the polemic that Western nations are current victims of "passive genocide":[22] "If two cultures compete for the same bit of 'turf,' and if one of the populations increases faster than the other, then year by year, the population that is reproducing faster will increasingly outnumber the slower one." This, Hardin proclaimed, "is genocide."[23] Hardin continues that in a truly laissez-faire system, genocide would pose no danger, and natural systems would quickly eliminate breeding populations. The issue? For Hardin, permissive immigration policy, international aid, and "the ideal of universal brotherhood."[24]

Hardin singled out Muslims as a supposedly self-aggrandizing group that had taken up the explicit goal to "outbreed" the West.[25] Similarly, he sounded the alarm for what he saw as an "aggressive ... takeover" of America by Latinx immigrants.[26] Citing an infamous French novel *Camp of the Saints* by Jean Raspail,[27] Hardin called for an enclosure of the American commons, asking, "Will America, like invaded France in Raspail's novel, continue to be immobilized by ambivalence in the face of a silent invasion? If we cannot muster the will to protect ourselves we will find that we have shared not wealth, but poverty with our invaders."[28]

---

[19] We do not rely on some single essay, affiliation, or expressed belief. Rather than state that the whole of Hardin's work is sullied by some racist comment or relationship, we recognize that each individual work – such as *The Tragedy* – ought to be interpreted in context.

[20] Hardin frequently published in venues closely tied to the far right and co-founded or affiliated with anti-immigration hate groups. Southern Poverty Law Center (SPLC), "Garrett Hardin," last accessed February 24, 2020: www.splcenter .org/fighting-hate/extremist-files/individual/garrett-hardin; Cairns, Jr., "Garrett Hardin," 417; SPLC, "The Social Contract Press," last accessed February 25, 2020: www.splcenter.org/fighting-hate/extremist-files/group/social-con tract-press; SPLC, "Federation for American Immigration Reform," last accessed February 25, 2020: www.splcenter .org/fighting-hate/extremist-files/group/federation-american-immigration-reform.

[21] Cairns, Jr., "Garrett Hardin," 414 (Multicultural societies inevitably experience social conflict, which is exacerbated by excessive immigration ... Harsh penalties are the result of exceeding carrying capacity); *id.* 418.

[22] Garrett Hardin, "Conspicuous Benevolence and the Population Bomb," *Chronicles* (September 1, 1991): 21.

[23] *Id.*

[24] *Id.* 22.

[25] *Id.* 21 ("The way this works was recently revealed in three remarks by Ali Akbar Hashemi Rafsanjani, the speaker of the Iranian parliament: 'One billion [Muslims] will become 2 billion tomorrow and 3 billion the day after tomorrow.' 'You [in the West] are afraid of our cultural presence in your countries.' '[Islam] is the sole determinant of man's future course.' Translated bluntly: 'We Muslims are going to outbreed you.'").

[26] Hardin, "Conspicuous Benevolence and the Population Bomb," 20–21; Craig Straub, "Living in a World of Limits – An interview with noted Biologist Garrett Hardin."

[27] Jean Raspail, *Le Camp des Saints* (Éditions Robert Laffont, 1973). For discussion of the book's racist legacy and broad influence into the present era, *see* Sarah Jones, "The Notorious Book that Ties the Right to the Far Right," *The New Republic* (February 2, 2018); Elian Peltier & Nicholas Kulish, "A Racist Book's Malign and Lingering Influence," *The New York Times* (November 22, 2019).

[28] Garrett Hardin, "An Ecolate View of the Human Predicament," *Alternatives*, 7, no. 2 (1981): 260. Hardin accuses immigrants and refugees of "fall[ing] out of their lifeboats and swim for a while in the water outside, hoping to be admitted to a rich lifeboat, or in some other way to benefit from the "goodies" on board. Garrett Hardin, "Living on a Lifeboat," *Bioscience*, 24, no. 10 (1974): 561–568.

Hardin proposed that eliminating immigration into the United States would be necessary for the sake of ecological safety[29] – restricting nonwhite immigration being the priority,[30] as he saw global benefits to ethnic segregation.[31] To Hardin, ecological safety and cultural purity were interrelated.[32] Hardin leveraged imagined catastrophes of ecological breakdown, immigration invasions, and passive genocide to justify a state crack down.[33]

Taking Hardin at his word, it seems unreasonable to believe he conceived of *The Tragedy*'s burden of "mutual coercion"[34] to be borne equally by all with respect to protected classes. Thus, although Hardin in *The Tragedy* limited himself to a general call for population control, only implying the need for segregated commons access and leaving his bogeyman races and religions unnamed, one need only consult his other writings. In this context, it becomes difficult to argue that Hardin's references to race, class, religion, equal rights, or coercion in *The Tragedy* are unlucky moments of innocent ambiguity.

Of course, it's not necessary to claim that everything Hardin wrote was code for white nationalism – sometimes ecology might just be ecology. But we reiterate that *The Tragedy* is not an ecology paper. It is a critique of morals, and one that is compromised by Hardin's radical and harmful view of humanity, expressed at times explicitly, at other times only implicitly.

And so, we're led to ask, given Hardin's extremist ideas, at times painfully apparent in *The Tragedy*, how did this essay end up as a centerpiece in environmental discourse?

Hardin's 1968 article was released with impeccable timing, coinciding almost exactly with a shift in national attention to issues pertaining to pollution and ecology.[35] Additionally, due to the tone of the early environmental movement, Hardin's paper (even its more startling propositions) did not stand out as much in 1968 as it might today. In fact, *The Tragedy of the Commons* spoke directly to what was, at that time, a very real concern over population growth.[36] The arguable culmination of the popular population movement came in the 1972 Declaration of the United Nations Conference on the Human Environment, which stated that "demographic policies ... should be applied in those regions where the rate of population growth or excessive population concentrations are likely to have adverse effects on the environment."[37]

---

[29] *Id.* Cairns, Jr., "Garrett Hardin," 417; Garrett Hardin, "Living on a Lifeboat," *The Social Contract* (Fall 2001): 37; Hardin, "Conspicuous Benevolence and the Population Bomb," 19 ("For rich nations like ours the most feasible partial solution is an immediate restriction of immigration."). *See also* Garrett Hardin, "Living on a Lifeboat," 44; Garrett Hardin, "The Toughlove Solution," *Newsweek* (October 26, 1981): 45 ("Our responsibility is to keep our country from being overwhelmed by immigrants. The responsibility of each poor country is to keep the excess population from being produced"); Hardin, "There is no Global Population Problem," 21.

[30] Hardin, "Conspicuous Benevolence and the Population Bomb," 19. *See also id.* 21–22 ("Diversity within the borders of a single state can become too great for the survival of all the competing ethnic groups. But, if borders are kept intact, diversity among nations is tolerable").

[31] Hardin, "Conspicuous Benevolence and the Population Bomb," 19 ("It's hard to see how there will be any peace until passionate ethnic groups are segregated from one another by effective borders").

[32] *See* Hardin, "Conspicuous Benevolence and the Population Bomb," 20; Hardin, "Limited World, Limited Rights."

[33] Hardin, "An Ecolate View of the Human Predicament," 260. *See also supra*, note 22; Garrett Hardin, "Lifeboat Ethics: the Case Against Helping the Poor," *Psychology Today* (September 1974), *available at* garretthardinsociety.org. In a modern setting, the state responses of Hungary and Russia to the COVID-19 pandemic, for example, demonstrate the opportunity posed by disaster to consolidate power.

[34] Hardin, "The Tragedy of the Commons," 1247.

[35] See Brigham Daniels, Andrew Follett & Josh Davis, "The Making of the Clean Air Act," 71 *Hastings Law Journal* (2020): 907–914.

[36] *See infra*, note 43.

[37] United Nations, *Declaration of the United Nations Conference on the Human Environment*, United Nations Conference on the Human Environment (1972): http://webarchive.loc.gov/all/20150314024203/http%3A//www.unep .org/Documents.Multilingual/Default.asp?documentid%3D97%26articleid%3D1503.

Congress, the White House, and premier environmental groups like the Sierra Club were all toying with state-sponsored population control efforts as a legitimate response to observed and projected environmental degradation in the late '60s and early '70s. Even popular news media at the time were often willing to laud the virtues of population control.[38] A March 1970 *U.S. News and World Report* article, for example, flaunts a term that would seem unthinkably problematic and inhumane to a modern audience: "people pollution."[39] Just a month later, the *Times* published an article recognizing a budding rhetoric of "control" over population growth – a euphemism for "family planning" – on which "pollution control" is seen as being contingent.[40] "We are on the verge," the article states, "of a massive education program to persuade the people that uncontrolled population growth can be disastrous for their children… The outlook is a horror story."[41] The *Star*'s Carl T. Rowan wrote, "[m]illions of Americans finally have become acutely aware that unless we deal with the population problem … it is self-delusional to talk about meeting the challenges of oxygen-depletion, air pollution, water contamination, food shortages, or any other things that affect the quality of life."[42]

A commission to investigate population growth and its potential consequences, known as the Rockefeller Commission, was called for by Congress and, in its final report, defended the ideological foundations of population control, finding that "no substantial benefits will result from further growth of the Nation's population … We have looked for, and have not found, any convincing economic argument for continued population growth."[43]

Nixon's July 1969 message to Congress made such an appeal to population growth, although the president did not frame it in explicitly environmental terms.[44] As the *Times* notes, Nixon was the first American President to send a message to Congress pertaining to the importance of population control.[45] Messaging from others in the administration was similarly oriented, often with even greater fervor. Dr. Roger O. Egeberg, Assistant Secretary at Health, Education, and Welfare (HEW), seemed to echo Hardin's commons dilemma when he asked in a speech, "what does freedom of choice in family planning imply in the present state of society? … The typical American family, if it can, will elect to have three children, not two. [This] will lead to intractable population growth—to 300 million Americans by the year 2000."[46] Similarly,

---

[38] In the following pages, we highlight a few articles that characterize our claim. However, our review of news media is by no means exhaustive. A range of media demonstrate the popular concern and population debate we outline here. *See, e.g.,* Barbara Hansen, "Population Control Vital, Says Expert," *Los Angeles Times* (May 21, 1970): I27A; C. G. McDaniel, "Population Control Center Proves to Be Successful," *Chicago Tribune* (September 26, 1971): S_A3; Paul R. Erlich, "Population Control—Earth's Last Chance?," *The Wall Street Journal* (December 3, 1968): 20; S. Fred Singer, "Calculating the Best Population for U.S.," *The Washington Post* (February 22, 1970): D4; "Need for Population Control," *The Atlanta Constitution*, (October 2, 1968): 4; "Mr. Nixon on Family Planning," *The New York Times* (July 29, 1969): 36; "Episcopal Diocese Asks Pope to Back Population Control," *The New York Times* (February 14, 1968): 19; Herbert Black, "Sterilization techniques suggested as means for population control," *The Boston Globe* (April 10, 1970): 7.

[39] "The Drive to Stop Population Growth," U.S. News & World Report (March 2, 1970); this phrase is analogous to Hardin's own invented term "popollution" – a portmanteau of population and pollution: Garrett Hardin, "Everybody's Guilty: The ecological dilemma," *California Medicine*, 113, no. 5 (1970): 40.

[40] James Reston, "Washington: Who Said 'Love Makes the World Go Round?," *The New York Times* (January 21, 1970): www.nytimes.com/1970/01/21/archives/washington-who-said-love-makes-the-world-go-round.html.

[41] *Ibid.*

[42] Carl T. Rowan, "What has Become of the Population Commission?," *Sunday Evening Star* (May 24, 1970).

[43] *Commission on Population Growth and the American Future, Population and the American Future* (Government Printing Office, 1972): 4; Thomas Silvert Lagomarsino, "A comparative study of population policy of three selected countries," PhD diss., Naval Postgraduate School (1976).

[44] "The Drive to Stop Population Growth," U.S. News & World Report (March 2, 1970).

[45] Reston, "Washington: Who Said 'Love Makes the World Go 'Round?"

[46] *Id.*

Nixon's science advisor, Dr. Lee A. DuBridge, explained to the *Report* in January 1970 that "it would be a very desirable goal in this country to reduce population growth to zero."[47]

It is worth noting the implicit, unstated premises underlying these arguments for no national population growth – natural growth must be halted through centralized family planning, as these officials admit, but what about the inflow of immigrants and refugees?

This was all well within bounds for the burgeoning environmental movement's mainstream, too. Esteemed biologist Paul Ehrlich's 1968 book *The Population Bomb*[48] sounded the alarm on environmental disaster stemming from human population growth, and was written at the request of Sierra Club executive director David Brower.[49] It argued that "nothing can prevent a substantial increase in the world death rate" – the population bomb was primed to explode, and catastrophe was imminent and unavoidable.[50] In 1970, even as Nixon's patience with the environmental issue at large was beginning to wear thin, Sierra Club president Phillip S. Berry responded to Nixon's earlier statement on population by insisting that the message failed to communicate the requisite "urgency."[51] Nothing short of an ethical "Renaissance" is required, Berry writes; "unfortunately the solutions discussed aim toward accommodating expected growth. To anticipate growth insures [sic] it will come." Berry adds that attitudes about overpopulation must be changed "by whatever means necessary."[52]

In the context of the media, government, and the environmental wave, Hardin's ideas seem to fit snugly into the accepted public discourse. Offering a pithy title and straightforward explanation to a perceived crisis, *The Tragedy* landed well and assumed its place in the academic conversation. As social attitudes concerning population control, reproductive rights, and other issues of morality shifted over the course of the '70s, however, so did the accepted meaning of *The Tragedy*.

In the years immediately following its publication, Hardin's central thesis of population control was retained in the scholarly conversation. Mainstream scientific journals continued to comment openly on the population crisis and, in some cases, the role of the welfare state and regulatory coercion in controlling population growth. In this growing body of literature, Hardin's article became a point of orientation, and Hardin's article was cited and represented (for the most part) correctly.[53]

Even after it was the population bomb became to be seen as a political dud, however, *The Tragedy* did not go away. Instead, Hardin's introduction and explanation of the herdsman at

---

[47] "The Drive to Stop Population Growth."

[48] Paul R. Ehrlich, *The Population Bomb* (Sierra Club/Ballantine Books, 1968).

[49] Paul R. Ehrlich & A.H., "The population bomb revisited," *The electronic journal of sustainable development*, 1, no. 3 (2009): 63.

[50] Charles C. Mann, "The Book that Incited a Worldwide Fear of Overpopulation," *Smithsonian Magazine* (January 2018): www.smithsonianmag.com/innovation/book-incited-worldwide-fear-overpopulation-180967499/.

[51] Phillip Berry to Richard Nixon, Washington, DC, April 9, 1970 (on file with author).

[52] *Id.*

[53] *See, e.g.,* Elliot, *et al.,* "U.S. Population Growth and Family Planning"; Donald T. Campbell, "On the Conflicts Between Biological and Social Evolution and Between Psychology and Moral Tradition," *American Psychologist*, 30, no. 12 (1975): 1103–1126; Joseph J. Spengler, "Population Problem: In Search of a Solution," *American Association for the Advancement of Science*, 166, no. 3910 (1969): 1234–1238; Paul R. Ehrlich & John P. Holdren, "Population and Panaceas," *BioScience*, 19, no. 12 (1969): 1065–1071; Harold L. Votey, Jr., "The Optimum Population and Growth: A New Look: A Modification to Include a Preference for Children in the Welfare Function," *Journal of Economic Theory*, 1, no. 3 (1969): 273–290; Carl Jay Bajema, "The Genetic Implications of Population Control," *BioScience*, 21, no. 2 (1971): 71–75; A. E. Kair Nash, "Pollution, Population, and the Cowboy Economy: Anomalies in the Developmentalist Paradigm and Samuel Huntington," *Journal of Comparative Administration*, 2, no. 1 (1970): 109–128; Richard A. Falk, "Toward Equilibrium in the World Order System," *American Journal of International Law*, 64, no. 4 (1970): 217–224.

pasture were retained while the rest of the article (including Hardin's explanation of his thesis and the need for an extension of morality to the issues of reproduction) was excerpted out.

Taking one such example of the excerpted restatement of *The Tragedy of the Commons* from a peer-reviewed research journal: "Hardin's primary objective was to convey that multiple rational actors, when faced with limited resources, will each make decisions based upon what is in their personal interest."[54] Some descriptions went a bit further and included references to privatization or free riding (generally the former), perhaps even setting the scene of the herdsman to provide an illustration of the problem. But again, all of this is only a small part of *The Tragedy*. Hardin's article lives on – misrepresented and mis cited, but thriving.

Granted, scholars have criticized Hardin on a number of fronts, although they generally focus their criticism on his framing of the commons generally and his proposed solutions, rarely venturing into his discussion of population and coercion.[55] The most prominent criticism of *The Tragedy of the Commons* pertains to Hardin's two proposed solutions to commons dilemmas – something Ostrom framed as the dichotomy between "socialism" and "the privatism of free enterprise."[56] The idea that the only way to address tragedies of the commons is through government regulation or privatization has been thoroughly and convincingly discredited by historically and empirically informed research, chiefly by the groundbreaking work of Elinor Ostrom.[57] In fact, Ostrom's findings, and the literature she inspired were so ground breaking that they eventually contributed to her being the first woman to win the Nobel Peace Prize for Economics.

Historians working on the commons similarly criticize Hardin for his broad assumptions and mischaracterization in presenting the commons analogy. After all, commons were (and are) a feature of the real world; rather than simply imagining a pasture open to all, as Hardin did, scholars such as Jane Humphries and Tine de Moor who study real-life commons and have come to conclusions far-removed, and at times entirely contrary to, those offered by Hardin.[58] The free-for-all grazing pastures presented in Hardin's imagined story, which seem to evoke English pastures, are, in reality, often maintained and regulated by bylaws and systems of co-produced rules, which at times are informal rather than codified. Commons are not doomed to tragedy, but instead, can be a "triumph."[59]

This post-Hardin empirical literature shows that, contrary to Hardin's claim that regulation and privatization are necessary to solve commons problems, communities around the world

[54] Justin Taillon, "Tragedy of the Commons: The Perils of Open Access Publishing," *Journal of Tourism & Hospitality*, 1, no. 6 (2012): 1–3. *See also supra*, note 5.

[55] *But see* Matto Mildenberger, "The Tragedy of The Tragedy of the Commons," *Scientific American* (April 23, 2019): https://blogs.scientificamerican.com/voices/the-tragedy-of-the-tragedy-of-the-commons/.

[56] Elinor Ostrom, Joanna Burger, Christopher B. Field, Richard B. Norgaard & David Policansky, "Revisiting the Commons: Local Lessons, Global Challenges," *Science*, 284, no. 5412 (1999): 278.

[57] Ostrom, *Governing the Commons*; Elinor Ostrom, Larry Schroeder & Susan Wynne, *Institutional Incentives and Sustainable Development: Infrastructure Policies in Perspective* (Westview Press, 1993); Elinor Ostrom, James Walker & Roy Gardner, *Rules, Games, and Common-Pool Resources* (University of Michigan Press, 1994); Elinor Ostrom & James Walker, *Trust and Reciprocity: Interdisciplinary Lessons from Experimental Research* (Russell Sage Foundation, 2003); Elinor Ostrom, *Understanding Institutional Diversity* (Princeton University Press, 2005); Elinor Ostrom & Charlotte Hess, *Understanding Knowledge as a Commons: From Theory to Practice* (MIT Press, 2007).

[58] Jane Humphries, "Enclosures, Common Rights, and Women: The Proletarianization of Families in the Late Eighteenth and Early Nineteenth Centuries," *The Journal of Economic History*, 50, no. 1 (1990): 21; Tine de Moor, "From historical institution to pars pro toto – The commons and their revival in historical perspective." In Blake Hudson, Jonathan Rosenbloom & Dan Cole (Eds.), *Routledge Handbook of the Study of the Commons* (Routledge, 2019).

[59] Susan Jane Buck Cox, 1985. "No Tragedy of the Commons," *Environmental Ethics*, 7, no. 1 (1985): 56–60.

have found ways to come together without rigid institutions or public oversight to manage commons systems sustainably.[60]

Nonetheless, because the commons are seemingly everywhere we look (and often appear to be riddled with tragedies), Hardin remains widely cited. But as racism, xenophobia, and Islamophobia are resurgent in the Western world today, and as the tenets of liberal democracy are falling out of favor around the world, the uglier aspects of Hardin and the world of his time should not be edited out of our collective memories, especially in the Academy. Now more than ever, introspection and an evaluation of the ideological roots of our canon seem worthwhile, if not urgent.

This is not so much a call to "cancel" Hardin as it is to give credit where credit is due. A healthy body of commons literature has all but dismantled Hardin's tragedy – when the commons are discussed, the trend of "drive-by citation"[61] of Hardin's article might be replaced with engagement and consideration of more recent and thoughtful commons scholars such as Ostrom.

Also, while we recognize that it is possible to harbor a genuine concern over the environmental impacts of a growing global human population, we insist that unqualified respect for individuals' liberty to make their own family choices must remain at the forefront of any conversation regarding reproductive rights. Otherwise, genuine concern for ecology risks succumbing to historical pitfalls of state overreach and illiberalism.

We must responsibly acknowledge and grapple with the fact that resurgent white supremacy and nationalist ideologies threaten the rise of a new kind of ecofascism, which may be hidden in policy programs which permit regulation of reproduction or human population growth. We note with dismay that, in fact, the shooters of tragedies in both El Paso and Christchurch attempted to make ecological arguments to justify their despicable acts of terror.[62]

Ultimately, it is not enough to criticize Hardin's thinking for historical inaccuracy or false dichotomies. Even if Hardin's writing is worth teaching or referencing, it should, at the very least, not be cited without disclaiming and recognizing its problematic ideological underpinnings.

These uglier elements of Hardin are, after all, far from a thing of the past.

---

[60] Ostrom, *Governing the Commons*, 2; Arun Agrawal & Clark Gibson, *Communities and the Environment: Ethnicity, Gender, and the State in Community-Based Conservation* (Rutgers University Press, 2001); Jean-Marie Baland & Jean-Philippe Platteau, *Halting Degradation of Natural Resources: Is There A Role for Rural Communities?* (Oxford University Press and FAO 1996); Daniel W. Bromley, *Making the Commons Work: Theory, Practice, and Policy* (ICS Press, 1992); Nives Dolšak & Elinor Ostrom, *The Commons in the New Millennium: Challenges and Adaptation* (MIT Press, 2003); Robert O. Keohane & Elinor Ostrom, *Local Commons and Global Interdependence: Heterogeneity and Cooperation in Two Domains* (Sage Publications, 1995); Clark C. Gibson, Margaret A. McKean, & Elinor Ostrom, *People and Forests: Communities, Institutions, and Governance* (MIT Press 2000); Blake Hudson, Jonathan Rosenbloom & Dan Cole, *Handbook of the Study of the Commons* (Routledge, 2019); Bonnie J. McCay & James M. Acheson, *The Question of the Commons: The Culture and Ecology of Communal Resources* (University of Arizona Press, 1987); Elinor Ostrom, Larry Schroeder, & Susan Wynne, *Institutional Incentives and Sustainable Development: Infrastructure Policies in Perspective* (Westview Press, 1993); Elinor Ostrom, James Walker, & Roy Gardner, *Rules, Games, and Common-Pool Resources* (University of Michigan Press, 1994); Elinor Ostrom & James Walker, Trust and Reciprocity: Interdisciplinary Lessons from Experimental Research (Russell Sage Foundation, 2003); Amy Poteete, Marco Janssen, & Elinor Ostrom, *Working Together: Collective Action, the Commons, and Multiple Methods in Practice* (Princeton University Press, 2010).

[61] Robert Stephen Hawkshaw, Sarah Hawkshaw & U. Rashid Sumaila, "The Tragedy of 'The Tragedy of the Commons': Why Coining Too Good a Phrase Can Be Dangerous," 3143.

[62] Joel Achenbach, "Two mass killings a world apart share a common theme: 'ecofascism,'" *The Washington Post* (August 18, 2019).

3

Kinship and Commons: The Bedouin Experience

Haim Sandberg

Strong kinship relations are rooted in tribal social structures and enable the efficient administration of tribal common properties. The clustering of tribal members in urban areas has gradually weakened tribal blood ties and altered the values of traditional tribal society. Modern urban culture emphasizes the autonomy and flourishing of individuals, rather than collective or communal continuity.[1] This change has reduced the power of natural social incentives to support sustainable common property regimes and fostered modern urban tragedies of the commons. Can modern urban society still maintain or redevelop social incentives strong enough to support efficient commons regimes? This is the political question at the heart of the Hardin-Ostrom debate. The main point of disagreement between Garrett Hardin and Elinor Ostrom was whether the contemporary management of public resources should lead to privatization, as Hardin argued, or whether there is an opportunity for effective collective management of those resources, as Ostrom thought.[2] This chapter argues that the tension between these two approaches reflects a larger issue: a major change in human social evolution. The version of the commons conceived by Ostrom was characteristic of earlier tribal societies, whereas the challenges posed by Hardin better reflect the dissolution of these earlier patterns of human life.

This chapter illustrates this argument through an analysis of the social evolution and urbanization processes experienced by the Bedouin society in Israel. Traditional Bedouin tribes or confederations of tribes are based on kinship relationships. Land resources such as grazing areas, water wells, and convergence sites have traditionally been held in common, rather than as private property. Beginning in the nineteenth century, Bedouin society underwent a process of sedentarization, primarily because of the inability to make a living from grazing. This process had a significant impact on both the Bedouins' patterns of life and the traditional regime that governed the commonly shared land. The development of agriculture gradually led to the allocation of exclusive property rights, though this process is still incomplete. When more and more Bedouins began to make their living from urban occupations, the movement away from the common property regime accelerated. Yet, the tribal social structure based on strong blood ties still remained in place. urbanization and sedentarization processes did not eliminate the pattern of sharing the commons, but altered them significantly: these patterns went through a metamorphosis.

---

[1] Gregory S. Alexander, *Property and Human Flourishing* (New York: Oxford University Press, 2018), 4–9.
[2] Garrett Hardin, "The Tragedy of the Commons," *Science* 162, (1968): 1243, 1247; Elinor Ostrom, *Governing the Commons: The Evolution of Institutions for Collective Action* (Cambridge University Press, 1990), 216.

This chapter first analyzes the debate on the most effective form of property regulation from an evolutionary perspective. Building on the current research literature, it highlights the link between strong tribal kinship relations and sustainable management of the commons. The article then describes how the sedentarization and urbanization of tribal Bedouin society in Israel have affected management of the commons.

EVOLUTIONARY THEORY AND THE COMMONS

The underlying assumption of the theory of evolution is that the purpose of each living species is to assure its genetic survival. Those species that develop the most effective strategies to carry out this mission will ultimately survive and flourish. At times, altruism supplements this genetic drive.[3] For example, when no workers in an ant nest are breeding but they continue to work, biologists give this behavior an evolutionary explanation: the workers may not be contributing to the survival of their own genes, but they are contributing to the survival of the genes of their genetic relative, the queen.[4]

Evolution can explain not only genetic development but also social development. Evolutionists try to explain how different social behaviors, such as parasitism, coexistence, territoriality, or cooperation, promote species survival.[5] King Solomon observed that ants collectively administer their commons "having no chief, overseer, or ruler"[6] and sent his subjects to learn from their ways.[7] Ostrom could certainly base some of her findings on the study of myrmecology.

Humans too have the instinct of living and largely also the instinct of reproduction. According to the evolutionary view, human beings, of course, are subject to the rules of natural selection. Evolution explains physiology and genetics as well as human social behavior patterns.[8] Indeed, the attempt of humanity to give an evolutionary explanation to its own behaviors is somewhat problematic. Human consciousness of the path of evolution, as well as human desires and views, can themselves influence analysis of the evolutionary virtues of our behaviors. Humankind tries not only to make predictions about its future evolution but also to influence it. Despite these interventions, human social behaviors have evolutionary significance. The choice of the form of societal organization have an effect on the survival of individuals, communities, and humankind as a whole.

The scholarly debate on the most effective common property regulation (CPR) is actually an effort both to identify and to influence the path of human evolution. Hardin and Ostrom may have been divided regarding the future of CPR, but they agreed that many societies in the past adopted efficient strategies of commons regulation.[9] They both identified patterns of behavior that characterized early human societies that survived over time. Ostrom based her well-known book, *Governing the Commons*, on her analysis of institutions that flourished more than a century to more than a millennium ago.[10] She attempted to show that sharing common

---

[3] William Donald Hamilton, *Narrow Roads of Gene Land: Evolution of Social Behavior* (Basingstoke, W. H. Freeman at Macmillan Press Ltd., 1996) 19, 31–32.

[4] Andrew F.G. Bourke and Nigel R. Franks, *Social Evolution in Ants* (Princeton University Press, 1995), 26–27.

[5] "Social Evolution—Latest Research and Reviews," *Nature*, accessed September 9, 2018, www.nature.com/subjects/social-evolution.

[6] Proverbs 6:7.

[7] Proverbs 6:6 ("Go to the ant, thou sluggard; consider her ways, and be wise").

[8] Jack Hirshleifer, "Economics from A Biological Viewpoint," *Journal of Law and Economics* 20, no. 1 (1977): 7–9.

[9] David B. Schorr, "Savagery, Civilization, and Property: Theories of Societal Evolution and Commons Theory," *Theoretical Inquiries in Law* 19, (2018): 507, 524.

[10] Ostrom, supra note 2, at 58.

resources may still be an effective evolutionary strategy, whereas Hardin, in contrast, argued that it should be abandoned.[11]

The debate between followers of Ostrom and supporters of Hardin is really between the advocates of commons regimes and supporters of private property. Critics of the commons see this regime as a barrier to progress and enlightenment. A romantic longing for the past and the natural motivates the supporters of sharing common resources.[12] Both regimes serve an evolutionary purpose by consciously promoting patterns of behavior. However, from a purely descriptive point of view, humankind has so far evolved in a very clear direction – from common ownership to private ownership.[13] If this is indeed the direction of development, this finding requires an evolutionary explanation. Why were effective common strategies the norm in early stages of human development, and why have some communities abandoned these strategies?

KINSHIP AND THE EVOLUTION OF THE COMMONS

To find the evolutionary explanation for why early societies chose – and many contemporary indigenous, tribal, and nomadic societies continue to choose – a commons strategy, we can consult several bodies of research. First, we can look at ethological studies of animal behavior because living cooperatively is not unique to human behavior. In nature, various species evolved systems of coexistence, whereas others live independently. From the biological evolutionary point of view, cooperation prevails when it serves genetic survival. Kin selection is one of the most commonly used mechanisms to produce cooperation, as in the ants example.[14] Likely, humankind chose a common resources strategy for the same reason that ants did: it increased the probability of survival.

Other scientific fields that can help us understand why early humans chose collaborative strategies include ancient archaeology and anthropological research into indigenous or tribal societies. Most ancient human societies, as well as many contemporary indigenous, tribal, and nomadic societies, are organized along common ownership and open-access systems to land resources.[15] We know that the way property was managed in such societies was closely related to their tribal structure. There was overlap between the property structure and the extended family structure. Societies tended to preserve property in a patriarchal or patrilineal manner. In a tribal patriarchal society, retaining lands within the patrilineal ancestor's tribe throughout the generations is considered of prime importance. Landowning is viewed as key to one's way of life and as an identity marker for the broader clan or tribe as their social unit. Allowing outsiders to own

---

[11] See citations, supra notes 2.

[12] Schorr, supra note 9, at 524.

[13] Harold Demsetz, "Toward a Theory of Property Rights," *American Economic Review* 57, (1967): 347, 350–353; Robert Ellickson, *Order Without Law: How Neighbors Settle Disputes* (Cambridge: Harvard University Press, 1991), 184; Daniel Fitzpatrick, "Evolution and Chaos in Property Rights Systems: The Third World Tragedy of Contested Access," *Yale Law Journal* 115 (2006): 996, 1010–1012.

[14] Daniel J. Rankin, Katja Bargumand, and Hanna Kokko, "The Tragedy of the Commons in Evolutionary Biology," *Trends In Ecology & Evolution* 22, (2007): 643, 648; F. L. W. Ratnieks et al., "Conflict Resolution in Insect Societies," *Annual Review of Entomology* 51, (2006): 581, 584; T. Wenseleers and F. L. W. Ratnieks, "Tragedy of the Commons in Melipona Bees," *Proceedings of the Royal Society–Biology Science* 271, (2004): 310, 312.

[15] Henry Schaffer, *Hebrew tribal economy and the Jubilee* (New York: G. E. Stechert & Co., 1922), III–V (A conclusion based on a comparative study of ancient Hebrew, pre-Islamic, Indian, Homer, Roman, Russian, German, Irish, Welsh, and English tribal societies); Rucha Ghate et al., "Cultural Norms, Cooperation, and Communication: Taking Experiments to the Field in Indigenous Communities" *International Journal of The Commons* 7, (2013): 498, 501; Samira Farahani, "Ecological Engagement in Tribal Communities in the Context of Common-Pool Resources" (MA thesis, Texas State University, May 2018), 22, 38, 42.

land, whether through a sale or inheritance, weakens not only the economy but also the very fabric of society.[16]

A broad definition of family has shaped adoption of the tribal commons strategies. Sharing resources seems to be directly related to the goal of evolutionary survival.[17] Strong kinship relations, having large families, and intergenerational stability facilitate several important components of sustainable commons, including trust among people, the free transfer of information, and soft enforcement mechanisms.[18] Hardin too assumed that breeding (or "overbreeding") is a Darwinian choice of "Homo Progentivus," calling it "a policy to secure the aggrandizement" of "the family, the religion, the race of the class (or indeed any distinguishable and cohesive group)."[19]

An evolutionary perspective on tribal societies allows us to better understand the reasons why humankind has gradually abandoned sharing as a central strategy of social behavior. The most cited historical explanation for the change is an increase in population size, which led to increased pressure to obtain essential resources, capitalism, and the transition to a market economy.[20] These changes led to change in social interactions as well. The social basis of sharing in modern urban society is not based on genetics. Modern urban communities are communities of genetic strangers. Once people abandon the tribal lifestyle and move into an urban environment that places at its center the individual or, at most, the small nuclear family unit, the power of the commons, and the ideas it is built upon, are weakened; the connection between cooperation and breeding becomes much less important. In some Western countries, the weakening of kin ties has even weakened the genetic motivation and the social incentive to reproduce, leading to a "demographic transition"; that is, a decline in fertility rates.[21] The trust and social conditions that naturally encouraged cooperation in a tribal society no longer exist in urban settings, where most people are genetically alien to one another.

Such an evolutionary perspective raises questions about the likelihood that approaches to revive the strategy of the commons will succeed. They seek to re-create in modern urban neighborhoods patterns of behavior that worked well in an environment where social norms sanctified kinship relations within an extended family, clan, or tribe. Whether modern urban life can produce human incentives to cooperate that will be as strong as kinship relations and genetics is too early to predict.[22] Indeed, guilds and corporations emerged in Western Europe despite the weakening of kinship relations.[23] There are also examples of some urban

---

[16] Numbers 27:1–11, 36:1–12; Schaffer, supra note 15, at 98–99; Jeffrey A. Fager, *Land Tenure And The Biblical Jubilee* (Sheffield: Sheffield Academic Press, 1993), 27–34; John Sietze Bergsma, *The Jubilee From Leviticus To Qumran: A History of Interpretation* (Leiden; Boston: Brill Academic Publishers, 2007), 8–12; Fitzpatrick, supra note 13, at 1028–1029.

[17] Joseph Henrich and Natalie Henrich, *Why Humans Cooperate: A Cultural and Evolutionary Explanation* (New York: Oxford University Press, 2007), 89–107.

[18] Ostrom, supra note 2, at 88; Schorr, supra note 9, at 525.

[19] Hardin, supra note 2, at 1246.

[20] Schorr, supra note 9, at 529.

[21] Lesley Newson et al., "Why Are Modern Families Small? Toward an Evolutionary and Cultural Explanation for the Demographic Transition," *Personality And Social Psychology Review* 9, (2005): 360, 370–372 (Indicates the link between the lack of support for reproduction on the part of a broad family framework and the decline in reproduction rates); John C. Caldwell, "Demographic Theory: A Long View," *Population and Development Review* 30, (2004): 297, 303 (Analyzes theoretical explanations for low fertility rates, some of which are based on "the fact that post-agricultural society did not need the traditional family").

[22] Alexandra Flynn, Below Ch. 7, at 155.

[23] Tine De Moor, "The Silent Revolution: A New Perspective on the Emergence of Commons, Guilds, and Other Forms of Corporate Collective Action in Western Europe," *International Review of Social History* 53, (2008): 179, 211.

communities with strong ties.[24] However, the fate of modern forms of communes, such as kibbutzim, does not augur well for their long-term, sustainable survival.[25] There may be other social modern incentives that encourage social obligations in modern communities.[26] Yet, the chances that humankind will produce collaboration incentives that will be as powerful as kinship relations is at best questionable.[27]

The next section analyzes how both kinship relations and the transition from a nomadic to an urban life affect a group's strategies toward common resources. It focuses on the Bedouins living in the northern Negev in Israel.

THE BEDOUIN METAMORPHOSIS

Kinship and Tribal Commons. The Bedouins are an ethnic group of nomads living in the deserts of the Middle East and North Africa; they have a tribal structure.[28] Each tribe or group of tribes is considered to stem from one ancestor. This social structure fits well with both the evolutionary rationale of genetic reproduction and survivability.[29] Bedouins traditionally made a living from raising camels and grazing sheep. They held land resources, mainly water wells and pasture, in common. Each tribal confederation provided its members with equal access to these resources and in certain circumstances would permit such a grant to members of other tribal federations.[30] This regime of the commons was motivated by survival: Bedouins, who had a common genetic background, shared this quest to survive.[31] In Bedouin society, there were conditions that supported a regime of common ownership, such as those enumerated by Ostrom: trust among blood relatives, tribal independence, and tribal tribunals that resolved disputes.[32] However, like many traditional societies, it had to confront changes that challenged the long-standing commons strategy

Sedentarization and Urbanization. The common ownership regime in the Bedouin community living in the Negev region in southern Israel has undergone change over the past century. The community numbers about 270,000 people, comprising about fourteen percent of Israel's Arab population and about 3 percent of the total Israeli population.[33] At the end of the nineteenth century, the Bedouins population began to experiment with agriculture because of the difficulty of making a living exclusively from the traditional raising of livestock. This change resulted in an internal allocation (not recognized by the government) of private and

---

[24] Stephen Glackin, "Contemporary Urban Culture: How Community Structures Endure in an Individualized Society," *Culture and Organization* 21, (2015): 23, 34–39; Lucie Middlemiss, "Individualized or Participatory? Exploring Late Modern Identity and Sustainable Development," *Environmental Politics* 23, (2014): 929, 933–941.

[25] Abraham Bell and Gideon Parchomovsky, "Property Lost in Translation," *University of Chicago Law Review* 80, (2013): 515, 520.

[26] Alexander, supra note 1, at 109–113.

[27] Gideon M. Kressel, *Descent Through Males: an anthropological investigation into the patterns underlying social hierarchy, kinship, and marriage among former Bedouin in the Ramla-Lod area (Israel)* (Wiesbaden: Harrassowitz, 1992), 254–255; Tamas David-Barretta and Robin I. M. Dunbar, "Fertility, Kinship and the Evolution of Mass Ideologies," *Journal of Theoretical Biology* 417, (2017): 20, 24–25.

[28] Austin Kennett, *Bedouin Justice: Law and Custom among the Egyptian Bedouin* (London: Cass, 1968), 1–12.

[29] Emanuel Marx, *Bedouin of the Negev* (Manchester: Manchester University Press, 1967), 63.

[30] Emanuel Marx, "The Tribe as a Unit of Subsistence: Nomadic Pastoralism in the Middle East," *American Anthropologist* 79, (1977): 343, 348–349; Clinton Bailey, *Bedouin Law From Sinai & The Negev: Justice Without Government* (New Haven, CT: Yale University Press, 2009): 263–264.

[31] Kressel, supra note 27, at 242–249.

[32] Bailey, supra note 30, at 16–22, 158.

[33] Israel Central Bureau of Statistics, Table 2.1: Population by population group & Table 2.15: Population by district, sub-district and religion, *Statistical Abstract of Israel* (2019).

non-common property rights, but only in cultivated agricultural areas.[34] It did not affect the open-access regime that prevailed in the rest of the territories of the tribal confederation. In addition, the private agricultural land was also kept within a tribal framework; when land was sold, the first right of purchase was reserved for members of the tribe, especially neighbors of the previous owner.[35] Some of the Arab agricultural villages in Israel are also organized in this manner.[36] In both Arab and Bedouin societies, the allocation of private property rights in agricultural land is still, albeit more loosely, linked to broad family patrilineal relations, reflecting the evolutionary quest for genetic survival.

The establishment of the State of Israel brought two changes that challenged the traditional mechanism of common ownership. First, most of the Bedouins had to leave their original territories and were relocated by the state in land near Beer Sheva that was designated for their new settlement (the Sayag area).[37] Second, both the nomadic grazing way of life and the sporadic agriculture that began in the nineteenth century ceased to be the main sources of income for the Bedouins, and they began to make their living by pursuing urban occupations such as providing services or trading.[38] Bedouin populations in other Middle Eastern countries have undergone a similar process of sedentarization.[39] These changes forced the Bedouin society as well as the State of Israel to adapt the old traditional proprietary system to these new circumstances. Because strong kinship and tribal relationships encourage the tendency to share common land and resist privatization, this trend toward sedentarization produced new patterns of behavior. Weakening this tribal structure can lead to chaos and harm the incentive to cooperate.

Remains of the Commons in New Towns. The threats to their traditional style of life led more than half of the Bedouin population to seek permanent settlement in the small towns created by the State of Israel for their resettlement. In these towns, each family was given the private property right to a residential plot.[40] The transition from a nomadic and open-space regime to a regime of private urban property was fraught with difficulties: many of the Bedouin found it hard to adjust to an urban way of life. Today, these towns and their populations have some of the lowest rankings on combined socioeconomic indices in Israel.[41]

However, in some of these state-established towns, certain neighborhoods are made up of residents only from a single Bedouin tribe, while other neighborhoods contain a mixed

[34] Gideon M. Kressel et al., "Changes in the Land Usage by the Negev Bedouin since the Mid-19th Century: The Intra-Tribal Perspective," *Nomadic Peoples* 28, (1991): 28, 31–40; Bailey, supra note 30, at 268.

[35] Bailey, ibid., at 269; Kressel et al., ibid., at 40.

[36] Rassem Khamaisi, "Housing Transformation within Urbanized Communities: The Arab Palestinians in Israel," *Geography Research Forum* 33, (2013): 184, 190–200; Rassem Khamaisi, "Land Ownership as a Determinant in the Formation of Residential Areas in Arab Localities," *Geoforum* 26, (1995): 211, 215–216.

[37] Havatzelet Yahel and Ruth Kark, "Israel Negev Bedouin during the 1948 War: Departure and Return," *Israel Affairs* 21, (2014): 48; Ghazi Falah, "The Spatial Pattern of Bedouin Sedentarization in Israel," *Geojournal* 11, (1985): 360.

[38] A. Allan Degen and Shaher El-Meccawi, "Livestock Trader Entrepreneurs among Urban Bedouin in the Negev Desert," *Entrepreneurship and Innovation* 9, (2008): 93, 95; Shaul Krakover, "Urban Settlement Program and Land Dispute Resolution: The State of Israel versus the Negev Bedouin," *Geojournal* 47, (1999): 551.

[39] Donald P. Cole, "Where Have the Bedouin Gone?" *Anthropological Quarterly* 76, (2003): 235, 240–251; Nancy A. Browning, "*I am Bedu: The Changing Bedouin in a Changing World*" (MA diss., University of Arkansas, 2013), 33–40; Andrew Shryock "Bedouin in Suburbia: Redrawing the Boundaries of Urbanity and Tribalism in Amman" *The Arab Studies Journal* 5, (1997): 40, 42, 29; 302, 311–313; Riccardo Bocco, "The Settlement of Pastoral Nomads in the Arab Middle East: International Organizations and Trends in Development Policies, 1950-1990" *Nomadic Societies in the Middle East And North Africa: Entering the 21st Century* (Dawn Chatty ed., Brill 2006): 302, 311–312.

[40] Havatzelet Yahel, "Land Disputes between the Negev Bedouin and Israel," *Israel Studies* 11, (2006): 1, 5, 13.

[41] Israel Central Bureau of Statistics, Table 1: Socio Economic Index 2015 of Local Authorities in Ascending Order of Index Values—Index Value, Rank and Cluster, www.cbs.gov.il/he/mediarelease/doclib/2018/351/24_18_351t1.pdf.

population including members of different tribes. Neighborhoods with a homogeneous tribal population have developed a version of "urban tribalism," maintaining traditional patterns of common area management in public urban spaces. Residents of neighborhoods with a mixed population have not maintained a common interest in similar public urban spaces.[42]

The state made a similar attempt to resettle Bedouins in northern Israel, where their adaptation to modern patterns of settlements has been more successful.[43] One of the reasons for this smoother adaptation was stated by a Bedouin in the north in a recent television interview when he stated, "[w]e are no longer Bedouins."[44] The property changes in northern Israel thus, in some cases, led to a change in group identity.[45] Bedouins in other countries in the Middle East have gone through a similar process of "detribalization" in which an overall Bedouin identity – one based on a common history and subculture – replaced the strong tribal boundaries of blood ties. In these societies communal rights are no longer recognized.[46]

In new towns, tribal blood ties may continue to be, at least for a while, an incentive for the effective management of common resources, even when the entire environment changes. When tribal tradition and blood ties loosen, the ability to cooperate weakens, and adaptation to a private property regime improves.

Spontaneous Tragedy of the Commons. Nearly half of all Bedouins have refused to move to towns and cities. On land that they consider to be their common grazing territory, they have begun independently to build unplanned residential constructions, mainly tin shacks. They are thus using open-access land for residential purposes. Such constructions preserve some of the characteristics of the traditional neighborhoods, but have slowly become more permanent.[47] These settlements of shacks spread quickly, occupying very wide areas of the open spaces.[48] They are a clear example of Hardin's tragedy of the commons.

Bedouins see these "spontaneous settlements" as a way to protect their land.[49] They demand that the government legally recognize them and invest in their development. Yet the government considers them to be illegal because they are being built without the necessary public infrastructure and do not meet urban construction standards. The government wants in principle to stop the expansion, but it has not acted decisively toward this goal. It prefers negotiating with the Bedouins and has even considered legalizing some of their settlements.[50]

The Bedouin response to their dispersion indicates again that common open-access patterns that were developed in traditional or nomadic societies do not suddenly disappear when there is a change in the circumstances of life. Traditional attitudes to common resources drive the

---

[42] S. Tamari et al., "Urban Tribalism: Negotiating Form, Function and Social Milieu in Bedouin Towns, in Israel," *City Territory and Architecture* 3, (2016): 1, 9–10; Yuval Karplus, *"The Dynamics of Space Construction among the Negev Bedouin"* (PhD diss., Ben-Gurion University of the Negev, 2010) (Hebrew), 239–241.

[43] Arnon Medzini, "Bedouin Settlement Policy in Israel: Success or Failure?" *Themes in Israeli Geography* 79, (2012): 37, 43–44.

[44] Gil Karni and Peleg Nathaniel, "Second Look: Permanent House for Nomads—On the Northern and Southern Solution to the Bedouin Localities," Kan 11: Israel Broadcasting Corporation, YouTube video, 6:57, February 13, 2014, www.youtube.com/watch?v=1FLE8-wk-oI (Hebrew).

[45] Arnon Medzini, "Tribalism Versus Community Organization: Geography of a Multi-Tribal Bedouin Locality in the Galilee," *Studia z Geografii Politycznej i Historycznej* 5 (2016): 237, 251–253.

[46] Cole, supra note 39, at 250–252; Browning, supra note 39, at 37.

[47] Isaac A. Meir and Ilan Stavi, "Evolution of the 'Modern' Transitory Shelter and Unrecognized Settlement of the Negev Bedouin," *Nomadic Peoples* 15 (2011): 33, 35, 41.

[48] Yahel, supra note 40, at 4–8.

[49] Falah, supra note 37, at 367.

[50] Deborah F. Shmueli and Rassem Khamaisi, "Bedouin Communities in the Negev: Models for Planning the Unplanned," *Journal of the American Planning Association* 77, (2011): 109, 115; Yahel, supra note 40, at 11–13.

creation of new versions of common resources as long as there are no governmental barriers and traditional kinship relations prevail in the changing society.

Claiming Commons as Private. Another strategy adopted by a small portion of the Bedouin who remain in their original territories is to file lawsuits for recognition of private property rights to their former open-access territories. They claim private property rights to an area of about 650 square kilometers.[51] For the sake of comparison, the entire urban built-up area of the State of Israel (excluding the Bedouin dispersion area) was about 840 square kilometers in 2003 and 900 square kilometers in 2007.[52] The entire area that is privately owned in the State of Israel is about 1,500 square kilometers.[53] The government opposes the Bedouins' lawsuits and claims that they have no legal basis. The Supreme Court rejected them, inter alia, on the grounds that collective rights cannot be given to individuals.[54] That the Bedouins have made these claims illustrates their adherence to the common-access traditional order while adapting to the newer and completely different standard of private property through legal means. The underlying motivation of both is keeping land assets within kinship groups.

CONCLUSION

This chapter focused on the role of kinship relations in the effectiveness of strategies for the management of common resources. This linkage is not only well known in legal writing about the commons but is also recognized in the literature dealing with the social evolution of nonhuman species and humankind and with the social structure of tribal societies. It reflects a strategy of social and genetic survival. Modern processes of urbanization and sedentarization have severed blood ties, so that urban societies usually comprise genetic strangers. The loosening of blood ties or their lack thereof weakens the incentives for sharing in a modern urban society and causes tragedies of the common. The political debate between Ostrom and Hardin deals with how to respond to this change in human evolution.

The importance of traditional kinship relations in fostering cooperation can be seen in modern Bedouin society in Israel, which has undergone both sedentarization and urbanization. These processes have led to the abandonment of the traditional regime of the commons; they also show how difficult it is for a tribal society to break away from the commons tradition and adapt to urban private ownership patterns. The tribal structure based on close blood ties still remains, if weakened. Traditional sharing patterns continue to influence attitudes to open and urban space held by residents of newly created towns in the south of Israel; however, this effect varies by the composition of the neighborhood.

In segregated Bedouin urban neighborhoods, there is a high degree of sharing common resources, but the weakening of tribalism has impaired the ability of Bedouins living in mixed urban neighborhoods to collaborate on public spaces. Among those Bedouin who have chosen to erect encampments on large tracts of grazing lands, some are waging lawsuits to claim them as

---

[51] Yahel, supra note 40, at 8.

[52] Amir Eidelman and Yael Yavin, "Built Areas and Open Spaces in Israel," in *Israel Sustainability Project 2030: Indices — Sustainability Yesterday, Today And Tomorrow* (Israeli Ministry of the Environment, 2011), 3 (Hebrew); Moti Kaplan et al., *Patterns of use of Built-Up Areas in Israel* (2007), 89 (Hebrew).

[53] Israel Land Administration, *Report on Activities for the 2012 Budget Year* (2013), 72 (Hebrew).

[54] C.A.4220/12 "Al-Uqbi v. The State of Israel," J. Hayut, par. 36, 42, 67, 81 (May 14, 2012) (Official English translation), https://supremedecisions.court.gov.il/Home/Download?path=EnglishVerdicts\12\200\042\v29&fileName=12042200 .V29&type=5.

privately-owned areas. At the same time, Bedouins who have settled in the north of the country seem to have a stronger capability to adapt to an individualistic urban lifestyle.

The significant contribution of blood ties to common resource management raises the question of whether societies in which kinship ties have loosened can produce strong enough incentives for collaboration. The answer to this question poses serious challenges for both Hardin's and Ostrom's models.

PART II

Averting New Tragedies

4

Averting Tragedy of the Resource Directory Anti-Commons

A Practical Approach to Open Data Infrastructure for Health, Human, and Social Services

Greg Bloom

WHAT IS COMMUNITY RESOURCE DATA?

Community resource information is comprised of data about the health, human, and social services that are made available by government agencies and non-profit organizations (NPOs) to people in need. This specifically entails the following factors: what services exist, where they are located, and how people can access them. This is public information, and yet it is persistently difficult to find.

This difficulty reflects the complexity of the health, human, and social services that are represented by resource data. Organizations provide various services in different combinations at different locations. Funding for services comes from fragmented, overlapping jurisdictions and sectors, with no central institution that can establish and coordinate common reporting practices. Access to services is limited by various criteria that delineate which kinds of people are eligible, under what circumstances. All of these details are in constant flux as a result of changes in funding, policy, staff, and any number of other factors. Complicating matters further, diverse actors in varying contexts might each use different vocabularies to describe the same concepts.[1]

I learned about these challenges first-hand while working at a large community-based anti-poverty organization that provides dozens of services across multiple departments and facilities.[2] I was responsible for managing "communications" – the primary purpose of which was fundraising. The organization's website, for example, was designed to generate donations. I chose to add additional pages with specific information about how to access our various services, but I wasn't expected to do so. Our peer organizations' websites, by comparison, often described their services with a broad mission statement (i.e., "we give support to our neighbors in need") alongside little more than a front-desk number to call for more information.

These experiences illuminated a conundrum at the root of resource information problem: many service providers lack strong incentives to attract new "clients."[3] Such providers often are

---

[1] For instance: "addiction therapy" and "outpatient behavioral health treatment program."

[2] Bloom, G. "Towards a Community Data Commons," *Beyond Transparency*. B. Goldstein and L. Dyson, eds. Code for America. (2013). https://beyondtransparency.org/chapters/part-5/towards-a-community-data-commons/

[3] In my experience, this claim is widely corroborated by practitioners in the field. I have not, however, found it reflected as such in relevant literature; that said, several literature reviews have observed that the quality of available research on human service capacities is poor. For some examples, see Lohr, A. M., M. Ingram, A. V. Nunez, K. M. Reinschmidt, and S. C. Carvajal. 2018. Community–clinical linkages with community health workers in the United States: A scoping review. *Health Promotion Practice* 19(3): 349–360; Bradley, E. H., M. Canavan, E. Rogan, K. Talbert-Slagle, C. Ndumele, L. Taylor, and L. A. Curry. 2016. Variation in health outcomes: The role of spending on social services,

not paid by their clients.[4] Furthermore, providers often don't receive funding on a per-client basis. Even among those who receive fee-for-service revenue or reimbursement from particular funding sources, such compensation often isn't sufficient to cover the full costs of service. As a result, the labor of disseminating information about their services is typically not a priority for already-overburdened staff.

One might assume that the funders of services, whether governmental or philanthropic, would require resource data to be reported as a condition of their funding, but this kind of policy is not typical. (The *potential* for such a policy is discussed below.) Funders tend to collect data about inputs (number of clients served) and outputs (results of services), but not data about how a service is actually accessed, such as what documents might be required, application processes, hours of operation, and so on. Through Forms 990 submitted to the IRS, the federal government asks broad questions about organizations' programming, to which organizations tend to submit their mission statements.

All of these factors combine to make information about "community resources" harder to find and less reliable than information about commercial services in a conventional market, where vendors have strong incentives to attract customers. The most accurate, detailed information about such services are often produced *ad hoc* by frontline staff, and scattered among emails, PDFs, and paper flyers posted across their facilities.

In the next section of this chapter, I'll explore the ways in which these misaligned incentives, which yield such ephemeral forms of critical public information, are refracted in the failure of a secondary market for resource data aggregation; subsequently, I will analyze that market's failure in the framework of a digital anti-commons. In the second half of this chapter, I will describe a strategic intervention – the Open Referral Initiative – that aims to correct this market failure through the development of open standards for resource data exchange; finally, I will describe a set of hypothetical institutional models that can sustainably provision resource data as a public good.

WHO MAINTAINS COMMUNITY RESOURCE DIRECTORIES?

In lieu of organizations' self-directed promotion of their own service information, resource data tends to be manually aggregated by third parties in "community resource directories." Many, if not most, community resource directories are produced by the people who use them on a daily basis. This, too, I learned about firsthand. Social workers at my organization built a Microsoft Access database of more than a thousand other organizations' services to which we would refer our clients; they would spend hours every week updating it. Other organizations would occasionally ask us for copies of this database and then use it to create their own community resource directories. This ad hoc collection and distribution process led to a proliferation of places, both online and in print, which needed ongoing maintenance that we and others had few real incentives to perform.

---

public health, and health care, 2000–2009. *Health Affairs (Millwood)* 35(5): 760–768; Pescheny, J.V., Pappas, Y. & Randhawa, G. Facilitators and barriers of implementing and delivering social prescribing services: a systematic review. *BMC Health Serv Res* 18, 86 (2018). DOI:10.1186/s12913-018-2893-4

[4] In the typology of "civil society organizations" and the associational goods thereof, as introduced by Swiney and DeMattee in Chapter 13 of this volume (236–240), most human service providers are "Common Pool Resource CSOs": their goods are subtractable, i.e. rivalrous, in that one person's use of a service depletes the availability of the service for others. Such organizations (or their funders) tend to compensate for this high subtractability by increasing the excludability of their services through boundary rules in the form of complex eligibility criteria.

This experience was in the late 2000s, when the emergence of Wikipedia (among other sites of open knowledge production) generated excitement about the prospect of "commons-based peer production."[5] It seemed at the time like the community resource directory data problem could soon be solved by "crowdsourcing." Many such sites did appear, like Code for America's Redirectory project and the San Francisco Homeless Wiki, yet they tended to be produced by one or two unusually committed individuals, and would be abandoned when that leadership moved on.[6] The potential for community resource directory information to be effectively managed by "the crowd" remains unrealized.

The aggregation and maintenance of community resource information poses a long-standing problem that the internet has, ironically, exacerbated. In the mid-twentieth century, local libraries maintained community resource directories as a service to their community.[7] In the '60s and '70s, increasing amounts of federal funding for nonprofit organizations fueled the formation of a professional sector known as "information-and-referral" (I&R). In 1973, the Alliance of Information and Referral Systems (AIRS) formed as a trade association for this field, setting standards and providing support to a membership that grew to include more than 1,000 organizations across the country. These conventional "I&R providers" typically operate call centers – such as local 2-1-1 hotlines, aging and disability resource centers (ADRCs), childcare resource and referral centers (CCR&Rs), and other specialist referral providers – in which inbound callers receive information from resource databases maintained through outbound calls to health, human, and social service organizations.

Since the turn of the century, a range of startups (both non-profit and for-profit) have taken entrepreneurial, web-based approaches to the I&R challenge. This emerging market is largely fueled by demand from the healthcare sector for "resource referral" solutions that can better address the "social determinants of health" by connecting patients with available social services, often through the aid of "community health navigators" who are trained for this task.[8] Similar startups are courting other sectors (such as education, corrections, homelessness, and workforce development); however, healthcare is where companies can find the most capital. As described by a recent report produced by the Social Interventions Research & Evaluation Network (SIREN), a "dizzying array of new technology platforms have emerged with the shared aim of enabling health care organizations to more easily identify and refer patients to social service organizations."[9] The SIREN Report observes that resource directory maintenance is a challenge common to all of these platforms; the vendors thereof tend to pass the cost of resource data maintenance onto their users, either through added fees or an expectation that users will produce and maintain this information themselves.

Across both markets of referral providers – the conventional call centers and emerging web-based startups – these information services tend to be bundled "end-to-end." Aggregation,

[5] Shirky, C. *Here Comes Everybody* (New York: Penguin Books, 2008), and *Cognitive Surplus* (New York: Penguin Books, 2010); Benkler, Y. *Wealth of Networks* (New Haven: Yale University Press, 2006).

[6] Fitch, D. "Wherefore Wikis?" *Journal of Technology in Human Services*, 25(4), 79–85. DOI:10.1300/j017v25n04_05

[7] Kate Williams and Joan Durrance consider this practice to be a key point of inception for the field of "community informatics" as a whole: "Community Informatics," Encyclopedia of Library and Information Sciences, Third Edition (2010). DOI:10.1081/E-ELIS3-120043669

[8] National Academies of Sciences, Engineering, and Medicine 2019. Integrating Social Care into the Delivery of Health Care: Moving Upstream to Improve the Nation's Health. Washington, DC: The National Academies Press. DOI:10.17226/25467.

[9] Cartier Y, Fichtenberg C, & Gottlieb L. "Community Resource Referral Platforms: A Guide for Health Care Organizations." San Francisco, CA: SIREN. (2019) Available at: https://sirenetwork.ucsf.edu/tools-resources/resources/community-resource-referral-platforms-a-guide-for-health-care-organization

maintenance, classification, curation, and delivery: each conducted by every intermediary. Today, most of these "information intermediaries" consider the resource data that they aggregate to be their private intellectual property, only available in bulk for a fee – as a commodity.[10]

THE ONGOING TRAGEDY OF THE RESOURCE DATA ANTI-COMMONS

We've discussed three distinct modes by which community resource data are produced, each of which tend to occur in isolation from the others:

- *Self-production:* Organizations that provide health, human, and social services can publish information about these services themselves. However, they often don't have strong incentives to do so.
- *Co-production:* Resource directories can be produced by the people who use them (often social workers and other care providers, professional or volunteer).[11] These co-produced directories typically struggle to reach any significant scale, or to sustain themselves.
- *Intermediary production:* Resource directories can be produced by third party providers – conventionally, call centers, or more recently, web-based software vendors. These intermediaries tend to treat the resulting data as their property and enclose it within their proprietary channels.

This state of affairs may be understood as a kind of "knowledge anti-commons." Initially coined by Heller, an "anti-commons" occurs when rights to a shared resource are held concurrently by multiple parties – each of whom can exclude others – leading to systematic underutilization of the resource.[12] Though digital resources are non rivalrous (in that they are not diminished by use) and non-excludable (in that, once published, they can be used by many parties simultaneously, in ways that are difficult if not impossible to restrict), they can still become tragic anti-commons.[13] In this case, when the same resource directory information is aggregated simultaneously across multiple databases by multiple parties, the result is a proliferation of data silos that each struggle to sustain themselves – while competing with each other,

---

[10] Such intellectual property claims would be difficult to enforce: longstanding legal precedent holds that publicly knowable facts, even when laboriously aggregated, cannot be subject to copyright without some degree of creative presentation. (See Feist Publications vs Rural Tel. Service Co. (1991), https://caselaw.findlaw.com/us-supreme-court/499/340.html). Resource directory maintainers may claim that their curation, especially categorization, of resource data is a creative work, but this still would not prohibit a third party from "scraping" resource data from a directory website, and repurposing that data in some other way. This precise right was recently affirmed in federal court – see Kerr, O. "Scraping A Public Website Doesn't Violate the CFAA, Ninth Circuit (Mostly) Holds," The Volokh Conspiracy. (November 1, 2019), https://reason.com/2019/09/09/scraping-a-public-website-doesnt-violate-the-cfaa-ninth-circuit-mostly-holds/

[11] In *Digital Dead End* (Cambridge: MIT Press, 2011, p. 110–120), Virginia Eubanks describes an instance of such co-production among clients of a local YWCA, who collaboratively published their own printed resource directory. Eubanks describes how this process amounted to more than the sum of the directory's parts, in that it fostered "relationship building" and "peer learning," enabling the co-producers to "[explore] ways of knowing," and "[create] spaces for collaborative analysis." The project was eventually rendered obsolete by the launch of a local 2-1-1 hotline. While the information intermediary may have been able to maintain data more efficiently, and at a greater scale, Eubanks observes that this shift in context of information production and consumption – from peer-based to provider-to-consumer – resulted in the loss of *tacit knowledge* that service users share with each other, along with a social setting in which such knowledge can be collectively acted upon.

[12] Heller, M. "The Tragedy of the Anticommons: Property in the Transition from Marx to Markets." William Davidson Institute Working Papers Series 40 (1997).

[13] Kamppari, S. "Tragedy of digital anti-commons," Helsinki University of Technology, Networking Laboratory (2004). www.netlab.tkk.fi/opetus/s38042/s04/Presentations/06102004_Kamppari/Kamppari_paper.pdf

directly or indirectly. With more and more sources of less and less reliable information, supply grows while demand remains unmet.

In any given community, at any given time, one might find multiple efforts to build a "centralized community resource clearinghouse" in various stages of design, launch, or decay. Successful instances of this method – in which a single community resource directory serves as a canonical and sustainable source of information for an entire community – are rare, perhaps even unprecedented. Given the vast, context-specific range of needs in a given community, one set of interfaces can not be effectively suited for all possible uses. When attempted anyway, this mode of intervention tends to repeat and reinforce the anti-commons pattern: yet another system ends up competing for resources and attention.[14]

This is not to dismiss the prospect of collective action. As Elinor Ostrom has shown, practical solutions to collective action problems may best be achieved through *polycentricity* – distributed, nested, and interconnected systems of production and decision-making. In this context, poly-centricity might entail cooperative alignment of the modes of resource data production described above, along with their associated actors and incentive structures, around standardized protocols and open infrastructures. Instead of being centralized within one monolithic system, *resource data as a commons* could circulate through a distributed ecosystem of heterogeneous technologies and institutional contexts.

TOWARD A POLYCENTRIC RESOURCE DATA COMMONS:
THE OPEN REFERRAL INITIATIVE

Through facilitated dialogues among various institutions involved in community resource data aggregation and/or dissemination (including AIRS, Code for America, Google.org, and others), the Open Referral Initiative was conceived and launched as a multi-stakeholder market inter-vention in support of standardization and open access for community resource data.[15] Open Referral's mission is to make it easier for community resource directory data to be provisioned as an interoperable, infrastructural common good.

In contrast to the concept of a "centralized platform," Open Referral is not a product but rather a community of practice that fosters cooperative capacities among actors who have previously been trapped in tragic anti-commons dilemmas. Similar in function to that of a Standard Setting Organization,[16] though less formal in structure, Open Referral facilitates participatory research and development processes through which priorities are set, and outcomes evaluated, by people working closest to the actual problem at hand – often service providers who maintain resource directories and/or provide referral services to people seeking help. This development process entails iterative, distributed cycles of research, deliberation, modeling, testing, and deployment, involving multiple stakeholders from multiple communities, each with their own socio-technical landscape and tactical objectives.[17] It is a live experiment in polycentricity.

---

[14] This reflects the classic characteristics of a "wicked problem." Rittel, H., and M. Webber; "Dilemmas in a General Theory of Planning" pp. 155–169, Policy Sciences, Vol. 4, Elsevier Scientific Publishing Company, Inc., Amsterdam, 1973.

[15] https://openreferral.org/about/history/

[16] Simcoe, T. "Governing the Anticommons: Institutional Design for Standard-Setting Organizations," *Innovation Policy and the Economy* 14 (2014): 99–128.

[17] Insights from these processes are reflected in claims made by this essay, and aggregated in Open Referral's website (https://openreferral.org/category/blog) and associated public documentation, viewable at https://docs.openreferral.org

SOLVING ONE PIECE OF THE PUZZLE:
INTEROPERABILITY THROUGH RESOURCE DATA STANDARDS

In 2014, Open Referral developed version 1.0 of the Human Services Data Specification (HSDS), a non-proprietary data interchange format. HSDS has been adopted by dozens of organizations to share resource data among various channels – from web and mobile applications, to call centers, and even printed directories. In 2017, Open Referral introduced version 1.0 of the Human Services Data Application Programming Interface protocols (HSDA),[18] modeled upon HSDS, to enable real-time data exchange. In 2018, AIRS formally endorsed the use of HSDS and HSDA as industry standards for resource data exchange among I&R providers.[19]

As a result, there is now a common method by which the same resource data can be used by many systems – and through which resource data from many systems can be synthesized for the same type of use. These protocols have already helped organizations reduce the costs of developing new resource directory websites, redeploying already-built websites and tools, and exchanging resource data among intermediaries.

The development of open standards is a necessary pre-condition to the establishment of resource data as a public good, provisioned through polycentric institutional cooperation; however, it is not sufficient. A formidable collective action dilemma is yet to be resolved: If resource data is to be openly accessible, yet it requires effort to maintain, how can such maintenance be sustained?

HYPOTHETICAL MODELS FOR SUSTAINABLE OPEN RESOURCE DATA PRODUCTION

To seek answers for this question of sustainability, we can draw upon an array of principles and pattern languages for the institutional design of data infrastructures from the emerging literature about "knowledge commons."[20] These principles have guided the strategic development of the Open Referral Initiative and its associated pilot projects, in which diverse sets of actors – from intermediary I&R providers, to emerging startups, to local community anchor institutions, governments and funders – work together to formulate and test hypotheses as to how resource data might be established as a commons.

A set of hypothetical institutional models have emerged through this process. Corresponding loosely with the modes of resource data production described above, we'll describe these models as:

- A service registry
- A data utility
- A data collaborative
- A data trust

[18] Application Programming Interfaces (APIs) enable computer programs to access the contents of databases. Standardized API protocols provide common conventions so that different APIs can "speak" the same language.

[19] https://openreferral.org/airs-recommends-open-referral-for-resource-database-interoperability/

[20] Frischmann B, Madison M, and Strandburg, K. *Governing Knowledge Commons*, Oxford University Press (2014). See also: Neylon, C. "Sustaining Scholarly Infrastructures through Collective Action: The Lessons that Olson can Teach us," *KULA: Knowledge Creation, Dissemination, and Preservation Studies* 1(1): (2017): 3. DOI: 10.5334/kula.7

These models should not be considered mutually exclusive. Indeed, hybridized institutional designs may be the most likely to succeed. Nevertheless, it will be helpful to consider each on its own terms.

The Service Registry: Publication by an Authority. A register is an official list.[21] A "service register" could be established by a funder to aggregate canonical information about the entire set of services that it funds. As such, a service registry model could address the resource directory problem at its root, by requiring as a condition of funding that service providers will produce up-to-date information about their own services as a public good.

This model is being tested by a range of institutions, both governmental and philanthropic. For instance, New York City's Mayor's Office of Opportunity is using HSDS to standardize data extracted from NYC's health, human, and social services contracting system, and has published the resulting register of contracted services on the city's open data portal.[22] Meanwhile, the Florida Legal Aid Resource Federation developed a shared registry of every legal aid provider in Florida that receives funding from the Legal Services Corporation and Florida Bar Foundation.[23] In this instance, each provider is expected to input their service information into a form deployed within their case management system, which outputs aggregated resource data that is shared among, and verified by, the peer network of providers.

The Data Utility: Sustainable "Infomediary" Infrastructure. A reimagined version of the 'centralized clearinghouse' concept, the "data utility" model takes an infrastructural "infomediary" approach to the resource data problem: rather than one "centralized" system that "everyone" would supposedly use, a data utility can serve as a supplier of resource data services that can be accessed via API by any third-party organizations and information systems. In turn, the utility can recover the costs of production through fees for value-added services, paid by organizations that require high-performance functionality associated with resource data.[24]

This data utility model takes a "club goods" approach to sustainability: one infomediary bears the costs of stewarding resource directory information as open data that any third party can leverage, and recoups these costs by generating revenue from a subset of institutions which have the resources and motivation to pay for value-adding premium features. Through market analysis and pilot experiments, Open Referral's Miami Open211 pilot has validated this hypothetical model: a range of organizations that currently maintain duplicative databases have indicated that they would instead use data supplied by a reliable third party, and a sufficient subset of these organizations indicated interest in paying for services such as unlimited API access and frequency of updates, and/or features such as customizable classification tools, white-labeled custom websites, special filters, reports, and other curatorial products.[25] Most promising of all, a successful data utility could analyze traffic patterns (search terms, clicks, etc.) across all of the channels that use its API, generating valuable insights about communities' needs, resource allocation, and program effectiveness at a scale and granularity that is not currently possible in the field.

---

[21] See the Open Data Institute's 2018 report, "Registers and collaboration: making lists we can trust." https://theodi.org/article/registers-and-collaboration-making-lists-we-can-trust-report/

[22] https://openreferral.org/nyc-government-publishing-open-data-for-municipally-contracted-service-providers/

[23] https://openreferral.org/the-florida-legal-resource-directory-project/

[24] For examples of open data business models, see Janssen M. and Zuiderwijk A. "Infomediary Business Models for Connecting Open Data Providers and Users" Social Science Computer Review 1–18 (2014) DOI: 10.1177/0894439314525902

See also Donker, F. W., and Loenen, B. "Sustainable Business Models for Public Sector Open Data Providers," *Journal of eDemocracy & Open Government* 8 (2016): 28–61. DOI: 10.29379/jedem.v8i1.390

[25] https://openreferral.org/miami-open211-developing-new-business-models-for-resource-data-as-a-service/

The Data Collaborative: A Cooperative Network of Resource Data Producers. In a "data collaborative" model, resource data is managed as a common pool resource, co-produced by multiple organizations that cooperatively align their efforts to distribute the burden of data production and maintenance, and share its benefits.[26]

This model assumes that even though intermediary organizations might compete with each other for funding and other resources, they share common interests in the quality of available resource data. If, by developing a "pre-competitive" resource data supply chain, such intermediaries could process more information of higher quality at lower cost, then they would be able to shift their own resource allocation to invest more into their core programmatic activities, such as curating and delivering this information in ways that are custom-tailored for their particular clients and contexts.

The prospect of a resource data collaborative poses serious, intersecting technical and institutional design challenges. Technologically, multi-lateral resource data management could be facilitated by the development of a "federated publishing platform" that enables records to be matched across databases, updates to be shared, conflicts to be identified and resolved, etc.[27] However, a successful federation will require more than just technology. Ostrom identifies a range of conditions that need to be established in the "struggle to govern the commons" – such as social capital shared among members, the development of monitoring capabilities, the means of enforcing norms, and the ability to exclude non-compliant actors from the common pool.[28]

There are few precedents for such cooperation in the field. A rare example is the Community Information Online Consortium (CIOC), which is a cooperative that provides a software platform to its organizational members, including dozens of infomediaries across Ontario, Canada. Over more than a decade, CIOC has developed data collaboration tools that enable its members to not only share data but also work together to improve its quality over time. CIOC's leadership has described a set of "lessons learned" from this experience, which appear to reflect the principles of Ostrom's Institutional Analysis and Development framework. For example, CIOC's successful data partnerships tend to emerge from strong relationships that establish clear boundaries around which resources will be stewarded by which infomediaries, and clear expectations about how those responsibilities should be upheld.[29]

The data collaborative approach is also being tested in the Service Net pilot, led by Benetech, among multiple referral providers in the San Francisco Bay Area. Through Service Net, Benetech is developing open source infrastructural tools for multi-lateral resource data management among previously siloed databases.[30] Specifically, Service Net enables a network of resource directory maintainers to compare the contents of their respective databases – and to suggest edits, verify information, and share updates with each other. This initiative, if successful, could be transformative for the field.

The Data Trust Model: Governing Resource Data as a Commons : The previous three models describe new potential methods of data production. A "data trust" may serve as a useful method of data governance, in that it can establish and coordinate the operational and legal activities of any given production method.

[26] See the GovLab's aggregation of research on data collaboratives at http://datacollaboratives.org
[27] Bloom, G. "An Open Data Approach to the Human Service Directory Problem," Bloomberg Data for Good Exchange Conference (2015). www.academia.edu/16449530/An_Open_Data_Approach_to_the_Human_Service_Directory_Problem
[28] Dietz T, Ostrom E, Stern P, "The Struggle to Govern the Commons," *Science* 302 (5652): (2003), 1907.
[29] Presented at the 2019 Workshop on the Ostrom Workshop at Indiana University. See also: http://opencioc.org/
[30] https://openreferral.org/introducing-benetech-service-net/

Data trusts are a new version of an old concept: as a fiduciary instrument, a trust can hold and execute assets on behalf of designated beneficiaries.[31] The concept of a data trust offers several benefits that help communities cope with the dilemmas that pertain to their data.

For example, a trust can establish a set of principles and priorities reflecting the interests of various stakeholders for whom the data is collected and maintained, and, accordingly, a set of rules pertaining to the use of this data. Those rules can change over time through processes that are transparent and accountable to the beneficiaries.

The trust can then serve as a coordinating mechanism, bringing to bear capacities such as legal expertise, technology, and scientific processes, while ensuring that these actors are constrained in accordance with the rules established by the data trust. The data trust can facilitate monitoring of these activities, and solicit appropriate consent for production and use of resource data and other associated assets. Finally, the data trust can manage the process of valuation and transactions involving services associated with the resource data. In this way, the data trust can disentangle the fate of community resource directory data from the actions of the parties that might temporarily collect, store, or use it, establishing a kind of collective ownership over the former and accountable stewardship of the latter.

CONCLUSION

This chapter has described the resource directory data anti-commons: many types of users need resource directory data, and many types of producers produce resource directory data, yet these activities are both concurrent and non-cooperative, resulting in a proliferation of resource data sources that don't actually satisfy demand. We explored the contours of this market failure by examining distinct methods in which resource data is produced: provided directly from an organization about its own services, co-produced by the users of the data themselves, or aggregated by an intermediary organization that supplies it as a service to third parties.

Finally, we've explored a set of hypothetical models that can address the points of failure for each of the above modes of production – from a "service registry" model that can be implemented directly by funders about their own contractors and grantees, to a "data utility" model through which an intermediary can sustainably monetize the provision of open data, to a "data collaborative" model in which multiple intermediaries can cooperate in the management of shared resource data. [See *Figure 4.1.*]

Various pilot experiments have already validated the plausibility of these hypothetical models; however, assessing their operational viability will require more time and investment. Further research could help articulate the various strengths and weaknesses for each of these models (and any others yet to be identified) across every part of the data supply chain as described above – from aggregation, to verification, to classification and curation, to delivery, analytics, and so on.

These models are complementary and likely require some hybridization to succeed. For example, the potential value of a service registry may be most practically realized when a funder contracts a data utility to deploy a registry, monitor it, and ensure compliance. And a data utility might be made more sustainable through the development of a data collaborative, which can

---

[31] Wylie B, McDonald S, "What Is a Data Trust?," Center for International Governance Innovation. (2018), www.cigionline.org/articles/what-data-trust

See also Porcaro K. "In Trust, Data: The Trust as a Data Management Tool." (2019). Available at SSRN: https://ssrn.com/abstract=3372372 or http://dx.doi.org/10.2139/ssrn.3372372

Modes of open resource data production.	**Intermediated** (produced by third parties)	**Direct** (produced by the source)
Authoritative (official records)	**A "Data Utility"** • Centralized platform (one-to-many). • Resource data via open API. • Sustained by revenue from "club goods" — value-adding services / premium features. *Examples: Miami Open211, Ontario Open211*	**A "Service Registry"** • Mandated by funder (gov or philanthropic) or network body (i.e., food bank). • Orgs required to update own service records. • Needs mechanisms for monitoring and compliance. *Examples: Florida Legal Aid Resource Federation, NYC gov's HHS contractors open dataset*
Co-produced (shared among peers)	**A "Data Collaborative"** • Federated network (many-to-many) • Data producers share updates in common pool • Decreases costs of maintenance, increases quality of data. *Examples: Benetech's Service Net, Community Information Online Consortium*	**Crowdsourcing** • "Peer production," i.e., a wiki • Maintained by service users and/or service providers • Few known examples of sustainability *Examples: San Francisco Homeless Wiki*

FIGURE 4.1 Modes of open resource data production

efficiently distribute responsibility for resource data maintenance among members' domains of expertise. In turn, stewardship from a trusted data utility may bolster the ongoing viability of a data collaborative. For any given community's unique institutional landscape, the most effective solutions may be best found through a process of research and development, dialogue and deliberation, and trial and error.

Such long-term, relational, and process-driven work is difficult to fund. Government procurement processes tend to expect complete workplans designed in advance, and philanthropies tend to expect simple solutions with linear, easily measurable impacts. However, governments and philanthropies are not merely sources of funding; they are also stakeholders, as prospective users of both the resource data itself and the analytics that can be gleaned from the monitored use of the data infrastructure. Future research and development should explore the great potential for resource data commons to enhance our collective capacities – governmental, philanthropic, and democratic – for needs assessment, programmatic evaluation, and data-driven decision-making.

5

Time and Tragedy

The Problem with Temporal Commons

Blake Hudson

[P]hilosophical arguments about future generations are symptomatic of a temporal myopia that infects modern society. The question of obligations to future generations is posed in terms of abstract obligations to possible future people who are strangers to us. The argument is premised on the lack of a sense of continuity of the present with both past and future. There is little sense in which our projects, and interests in the success of such projects, are understood as tied to the future. What is the source of that myopia?[1]

Philosopher John O'Neill answers his own question about why society struggles to fulfill its obligations to future generations by identifying a familiar culprit: "the tragedy of the commons."[2] Indeed, O'Neill's 1993 article *Future Generations: Present Harms* was the first – and virtually only scholarly work since–to meaningfully wrestle with the role of time in contributing to the tragedy befalling common-pool resources and their users. O'Neill argued, without exploring in detail, that "successive generations occupy a temporal 'commons,'" regardless of whether resources are owned publicly or privately.[3] Present and future generations share a common pool not only of physical resources, but of time. O'Neill then reimagines Garrett Hardin's popular example by considering a plot of land owned by successive generations of herders: "Each generation, if they are rational self-maximizers, will add to their herd and graze the land to its limits within that generation; the benefit accrues to themselves, while the loss is shared by all successive generations . . . we should expect each generation to deplete the resources it passes on to following generations."[4]

We might, as does O'Neill, characterize resource consumption through time as a commons in and of itself (a "new commons"[5]) or rather look at time as one of the primary commons dilemmas that contributes to resource management failures. This chapter does not seek to answer the proper frame for assessing "temporal commons," which I will leave for future work. Regardless of frame, the role of time in exacerbating resource management is understudied and should be given more attention if society is to better account for temporality in making resource management decisions. While not an exhaustive study, this chapter attempts to establish a

---

[1] John O'Neill, *Future Generations: Present Harms*, 68 PHILOSOPHY 46 (1993).
[2] *Id.*
[3] *Id.*
[4] *Id.*
[5] Charlotte Hess, *Mapping the New Commons* (July 1, 2008) (unpublished manuscript), available at http://papers.ssrn.com/sol3/papers.cfm?abstract_id=1356835.

baseline for viewing the relationship between time and common-pool resources by first eluci-
dating the nature of temporal commons. Second, the chapter details how the typical solutions to
the tragedy of the commons – private property, government regulation, and Elinor Ostrom's
successful collective action model – fail to adequately account for temporal commons. Third,
the chapter explores some factors that distinguish temporal commons from traditionally studied
commons, making them arguably more likely to devolve into tragedy. The chapter concludes
with initial thoughts on avenues for better addressing temporal commons dilemmas.

THE ROLE OF TIME IN COMMONS TRAGEDIES

Regardless of one's perspective on the value of the tragedy of the commons as a frame for
analyzing natural resource management decisions, it remains a powerful lens for describing
resource management problems. The empirical strain of commons scholarship prioritizes data
and its predictive capacity for forecasting and influencing the decisions that resource managers/
users will make.[6] While it is true that management of common-pool resources does not inevitably devolve into tragedy, and that private property, government regulation, and self-
coordination can help avoid tragic over-appropriation of resources,[7] tragedy is nonetheless an
outcome witnessed repeatedly in the real world, from the global loss of wetlands and biodiversity,
to crashing fish stocks, to deforestation of the Amazon, to the dangerous climate precipice upon
which we currently rest.

   While the descriptive power of the theory is quite strong, the paucity of attention given to time
and how to account for it in present-day resource management decisions renders the theory
incomplete. When nonexcludable users have rivalrous access to common-pool resources, several
dilemmas contribute to potentially tragic resource management, including (but not limited to)
problems of free-riders, collective action, and vulnerable and sticky institutional dynamics.[8]
Time, though under-analyzed in the literature to date, should hold a more prominent position
among these contributing dilemmas, if not be viewed as a new commons in and of itself (the
common pool of time across generations).

   Commons dilemmas arise out of an inability of resource users to coordinate, and while we
tend to think primarily of tragedies arising out of an inability to coordinate across spatial planes,
perhaps the bigger threat is the failure to coordinate through time. In other words, the commons
dynamic has both spatial (or "tangible") and temporal (or "intangible") dimensions, with the
tangible aspect receiving the bulk of focus in the literature – an appropriator consumes X
amount of resources at a particular point in time, and it reduces another appropriator's access to
those resources, potentially tending toward tragic overconsumption among a group of identifiable appropriators at a later identifiable Y point in time. All data points are known or are
projectable. Solutions touted to avoid commons tragedies, such as private property rights and
Ostrom's design principles for self-governance, are largely focused on activities taking place in
the present. Other solutions, like government regulation, contemplate the future, but all too
often prove inadequate at both projecting future resource needs and at implementing policies in
the present that will ensure future resource availability.

   In reality, most resources are either government owned and regulated, or owned by private
parties and subject to varying degrees of government regulation (including no regulation at all).

---

[6] *See* ROUTLEDGE HANDBOOK OF THE STUDY OF THE COMMONS (EDS., BLAKE HUDSON, JONATHAN ROSENBLOOM &
DAN COLE) (2019).

[7] ELINOR OSTROM, GOVERNING THE COMMONS: THE EVOLUTION OF INSTITUTIONS FOR COLLECTIVE ACTION 90 (1990).

[8] Brigham Daniels, *Emerging Commons and Tragic Institutions*, 37 ENV. L. 515 (2008).

Designing policies to add a sufficient overlay of regulation on natural resources subject to public or private ownership is a particularly wicked problem,[9] meaning "an issue highly resistant to resolution."[10] And one of the most significant elements contributing to that wickedness is time. How does society avoid a tragic over-appropriation of resources through time, when over any given time frame appropriators are unable to comprehend the larger temporal appropriation context in which they are embedded? Resource management decisions are made during discrete time periods, within which the individual harm caused by the removal of a discrete set of resources is nearly always justifiable. On the other hand, the appropriation's contribution to aggregated harm far into the future is virtually imperceptible. Thus, an appropriator rationally discounts and undervalues presumptions regarding a collection of similar harms aggregated through time.

Indeed, time, and the ways in which it intersects with human behavior, is perhaps the most difficult resource management complication to articulate and analyze. Like the grandfather paradox of time travel, how does one begin to process all the ways in which today's use of resources impacts the ability of others to have access to and use of those resources in a distant and unknowable future? While society has been successful in some areas, like placing the hole in the ozone layer on a trajectory to recovery (eventually), other areas have proved far more intractable – like the continued degradation of ecosystems caused by land development.[11] Jared Diamond provided insight into this phenomenon with his perspective on the destruction of resources on Easter Island, once a sophisticated society, as evidenced by its iconic Moai.[12] The island had once been heavily forested, but was completely deforested by the fifteenth century.[13] Critical species went extinct with the loss of forest cover, while soil erosion and leaching of nutrients reduced agricultural productivity.[14] Without timber, islanders had no wood to burn or for constructing wooden houses, and were forced to retreat into caves.[15] They could no longer build canoes, so fishing declined, which meant the loss of a key protein in islander diets.[16] When the first European explorers visited Easter Island in the eighteenth century, they found a starving, cannibalistic society, and a landscape of degraded natural resources.[17]

The Easter Island collapse is a stark cautionary tale regarding the interplay between the passage of time and resource management:

> [A]ny islander who tried to warn about the dangers of progressive deforestation would have been overridden by vested interests of carvers, bureaucrats, and chiefs, whose jobs depended on continued deforestation … The changes in forest cover from year to year would have been hard to detect … Only older people, recollecting their childhoods decades earlier, could have recognized a difference.[18]

From Diamond's perspective, time, and people's inability or unwillingness to perceive incremental resource damage through time, contributed to the collapse.

---

[9] *See* Blake Hudson, *Land Development: A Super-Wicked Environmental Problem*, 51 Ariz. St. L.J. 1123 (2019).

[10] *Tackling Wicked Problems: A Public Policy Perspective*, Austl. Pub. Serv. Comm'n, www.apsc.gov.au/tackling-wicked-problems-public-policy-perspective.

[11] *See* Hudson, *supra* note 9.

[12] James Rasband, James Salzman, & Mark Squillace, Nat. Res. Law & Pol. 41 (2011).

[13] *Id.* at 42.

[14] *Id.*

[15] *Id.*

[16] *Id.*

[17] *Id.*

[18] Jared Diamond, *Easter's End*, Discover Mag. (Aug. 1, 1995), http://discovermagazine.com/1995/aug/eastersend543 [https://perma.cc/4XAH-4W76].

Other scholars disagree with Diamond's perspective on the cause of Easter Island's decline, arguing that the islander's exploitation of resources was not responsible for the environmental collapse on their island. Terry Hunt and Carl Lipo argue that stowaway Polynesian rats in canoes were responsible for rampant deforestation on the island, resulting in a cascade of other animal and plant species' loss.[19] The rats multiplied furiously, and so islanders, again with no trees to make canoes for fishing, turned to the rats for food. As for population decline, Hunt and Lipo argue it was due to sexually transmitted diseases from Europe.[20] Nonetheless, the culture was fundamentally altered, since over generations the islanders adapted to view a deforested wasteland full of only rats to eat as an acceptable outcome for their society.

Even if the Easter Islanders were not as responsible for their own collapse as Diamond posits, and Hunt and Lipo are correct, time remains a culprit in the collapse. What happened in either case represents a "shifting baseline," whereby the incremental degradation of resources through time causes each new generation to view resources as abundant or in high quality, when in reality those resources are declining or becoming increasingly degraded across generations. It very much "... is like the story people used to tell about Tang, a sad, flat synthetic orange juice popularized by NASA. If you know what real orange juice tastes like, Tang is no achievement. But if you are on a 50-year voyage, if you lose the memory of real orange juice, then gradually, you begin to think Tang is delicious."[21] While the scholarship on shifting baselines is deep[22] they are only indicia of a temporal commons problem. The reason that baselines shift is because the passage of time affects human perception of resource availability. Each generation only quantifies the resources it sees, without appreciating how abundant resources had been in the past. As with Easter Island, in the context of much of modern resource management and/or regulation, "[c]orrective action is blocked by vested interests, by well-intentioned political and business leaders, and by their electorates, all of whom are perfectly correct in not noticing big changes from year to year. Instead, each year there are just somewhat more people, and somewhat fewer resources, on Earth."[23]

O'Neill describes temporal commons as situations where benefits accrue to present users while harms are dispersed across future generations. In public-choice terms, present generations have a concentrated collective interest in using resources now, and only a diffuse interest in ensuring that those resources are available for future generations. Because certain forms of natural resource loss are diffused through time, any one generation has difficulty discerning how those harms will aggregate to cause a resource management tragedy.

By way of a modern example, consider the rapid development that has consumed thousands of acres of natural capital around the rapidly expanding city of Houston, Texas. Over a period of fifty years the replacement of those natural resources has occurred incrementally, a little more pavement each year, somewhat fewer trees. No one development can be pinned as leading to

---

[19] *See* Robert Krulwich, *What Happened On Easter Island — A New (Even Scarier) Scenario*, NPR, www.npr.org/sections/krulwich/2013/12/09/249728994/what-happened-on-easter-island-a-new-even-scarier-scenario.

[20] *Id.*

[21] *Id.*

[22] *See, e.g.,* Frank Sturges, Humane Society of the United States v. Zinke (D.C. Cir. 2017): *Shifting Baselines in the Endangered Species Act*, 43 HARV. ENVTL. L. REV. 225 (2019); Guerrero-Gatica, Matías, Enrique Aliste, and Javier Simonetti, *Shifting Gears for the Use of the Shifting Baseline Syndrome in Ecological Restoration*, 11 SUSTAINABILITY 1458 (2019); Masashi Soga and Kevin J. Gaston, *Shifting Baseline Syndrome: Causes, Consequences, and Implications*, 16 FRONT. ECOL. & ENV. 222 (2018); S.K. Papworth, J. Rist, L. Coad, and E.J. Milner-Gulland, *Evidence for Shifting Baseline Syndrome in Conservation*, 2 CONSER. LET. 93 (2009).

[23] RASBAND, *supra* note 12, at 42.

greater flood risk, and yet we know that the unprecedented flooding during Hurricane Harvey,[24] and during intense rain events since,[25] were worse because of the aggregated effects of past developments. How much so is virtually unquantifiable. When Houston approved the development of 800 homes in a current greenspace located in the 100-year flood plain *after* Hurricane Harvey,[26] the temporal commons dilemma was made manifest. The loss of the greenspace may be justifiable at the present point in time. The 800 homes may not flood, at least for a while, because they will be built higher than the surrounding area. But additional impervious rooftops and roadways from both this development and future developments will send more water into floodways – and will send it there faster – during extreme weather events than would undeveloped green spaces, like forests and wetlands. Of course, it is impossible to calculate exactly how much worse a specific development makes flooding downstream or in the surrounding area in the future. But we can conclude that when combined with both past and future developments, more flooding occurs in the aggregate.

In short, time makes it exceedingly difficult if not impossible to assess the long-term aggregated harm caused by individual development or extraction decisions. No one resource appropriation may cause a species to go extinct, or a downstream neighborhood to flood, and nearly all developments, appropriations, or extractions can be justified over a certain time frame – "clearing *this* forty acre plot of land will not cause a significant amount of additional flooding or reduce habitat by enough to threaten a species." But what about fifty years from now, when other, also individually justifiable developments synergize with today's development to cause an aggregated increase in flooding or threat to habitat or other natural resources? Or when the baseline ecosystem has been so fundamentally altered as to make removal of its last vestiges not particularly alarming to future extractors who have no conception of its past abundance. As time passes, our ability to perceive and understand the implications of resource loss when aggregated with both past appropriations and future ones over a period of years declines. In this way, time makes many forms of resource management the quintessential frog in the boiling pot.[27] Except unlike the frog, we understand the dangers we face, but simply do not maintain an adequate mechanism for calculating, internalizing, and acting in response to the totality of probable danger.

Given that the temporal commons dilemma has been largely under-analyzed, it is useful to review the primary solutions proposed for addressing commons problems to evaluate how useful they are for tackling temporal commons, including private property, government regulation, and Elinor Ostrom's successful collective action model.

PRIMARY COMMONS MANAGEMENT STRATEGIES AND TEMPORAL COMMONS

Private Property. One way to manage commons resources is to privatize them – place a fence around a portion of the open pasture and herders will presumably only maintain as many sheep

---

[24] *See* Hudson, *supra* note 9.

[25] Timothy Bella and Jayla Epstein, *Torrential rain in Houston leaves roads flooded and schools closed*, THE WASHINGTON POST, May 10, 2019, www.washingtonpost.com/nation/2019/05/10/really-genuinely-scary-torrential-rain-houston-strands-cars-leaves-thousands-without-power/.

[26] Blake Hudson, *Houston must stop developing in the 100-year floodplain*, November 17, 2017, www.houstonchronicle.com/opinion/outlook/article/Hudson-Houston-must-stop-developing-in-the-12364026.php.

[27] Nevermind that the metaphor of the frog is a myth, debunked by science. James Fallows, *The Boiled-Frog Myth: Stop the Lying Now!*, ATLANTIC (September 16, 2006), www.theatlantic.com/technology/archive/2006/09/the-boiled-frog-myth-stop-the-lying-now/7446/ [https://perma.cc/8HEF-DAUT].

as can be sustained by the grass resource. Yet, as I have argued previously,[28] privatizing resources may make them no less subject to the commons dynamic, since the resources spread across private properties remain a commons pool that is depletable (e.g., there is rivalry over them) and it is difficult if not impossible to exclude appropriators from accessing the resource system made up of private properties.

Similarly, O'Neill argued that private property is no better solution for avoiding temporal tragedies because the tragic result occurs even in the presence of private ownership within each generation.[29] Private property may have been a more workable solution to temporal tragedies when families would pass the same land down to successive familial generations, and thus "land across generations was seen as the common property of particular families or communities."[30] Under those circumstances "[e]ach generation had a sense of identity over time with future owners ... members of a collective with continuity over time," whereas in modern society this continuity is missing. O'Neill posits that "the present generation acts on the land in terms of a temporally local horizon without a sense of identity or projects spread over time ... engag[ing] knowingly in resource depletion ... concerned for immediate high returns from the land" because of economic development pressures.[31] O'Neill specifically calls out the "mobility in ownership of land" in commercial society as undermining the role of private property in avoiding commons dilemmas for natural resources, since the "family as an intergenerational owner of the land often no longer exists" and there is no continuity with future owners of the land.[32] Thus individual landowners "roam" the commons through real estate transactions, with each successive owner having a right to permanently appropriate resources to the detriment of the common-pool over time.

In our modern commercial society, private property owners compete over resources and development activities that maximize the short-term value of their land, and "when individuals compete, they effectively disregard (or even intend) the negative impact of their decisions on the well-being of others."[33] Destruction or exploitation of resources on private property can only be avoided if private property owners "curtail their use of the commons in order to coordinate with other users to preserve the stock of resources and ensure the long-run health of the commons.[34]"

Peter Gerhart echoes O'Neill's view of sequential property owners as "common owners (over time rather than during a period of time)," arguing that the law already recognizes to a degree that property owners have obligations to future owners.[35] The U.S. legal doctrine of waste, for example, stands for the proposition that a current owner owes duties to future owners "by virtue of their sequential relationship," which "requires each owner/possessor who gets the present benefits of the property to also accept the burdens of saving appropriate benefits for future owners."[36] But property doctrines like waste, while incorporating temporal considerations, are narrowly tailored, applying to only rare resource management scenarios and requiring identifiable (and immediate) successors in interest who would be affected by present-day resource decisions. They do not contemplate the status of property owner access to or stewardship of important ecological resources 100 years hence.

---

[28] Blake Hudson, *Federal Constitutions: The Keystone of Nested Commons Governance*, 63 ALA. L. REV. 1007 (2012).
[29] O'Neill, *supra* note 1, at 46.
[30] *Id.* at 47.
[31] *Id.*
[32] *Id.* at 48–49.
[33] PETER M. GERHART, PROPERTY LAW AND SOCIAL MORALITY 67 (Cambridge Univ. Press 2013).
[34] *Id.* at 220.
[35] *Id.* at 232–233.
[36] *Id.* at 59.

Waste and similar temporally oriented property doctrines also "ask which individual can avoid the harm at least cost."[37] Future generations have no ability to avoid costs associated with how resources are managed today, while current property owners do. And it is impossible for future owners/resource users to exclude current owners from accessing or exploiting resources today. Yet the value of private property in modern society is most often not in the natural resources present on the land, but the land itself. Private property is often an individual's most significant investment, and when the sale of the dirt can lead to a higher value (as in the case of development in rapidly sprawling metro areas), then the natural capital present on the land is disregarded in the exchange (and in the ultimate conversion of the land from a natural habitat). While some forms of private ownership may be used to address the temporal commons, such as conservation easements restricting uses of property through time or ownership by land trusts whose purposes are strictly conservation in perpetuity, for the most part private property is a poor vehicle for managing temporal commons absent some form of government regulation, especially since current legal doctrines provide limited protection for future interests.

Government Regulation. Government regulation is a second mechanism for addressing commons dilemmas, but – while it would seem the most likely commons solution to address temporal commons – it too has proven inadequate in practice – not because of a deficiency in the tool, but rather the unwillingness of society to wield it effectively. Public law is crucial to reigning in over-appropriation of natural resources through time, since "the appropriate division of decision-making responsibility over time occurs when a present owner is required to take into account the well-being of future owners …"[38] As Gerhart argues, legal regimes should contemplate "the relationship between sequential owners that understands the role of the market in protecting owner autonomy over time and that situates the role of the law in intervening when the market cannot play its coordinating role."[39] When private law is "inadequate to successfully coordinate decisions over time," we now have "a justification for legislative intervention as a response to the deficiencies of private law and the market."[40] Positive law is to intervene when "the market is unable to fulfill its function as a stand-in for future owners because an owner can escape the consequences of her decisions."[41] So future private property owners are to be protected by today's government. As Gerhart argues:

> Without legislative regulation, [future] interests would not be accounted for by the legal system … wetlands preservation laws, for example, involve a conflict between present and future generations and an intra-generational conflict between those who find preservation to be worthwhile and those who do not. Because trees, endangered species, and future generations do not have standing, those with an interest in trees, endangered species, and future generations can use the legislative outlet to express their interests. The resolution of disputes over these kinds of interests requires consideration of both the harm to the owners and the benefits to a widely diffuse and heterogeneous population (over time) and are best dealt with in the aggregation process that only legislative regulation can provide.[42]

Government regulation is in theory intended to ensure resource availability for the future, yet in many circumstances it has largely failed to do so. The private interests and economic inertia described in the previous section undermine the political will of those who elect government

[37] *Id.* at 200.
[38] *Id.* at 227.
[39] *Id.* at 229–230.
[40] *Id.* at 200.
[41] *Id.* at 232.
[42] *Id.* at 235.

officials, rendering it incredibly difficult to account for the interests of future users of resources appropriated by today's private landowners. Until society decides wholesale to effectively harness the powers of government to ensure that future generations' preferences are being represented by today's governmental policies – that is, to account more directly for temporal commons – then government regulation will remain a limited approach for addressing resource management dilemmas.

OSTROM'S COLLECTIVE ACTION MODEL

Nobel Laureate Elinor Ostrom identified circumstances under which groups of individuals have engaged in successful collective action to sustainably manage resources in the absence of private property rights or governmental regulatory intervention.[43] Consider each in the context of temporal commons.

First, the boundaries of both the resource system and the parties who may appropriate resources should be clearly defined. For temporal commons, the boundaries of the resource system (which refers to resources managed across time) is boundless and undefinable, as are the parties who may appropriate resources. (How long will humanity be around and how long would they need those resources?)

Second, appropriation and provision rules should match (or be "congruent" with) local conditions, meaning rules restricting time, place, technology, and quantity of resource units that may be appropriated are related to those conditions. But there can be no congruency within temporal commons because local conditions are unknowable through an unknown quantity of time.

Third, most all appropriators should maintain collective choice rights allowing them to participate in modifying operational rules. Future generations have no collective choice rights regarding operational rules for managing today's resources.

Fourth, monitors of rules and behavior must be accountable to appropriators or be appropriators themselves. Yet monitors of rules cannot be accountable to future appropriators nor can they be future appropriators themselves.

Fifth, appropriators who violate rules should face graduated sanctions. While present day appropriators may indeed receive such sanctions, if those sanctions are not designed to curb behavior today and in the future for the sake of future generations, then they are likely to be ineffective.

Sixth, adequate conflict-resolution mechanisms should be low-cost and must be accessed quickly. Such mechanisms are inaccessible by future generations, who have no ability to adjudicate resource-management decisions made in the present.

Seventh, the rights of appropriators to devise their own institutions should not be challenged by external governmental authorities. Future generations have no rights to devise their own institutions, period.

Finally, appropriative, monitoring, enforcement, and conflict resolution activities should be organized in multiple layers of nested enterprises. These enterprises are nested in the present day, and there may be no enterprise representing the future (unless it is present day government regulators).

So, while Ostrom's collective action model is meant to ensure that future generations have access to resources, future generations along the temporal commons spectrum cannot fully participate in decision-making necessary for collective action across generations.

---

[43] ELINOR OSTROM, GOVERNING THE COMMONS (1990).

WHY TEMPORAL COMMONS MAY BE MORE LIKELY TO DEVOLVE INTO TRAGEDY

We must give more careful consideration to temporal commons and the difficulties that time poses for resource management. There are some key differences between temporal commons and the traditionally analyzed commons scenario, which may make the risk of a tragic resource outcome more likely than is currently contemplated.

Rate of Consumption. When considering the dangers posed by the traditionally analyzed tangible commons (where the users of the commons and its resources are all present, vying for use of the resource), one primary concern is a *fast* rate of consumption (that is, when resources are consumed at a rate greater than they can replenish, or, overconsumption). The tragedy unfolds when a user is incentivized to remove as much of the resource as quickly as possible[44] before others can consume their share of the resource. Such consumption may certainly occur over many years before the resource is exhausted, such as fisheries,[45] or buffalo,[46] or an underground aquifer[47] depleted in only a matter of decades. A rapid rate of consumption is what yields tragedy in this instance, and one or two generations can see it unfold before their eyes. But when considering, for example, the loss of natural landscapes due to urban development over 100+-year periods, where the physical change is incremental and imperceptible year to year, it is the *slow* rate of consumption that yields tragedy. Indeed, it is because the rate is so slow that society is blinded to its progression and ends up in a tragic plight. Only future generations, who share the commons pool of time and have no say in how resources are incrementally consumed in the present, will be able to assess the gravity of resource loss and it is they who will bear its full cost.

Rivalry. With temporal commons, excludability plays out the same as in a traditional commons, since it impossible to exclude both present or future appropriators from appropriating resources from the resource system that spans time. But the rivalry aspect between today's users and future users plays out quite differently. In the traditional rivalry sense, each rivalrous party is appropriating within the same space and within the same basic time period. So, my appropriation of resources today means less for you today (and tomorrow). But rivalry is a one-way street in the temporal commons context. Future users need resources that exist in physical form today (or that must be maintained in physical form today to propagate new resources in the future). Yet future users have no access to those resources unless today's users curb their consumption. Today's users have access to resources and can do with those resources what they will even though future users need them. This is a rivalry akin to the Harlem Globetrotters and the Washington Generals, where the Globetrotters are today's users and the Generals are future generations. One side always wins. But it remains rivalry, nonetheless.

Collective Action. In a traditional commons situation, you may have those who overconsume and do not want to collectively act to curb overconsumption, those who overconsume and would like to act, and those who do not overconsume and would like to act. Collective action by

[44] *See* Suzanne Iudicello et al., Fish, Markets, and Fishermen: The Economics of Overfishing 147 (1999).

[45] David Ropeik, *Atlantic Cod and The Human 'Tragedy of The Commons,'* WBUR.Org, December 3, 2014, www.wbur .org/cognoscenti/2014/12/03/overfishing-georges-bank-david-ropeik.

[46] Gilbert King, *Where the Buffalo No Longer Roamed*, Smithsonianmag.com, July 17, 2012, www.smithsonianmag .com/history/where-the-buffalo-no-longer-roamed-3067904/.

[47] Jeremy Frankel, *Crisis on the High Plains: The Loss of America's Largest Aquifer – the Ogallala*, duwaterlawreview. com, May 17, 2018, http://duwaterlawreview.com/crisis-on-the-high-plains-the-loss-of-americas-largest-aquifer-the-ogal lala/.

those who would like to stop overconsumption by themselves or other users is difficult (maybe exceedingly so), but not impossible in the tangible commons sense. The parties can overcome collective action difficulties to act. But in the temporal context, it is impossible for some of those who would stop present over-appropriation to act. Future generations are simply unable to act in any capacity to protect resources today. They rely solely on current appropriators, so collective action for them is impossible.

HOW TO BEGIN ACCOUNTING FOR TEMPORAL COMMONS

This chapter aims to bring greater focus on temporal commons and will leave a thorough articulation of how to address them for future work. Yet some initial conclusions and suggestions emerge from the foregoing analysis.

First, Ostrom's collective action model requires the participation of all actors on the commons, and we have established that future generations cannot participate or collectively act today. Property rights tend toward preserving present interests over future interests. It seems, as a result, that government regulation is the only mechanism capable of taking into account future generations and the temporal commons. Many natural resource and environmental policies have this as their explicit goal, to make such resources available for future generations. While the scholarship is vast on the inadequacies of government regulation and centralized decision-making, in the temporal commons context it does seem to emerge as the preferential tool for considering future generations.

Second, debate over just how precautionary society should be in resource management is a lynchpin of modern policy debates. And discussion is often stark – should we adopt a precautionary principle or not. But it is time the debate became more nuanced. There are circumstances, like the temporal commons, where a precautionary approach is even more important. Air can become clean again 100 years hence if pollution stops today, so perhaps there is an acceptable level of pollution and harm to the environment today so long as more benefit accrues to society in total, and clean air can be returned to future generations. Thus, clean air might warrant a less precautionary approach. But a natural ecosystem (forest, wetland, endangered species, etc.) once destroyed cannot be fully restored to its natural condition once it has been paved over, and therefore the future implications are starker (especially when aggregated with related actions through time). A more precautionary approach is warranted here to protect the interests of future generations. Making John Rawls' *Veil of Ignorance* more concrete in policy decisions would help integrate more precaution into decision-making. Rawls asks how you would want society to operate if you did not know who you would be in that society – rich or poor, male or female, black or white. In the environmental context we can ask how would you want resources to be managed today if you did not know *when* you would be born? We need to identify and track areas where temporal commons tragedies are most likely to play out and then adjust how cost-benefit analysis proceeds. Conventional air pollution, food and drug administrative decisions regarding the safety of pharmaceuticals or other products, nutrient pollution in the Gulf of Mexico, and similar issues may not implicate the temporal commons as directly, since each can be rectified fairly quickly for future generations (that is, the harm is borne mostly by those in the present). But incremental land development, climate change, and all forms of habitat destruction are harms that are unlikely to be undone (or are incredibly difficult to undo), with future generations suffering the consequences.

Finally, while not a novel insight, Douglas North's perspective on creating informal institutions and norms is instructive. On temporal commons issues, we must focus on the creation of norms that effectively shame people into accounting for future generations, or at least make society more aware of them. Climate change is a good example, and what we have witnessed with Greta Thunberg and the children's public trust cases has been evidence of a shift toward bringing future generations more directly into legal and policy discussions. The entire rhetoric of talking about harm to our grandkids is an attempt to bring future generations into rivalry with current generations. We can say that those in the present have a stake in the future and therefore it should matter to those in the present. As articulated earlier, grandchildren cannot step into the present and rival present users of resources. But present users can step into the future and rival with them, by representing them in today's policy discussions.

CONCLUSION

In conclusion, the temporal commons deserves more attention and study. The passage of time can lead to human behaviors that cause resource management to tend toward tragedy. When baselines shift from one generation to the next, resources only appear to become somewhat scarcer. Future generations are left to suffer tragic resource depletion as rival appropriators—those appropriating resources within each baseline generation—chip away further at the resources before them to a degree that appears justifiable. Ostrom's collective action model and private property are insufficient vehicles for addressing temporal commons, while government regulation in many resource management contexts has failed to fulfill its role of representing future generations. Studying the ways in which temporal commons differ from traditional commons (regarding rate of consumption, rivalry, and collective action), gaining a more precise understanding of which resources deserve a precautionary management approach, and focusing on norms that integrate future generations into government policy discussions will each be critical to mitigating the likelihood of tragedy that can result from the incremental, hardly noticeable loss of critical resources over time.

6

Transforming Climate Dilemmas from Tragedy to Cooperation

Bryan Bruns

Controlling emissions of greenhouse gasses (GHGs) has often been analyzed as a tragedy of the commons, a social dilemma where cooperation would be better for everyone but in which incentives lead individuals, businesses, and nations to keep on polluting.[1] This chapter shows how a simple game theory model of tragedy of the commons, Prisoner's Dilemma, is only one of many possible models for climate conflict and cooperation. Changing the ranking of outcomes transforms one game model into another.[2] Mapping these transformations displays pathways for turning tragedy into cooperation.

This chapter first describes how three famous games – Prisoner's Dilemma, Chicken, and Stag Hunt – can transform into each other or into a stable win-win game of Concord. The second section looks at relationships between some previous game theory models for international climate negotiations.[3] The third section presents a more complete map of diversity and potential transformations in climate situations. The fourth section analyzes how the incentive structures in climate situations can change as resource problems worsen and explores pathways for escaping from climate dilemmas by avoiding catastrophe, improving gains from cooperation, or asymmetrically restructuring incentives. The fifth section discusses limitations and extensions of two-person two-choice (2 × 2) game models for understanding cooperation in coping with climate problems. Overall, this analysis shows that tragic temptation to defect from cooperation is neither inevitable nor the only kind of challenge posed by GHG emissions. A map of how payoff swaps link games displays the diversity of situations, their potential transformations, and multiple pathways to change climate dilemmas from tragedy into cooperation.

---

[1] For example, see Marvin S. Soroos, "Global Change, Environmental Security, and the Prisoner's Dilemma." *Journal of Peace Research* 31, no. 3 (1994): 317–332; Stephen M. Gardiner, "A Perfect Moral Storm: Climate Change, Intergenerational Ethics and the Problem of Moral Corruption." *Environmental Values* 15, no. 3 (2006): 397–413; Stephen M. Gardiner. *A Perfect Moral Storm: The Ethical Tragedy of Climate Change.* (Oxford: Oxford University Press, 2011); Rony Smead and Ronald Sandler, "Game Theory and the Ethics of Global Climate Change." *Philosophy and Public Issues* 3, no. 1 (2013): 13–23; William Nordhaus, "Climate Clubs: Overcoming Free-Riding in International Climate Policy." *American Economic Review* 105, no. 4 (2015): 1339–1370.

[2] David Robinson and David Goforth, *The Topology of the 2x2 Games: A New Periodic Table* (London: Routledge, 2005); Bryan Bruns, "Names for Games: Locating 2 × 2 Games." *Games* 6, no. 4 (October 22, 2015): 495–520.

[3] Stephen J. DeCanio, and Anders Fremstad, "Game Theory and Climate Diplomacy," *Ecological Economics* 85 (2013): 186; Kaveh Madani, "Modeling International Climate Change Negotiations More Responsibly: Can Highly Simplified Game Theory Models Provide Reliable Policy Insights?" *Ecological Economics* 90 (2013): 68–76. This chapter expands on comments sent to DeCanio and Fremstad about transformations between games, which they acknowledged and discussed in their 2013 journal article.

FROM SOCIAL DILEMMAS TO CONCORD

The essence of a tragedy of the commons is that pursuing individual interests could lead to collective ruin, even though cooperation would be better for everyone.[4] In Hardin's fable, a farmer who adds another animal to a shared pasture gets all the benefits, while only suffering a fraction of any losses from overgrazing, but if everyone acts this way the pasture itself may be destroyed. The same logic applies to pollution, if each is free to dump their wastes into the environment while others suffer most of the costs. Similarly, if everyone shares in the benefits from reducing GHGs, then potential contributors may be tempted to free-ride,[5] enjoying benefits while continuing to pollute.

The game theory story of the Prisoner's Dilemma illustrates a simple model of such conflict between individual and collective interests. Two prisoners are each offered a deal, while held separately and unable to communicate.[6] If one confesses and the other stays silent, then the one who confesses goes free while the other serves a long sentence. If both confess, they receive a moderate sentence. If both keep silent, they still receive a short sentence. Mutual silence would be better than both confessing. However, examining the logic of choices shows that if the other does not confess, it is best to confess. Furthermore, if the other confesses, then it is better to confess. In each case, confessing does better, posing a dilemma for cooperation (at least under the assumed conditions).

The payoff matrix for Prisoner's Dilemma at the top of Figure 6.1 shows the outcomes from choices to cooperate (C) or defect (D) with preferences for the four outcomes ranked from worst

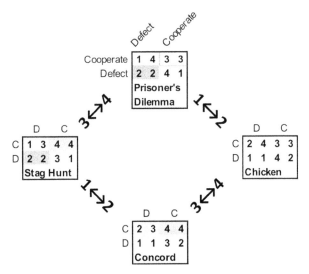

FIGURE 6.1 Changes in the ranking of outcomes (payoff swaps) turn Prisoner's Dilemma into Stag Hunt or Chicken and then into Concord

[4] Garrett Hardin, "The Tragedy of the Commons." *Science* 162 (1968): 1243–1248; Elinor Ostrom, "Tragedy of the Commons," *The New Palgrave Dictionary of Economics* 2 (2008).

[5] Mancur Olson, *The Logic of Collective Action: Public Goods and the Theory of Groups* (Cambridge, MA: Harvard University Press, 1971).

[6] A. W. Tucker, "The Mathematics of Tucker: A Sampler. A Two-Person Dilemma: The Prisoner's Dilemma." *The Two-Year College Mathematics Journal* 14, no. 3 (1983): 228–232. Originally presented in a lecture at Stanford University in 1950.

(1) to best (4). In game theory terms, defection is a dominant strategy, better regardless of what the other does. Defection by both leads to a situation from which neither can improve their payoff unilaterally, a Nash equilibrium (shaded). The distinguishing problem in Prisoner's Dilemma is that defection from cooperation (with 3,3 payoffs) leads to an equilibrium with payoffs that are worse for both (2,2) (a Pareto-inferior equilibrium).

However, if both actors defecting from cooperation would lead to the worst outcome (1,1) then the payoff structure is not Prisoner's Dilemma.[7] The game of Chicken takes its name from the story of two cars driving toward each other. If one swerves the other wins, but crashing is worst for both. Both want to avoid disaster. Both swerving is a cooperative second-best outcome. However, rather than cooperating, each would be tempted to defect, seeking to win while the other gets second-worst. If catastrophic climate change could be avoided by only one country reducing (abating) emissions, then each would prefer to get the benefits of abatement by the other without paying the costs. In biology, this incentive structure is sometimes called Hawk-Dove. One aggressor could win, but two hawks playing against each other do worse. In politics and climate negotiations, Chicken can model brinkmanship, where two nations try to intimidate or bluff the other into conceding.

Alternatively, cooperation to control GHGs might be best for everyone as long as enough others cooperate, as in a Stag Hunt (assurance) game.[8] Rousseau described a hunter choosing whether to catch a rabbit for sure or getting a stag but only if others cooperate and otherwise getting nothing.[9] A transition from fossil fuels to renewable energy might be similar, where a critical mass of innovation and investment produces the best outcome, as long as enough others also cooperate. The crucial distinction between Prisoner's Dilemma and Stag Hunt is: assuming everyone else cooperates, is there still a temptation to defect?[10]

In the game of Concord,[11] incentives align so cooperation is better regardless of what the other does. If both players cooperate, both get their best payoff (4,4). Recommendations for carbon fees and abolishing subsidies that distort prices for fossil fuels aim to have the "invisible hand" of market prices lead individual decisions to an outcome that is best for all.[12] Some research suggests that investing in efficiency and renewable energy is worthwhile even at current (distorted) prices,[13] in which case reducing GHG emissions might already be the best strategy without depending on how others act. Redesigning carbon fee policies to better attract voters could further improve incentives to reduce emissions.[14]

---

[7] In "Game Theory and Climate Diplomacy" DeCanio and Fremstad repeatedly use the term "catastrophe" for situations in which both polluting is only the second-worst outcome, with abating while the other pollutes as the worst outcome.

[8] This, arguably, is the case for controlling gasses that damage the ozone layer, as DeCanio and Fremstad suggest in "Game Theory and Climate Diplomacy."

[9] Jean-Jacques Rousseau, *A Discourse upon the Origin and the Foundation of the Inequality among Mankind*, 2004, www.gutenberg.org/ebooks/11136; Brian Skyrms, *The Stag Hunt and the Evolution of Social Structure* (Cambridge: Cambridge University Press, 2004); A. K Sen, "Isolation, Assurance and the Social Rate of Discount," *The Quarterly Journal of Economics* 81, no. 1 (1967): 112–124; Carlisle Ford Runge, "Common Property Externalities: Isolation, Assurance, and Resource Depletion in a Traditional Grazing Context," *American Journal of Agricultural Economics* 63, no. 4 (1981): 595–606; Daniel H. Cole and Peter Z. Grossman, "Institutions Matter! Why the Herder Problem Is Not a Prisoner's Dilemma.," *Theory and Decision* 69, no. 2 (2010): 219–231.

[10] S. M. Amadae, *Prisoners of Reason: Game Theory and Neoliberal Political Economy* (Cambridge: Cambridge University Press, 2016).

[11] Names are from Bruns, "Names for Games." Robinson and Goforth used the name "No Conflict."

[12] Nordhaus, "Climate Clubs."

[13] Amory Lovins, *Reinventing Fire: Bold Business Solutions for the New Energy Era*. Chelsea Green Publishing, 2013.

[14] David Klenert, Linus Mattauch, Emmanuel Combet, Ottmar Edenhofer, Cameron Hepburn, Ryan Rafaty, and Nicholas Stern, "Making Carbon Pricing Work for Citizens," *Nature Climate Change* 8, no. 8 (2018): 669–677.

Changes can swap the ranking of outcomes and transform one game into another, as Figure 6.1 shows. Swapping the two lowest-ranked outcomes (1↔2) turns Prisoner's Dilemma into Chicken. Swapping the two highest-ranked outcomes (3↔4) turns Prisoner's Dilemma into Stag Hunt. Swapping the top-ranked outcomes in Chicken to make cooperation more rewarding turns Chicken into Concord; Swapping the lowest-ranked outcomes in Stag Hunt so that cooperation also minimizes risks turns Stag Hunt into Concord.

For understanding climate problems and solutions, crucial questions concern the current incentive structure and how that could be changed. Are we in a situation where both failing to cooperate leads to the worst outcome as in Chicken, or trapped in a potential tragedy like Prisoner's Dilemma? Could we control emissions in a way that would be best for everyone? The climate literature has sometimes recognized the potential for transformation between games, but usually only for change between a few neighboring games.[15]

CLIMATE NEGOTIATIONS: ABATE OR POLLUTE?

DeCanio and Fremdstad explored 2 × 2 game models for climate negotiations.[16] They restricted their analysis to games where both abating was better than both polluting and where polluting rather than abating always made the other worse off. They examined all possible 2 × 2 games with a strict rank ordering of outcomes. Out of 144 order games, DeCanio and Fremstad found twenty-five relevant to climate negotiations.

Five of the climate games were symmetric, where the two actors each face the same pattern of payoffs, including Prisoner's Dilemma, Chicken, Stag Hunt, and Concord.[17] Swapping the ranking of the middle outcomes (2↔3) turns Concord into Harmony, where dominant strategies also lead to win-win.

Although DeCanio and Fremstad used Robinson and Goforth's "New Periodic Table" to identify 2 × 2 climate games,[18] they presented their results as a series of separate tables for different groups of games. Figure 6.2 uses the structure of payoff swaps in the "New Periodic Table" to display the five symmetric games along a diagonal axis. Their payoffs combine to form the twenty asymmetric games, compactly displaying the relationships among climate games in a single table.[19]

The twenty asymmetric games are composed of ten pairs on either side of the diagonal that differ by exchanging positions for the Row and Column players (reflections). In the lower left of

---

[15] See, for example, Jason K. Levy, Keith W. Hipel, and N. Howard, "Advances in Drama Theory for Managing Global Hazards and Disasters. Part II: Coping with Global Climate Change and Environmental Catastrophe." *Group Decision and Negotiation* 18, no. 4 (2009): 317–334; Karen Pittel and Dirk T. G. Rübbelke, "Transitions in the Negotiations on Climate Change: From Prisoner's Dilemma to Chicken and beyond." *International Environmental Agreements: Politics, Law and Economics* 12, no. 1 (2012): 23–39. Scott Barrett, "Collective Action to Avoid Catastrophe: When Countries Succeed, When They Fail, and Why," *Global Policy* 7 (2016): 45–55.

[16] "Game Theory and Climate Diplomacy."

[17] Under some conditions, a competitive person might "defect" in Concord to try to get the outcome where they do better (3,2), for example if they could choose first so the other has only a choice between worst and second-worst. Due to this susceptibility to a competitive concern to maximize the difference in payoffs, some social psychologists call this payoff structure Max-Diff. See Harold H. Kelley, and John W. Thibaut. *Interpersonal Relations: A Theory of Interdependence.* (New York: John Wiley & Sons Inc, 1978). If nations pursue relative advantage, not absolute gains, this could pose an issue in Concord-type situations, especially if one actor could take initiative and commit themselves.

[18] Robinson and Goforth, "Topology of 2x2 Games."

[19] The symmetric games also act as coordinates to name and locate the asymmetric games, Bruns, "Names for Games." Figures 6.2 and 6.3 also show layer, row, and column numbers that compose Robinson and Goforth's game index numbers, as used by DeCanio and Fremstad and by Madani.

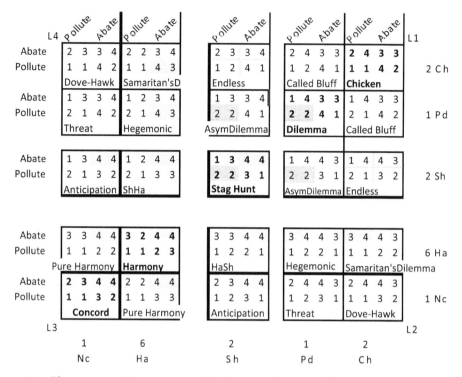

FIGURE 6.2 Climate negotiation games model choices to abate or pollute. Symmetric games form a diagonal from lower left to upper right. Their payoffs combine to form asymmetric games

Figure 2, Harmony, Concord, and three pairs of asymmetric games have dominant strategies for one or both that lead to a single "no conflict" equilibrium where both abate. In the center, Prisoner's Dilemma and a pair of asymmetric neighbors have an inefficient "tragic" equilibrium where both pollute. In five pairs of "unhappy" asymmetric games, one pollutes while the other abates and does worse. Another pair of games have no equilibrium (in pure strategies) and a cyclic incentive structure where one or the other always wants to change their move. However, the 4,3 outcome could be a prominent focal point[20] for agreeing to abate.

A MAP FOR CHANGING GAMES

The set of five symmetric games on the diagonal in Figure 6.2 extends to include five more games, rivalrous, second-best, and harmonious climate situations that DeCanio and Fremstad's restrictions excluded. Payoffs from the twelve symmetric games combine to form asymmetric games, making a more complete map of transformations between situations. This section describes the additional symmetric games, and the "Periodic Table of 2x2 Games" in more detail.

In Chicken, one or the other does much better at the rival equilibria, best versus second worst (4,2). The rival equilibria in the neighboring games of Hero and Leader (Battle) are less unequal, best versus second best (4,3).[21] They could model situations where it would be more efficient for only one to abate. Hero could model where both abating would be too much, as

---

[20] T. C. Schelling, *The Strategy of Conflict*. (Cambridge, MA: Harvard University Press, 1960).

[21] Gardiner's discussion of "battle of the sexes" mainly concerns a dynamic coordination problem of assembling an effective coalition, not rivalry over which of two mutually desirable equilibria to select.

might occur with geoengineering. Other choices could also require coordination but be mutually exclusive and offer advantages to one nation or the other (or group of countries, such as fossil fuel exporters versus importers). One climate debate concerns directly switching to renewable energy versus using natural gas during a transition. Everyone wants to avoid the worst outcome of climate catastrophe and the second-worst outcome of uncoordinated and inefficient investment. However, countries may differ over which path to take.

Stag Hunt has one win-win equilibrium and an inferior equilibrium where both get second worst (2,2). By contrast, Assurance and (Strict) Coordination have an inferior equilibrium where both get second-best (3,3). These two games could model a situation where only concerted strategies can succeed and such an effort by only one would make the other worse off (unlike DeCanio and Fremstad's assumptions). For two big developing countries the only feasible strategy might be to first rely on fossil fuels, temporarily worsening global warming, to reach a level of economic development where they both could switch to renewable energy and carbon capture. Only a joint effort might be sufficient to gain synergies or cross a threshold for success. If such a strategy by one big developing country alone were at least able to avoid a catastrophic outcome for that country, then the situation would be like Strict Coordination. If such a solo strategy led to that country getting their worst outcome, then the situation would be like Assurance. These six games all pose coordination problems of selecting between alternative equilibria, where failure to successfully coordinate would be worse for both (a Pareto-inferior outcome).

In the games of Deadlock and Compromise, dominant strategies lead to second-best, differing only by the location of the two lowest-ranked payoffs. As long as impacts are not severe, some level of GHG emission may be tolerable, even if not ideal. This could be the case if abatement was not economically worthwhile or if each nation would most prefer to pollute while the other abates. However, if mutual abatement would be better than both continuing to pollute, that would swap the middle-ranked outcomes and convert the payoff structure from Deadlock into Prisoner's Dilemma.

Middle swaps turn Harmony into Peace, where dominant strategies also converge on win-win. This game could model a situation where one side's choice to cooperate makes things worse for the other unless they also cooperate. For example, a climate treaty between nations could impose trade restrictions that penalize those continuing to pollute. Contrary to DeCanio and Fremstad's assumptions (restrictions), there are relevant climate situations where abatement by one might be better than by both or where abatement by one could make the other worse off unless they also abate.

Figure 6.3 displays Robinson and Goforth's "Periodic Table of 2x2 Games" where payoff swaps link neighboring games.[22] The twelve strict symmetric ordinal games discussed above form a diagonal axis. Their payoffs combine to make asymmetric games, elegantly revealing relationships between 2 × 2 games.

In the detailed structure of the topology, low swaps (1↔2) form "tiles" of four games. Middle swaps (2↔3) link tiles within four "layers." In the display, each layer wraps top-to-bottom and side-to-side like a doughnut (torus). In each layer, the top two payoffs have the same alignment: in a win-win cell as in Harmony; diagonally opposed as in Prisoner's Dilemma and Chicken; or in the same row or column. High swaps (3↔4) connect games across layers and link the entire table top-to-bottom and side-to-side [this should be consistent with above, either all with dashes or all without.] . Thus, at the center of the table, high swaps change Prisoner's Dilemma into an

[22] Robinson and Goforth, *Topology of 2x2 Games*. Bruns, "Names for Games."

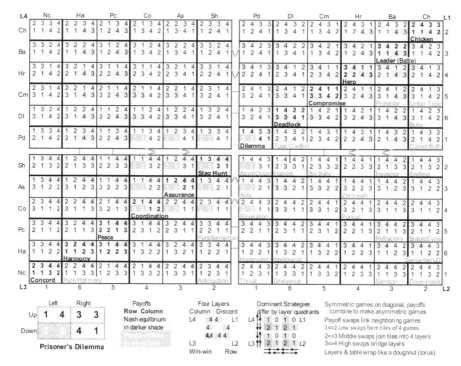

FIGURE 6.3 The topology of 2 × 2 games shows potential transformations. Payoff swaps link neighboring games. Symmetric games lie on a diagonal axis; their payoffs combine to form asymmetric games. High swap transformations link layers

Asymmetric Dilemma and then Stag Hunt. High swaps for one or the other also transform the coordination problems in Strict Coordination and Assurance into rivalries on the Layer 1 tile with Hero and Leader. High swaps for both transform Deadlock into Peace and Compromise into Harmony.[23]

PATHWAYS FOR TRANSFORMATION

As greenhouse gasses accumulate, impacts worsen, and gains from abatement increase, the situation could move through a series of games.[24] This can be visualized in transformations between games in Figures 6.2 and 6.3, looking first at symmetric transformations along the diagonal axis. Initially, each nation might prefer to pollute while the other abates but would settle for second-best where both pollute, in which case they would start in Deadlock. As climate impacts become more severe, abatement may be worthwhile if both cooperate, becoming a Prisoner's Dilemma, where each would be tempted to defect, trying to gain the benefits of the

---

[23] To visualize more high swaps, horizontally switch the Harmony row of six games with the equivalent row on Layer 2; high swaps for row payoffs then transform into the game in the row above. Harmony turns into *PcDl* and Samaritan's Dilemma, *HaCh*, turns into Pure Samaritan, *PcSh*. High swaps for row payoffs similarly link the rows with Deadlock and Compromise. Similar column swaps slide vertically. Rows (and columns) for coordination and cyclic tiles cross diagonally between layers.

[24] Kaveh Madani, "Game Theory and Water Resources." *Journal of Hydrology* 381 (2010): 225–238; Madani, "Modeling Climate Change;" Bora Ristić and Kaveh Madani, "A Game Theory Warning to Blind Drivers Playing Chicken with Public Goods," *Water Resources Research* 55, no. 3 (2019): 2000–2013. Madani and Ristić use formulas and cost curves to model changes between payoff structures, which this chapter visualizes for a broader range of transformations between games.

other's efforts without paying the costs. As conditions worsen the situation could turn into Chicken, where both polluting is worst for both.[25] Cooperation would be second-best, but each would still be tempted to defect from cooperation so they could keep polluting while the other abates enough to avoid catastrophe. As conditions further deteriorate, each might have sufficient incentive to act alone to mitigate disaster regardless of what the other does. This would be like Concord, where dominant strategies converge on abatement. However, by then it might be long past climate tipping points that lead to catastrophic changes.[26]

Outcomes of climate situations, and their rankings, could change for many reasons. Improvements in technology, institutions, and financing, such as for renewable energy, could make cooperation more efficient and profitable. Governments, businesses, and other organizations could develop shared strategies, support norms favoring a particular outcome, or establish rules that regulate behavior and incentives.[27] Expectations could shift, for example, based on new information or greater fear of risks.[28] The ranking of outcomes could also change due to sympathy, more concern for what happens to others or a change in moral judgements. If the payoff pattern changes only for one player, the situation becomes asymmetric, a possibility that can help think about more options for escaping climate dilemmas.

Depending on the starting point, multiple pathways may reach climate cooperation. The solution for Prisoner's Dilemma is often to turn it into a Stag Hunt, where cooperation is best for both.[29] A governance solution, unsuccessful so far, would be an enforceable international agreement imposing penalties or rewards that overcome temptation to defect. Concern for others, including all humans alive now, future generations, and nature, should transform the evaluation of outcomes so that cooperation is the only morally acceptable choice.[30] Or, as mentioned above, technological changes and coordinated investments might suffice to make abatement best for all.

If both not cooperating would be the worst outcome, that poses a problem like Chicken. If the benefits of cooperation can be increased and temptation to defect reduced symmetrically, that turns Chicken into Concord. Abatement by one nation or other actor, asymmetrically, might initially lead them to do worse than the other, as in the game of Dove versus Hawk. However, this inequality might be accepted as a necessary "strategic loss."[31] This could facilitate learning, negotiation, and further transition.[32]

Even if one nation (or set of nations) never believes both polluting would be the worst outcome, there might still be ways to reach a situation where incentives lead both sides to abate.

---

[25] If costs are asymmetric, then one will have a Chicken payoff sooner, making a game of Called Bluff. One keeps polluting, while the other starts abating, incurring costs and doing worse. In Figure 8 in Ristić and Madani, "Game Theory Warning" this is the red zone on the asymmetric path from Prisoner's Dilemma to Chicken.

[26] Scott Barrett, and Astrid Dannenberg, "Sensitivity of Collective Action to Uncertainty about Climate Tipping Points," *Nature Climate Change* 4, no. 1 (2014): 36–39. Barfuss, Wolfram, Jonathan F. Donges, Vítor V. Vasconcelos, Jürgen Kurths, and Simon A. Levin, "Caring for the Future Can Turn Tragedy into Comedy for Long-Term Collective Action under Risk of Collapse," *Proceedings of the National Academy of Sciences*, 2020

[27] Elinor Ostrom, *Understanding Institutional Diversity*, Princeton, NJ: Princeton University Press, 2005).

[28] Changing the perceived ranking of outcomes creates a different "effective matrix." Kelley and Thibaut, *Interpersonal Relations* "Social Dilemmas: The Anatomy of Cooperation," *Annual Review of Sociology* 24, no. 1 (1998): 183–214; Peter Kollock, "Transforming Social Dilemmas: Group Identity and Cooperation." *Modeling Rational and Moral Agents*, 1998, 186–210.

[29] Skyrms, *The Stag Hunt*.

[30] Gardiner, *Perfect Moral Storm*. The chapter by Hudson in this volume examines challenges that time poses for commons governance and intergenerational equity.

[31] Ristić and Madani, "A Game Theory Warning."

[32] Navroz K. Dubash, "Revisiting Climate Ambition: The Case for Prioritizing Current Action over Future Intent," *Wiley Interdisciplinary Reviews: Climate Change* 11, no. 1 (2020): e622.

If one nation thinks abatement is worth doing even without cooperation, that changes their payoff pattern to Chicken, changing the game from Prisoner's Dilemma to Called Bluff, where they abate and get second worst. If that nation comes to believe that mutual abatement would be the best outcome (rather than preferring to free ride if the other abates), then their payoff becomes that in Concord and the game would become Threat.[33] They might decide abatement is a moral imperative, or raise their expectations about the mutual benefits of a sustainable economy based on renewable energy, or see abatement it as a necessary transitional step that will be followed by others. The other nation might continue to pollute and get their "best" outcome. However, Threat is susceptible to transformation. The abater could threaten to resume polluting, a veto that would block the other nation from getting best or second-best. If the other changes to rank abatement as better than polluting, for whatever reasons, including information, persuasion, moral reconsideration, reputational risks, side payments, linkage, sanctions, or other pressures, that would reach a stable win-win game of Anticipation. This pathway illustrates how assuming symmetry or conditional cooperation only when others cooperate could blind analysts and decisionmakers to less symmetrical, less ideal, and less equitable but potentially feasible pathways to solutions.

Figure 6.4 shows the games formed by combining payoffs from Chicken, Prisoner's Dilemma, Stag Hunt, and Concord. This makes a simpler microcosm (subspace) of possible games showing the three pathways for 1) turning Prisoner's Dilemma into Stag Hunt at the center of

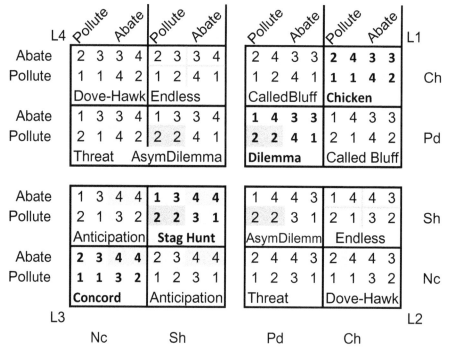

FIGURE 6.4 In a microcosm for transforming from pollution to abatement, changes that swap the ranking of outcomes turn tragic conflict in Prisoner's Dilemma into win-win cooperation

[33] Melvin J. Guyer, and Anatol Rapoport. "Threat in a Two-Person Game," *Journal of Experimental Social Psychology* 6, no. 1 (1970): 11–25.

the diagram and then into Concord, 2) converting Chicken into Concord (perhaps via Dove-Hawk), and 3) transforming asymmetrically from Prisoner's Dilemma through Called Bluff to Threat and win-win cooperation in Anticipation.

LIMITATIONS AND EXTENSIONS OF SIMPLE 2X2 MODELS

Game theory models offer insights into climate problems, but have many limitations,[34] especially if models make assumptions typical of early mathematical game theory, such as no communication, single-shot interaction, simultaneous decisions, irreversible moves, complete information, payoffs that already incorporate other-regarding preferences, risk-neutrality, no external enforcement, no side payments, and no links to other situations. Conversely, research has shown how different conditions can contribute to cooperation, even in Prisoner's Dilemma and multi person dilemmas.[35] Cooperation may be more successful with repeated interaction, communication, and incremental commitment. Most people are inclined to cooperate and willing to cooperate as long as others do so. Most care about what happens to others and are willing to punish those who do not cooperate. People are not prisoners, and often can "change the game" by making rules and other institutions that enable them to cooperate, including sustainably governing commons.[36]

Promising opportunities for further analyzing transformations between climate dilemmas include systematically applying multiple models beyond Prisoner's Dilemma and exploring asymmetric pathways where unequal and unsatisfactory outcomes could encourage efforts to find more equitable and mutually acceptable results. A broader menu of models may also help to understand the diversity of interconnected action situations between and within nations.[37]

CONCLUSIONS: TRANSFORMING CLIMATE DILEMMAS

Changes in the ranking of outcomes show how the tragic temptations of Prisoner's Dilemma can turn into potential coordination in Stag Hunt or shared fear of a worst outcome in Chicken, and then transform into convergent incentives to win-win in Concord. Combining payoffs from symmetric games to form asymmetric games reveals relationships between models of climate

---

[34] Madani, "Modeling International Climate Change."

[35] Some useful sources in a vast literature include Anatol Rapoport, Melvin J. Guyer, and David G. Gordon. *The 2 × 2 Game*. (Ann Arbor: University of Michigan Press, 1976); Robert Axelrod, *The Evolution of Cooperation*. (New York: Basic Books, 1984); Kollock, "Social Dilemmas"; Martin A. Nowak, "Five Rules for the Evolution of Cooperation," *Science* 314, no. 5805 (2006): 1560–1563; Michael Taylor, *Rationality and the Ideology of Disconnection*. (Cambridge: Cambridge University Press, 2006.)

[36] Elinor Ostrom, *Governing the Commons: The Evolution of Institutions for Collective Action*. (Cambridge: Cambridge University Press, 1990); Elinor Ostrom, Roy Gardner, and James Walker, *Rules, Games and Common-Pool Resources* (Ann Arbor: University of Michigan Press, 1994).

[37] Robert D. Putnam, "Diplomacy and Domestic Politics: The Logic of Two-Level Games," *International Organization* 42, no. 3 (ed 1988): 427–460. Michaël Aklin, and Matto Mildenberger. "Prisoners of the Wrong Dilemma: Why Distributive Conflict, Not Collective Action, Characterizes the Politics of Climate Change," *SSRN*, 2018. Elinor Ostrom, "A Polycentric Approach for Coping with Climate Change," *The World Bank*, 2009; Daniel H. Cole, "Advantages of a Polycentric Approach to Climate Change Policy." *Nature Climate Change* 5, no. 2 (2015): 114–118; Andrew Jordan, Dave Huitema, Harro van Asselt, and Johanna Forster. *Governing Climate Change: Polycentricity in Action?* (Cambridge: Cambridge University Press, 2018).

negotiations about whether to abate or pollute. The topology of payoff swaps in 2 x 2 games maps potential transformations and shows symmetric and asymmetric pathways to climate cooperation through fear of catastrophe if both pollute, changes that make cooperation best for both, or restructuring incentives even if a polluter always sees abating while the other pollutes as the worst outcome. A map for changing games displays the diversity of climate dilemmas and potential pathways to cooperation.

PART III

New Forms of Contested Commons

7

Reimagining Urban Public Housing as a Commons

Andrea McArdle

INTRODUCTION

This chapter offers an opening argument for a more democratic approach to governance of public housing in the United States based on an extension of commons scholarship to the context of an urban commons. Drawing on Sheila Foster and Christian Iaione's generative work, "The City as a Commons,"[1] the chapter uses New York City's Housing Authority (NYCHA), the nation's largest public housing agency, as a case study. Despite decades of disinvestment, mismanagement, and often dangerously deteriorating conditions, access to public housing remains a significant asset for economically vulnerable people. Although public housing and the land on which it is built typically are owned and managed by local government authorities,[2] supported in part by federal funding and subject to federal as well as local regulatory oversight,[3] the pressing reality of public disinvestment, and the concentration of economically precarious urban families in public housing's deteriorating spaces, have led to various rescue scenarios identifying private capital as essential to preserving this public resource. This shifting orientation from public to private has occurred during an extended period of regulatory slippage, a time when enforcement of public regulatory standards has significantly diminished.[4]

Foster and Iaione's urban commons analysis identifies resources that, under some legal regimes, qualify as non excludable open-access resources.[5] Further, and relevant to this chapter's argument, they consider a normative basis for urban residents to claim other resources, such as abandoned or unutilized urban spaces, particularly when these resources are in transition from one form of recognized ownership to another (private to public or vice versa)[6] under conditions of regulatory slippage.[7] This normative dimension identifies the social value of opening up urban assets in transition to economically vulnerable people who could benefit from them,[8] and

---

[1] Sheila R. Foster and Christian Iaione, "The City as a Commons," *Yale Law & Policy Review* 34 (2016): 281.

[2] United States Housing Act of 1937, 42 U.S.C. §1437 et seq.

[3] "Public Housing," National Housing Law Project, accessed December 1, 2019, www.nhlp.org/resource-center/public-housing/.

[4] Sheila R. Foster, "Collective Action and the Urban Commons," *Notre Dame L. Rev.* 87 (2011):57, 67.

[5] Foster and Iaione, "City as Commons," 315–21.

[6] Ibid., 288–289, 301–306.

[7] Foster, "Collective Action and the Urban Commons," 67–68 (defining regulatory slippage).

[8] Ibid., 306–311.

treating such assets as essentially a common or community good, as distinguished from a good owned privately or by the government.[9]

Foster and Iaione's capacious understanding of the implications of urban commons theory builds on Elinor Ostrom's groundbreaking studies of self-organized cooperative action, which offered hybrid governance mechanisms for common-pool natural resources involving both public and private spheres as alternatives to government regulation and private property regimes.[10] Applying these principles to the broader urban context, Foster and Iaione develop a rationale grounded in a social theory of property[11] for expanding the equitable use of urban space and resources from which a community can derive benefit and to which they are bound by a shared stake and sense of connection.

The increasing transition of public housing assets to private control heightens the urgency of developing a theoretical basis for reimagining NYCHA land and assets under an urban commons framework. Although public housing is not a classic common-pool resource, the chapter argues that, at a time of failed public stewardship and increasing private-sector access to public housing assets, the democratizing implications of urban commons theory that Foster and Iaione tease out can reorient use of NYCHA's space – its land, improvements, and air space – and ensure residents' meaningful participation in decisions concerning the sustainability of a significant community resource in New York City.

PUBLIC HOUSING IN TRANSITION

With its origins in the Depression-era National Housing Act of 1937,[12] publicly constructed housing was, in part, the federal government's response to widespread problems of unemployment[13] as well as to the accompanying need for affordable housing for persons of low income.[14] The commitment of national funding was balanced by a delegation of authority to local government housing authorities to oversee the creation and management of public housing.[15] The resulting statutory scheme included income eligibility criteria[16] for residents to ensure that public housing units were available to low-income persons in need, but the underlying regulatory framework established a structural role for tenants to participate in the policy and management decisions associated with these units. This role requires membership of at least one public housing resident in the governing body of the public housing agency[17] and establishment

---

[9] Ibid., 306–308. For a close analysis of the distinction, see James B. Quilligan, "Why Distinguish Common Goods from Public Goods?" http://wealthofthecommons.org/essay/why-distinguish-common-goods-public-goods (arguing that "in practice," public equates to government which, in a neoliberal political economy, is heavily responsive to the "private") *in* David Bollier and Silke Helfrich, eds., *The Wealth of the Commons: A World Beyond Market and State* (The Commons Strategy Group, 2012), www.wealthofthecommons.org/essay/introduction-commons-transformative-vision.

[10] Elinor Ostrom, *Governing the Commons: The Evolution of Institutions for Collective Action* (Cambridge: Cambridge University Press, 1990, 2015), 8–14, 14–15, 182–216.

[11] Foster and Iaione, "City as Commons," 307–311.

[12] The United States Housing Act of 1937, 42 U.S.C. §1437 et seq. (Westlaw, current through P.L. 117–30 except PL 116–283, Div. A, Title XVIII, takes effect 1/1/2022).

[13] Maggie McCarty, "Introduction to Public Housing," *Congressional Research Service*, January 3, 2014, https://fas.org/sgp/crs/misc/R41654.pdf.

[14] The United States Housing Act of 1937, 42 U.S.C.§ 1437a (Westlaw, see note 12 for currentness).

[15] National Housing Law Project, "Public Housing."

[16] 42 U.S.C.§ 1437a.

[17] 42 U.S.C. § 1437(b)(1).

of resident advisory boards,[18] recognizes residents' right to organize and elect a resident council,[19] and authorizes resident councils' working partnership with housing authorities to advise and assist in all aspects of public housing operations.[20]

In the post–World War II era, public housing's role was circumscribed as the National Housing Act of 1949[21] prioritized urban renewal carried out by the private sector.[22] Increasingly, the political economy of urban redevelopment pointed away from publicly owned and managed housing to a paradigm of private-sector construction of housing, in which government subsidies and other incentives promoted the creation of units for middle-income families.[23] This increasing turn to private-sector housing, in combination with federal disinvestment from aging public housing stock and programmatic limits on rental payments, eventually led many localities to demolish their severely distressed public housing, and to replace it with mixed-income housing developments, which late twentieth-century changes in federal law permitted.[24] Although New York has retained its public housing assets, these funding and maintenance issues increasingly have plagued New York's public housing stock as well.[25]

Created by state legislation in 1934,[26] NYCHA was envisioned by New York mayor Fiorello LaGuardia, an early champion of public housing, as an antidote to unhealthy conditions in crowded tenement buildings.[27] The norm for NYCHA housing soon became high-rise towers on superblocks[28] where only a percentage of space was built upon, providing a source of "light and air."[29] With its income and other eligibility criteria,[30] NYCHA housing differs from the classic conception of an open resource to which access is not excludable.[31] However, NYCHA's aggregated land and population in New York approximate a mid-sized city in scale,[32] and, when it functions as envisaged, it operates within the conceptual and normative frame of an urban commons, in which vulnerable individuals across New York City share access to its housing, social services,[33] and accessory spaces.[34]

---

[18] 42 U.S.C. § 1437c-1(e) (Westlaw, see note 12 for currentness).

[19] 24 C.F.R. § 964.11 (Westlaw, current through July 29, 2021; 86 FR 40789).

[20] 24 C.F.R. § 964.100 (Westlaw, see note 19 for currentness).

[21] 42 U.S.C. §§ 1441 et seq. (Westlaw, see note 12 for currentness).

[22] Nicholas Dagen Bloom, *Public Housing that Worked: New York in the Twentieth Century* (Philadelphia: University of Pennsylvania Press, 2008), 117.

[23] Early examples in New York City included multifamily developments designed for postwar middle-income families such as Stuyvesant Town. Samuel Zipp, *Manhattan Projects: The Rise and Fall of Urban Renewal in Cold War New York* (New York: Oxford University Press, 2010), 73–113.

[24] "About Hope VI," HUD.gov, accessed December 1, 2019, www.hud.gov/program_offices/public_indian_housing/programs/ph/hope6/about.

[25] Victor Bach, *Public Housing: New York's Third City* (Community Service Society, March, 2017), 3–4, https://smhttp-ssl-58547.nexcesscdn.net/nycss/images/uploads/pubs/Third_City_-_web_3_1_2017.pdf

[26] Bloom, *Public Housing that Worked*, 13, 26–27.

[27] Michael Markowitz, "Public Housing," *Gotham Gazette*, February 17, 2003, http://www.gothamgazette.com/index.php/housing/1721-public-housing.

[28] Bloom, *Public Housing that Worked*, 142-148; Robert Fox Elder, "Protecting New York City's Community Gardens," *N.Y.U. Environmental Law Journal* 13 (2005): 769, 771–773.

[29] Bloom, *Public Housing that Worked*, 135, 140–143, 148, 150; Zipp, *Manhattan Projects*, 14–15, 287–288.

[30] National Housing Law Project, "Public Housing."

[31] Foster and Iaione, "City as Commons," 287-288.

[32] "Urban Population by City Size," OECD Data, accessed December 1, 2019, https://data.oecd.org/popregion/urban-population-by-city-size.htm.
   (population range between 200,000–500,000).

[33] NYC Open Data, Directory of NYCHA Community Facilities, https://data.cityofnewyork.us/Social-Services/Directory-of-NYCHA-Community-Facilities/crns-fw6u

[34] "NYCHA 2019 Fact Sheet," New York City Housing Authority, March 2019, www1.nyc.gov/assets/nycha/downloads/pdf/NYCHA-Fact-Sheet_2019_08–01.pdf

Once lauded as "public housing that worked,"[35] the City's 326 developments, 2,462 residential buildings, approximately 175,000 apartments, and nearly 400,000 residents,[36] now serve as the public face of failed stewardship, far from the governing norm of "decent, safe, and sanitary housing."[37] The combination of badly deteriorated housing stock, loss of federal and state funding sources, and system-wide management failures has led to a crisis in sustainability. These failures are documented in an 80-page complaint from a recently settled lawsuit brought by the U.S. Department of Housing and Urban Development (HUD), NYCHA's oversight agency, detailing NYCHA's breach of serious health and safety obligations and its attempt to conceal these derelictions.[38] Despite NYCHA's early exemplary reputation,[39] the conditions brought to light in HUD's lawsuit were the inevitable outcome of regulatory slippage: declining government funding and lack of robust regulatory oversight. The effects of mismanagement and corruption[40] have been reflected in a raft of legal proceedings challenging NYCHA's failure to maintain its housing stock to the basic standard required under federal law.[41]

In January 2019, after a federal district court judge had earlier disapproved a proposed settlement of the HUD lawsuit,[42] NYCHA, New York City, and HUD entered into an administrative agreement requiring NYCHA to reform its operations and management, adopt new performance standards and deadlines to remedy conditions threatening health and safety, hire a new chief executive, and answer to a federal monitor, which New York City is obligated to pay for, along with committing to more than $1.2 billion in additional capital funds over the ensuing five years.[43]

To encourage that settlement, in late 2018 New York City announced a ten-year NYCHA 2.0 plan, billed as an initiative to generate revenue to preserve public housing.[44] Added to commitments to increase accountability and prioritize areas of needed repair,[45] the plan

[35] Bloom, _Public Housing That Worked._
[36] "About NYCHA," New York City Housing Authority, accessed December 1, 2019, www1.nyc.gov/site/nycha/about/about-nycha.page.
[37] 24 C.F.R.§ 5.703; 24 C.F.R. §902.21 (physical condition standards for public housing, requiring decent, safe, and sanitary housing in good repair) (Westlaw, see note 19 for currentness).
[38] United States of America v. New York City Housing Authority (18 Civ. 5213), June 11, 2018, www.justice.gov/usao-sdny/press-release/file/1070551/download.
[39] Bloom, _Public Housing That Worked_, 1-10, 266-68; Linda I. Gibbs and Caswell F. Holloway, NYC _Hurricane Sandy After Action: Report and Recommendations to Mayor Michael R. Bloomberg_, May 2013, 8–10, 20.
[40] The federal lawsuit brought against NYCHA in June 2018 details the factual basis for these charges. United States v. NYCHA, ¶¶ 215–267.
[41] For example, in 2013, NYCHA entered a consent agreement in a class action under the Americans with Disabilities Act on behalf of residents with asthma to correct mold problems in apartments. "NYC to Address Rampant Mold and Moisture Problems in Public Housing Following NRDC Lawsuit," Natural Resources Defense Council, December 17, 2013, www.nrdc.org/media/2013/131217. NYCHA's failure to meet the remediation timeline has led to appointing a special master to enforce provisions of the consent decree, and an amended settlement that appointed independent data and mold analysts and an ombudsman, among other measures. "Baez v. New York City Housing Authority," Natural Resources Defense Council (last updated October 18, 2019), www.nrdc.org/court-battles/baez-v-new-york-city-housing-authority.
[42] United States of America v. New York City Housing Authority (November 14, 2018, S.D.N.Y.), 1-18CV05213_DocketEntry_11–14-2018_64(2).pdf.
[43] "Manhattan U.S. Attorney Announces New Agreement for Fundamental Reform at NYCHA," Department of Justice, U.S. Attorney's Office, Southern District of New York, January 31, 2019, www.justice.gov/usao-sdny/pr/manhattan-us-attorney-announces-new-agreement-fundamental-reform-nycha.
[44] "NYCHA 2.0, Part 1, Invest to Preserve," The City of New York, December 12, 2018, www1.nyc.gov/assets/nycha/downloads/pdf/NYCHA-2.0-Part1.pdf.
[45] "NYCHA 2.0, Part 2, Fix to Preserve," The City of New York, December 12, 2018, www1.nyc.gov/assets/nycha/downloads/pdf/NYCHA-2.0-Part2.pdf.

includes three investment pillars: infill construction[46] – permitting private development of new, mainly market rate, rental housing on existing NYCHA campuses under long-term leases;[47] creation of public–private partnerships to underwrite the renovation of thousands of units;[48] and transfer of NYCHA development rights to adjoining private properties.[49] To be sure, this shift in focus to greater private-sector involvement is made possible in part by the substantial amount of unbuilt space inside NYCHA campuses, one of NYCHA's signature features.[50] However, given continuing opposition by some residents and public officials[51] to plans for disposition of this undeveloped space, and lack of evidence that alternative uses of unbuilt spaces have been considered,[52] the development framework envisioned to preserve NYCHA remains highly contested.[53]

APPLYING COMMONS THEORY TO EXPAND EQUITABLE ACCESS TO DECENT, AFFORDABLE PUBLIC HOUSING

As federal policy underpinning the regulatory framework for public housing requires, public housing tenants have a substantial stake in how these public assets are managed. Applied to an urban context, where residents' access to public space, and opportunities for a role in managing it, generally have been shrinking, commons principles offer strong theoretical and normative support for this federal policy. In a time of disinvestment from urban properties, community-based claims to use or occupy these types of properties (for example, homesteading to address displacement and homelessness,[54] community gardening to address the urban green space deficits[55] and to enhance "social capital")[56] derive their legitimacy from the social benefits

---

[46] University of Delaware, Complete Communities Toolbox, "What Is Infill and Redevelopment?," www .completecommunitiesde.org/planning/landuse/what-is-infill/.

[47] "NYCHA 2.0, Part 1, Build to Preserve," www1.nyc.gov/assets/nycha/downloads/pdf/NYCHA-2.0-Part1.pdf. Earlier versions of this idea of "infill" construction on NYCHA land included a proposal in 2013 during Mayor Michael Bloomberg's administration, Sam Spokony, "Judge Halts City Council's Suit Against NYCHA Infill Plan, For Now," *The Villager*, December 12, 2013, http://thevillager.com/2013/12/12/judge-halts-city-councils-suit-against-nycha-infill-plan-for-now/), and, in 2015, a reconceived plan under the de Blasio mayoral administration. "Next Generation NYCHA," The City of New York, May 2015, www1.nyc.gov/assets/nycha/downloads/pdf/nextgen-nycha-web.pdf.
  Since NYCHA 2.0 was launched, the announced projects under the 2015 deBlasio plan have been delayed. Citizen's Budget Commission, NYCHA 2.0: *Progress at Risk*, September 17, 2019, https://cbcny.org/research/nycha-20-progress-risk.

[48] "Rental Assistance Demonstration," U. S. Department of Housing & Urban Development, accessed December 1, 2019, www.hud.gov/RAD.

[49] The first of these transfers has reportedly gone to a substantial donor of the City's current Mayor de Blasio. Shant Shahrigian, "NYC Is Selling 'Air Rights' to City Housing Buildings, First Big Deal Goes to de Blasio Donors," *New York Daily News*, November 10, 2019, 12:01 A.M., www.nydailynews.com/news/politics/ny-de-blasio-nycha-deal-jorge-madruga-eli-weiss-20191110-pxol35ffcbhmbfyii4igf4vgpa-story.html.

[50] Bloom, *Public Housing that Worked*, 59, 138, 142-43, 148, 150.

[51] Citizen's Budget Commission, NYCHA 2.0: *Progress at Risk* (September 17, 2019), https://cbcny.org/research/nycha-20-progress-risk.

[52] See discussion of text accompanying notes 76-90.

[53] Elizabeth Kim, "Facing Opposition to Redevelopment Plan, City Establishes Working Group to Decide Future of NYCHA's Chelsea Complex," *Gothamist*, October 11, 2019. https://gothamist.com/news/facing-opposition-redevelopment-plan-city-establishes-working-group-decide-future-nychas-chelsea-complex.

[54] Andrea McArdle, "[Re]Integrating Community Space: The Legal and Social Meanings of Reclaiming Abandoned Space in New York's Lower East Side," *Savannah Law Review* 2 (2015): 247, 257-262.

[55] Robert Fox Elder, "Protecting New York City's Community Gardens," *N.Y.U. Environmental Law Journal* 13 (2005): 769, 792-795.

[56] Foster and Iaione, "City as Commons," 306-307; Elder, "Community Gardens," 789-790.

inherent in these uses.[57] The consideration of these potential benefits is bolstered by the idea that property as an institution encompasses a social function and an obligation to prioritize human needs, even when this requires adjustment, or subordination, of formal property ownership interests.[58]

When commons theory is applied in an urban context, its grounding in social need and the well-being of local residents recognizes those residents' stakes in resources that are capacity-enhancing and thus likely to produce community benefits. In urban commons thinking, the community stake in urban resources extends not only to their use but, critically, to governance – participation in decisions on managing their use and allocation.[59]

In related housing contexts, studies of resident participation in decision making offer empirical support for the benefits of strengthening participation norms. Analysis of the Demonstration Disposition Program, a late twentieth-century federal housing rehabilitation project designed to transition low-income residents to ownership of redeveloped properties, illustrated how residents could be successfully engaged in decision making throughout the development process.[60] Program studies documented gains in residents' voice, sense of self-efficacy, and community-building,[61] as well as residents' improved relationships with the local police department.[62] Resident participation in initiatives to preserve HUD affordable housing projects has yielded evidence of improved housing conditions, increased connections among residents, and gains in individual residents' capacity and confidence.[63]

The democratic implications of applying commons principles have particular relevance for the concern that NYCHA residents have been excluded from meaningful involvement in transfers of long-term control over NYCHA properties to private developers, despite the regulatory framework that ordains that residents have a structural role in NYCHA's governance.[64]

STATUTORY AND NORMATIVE BASES FOR CLAIMING A STAKE IN DECISION MAKING

The suite of investment proposals authorized under NYCHA 2.0 would significantly reallocate control of NYCHA assets to the private sector.[65] As noted, one aspect of the plan contemplates private infill construction within selected NYCHA campuses under long-term leases. Revenue generated by the development would help pay for improvements to existing NYCHA housing, mainly housing on the same NYCHA campuses slated for new construction.[66] In the current iteration of this plan, 70% of the units built on NYCHA land would be market rate, and 30% would be offered at rents below market rate in accordance with New York City's Mandatory

[57] Foster and Iaione, City as Commons," 307–311.
[58] Ibid. (discussing social function property theorists); 321–324.
[59] Ibid., 324–334.
[60] Carolyn C. Leung, *Resident Participation: A Community-Building Strategy in Low-Income Neighborhoods*, NeighborWorks America, Joint Centers for Housing Studies of Harvard University 10, 24 (2005).
[61] Ibid., 24.
[62] James Jennings et al., *The Demonstration Disposition Program in Boston, Massachusetts, 1994-2001: A Program Evaluation, Final Draft Report*, Submitted to MassHousing, Boston, Massachusetts 33 (March 2002).
[63] Deb Goldberg Gray, *Resident Participation in HUD Affordable Housing Preservation Projects: What Works?* 25 (University of California Center for Cooperatives, September 2000).
[64] See statutes and regulations cited in text accompanying notes 17–20.
[65] Abigail Savitch-Lew, "NYCHA Responds to Fiscal Crisis with Embrace of Private Sector," *City Limits*, June 20, 2016, https://citylimits.org/2016/06/20/nycha-responds-to-fiscal-crisis-with-embrace-of-private-sector/.
[66] "NYCHA 2.0, Part 1, Build to Preserve," www1.nyc.gov/assets/nycha/downloads/pdf/NYCHA-2.0-Part1.pdf.

Inclusionary Housing legislation.[67] Another prong of NYCHA 2.0 is built on HUD's Rental Assistance Demonstration (RAD) project, which converts tenants to a different statutory status and authorizes formation of public–private entities that can draw on private funding for renovations and take over ownership of the renovated buildings, but not the underlying land.[68] Tenants of the public–private partnerships are guaranteed the same rights and protections that they would have as public housing residents,[69] though reports of higher eviction rates in RAD buildings,[70] and a lack of transparency about the status of repairs,[71] have raised concerns. A third NYCHA 2.0 proposal authorizes transfer of NYCHA property air rights to nearby private property owners.[72] Notwithstanding the apparent economic benefits these initiatives may confer, their implications for the structural role and stake of NYCHA residents in governance must first be addressed in a meaningful way, in light of the regulatory framework requiring that NYCHA residents have input over matters affecting their tenancy.[73]

Addressing this inquiry, commons analysis provides important theoretical and conceptual support for fully implementing the policy to foster participation in decisions that affect residents' tenancy. NYCHA's approximately 400,000 residents are bound together by a shared need for affordable, safe, and habitable housing.[74] These considerations support treatment of NYCHA properties, including currently unbuilt spaces, as communal resources in which its residents, a community of shared urban knowledge, experience, and economic vulnerability, hold a stake, both by statute, as noted, and under ideas grounded in democratic theory and the social function of property. As Foster and Iaione develop, these theoretical frameworks identify a social responsibility to use property in ways that benefit the common good, such that all community members have access to baseline resources needed to ensure the capacity to thrive.[75] Arguably those resources would include an assurance of safe and affordable housing; opportunities to acquire information, knowledge, and skills; and a right to participate in decision-making that affects one's well-being. Informed by this social obligation norm, commons theory supports prioritizing a role for NYCHA residents to participate in the decision-making process when NYCHA assets are transferred to the private sector.

CONSIDERING ALTERNATIVE BENEFICIAL USES OF UNBUILT SPACES

The seemingly reflexive shift from public ownership and regulation to "rescue" by an enhanced private-sector stake insufficiently accounts for public housing's role as a resource providing access to urban space, services, and support for its residents. Given the serious degradation of NYCHA properties, initiatives that would directly improve conditions (RAD), or generate

---

[67] NYC Planning, "Mandatory Inclusionary Housing," www1.nyc.gov/site/planning/plans/mih/mandatory-inclusionary-housing.page.

[68] "Permanent Affordability Commitment Together," New York City Housing Authority, accessed September 5, 2020, www1.nyc.gov/assets/nycha/downloads/pdf/pact-factsheet.pdf. See also "Rental Assistance Demonstration," U.S. Department of Housing & Urban Development, accessed December 1, 2019, www.hud.gov/RAD.

[69] "Permanent Affordability Commitment Together (PACT), Frequently Asked Questions," New York City Housing Authority, accessed December 1, 2019, www1.nyc.gov/assets/nycha/downloads/pdf/nextgen-pact-faq.pdf.

[70] Harry DiPrinzio, "Hundreds of NYCHA Evictions Raise Questions about Process," *City Limits*, August 14, 2019, https://citylimits.org/2019/08/14/nycha-evicitons-rad-oceanbay/.

[71] Greg B. Smith and Trone Dowd, "Tenants in Privately Managed NYCHA Homes Kept in Dark on Building Repairs," *The City*, February 3, 2020, https://thecity.nyc/2020/02/nycha-rad-privately-run-building-tenants-lack-repair-info.html.

[72] "NYCHA 2.0, Part 1, Transfer to Preserve," www1.nyc.gov/assets/nycha/downloads/pdf/NYCHA-2.0-Part1.pdf.

[73] See statutes and regulations cited in text accompanying notes 17–20.

[74] Based on its population, NYCHA would rank 32nd in size in the U.S. "NYCHA 2019 Fact Sheet."

[75] Foster and Iaione, "The City as a Commons," 307–311.

funding, such as NYCHA 2.0 infill projects, do offer potential benefits that NYCHA residents should have the opportunity and time to consider. Realizing this objective entails a level of engagement needed to gauge the will of residents, including ways in which infill projects on NYCHA campuses could be implemented without altering the animating value of preserving open space, and, in particular, green space,[76] within NYCHA developments.[77] This emphasis on providing open space was a public-health objective that NYCHA's founders embraced to ensure that the properties offered sufficient light and air,[78] replacing the close-quarter tenement buildings from an earlier era.[79] Before NYCHA transfers a long-term interest in unbuilt space in its properties, residents also must have the opportunity to fully vet alternative uses, including those that would serve some of the same purposes as infill projects, as well as others that would benefit residents differently.

For example, a key justification offered for the infill projects is their capacity to generate revenue for renovations. However, infill construction is not the only potential funding source for this purpose. The early planning for NYCHA developments had included recommendations that certain space be allocated for commercial retail.[80] NYCHA ultimately did not provide on-site retail establishments in most developments, except in more isolated areas.[81] Despite this early decision limiting the inclusion of retail stores within NYCHA,[82] residents should have the opportunity to consider whether on-site retail stores could add greater convenience for residents, offer more opportunities for social interaction[83] and employment,[84] and provide alternative revenue sources to fund needed renovations. These potential benefits could be weighed against possible disruption and negative health impacts to residents during the infill construction process, impacts that might also occur during renovations of buildings approved for RAD conversions.

NYCHA residents should also have the opportunity to explore the alternative of cultivating open spaces to enhance NYCHA's existing urban agriculture projects.[85] Such initiatives could address the serious health and environmental implications of the green deficit in vegetation–starved urban neighborhoods.[86] They could also enable residents to market their own produce to surrounding neighborhoods as a commercial venture. Further, where proposed infill construction is located in flood zones, residents should be able to consider the environmental impact of

---

[76] Bloom, *Public Housing that Worked*, 64–68, 160–161, 163–164, 166. Bloom's history of NYCHA in the 20th Century described the grounds, then open to the public, as "beachheads of green in a crowded, polluted environment." Ibid., 66.

[77] Ibid., 57–59, 64, 138.

[78] Ibid., 135, 140–143, 148, 150.

[79] Ibid., 25–26, 62, 118–119, 123.

[80] Ibid., 59, 143.

[81] Ibid., 143–144.

[82] Ibid., 148.

[83] Ibid., 144, 146.

[84] Section 3 of the Housing and Urban Development Act of 1968, codified at 12 U.S.C.§1701u, reflects the role that public housing authorities are to play in improving opportunities for employment and job training for NYCHA residents.

[85] "Farms at NYCHA," Green City Force, accessed December 1, 2019, www.greencityforce.org/farmsatnycha/ (noting multi-party collaboration involving community partners and the Fund for Public Health in which 18-to-24-year-old NYCHA residents manage six farms on NYCHA properties to provide produce for NYCHA residents).

[86] Nevin Cohen, Nick Freudenberg, and Craig Willingham, *Nourishing NYCHA: Food Policy as a Tool for Improving the Well-Being of New York City's Public Housing Residents* (CUNY Urban Food Policy Institute, February 2017), https://static1.squarespace.com/static/572d0fcc2b8dde9e10ab59d4/t/58c98e01f7e0ab19ba66d6c3/1489604100091/Brief-NYCHA+Food-20170227-Final.pdf.

the proposed projects,[87] such as whether they would be vulnerable to storm surges, a risk shown to be painfully real during Superstorm Sandy in 2012 for NYCHA developments located along the City's waterfront.[88]

Although the planned infill projects will add a number of privately developed affordable housing units, the attractiveness of infill projects to developers, and the revenues the projects could generate for NYCHA to refurbish its existing developments, generally hinge on whether developers can recoup their investment via market-rate units.[89] However, NYCHA residents should have input concerning whether, and otherwise in what proportion, infill housing units should be rented at market rates, especially in light of the predictable gentrifying effects that flow from locating such housing in transitioning urban neighborhoods.[90]

THE RIGHTS TO PARTICIPATION AND INFORMATION

The well-documented deterioration of NYCHA properties in the last decade suggests that permitting some private-sector involvement in infill construction and RAD conversions might be feasible. Such involvement is not inconsistent with commons norms, which recognize the potential value of a broad spectrum of participants in governing institutions, so long as the residents most affected by the decisions concerning use of NYCHA property are included in the planning and decision-making process.[91] The statutory mandate that NYCHA residents participate in decision making in matters affecting the developments requires that residents have a meaningful opportunity to be heard about the desirability and extent of market-rate infill development, as well as other transfers of control of NYCHA assets to the private sector. A robust participation norm which values NYCHA residents' knowledge, perspectives, and experience, and in which residents play a genuine role in governance, would ensure that the issues of greatest practical import to residents would be aired.

Giving effect to a more fully realized right to resident input and participation would require assurances that residents are given access to information about the feasibility of alternative uses and available funding sources. The engagement of NYCHA residents contemplated by commons principles requires more than an after-the-fact consultation, or ratification of decisions that are already fait accompli.[92] Urban commons theory calls for more robust forms of engagement, and at the earliest stages of planning, that involve residents in discussions about the full spectrum of costs, benefits, and consequences entailed in private infill development, RAD public–private partnerships, and other transfers of NYCHA assets to private entities.

---

[87] The Bloomberg administration's 2013 infill plan prompted a lawsuit citing the City's failure to carry out environmental and floodplain studies. Sam Spokony, "Advocates to File Suit Against NYCHA Infill Plan," *The Villager* (November 14, 2013) (originally published November 8, 2013), http://thevillager.com/2013/11/14/advocates-to-file-suit-against-nycha-infill-plan/.

[88] Andrea McArdle, "Storm Surges, Disaster Planning, and Vulnerable Populations at the Urban Periphery: Imagining a Resilient New York after Superstorm Sandy," *Idaho Law Review* 50 (2014): 19, 28–29, 43–44.

[89] NYU Furman Center, *Gentrification Response: A Survey of Strategies to Maintain Neighborhood Economic Diversity* (October 2016), 12–13, http://furmancenter.org/files/NYUFurmanCenter_GentrificationResponse_26OCT2016.pdf.

[90] Ibid., 5–7.

[91] Foster and Iaione, "City as Commons," 329–332. The potential of public-private partnerships is explored at length in Ostrom, *Governing the Commons*.

[92] The petition of the NYCHA-wide resident body complained of its lack of meaningful input into NYCHA management, that NYCHA "makes unilateral decisions on virtually every important policy matter that affects Tenants' lives," The City-Wide Council of Presidents v. NYCHA, ¶ 191, and fails to provide sufficient advance information. Ibid., ¶¶ 191–194.

CONCLUSION

Applying an urban commons analysis to the capital and managerial challenges faced by NYCHA is fundamentally a question of reorienting its governance to an equity-based and participatory norm that responds to the political, social, and economic realities of contemporary cities, and the inequities that have resulted. This reorientation is essential to ensure a meaningful role for residents in decisions affecting their shared environment, degraded as it has become by the actions or omissions of political and market actors who have long dominated the political economy of cities.[93]

In New York's public housing context, the transition in ownership and control from public to private under conditions of regulatory slippage implicates the normative dimensions of urban commons theory and legitimizes a claim to more robust resident participation in governance of resources over which NYCHA continues to exercise jurisdiction. The urban strand of commons scholarship adds theoretical and normative heft to that claim, reinforced in related empirical evidence,[94] a claim traceable to residents' experience, circumstances, and social need,[95] and NYCHA's failing stewardship of the resource entrusted to it. Urban commons theory offers an enduring basis—one that will survive a change in law or capriciousness in its enforcement – for recognizing residents' voice concerning a resource that has demonstrated meaning and utility for the NYCHA community. It inheres in the prospective benefits that an amplified voice can bring to NYCHA residents, as they draw on their urban experience and knowledge, work collectively to shape their shared environment, and, by participating in decisions that will affect its use, speak and act for themselves.[96]

[93] David Bollier and Silke Helfrich, "Introduction: The Commons as Transformative Vision," – www.wealthofthecommons
       .org/essay/introduction-commons-transformative-vision (discussing the limitations of the "market/state duopoly" and calling
       for developments in policy and law to strengthen commons institutions) *in* Bollier and Helfrich, *Wealth of the Commons*;
       David Bollier, *Think Like a Commoner: A Short Introduction to the Life of the Commons* (Gabriola Island: New Society
       Publishers, 2014), 4–5.
[94] See text and accompanying notes 60–63.
[95] Foster and Iaione, "The City as a Commons," 308–311, 322–324; Bollier, *Think Like a Commoner*, 89–90, 98 (noting
       the value of day-to-day experience and social norms in forming commons institutions).
[96] For a discussion of residents' struggle with lack of voice, see Jeffery C. Mays, "Tenants Sue New York City Housing
       Authority: 'We Have Let Other People Speak for Us for Too Long,'" New York Times, February 27, 2018, www
       .nytimes.com/2018/02/27/nyregion/nycha-lawsuit-nyc-housing.html.

8

Humanitarian Aid as a Shared and Contested Common Resource

Michelle Reddy

Perceptions of humanitarian intervention center around images of United Nations blue helmets and Doctors Without Borders. However, the vast majority of first responders during a crisis are one's neighbors.[1] Individual and community networks facilitate information flows, aid, resources, and support[2] and oftentimes are more trusted than outside organizations.[3] Therefore, humanitarian intervention is a shared space, combining the efforts of international organizations, governments, and increasingly the private sector in addition to the actions of everyday individuals and professionals. Across contexts, individuals organize groups informally and act before formal organizations are able to mobilize.[4] In addition, local participation in decision-making improves recovery (see for example, the Kobe earthquake in Japan).[5] The role of localized humanitarian aid is widely acknowledged as a policy goal in terms of efficiency, preparedness, improving outcomes, capacity-strengthening, and resilience. However, during humanitarian disasters decision-making usually remains within the realm of international or national policy, adversely impacting not only disaster outcomes, but also recovery and reconstruction.[6]

---

[1] Daniel P. Aldrich and Michelle A. Meyer, "Social Capital and Community Resilience," *American Behavioral Scientist* 59, no. 2 (October 2012): 254–269.

Daniel P. Aldrich, "Social, Not Physical, Infrastructure: The Critical Role of Civil Society in Disaster Recovery," *Disasters Studies* 36, no. 3 (July 2012): 398–419.

George Horwich, "Economic Lessons of the Kobe Earthquake," *Economic Development and Cultural Change* 48, no. 3 (April 2000): 521–542.

Rajib Shaw and Katsuihciro Goda, "From Disaster to Sustainable Civil Society, the Kobe Experience," *Disasters* 28, no. 1 (April 2004): 16–40.

[2] Jeanne S. Hurlbert, Valerie A. Haines, and John J. Beggs. "Core Networks and Tie Activation: What Kinds of Routine Networks Allocated Resources in Nonroutine Situations? *American Sociological Review* 65 no. 4 (August 2000): 598–618.

[3] Michelle Reddy, "The NGO-ization of Civil Society and the 2013-2016 Ebola Epidemic," *Working Paper* February 2020.

[4] Beverley Raphael. *When Disaster Strikes: A Handbook for the Caring Professions* (London: Hutchinson, 1986).

[5] Shaw and Goda, "From Disaster," 16–40.

[6] Organization for Economic Cooperation and Development (OECD), "Localising the Response: World Humanitarian Summit," *OECD* (2017): 1–19.

International Federation of the Red Cross Red Crescent (IFCRC), "Localization – What it Means and How to Achieve it," *IFCRC Policy Brief* (May 2018): 1–6.

Accelerating Localisation through Partnerships, "Pathways to Localisation: A framework towards locally-led humanitarian response in partnership-based action." Christina Schmalenbach with Christian Aid, CARE, Tearfund, ActionAid, CAFOD, Oxfam (October 2019): 1–24.

Disasters, as well as other humanitarian crises, are events in which the need for collective action is unprecedented. However, collective action is complex in disasters as they often times mandate massive behavior change and the reallocation and distribution of extensive resources, whether financial, material, or human resources. The relevance of Ostrom's contributions around institutions in diverse contexts, to collective action dilemmas in humanitarian crises, has already been acknowledged to a small extent.[7] For instance, Ostrom maintains that development aid creates unique patterns of incentives undermining sustainable development.[8] Relatedly, Barnett and Ramalingam argue that incentives in the humanitarian system inhibit inter organizational cooperation due, in part, to competition for donor support.[9] While incentives, and the desire to respond rapidly in light of a crisis, explain the humanitarian dilemma, they only partially do so. In particular, humanitarian intervention faces challenges in designing collective action interventions. Therefore, Ostrom's design principles remain to be empirically applied in humanitarian settings.[10]

In this chapter, I aim to expand on this earlier work by discussing how humanitarian aid is viewed as a common pool resource by recipients in developing countries, and as a private resource to be managed, measured, and monitored by international organizations and donor governments. This leads to not only tension in the aid relationship particularly when a huge influx of aid arrives during a disaster, but also free-riding and conflict, that can be overcome once the rules of the game are co designed by institutional actors on all levels. While rational choice theory partially explains this tension, another impediment to local cooperation is that the rules – which increasingly include metrics, monitoring, and evaluation[11] – exclude local organizations that oftentimes lack technical capacity in terms of implementation yet are successful in terms of buy-in. As a result, response, recovery, and resilience to an epidemic, or another disaster, are adversely impacted. During an epidemic, and indeed in other humanitarian settings mandating behavior change, the rules may change rapidly and in unprecedented ways.

I use the example of the 2013–2016 West Africa Ebola Response, which occurred along the border of three countries with different institutional histories, to illustrate that individuals in contexts of national and international policy failure can indeed co-manage shared aid resources during disasters once rules are co-designed. To achieve this, I draw on Ostrom's core design principles as applied to the management of humanitarian assistance during the West Africa Ebola Response. Contrary to Hardin's "Tragedy of the Commons" thesis, Ostrom illustrated that individuals are capable of collaborating to co-manage shared resources even in the absence of government regulation or private ownership.[12] As a result, the core design principles consist of defining clear boundaries, matching governance rules to local conditions, as well as ensuring community participation, monitoring, graduated sanctions, affordable dispute resolution, and mechanisms for responsible governance at each level.[13]

[7] Michael Barnett and Ben Ramalingam, "The Humanitarian's Dilemma: Collective Action or Inaction in International Relief?," *Overseas Development Institute* (August 2010): 1–8.

[8] Clark C. Gibson, Krister Andersson, Elinor Ostrom, and Sujai Shivakumar, *The Samaritan's Dilemma* (Oxford: OUP, 2005) in Barnett and Ramalingam, 2010.

[9] Ben Ramalingam, *Aid on the Edge of Chaos* (Oxford: Oxford University Press, 2013), 1–440.

[10] Barnett and Ramalingam, "The Humanitarian's Dilemma," 1–8.

[11] Hokyu Hwang and Walter W. Powell, "The Rationalization of Charity: The Influences of Professionalism in the Nonprofit Sector," *Administrative Science Quarterly* 54, 2(2009): 268–298.

[12] Garrett Hardin, "The Tragedy of the Commons," *Science* 162, no. 3859 (December 1968): 1243–1248.

[13] Elinor Ostrom, "A Behavioral Approach to the Rational-Choice Theory of Collective Action," *American Political Science Review* 92, no. 1 (March 1998): 1–22.

As the number of disasters and humanitarian crises rise, humanitarian organizations are confronted with increased challenges to cooperation and coordination among actors.[14] One solution has been for international organizations to work more locally in order to improve disaster response[15] as well as resiliency, particularly for the local social sector.[16] During Ebola, aid delivered by local organizations was often faster, cheaper, and more 'culturally appropriate.'[17] However, local NGOs only receive approximately 1.6% of humanitarian aid.[18]

The 2013–2016 West Africa Ebola Response illuminates tensions in how international, national, and local organizations view aid resources. Despite the importance of local actors, the humanitarian aid system was designed for international organizations and NGOs.[19] I find that first, local cooperation is necessary during humanitarian intervention because the rules of the game may change rapidly and in unprecedented ways, mandating behavior change and thereby necessitating local buy-in. Secondly, during the Ebola Response, local individuals, often labeled as "beneficiaries" by international donors, viewed humanitarian aid as a common pool resource, whereas donor agencies view aid as a top-down resource to be delivered and managed by international experts, resulting in tensions and inefficiency in disaster relief and overall in the aid relationship. In addition, humanitarian aid was also viewed as a government resource (as well as an individual resource by some government officials), and in addition, as a political campaign resource by political elites. This contested view of humanitarian aid resources, as a common pool resource, as a resource to be managed, and as a resource to enrich oneself politically and or materially, inhibited the necessary collective action during Ebola, and led to massive social resistance and resentment in the aid relationship.

Intuitively, existing commons research focuses on collaborative governance of natural resources. While disasters are closely tied to environmental conditions, commons research has yet to extend into disaster management. Due to the pressures of climate change, the number of natural disasters is only expected to increase. As a result, I aim to extend this line of inquiry in my discussion of disaster management. During the 2013–2016 West Africa Ebola epidemic, local organizations and individuals, with limited to no funding, self-organized, engaged in community health education, and eventually partnered with international organizations.

Through interviews with 100 civil society organizations and domestic NGOs, I illustrate how top-down management of the epidemic by governmental and international organizations resulted in social resistance and inhibited epidemic control measures. While international intervention was necessary to curb the epidemic, given limited resources and materiel, a top-down approach reduced efficiency and at times catalyzed collective action against the international response. Policy aiming to improve collective action approaches to social

---

[14] Mizan B. F. Bisri, "Comparative Study on Inter-Organizational Cooperation in Disaster Situations and Impact on Humanitarian Aid Operations," *Journal of International Humanitarian Action* 1 no. 1 (July 2016): 8.

[15] Paul Richards. *Ebola: How a People's Science Helped End an Epidemic* (2016) London: Zed Books Ltd.

[16] Spencer Moore, Eugenia Eng and Mark Daniel. "International NGOs and the Role of Network Centrality in Humanitarian Aid Operations: A Case Study of Coordination During the 2000 Mozambique Floods." *Disasters* (2003) 27: 305–318.

Myroslava Tataryn and Karl Blanchet. "Giving with One Hand…Evaluation of Post-Earthquake Physical Rehabilitation Response in Haiti, 2010—a Systems Analysis." (2010). International Centre for Evidence in Disability. London: London School of Hygiene and Tropical Medicine.

[17] Bibi van der Zee, "Less than 2% of Humanitarian Funds 'Go Directly to Local NGOs'," *The Guardian*, October 16, 2015, accessed October 10, 2017, www.theguardian.com/global-development-professionals-network/2015/oct/16/less-than-2-of-humanitarian-funds-go-directly-to-local-ngos.

[18] International Federation of Red Cross and Red Crescent Societies (IFCRC). "World Disasters Report 2015: Focus on Local Actors, the Key to Humanitarian Effectiveness." (2015). Geneva: IFCRC.

[19] OECD, 2017, 1.

dilemmas must enhance trust,[20] and during the Ebola response, communities lacked trust of top-down interventions because they were not included. Policy failure during the Ebola response was due to a reliance on a top-down conventional theory of collective action viewing affected individuals as unable to act. Rather, individuals and local organizations were limited in their ability to act because they lacked equipment, funds, doctors, and other technical experts due to underdevelopment. However, the lack of technical equipment, institutions, personnel, and funds did not indicate a lack of local participation: as this chapter shows, local organizations were successful at dissipating rumors and working alongside international responders once included.

"BEYOND STATES AND MARKETS": CIVIL SOCIETY ORGANIZATIONS IN WEST AFRICA

Civil society organizations, which also comprise community-based organizations, expanded greatly in sub-Saharan Africa and elsewhere during the democratization wave of the 1990s, as a means to ensure local participation in development and democratization, separate from the state and the market. These organizations are thought to help mitigate the continent's proclivity to political conflict due to weak institutions and underdevelopment, as well as susceptibility to natural disasters brought on by climate change. However, despite decades of international aid to West African civil society, the international response to Ebola initially largely ignored local organizations.[21] Though participatory approaches improve upon crisis responses,[22] there is usually limited collaboration between international and local organizations. As a result, the international policy response to Ebola failed until it worked with local civil society organizations, as they were trusted locally and well-positioned to design new rule configurations.

Convinced by the capacity of individuals to solve commons problems, Ostrom was intrigued by the creation and modification of institutional arrangements for collective action, as Bloomquist indicates in Chapter 1. The need for institutional arrangements to support global policy at the national, regional, and local level is well-documented in the development and peacebuilding literatures, however questions remain about exactly how to achieve participation.[23] In terms of the governance of civil society, for example, in Chapter 13, DeMattee and Swiney note tensions around the institutional arrangements structuring, organizing, and regulating civil society organizations (CSOs).[24] DeMattee and Swiney introduce the concept of an *associational good*, achieved through voluntary organization. In addition, even when there is civil society participation in donor-managed projects, tensions exist in terms of how participation is envisioned and implemented. For example, in Chapter 3, Mishra notes that NGOs undertake 'commons' projects involving awareness-raising and bolstering community-based institutions around the management of natural resources. However, Mishra argues that external involvement in local institutions is both successful and unsuccessful, particularly as donor organizations envision participatory processes differently than traditional institutions, and at times ignoring the

---

[20] Ostrom, "Beyond Markets and States," 641–72.

[21] Reddy, "Aftershock," 2.

[22] Barnett, Michael, *The International Humanitarian Order* (New York: Routledge, 2010).

[23] Elinor Ostrom, "Polycentric Systems for Coping with Collective Action and Global Environmental Change." *Global Environmental Change* 20 no. 4 (October 2010): 550–557.

　　Peter Sampson, "Conceptual Shifts in Multi-Track Mediation in West Africa," in *New Mediation Practices in African Conflicts*, ed. Ulf Engle (Leipzig: Leipziger Universitätsverlag, 2012), 237–254.

[24] See Chapter 13 for definition.

needs of communities and weakening traditional governance systems. In Chapter 5, Ogbaharya notes similar tensions in terms of encouragement of local ownership on the one hand in terms of land resources, and the fear of neoliberalism via these policies on the other. Policies with good intentions are oftentimes "mistranslated" due to the lack of proper consultation.

Ostrom's design principles, due to an over emphasis on the rational actor, are limited in their guidance on inclusion of local norms and interactions.[25] Rational choice theory, which represents the prevailing theoretical framework for most development analysis, assumes that individuals make their own individual decisions rationally. However, during the Ebola response, there was a tension in the rules of the game – with traditional practices on the one hand as a source of "local rationality" and Western rational, scientific approaches to epidemic control on the other. Thus, there were competing rationalities over the epidemic response, leading to lack of buy-in and even social resistance.

Particularly in developing countries, local norms are socially embedded on a variety of scales.[26] Neo-institutional theory emphasizes the role of the external environment on the diffusion of practices and ideals. The external environment in which individuals and communities are embedded provides contextual differences that inform decision-making.[27] Sociological institutionalism maintains that organizations are reflections and carriers of contemporary global norms.[28] West Africa, in particular, due to the international aid relationship, is enmeshed in a complex web of global, national, and local organizational environments.

In the case of international NGOs, contemporary global norms include rational, scientific approaches to epidemic control, and the monitoring and evaluation of resources. Thus, the rules of the game may vary at each institutional level based on the norms they reflect, excluding different rationalities from participation, leading to a club of experts in terms of those who can participate, providing opportunities for free riders, as well as conflict and inefficiency in the delivery and management of community resources.

THE 2013–2016 WEST AFRICA EBOLA EPIDEMIC: A TEST

This chapter builds on fieldwork across Guinea and Sierra Leone, including interviews with 100 domestic NPOs.[29] I conducted interviews across four field sites. In addition to the capital cities, Freetown and Conakry, I also visited the towns of Koidu and Nzérékoré in the rural interior of Guinea and Sierra Leone, which were close to the epicenter of the epidemic and struck by Ebola at relatively the same time.

While the West Africa Ebola epidemic peaked from 2014 to 2015, the epidemic actually spanned the 2013–2016 time frame. Nearly all 28,000 cases and 11,000 deaths occurred in the three most-affected countries: Guinea, Liberia, and Sierra Leone.[30] Ebola spread rapidly due to

[25] Fred P. Saunders, "The Promise of Common Pool Resource Theory and the Reality of Commons Projects," *International Journal of the Commons* 8, no. 2 (August 2014), 636–656.

[26] Saunders, "Common Pool," 636–656.

[27] Craig Johnson, "Uncommon Ground: The 'Poverty of History' in Common Property Discourse," *Development and Change* 35, no. 3 (July 2004): 407–433.

[28] John W. Meyer, John Boli, George M. Thomas, and Francisco O. Ramirez. "World Society and the Nation-State." *American Journal of Sociology* 103, no. 1 (July 1997): 144–181.

[29] Michelle Reddy, "Aftershock," 16.

[30] Center for Disease Control (CDC), "2014 Ebola Outbreak in West Africa – Case Counts," Accessed March 1, 2020, www.cdc.gov/vhf/ebola/history/2014-2016-outbreak/index.html.

World Health Organization (WHO), "Ground Zero in Guinea: The Ebola Outbreak Smoulders - Undetected - for more than 3 Months: a Retrospective on the First Cases of the Outbreak," Accessed March 1, 2020, www.who.int/csr/disease/ebola/ebola-6-months/guinea/en/.

its highly contagious nature, weak institutions, and social resistance, especially since epidemic containment practices ran counter to cultural practices of caring for the sick and dying in a collectivist, religious society.

THE INTERNATIONAL HUMANITARIAN RESPONSE TO EBOLA

The International Crisis Group (ICG) warned that Ebola threatened regional stability, leading to a U.N. peacekeeping mission and foreign military intervention.[31] Governments were reluctant to acknowledge the outbreak, particularly due to concerns about foreign direct investment flows, and lacked the resources and institutions to adequately respond.[32] As a result, international organizations intervened. Social resistance to international as well as national responders was pervasive. The border regions at the epicenter of the epidemic were all home to marginalized ethnic groups, leading to stereotypes about Ebola and initial indifference at the national level. Rumors about Ebola proliferated due to the failure of governments, and then international organizations, to effectively communicate about the disease,[33] and this fueled social resistance in the form of non-compliance, riots, threats to burn down treatment centers,[34] massacres, and general violence against Ebola responders.[35] In addition, the contrast between medical treatments and more traditional methods of healing catalyzed rumors and social resistance, especially with the marginalization of traditional healers, who held positions of authority in many communities.

Understanding how norms around humanitarian aid delivery and management emerge and diffuse is important in examining collective action problems in the aid relationship. Ostrom noted the need for more configural approaches to the emergence of variables influencing collective action in diverse, multilevel, polycentric systems.[36] During the Ebola response, on the one hand, there were the rules of epidemic control and the rules of managing foreign aid. On the other hand, there were the implicit rules that reflected the social and cultural norms of those communities receiving aid. International organizations already believed that their rules governing the humanitarian commons were the most effective, as they were based on the technical and organizational capacity of partner organizations to deliver services accompanied by monitoring, evaluation, and metrics to enhance transparency. However, the emphasis on Western organizational rationality excluded local organizations led to free-riding and driving

[31] Ibrahim Al-bakri Nyei, "Beyond the Disease: How the Ebola Epidemic Affected the Politics and Stability of the Mano River Basin", *African Centre for the Constructive Resolution of Disputes*, (August 2016), accessed March 1, 2020, https://reliefweb.int/report/liberia/beyond-disease-how-ebola-epidemic-affected-politics-and-stability-mano-river-basin.

The UN Mission for the Emergency Ebola Response (UNMEER) was located in Ghana, though set up to respond to Ebola in Guinea, Liberia and Sierra Leone. The UK military intervened in Sierra Leone and the US military intervened in Liberia. Guinea declined foreign military assistance.

[32] Monica Rull, Ilona Kickbusch, and Helen Lauer, "International Responses to Global Epidemics: Ebola and Beyond," *International Development Policy* 6, no. 2 (December 2015).

[33] John Idriss Lahai, *The Ebola Pandemic in Sierra Leone* (London: Palgrave Macmillan, 2017), 1–140.

[34] Saffa Moriba, "Insane MCH Aid Nurse Sends Kenema into Turmoil," *Awoko Sierra Leone News*, July 31, 2014, http://awoko.org/2014/07/31/sierra-leone-news-insane-mch-aid-nurse-sends-kenema-into-turmoil/

[35] Monica Mark, "Thankless, dangerous – The task of the Ebola burial boys in Sierra Leone," *The Guardian*, September 4, 2014, www.theguardian.com/society/2014/sep/04/ebola-kailahun-sierra-leone-burial-boys-west-africa

Comité International de la Croix-Rouge (CICR), "Ebola: le movement Croix-Rouge est inquiet des violences contre ses volontaires en Guinée," *Guinéenews*, February 12, 2015, http://Guinéenews.org/ebola-le-mouvement-croix-rouge-inquiet-des-violences-contre-sesvolontaires-en-Guinée/

[36] Ostrom, *Beyond Markets and States*, 641–672.

social resistance during the Ebola response. Relatedly, regarding development aid, in Chapter 3, Mishra, citing Morrow, notes that donor-funded projects often focus on targets instead of institutional solutions amenable to communities.[37] In West Africa, most local organizations lacked technical capacity in terms of service delivery, monitoring, and evaluation. However, their added value was their access to communities, given their experience in advocacy and community education projects where they translated Western development and democratic norms and practices guided by dialogue with local communities.

Ostrom notes that solving collective-action problems at a single governance level is unsuccessful because of global impacts.[38] The locus of international decision-making was far from the epicenter of Ebola. In contrast, a polycentric system, therefore, which involves multiple governing authorities, enables the use of local knowledge[39] and therefore provides an important conceptual framework for humanitarian response. For instance, disposing of bodies in trash bags during Ebola may have made sense according to the rules of epidemic control but not according to the rules of Muslim burial practices, which involve rinsing the body and wrapping it in white linen. This tension between these two bodies of "rules" was compounded by misinformation and miscommunication. Thus, local beneficiaries not only lacked technology, but they also lacked information, which complicated rule configurations and led to free-riding, collective action problems, leading to the mismanagement of Ebola funds, particularly as decisions in large complex emergencies are usually delegated to international NGO workers and public officials. At the same time, there was also free-riding among local organizations. Humanitarian aid involves a large influx of money in an underdeveloped context where there are fewer market opportunities, which at times leads individuals at all levels to seek personal enrichment.

THE MISSING EBOLA MONEY AND THE "EBOLA BUSINESS"

Ebola unveiled bureaucratic malfeasance and the inability of international organizations and the Guinean, Liberian, and Sierra Leonean governments to garner popular support for epidemic control measures. For instance, in Sierra Leone 84 billion Leones (approximately 9.8 million USD) disappeared during the administration in power at the time of Ebola,[40] allegedly to construct houses for those in power in Freetown and to fund upcoming election campaigns.[41] National auditors suggest that this loss of funds, due to inadequate controls and at times disregard of laws, slowed the response and may have led to more deaths.[42] Ministry of Health contracts were poorly drawn up and under specified.[43] The large influx of humanitarian cash led locals to wonder "who ate the Ebola money?" and to coin the phrase "the Ebola business." Many viewed international aid workers as there to "make money" and were dubious of the epidemic. Others were suspicious of the government efforts and blamed the government for embezzlement of funds, as an Ebola survivor illustrates below:

[37] Morrow, C. E., and T. E. Hull, "Donor-Initiated Common Pool Resource Institutions: The Case of the Yanesha Forestry Cooperative," *World Development*, Vol. 24, no. 10 (1996): 1641–1657.

[38] Ostrom, *Polycentric Systems*, 550–557.

[39] Ostrom, *Polycentric Systems*, 550–557.

[40] Lisa O'Carroll, "A Third of Sierra Leone's Ebola Budget Unaccounted for, Says Report," *The Guardian*, 16 February, 2015, www.theguardian.com/world/2015/feb/16/ebola-sierra-leone-budget-report.

[41] O'Carroll, *Ebola Budget.*

[42] Reddy, "Aftershock," 130.

[43] Lahai, "Ebola Pandemic."

Funds for Ebola received from local and international donors did not reach us and even the president himself was a receiver of the Ebola funds; if you raised up alarm about that you will be beaten to death. And this kind of corrupt practice is common with the [ruling] party. One prominent civil society activist exposed the corrupt practices of government officials that were involved in the fight against Ebola. He was locked up for a week.

Ebola only came to a halt when we survivors came from treatment centers and started sensitizing people; then they started believing the existence of Ebola.[44]

In addition to mismanagement of funds at the governmental level, both local NGO employees and international NGO employees noted that the "Ebola money" also disappeared among international organizations. In part, this was due to the urgency of the crisis – money was spent without proper accounting.

I think that part of the funds arrived to the beneficiaries, but it is obvious that a lot of money was ... can I say some money misapplied, some money misused, and some money stolen. Misapplied in sense that you were asked to buy medicine, then you used it to buy a car, for example, or buy a generator. Some funds were stolen and some misused.[45]

HUMANITARIAN AID: A COMMON POOL RESOURCE?

In addition, the 2013–2016 Ebola response illuminates discrepancies in how international aid resources are viewed. Local individuals ("beneficiaries") viewed humanitarian aid as a pooled resource during Ebola, however many viewed the international intervention as the ultimate beneficiaries from the common pool resource, especially since local groups hardly received any funding, citing the perceived high salaries of international experts.[46]

The government had a whole lot of hands in it and those who were involved. I think there was even an auditory report which was not implemented. Thank God I don't have any hands in it. One thing I know is that international bodies always send their monies with expatriates. So it is like taking back some percentage of what they send. At times again what happened in the Ebola is that procedures were bypassed because of the urgency of the moment. So it is during those periods that people will take chances and play their funny games.[47]

This contestation of resources, viewed as a "commons" by recipients and as "private" by international aid organizations, fuels tensions in the aid relationship, and particularly during a crisis where local buy-in is essential. Donor organizations often state that they gave X million dollars of aid to a certain project or country, however several interviewees remarked that the money is in fact reverted to aid professionals sent from Western countries. At the same time, given the lack of institutional capacity of developing country governments to respond to crises, international aid organizations and donor governments bring in aid workers to deliver services as well as provide monitoring and evaluation, to understandably ensure proper accounting of funds.

LOCAL ORGANIZATIONS AND CONSORTIA

The institutional rules of inter organizational cooperation excluded most local organizations, because they could not meet the technical capacity threshold. Though these norms appear to be

[44] Anonymous interview, Michelle Reddy. "*Aftershock.*"
[45] Anonymous Interview, Freetown, Sierra Leone, "*Aftershock,*" interview by Michelle Reddy.
[46] Michelle Reddy, "*Aftershock: Aid, Ebola, and Civil Society in West Africa*" (PhD diss., Stanford University, 2019).
[47] Anonymous interview, Freetown, Sierra Leone, "*Aftershock,*" interview by Michelle Reddy.

motivated by efficiency, they are also largely motivated by legitimacy. Organizations adhering to these rules appear to be proper, legitimate actors to international funding agencies. During the Ebola crisis, though local organizations did not outwardly look efficient, they were efficient brokers of these international norms once included.

A reliance solely on Western rationality with the goal of efficiency in controlling the outbreak in fact led to inefficiency. A lack of coordination between organizations during a crisis often-times amplifies the crisis.[48] Numerous interviewees noted that international aid came too late.[49] As an example, in Nzérékoré, fifteen different ambulances arrived for the same woman, at different times and from different organizations.[50] The top-down approach of international responders fueled social resistance, as international organizations lacked community buy-in. As a result, the management of the humanitarian commons largely excluded aid beneficiaries. However, the local organizations themselves knew the local institutional rules of how to achieve buy-in with communities due to trust generated by pre existing relationships. International organizations faced significant challenges in educating communities, in a context with low educational attainment, alongside different cultural approaches. At the same time, local organizations and traditional healers lacked the training and resources to combat Ebola on their own. Once met with social resistance, the international response worked more with local organizations, to harness local knowledge alongside scientific responses to epidemic control, and as a result, had more success.[51]

As Ostrom notes, empirical research on collective action illustrates that access to information enables individuals to build settings of trust and reciprocity, resulting in management of community resources.[52] These settings of trust emerged from local discussions and meetings. Local organizations in Guinea and Sierra Leone lacked technical equipment however had expertise in community outreach. Community meetings that allowed for open exchange, and local consortia of organizations, led to information exchange reconciling the tensions between traditional approaches to caring for the sick and dying with rational, scientific approaches to epidemic control. As a result, individuals were able take socially costly actions to reduce the threat of Ebola, as well as adopt new practices. Local organizations facilitated buy-in to the international response by using educational techniques in informal settings, known as "sensitiza-tion," entailing group discussion of an issue through active dialogue and meaning-construction with participants, tapping into local understanding and knowledge.

My analysis of the West Africa Ebola response reveals how communities were able to pool together their resources and conduct outreach, and that this capacity was enhanced once they worked in collaboration with international organizations. I conducted interviews in four com-munities – two capital cities, and two rural towns. The differences in the response between the communities were largely due to differences in the social infrastructure between the two countries and between rural and urban areas. There was more local-international cooperation in Sierra Leone than in Guinea, given more longstanding relationships with international NGOs. In the rural towns (in both countries), which are quite far from the capital, international donors eventually encouraged the formation of consortia to manage fiduciary risk. Each consortia had a trusted, well-established organization at its helm, coordinating all meetings

[48] Laura E. Pechta. "A Study of the Effect of Organizational Communication Cultures on Interorganizational Collaboration of Crisis Response." *Dissertation.* Graduate School of Wayne State University. Detroit, Michigan, 2013.
[49] Anonymous interview, Nzérékoré, Guinea, "*Aftershock*," interview by Michelle Reddy.
[50] Anonymous interview, Nzérékoré, Guinea, "*Aftershock*," interview by Michelle Reddy.
[51] Richards, Ebola, 2016.
[52] Anonymous Interview, Freetown, Sierra Leone, "*Aftershock*," interview by Michelle Reddy.

and other smaller organizations. The lead organization had previous contracts with international NGOs, and during the response managed a small amount of resources and coordinated the response with smaller NGOs, which discouraged rent-seeking and defection. Given the proximity of the epidemic to the communities receiving the funds, organizations were incentivized to work even on a voluntary basis, to fight Ebola.

The majority of the organizations interviewed in Koidu, Sierra Leone came together in a consortium as part of the Civil Society Network. This network, funded by IBIS (a Danish organization that later merged with Oxfam) and the Christian Aid program "Enhancing the Interaction between Citizens and the State in Sierra Leone" (ENCISS), provided leadership and coordinated civil society organization activities during the Ebola response. Advocacy for Social Justice and Development – Sierra Leone (ASJD) was the lead organization in the consortium formed from the Civil Society Network, as it had the most experience in managing funds and delivering programs. The lead organization, therefore, had extensive knowledge of the prevailing norms of behavior with respect to problem solving, given their previous relationships with both international organizations and smaller civil society organizations. As a result, organizations across levels were able to design an Ebola intervention satisfying the two sets of institutional rules in tension, and local organizations were able to collaboratively monitor this process. In Koidu, the Civil Society Network comprises twenty-four CSOs, one national NGO, and six international NGOs. While the Civil Society Network received funding from the United Nations Development Program, the amount of money reported was minimal.

Similarly, in Nzérékoré, the consortium of local organizations with international organizations, helped to integrate local capacity and voice into the international response. While many smaller organizations lack financial guarantees, larger organizations are more accustomed to leading and managing more expensive projects. As noted by an NGO in Conakry:

> We give advice to some institutions that want to intervene of the good NGOs to work with. This is often done with many institutions here. Sometimes we try to put small NGOs with us in consortiums for them to be strengthened. That's how we have helped a lot of NGOs. For example, we took a lot of financial guarantees for some local associations.[53]

Consortia enable organizations to pool funds and therefore prove that they can handle large amounts of money. Organizations in Guinea and Sierra Leone are increasingly encouraged to form consortia by donors. Donor organizations maintain that consortia help local organizations to effectively apply for international grants, and to share grant and evaluation documents and strategies, materials in which they are otherwise hesitant to share with potential competitors. As Rios de Souza and Martins note in Chapter 4, governmental bodies and civil society leaders alike need to view themselves as belonging to a dynamic, adaptive, multi layered polycentric management system inclusive of those that use the resource. Information-sharing and deliberation are key, as mentioned by Rios de Souza and Toledo Martins, and consortia enabled information exchange, dialogue, and coordination during the 2013–2016 West Africa Ebola Response.

CONCLUSION

The Ebola response reflects wider international policy failure both in terms of humanitarian aid and development aid in sub-Saharan Africa, a continent viewed more as a place in need of help than a continent of actors in need of institutional strengthening, equipment, infrastructure, and

---

[53] Anonymous Interview, Conakry, Guinea, Interview, *"Aftershock,"* interview by Michelle Reddy.

accompaniment. As Ostrom notes, institutional rules that incentivize cooperation in one setting may not work in another.[54] Management of the Ebola crisis mandated rapid behavioral change, for example, widespread adoption of hand-washing in a context of limited running water, isolation of the sick, and different burial practices. "Getting institutions right" relies on participants understanding "how to make the new rules work."[55]

A first challenge during Ebola was to adjust the rules of epidemic control to alter behavioral norms sustainably. Governmental and international institutions addressing the crisis initially failed to get the new rules of epidemic control to work, in large part because they excluded communities in a context of deep-seated social and political distrust. A second challenge is that humanitarian aid during the 2013–2016 Ebola response was viewed as a common resource by local beneficiaries, a top-down resource to be expertly designed, monitored and managed, by international donors, and a government and political resource by elites. As a result, this led to social resistance and resentment over the use of aid resources. Aid workers who understandably viewed themselves as risking their lives were viewed by many locals as coming to make money off of them during the "Ebola business."

Overall, the 2013–2016 West Africa Ebola epidemic illustrates that a sole reliance on top-down humanitarian aid management is unsuccessful without institutional arrangements with local organizations, which have the access and trust of communities. Top-down humanitarian aid management, as evidenced by Ebola, did not eliminate bureaucratic malfeasance. When organizations collaborated together in consortia, funded by international NGOs with a lead local or national organization known in the region and accustomed to managing international funds, multiple governing authorities were able to harness localized knowledge while ensuring checks and balances. Once local organizations were included in the humanitarian response, communication and outreach with communities improved immensely and the response succeeded. Implications of this new research strand extend to other epidemics, and potentially inform the management of other humanitarian crises, particularly in the developing world and for vulnerable communities even beyond West Africa.

[54] Ostrom, "Beyond Markets and States," 641–72.
[55] Ostrom, "Beyond Markets and States," 641–72.

9

The Economic System as a Commons

An Exploration of Shared Institutions

John Powell

Elinor Ostrom developed a set of basic principles for long enduring commons governance, but she was also clear that there is no single panacea for all commons problems,[1] instead highlighting the need for both flexible approaches and institutional diversity. This is particularly true, she posited, with respect to large-scale commons resources such as the global climate, antibiotic resistance, and biodiversity. Yet, when Ostrom's principles of commons governance are applied to large-scale commons, they appear insufficient. More recent work suggests that additional requirements, such as 'meaningful participation' and engagement with a hierarchy of institutions from the local to global levels might also be required.[2] One area where this newer research, in combination with Ostrom's foundational insights, could be useful is with respect to the economic system and some commentators and researchers have begun to examine the opportunities brought about by new technologies and forms of collaboration, which are designed to "co-create" shared resources resulting in changes in prevailing value systems (see, for example, in this volume: Iaione and De Nictolis, Polko, and Bratspies, Chapters 6, 9, and 12, respectively).[3] Looking at the different conceptions of commons, and the various types of institutional arrangements utilized to manage commons resources in complex ways, suggests there may be some benefit from exploring the structures within larger socio economic systems as "commons" in their own right.

  This chapter looks at how different conceptions of commons are embedded in the economic system, and the extent to which the increasing range of goods, services, and economic activities labelled as 'commons' can be linked. The term: "economic system" is defined here as the current organization of political and economic institutions we see in most developed nations that are based around some form of state regulated capitalist market economy, where decisions about what should be produced are largely determined by the operation of a free market (i.e., not planned by a central authority). Modern market economies tend to be mixed systems relying on varying levels of state involvement that support productive growth through the market-led allocation of resources (primarily land, labor, and capital) and to a greater or lesser extent make

---

[1] Elinor Ostrom, *Understanding Institutional Diversity*. Princeton University Press.

[2] Michael Cox, M. "Understanding large social-ecological systems: introducing the SESMAD project," *International Journal of the Commons* 8, no. 2 (2014): 265–276. DOI: 10.18352/ijc.406.
  Paul Stern. "Design principles for global commons: Natural resources and emerging technologies," *International Journal of the Commons* 5, no. 2 (2011): 213–232.

[3] Michel Bauwens and Vasilis Niaros, *Value in the Commons Economy* (Co-published by Heinrich-Böll-Foundation & P2P Foundation, 2017).

decisions about the distribution of benefits arising from economic activity. The term "economic system" used throughout this chapter thus describes a state regulated capitalist market economy.

THE ECONOMIC SYSTEM AS A SET OF RULES

North defined economic systems in terms of their institutional arrangements.[4] It is not a huge step to go from that perspective into ideas arising from evolutionary economics where, rather than viewing the economic system as a series of transactions based on the allocation of property rights, it is explored as a set of rules, where knowledge is defined as a "rule structure."[5] This approach explores the economic system as a "population of rules, a structure of rules, and a process of rules," which together are referred to as the "meso-scale" (i.e., the space between micro- and macro- economic activities). The economic system is construed as a set of micro level interactions between elements within the meso (which could consist of individuals, organizations, or a mix), while the macrosystem consists of the structure and interactions between elements at the meso-scale (which could be sectors of the economy). The foundations of the economic system are explained in terms of rules governing interactions between individuals, organizations, and the resources they seek to utilize to achieve desired outcomes. Under this perspective the key mechanisms for change within a particular economic system are the processes by which new rules are designed and integrated at the meso-scale.

Focusing on rule structures as a means of understanding economic change has similarities with Ostrom's focus on rules as a means for analyzing the action arenas governing common pool resources (CPRs). The significance of rule structures has been identified by a number of authors in this volume (see, for example, chapters by Blomquist, De Matte and Swiney, and Hudson). Where Ostrom emphasizes the need for boundary rules, constitutional rules, and operational rules to ensure long-term governance of commons resources, evolutionary economists[6] emphasize "rule structures" describing "deep structure" (i.e., how generic rules fit together and are coordinated) and surface structure (how the deep structure itself is manifested in the macroeconomy). Changes in rules at the meso-level are identified as the source of economic change (as opposed to more simplistic notions of "market failure"). In other words, the focus is on interactions between people, and between people and the institutions creating the context in which they operate. In both cases, learning how rules and rule structures are created, operate, and decay, is critical to understanding how governance structures evolve over time, and their impact on the management of resources, whether they are within or outside the market economy, and whether they are public, private, or some form of commons.

Institutional arrangements that have developed to provide efficient means of governing transactions within markets can also be conceptualized as sets of knowledge-based rule structures,[7] or even as commons resources themselves, since such activities are often created by groups and are not 'owned' (or enclosed) by any individual or organizational entity, although individuals and organizations may benefit from their existence and operation. A national currency, for example, that is available to almost everyone within a defined area reduces the

---

[4] Douglass North, "Institutions", *Journal of Economic Perspectives* Vol. 5, No. 1 (1991): 97–112.

[5] Kurt Dopfer, John Foster, and Jason Potts, "Micro–meso–macro," *Journal of Evolutionary Economics* Vol. 14, No. 3 (2004): 263–279.

[6] Kurt Dopfer, John Foster, and Jason Potts, "Micro–meso–macro," *Journal of Evolutionary Economics* Vol. 14, No. 3, (2004): 263–279.

[7] Brian Loasby, "Time, knowledge and evolutionary dynamics: why connections matter," *Journal of Evolutionary Economics* Vol. 11 (2001): 393–412. https://link.springer.com/article/10.1007/PL00003867

transaction costs of exchange, maximizing total societal benefits when the largest number of people have access. New technology enabling the development of electronic payment systems can reduce transaction costs even further, although these systems are seldom available to everyone (the need for a bank account, for example), which is likely to create problems in attempting to move towards a "cashless" society, and potential exclusion of some sectors of the population from sharing in the benefits generated. Such arrangements need to be flexible and adaptable to the changing contexts in which they operate. Governance regimes within economic systems (whether related to common pool resources or more intangible resources, such as knowledge and outcomes of other shared institutional arrangements) need to be able to evolve in relation to changes in: knowledge/technology; the ethical principles and values that underlie policy; institutional decay and the non permanence of dominant economic organizations, and, changes in environmental systems. Governance structures or economic systems that become too rigid are doomed to fail in the long run,[8] and may also create inequalities and conflict.

If change is a defining characteristic of a socio economic and ecological system (of which the market economy would be a component part) then the nature of commons, the governance of commons, and the wider socio-economic system within which they are embedded can all be explored from the perspective of changes in rule structures, providing potential scope for developing a shared set of analytical tools (see Polko, Chapter 9 in this volume, for a discussion of the relationship between shared urban resources and the market). Dopfer et al. describe one approach to conceptualizing how a rule structure might change[9] following a familiar path taken from diffusion of innovation studies based on three phases of activity: origination (some person or organization develops an idea); diffusion (the idea is adopted and adapted in different places in a learning process); retention (the rule is widely accepted and reinforced), which inevitably leads to time lags and variability as rules change and are adapted, complicating the picture.

Understanding the multiple variants of rules that exist in different contexts can be difficult Knowing when and what kind of rule changes are required, and the time lags involved, is a similar problem whether faced with relationships between elements of an economic system, or managing some form of commons resource. Understanding how rule changes occur, the barriers facing those who see the need for change, and the costs and benefits of a new rule is the essence of being able to improve governance structures. A rule change (such as the introduction of new technology) alters a user's relationship to a resource (which may or may not be a commons resource shared in some way with others) due, for example, to the increased potential for overharvesting offered by new technology, or potential loss of economic value if new entrants are able to access the resource in an uncontrolled manner (one recent example is Uber, undercutting local taxi firms through lower costs). Changes in rules are then required in the governance regime to adjust how the resource is accessed and utilized (the recent ruling in California in relation to Uber is an example of continuing adjustment resulting from the development of new forms of employment[10]).

---

[8] Brendan Markey-Towler, "Monopolies can't survive forever: An evolutionary-institutional and behavioural perspective on the non-permanence of market power," University of Queensland Preprint (March 2018). DOI: 10.13140/ RG.2.2.25291.49446.

[9] Kurt Dopfer, John Foster, and Jason Potts, "Micro–meso–macro," *Journal of Evolutionary Economics* 14, no. 3 (2004): 263–279.

[10] Bobby Allyn, "California Judge Orders Uber And Lyft To Consider All Drivers Employees" (August 10, 2020). www.npr.org/2020/08/10/901099643/california-judge-orders-uber-and-lyft-to-consider-all-drivers-employees?t=1598525742318 accessed August 27, 2020.

In addition, where economic value declines, some characteristics of a resource may become marginalized quite quickly, while institutional change can be much slower to respond. One current example is the potential for reduced use of upland grazing commons in some parts of the United Kingdom due to changes in food preferences, meat consumption, and the anticipated reduction in agricultural subsidies as a result of leaving the European Union. On the one hand, this change may provide space for state or private interests to step in and capture the resource rights (e.g., for meeting alternative policy objectives such as re-wilding, biodiversity, renewable energy generation, and carbon sequestration), while on the other hand, the institutional arrangements (e.g., the property rights regime and ownership of grazing rights) may change more slowly, delaying opportunities for utilization of the resource in new or different ways. Institutional lags tend to hinder and influence change, slowing down adoption and creating variability within new rule structures in relation to both commons resource governance and economic systems.

COMMONS WITHIN THE ECONOMIC SYSTEM

Exploring the economic system from a commons perspective is not a new idea. The commons concept has been applied from its earliest days as a means of looking at various aspects of the market/economic system, most significantly in relation to property rights. Early work transferred the developing knowledge on how to control overharvesting from open access resources, such as fisheries, to other areas of activity such as retail markets.[11] Carroll et al., for example, focused on the tension between operational efficiency, which requires unfettered access, and the need for property rights to protect resource owners but creates friction through transaction costs.[12] In their analysis property rights were presented as providing the protection that enables individuals to gain from the efficiencies of exchange that the market provides, while the "market" was presented as a battleground where producers constantly try to increase security of value (and prices) through a range of monopolistic actions that reduce 'market efficiency' by excluding competition. Exclusion that leads to oligopolistic or monopolistic power can be interpreted as the creation of property rights in a market (i.e., the right to exclude others), effectively turning an "open access resource" (the market for a product) into some form of club or private property. Commons scholars have thus previously identified a range of institutional arrangements within the economic system as different forms of "commons," and more recent application of Ostrom's theories are leading to a re-consideration of some economic activities as amenable to a commons governance regime.[13]

A key issue has been the way in which the relationship between commons resources, the market, and the wider economic system has been conceived.[14] Until recently commons resources (i.e., resources managed by a user group through agreed rules controlling access and extraction) were routinely described as being outside, apart from, or 'beyond' the market-state binary, coloring much of the commons discourse[15]. Ostrom's early work, for example,

---

[11] Parzival Copes, "The market as a commons: open access vs price adjustment," *De Economist* 133, no. 2 (1985): 225–232.

[12] Thomas Carroll, David Ciscil, and Roger Chisholm, "The Market as a Commons: An Unconventional View of Property Rights," *Journal of Economic Issues* 2 (1979): 605–627.

[13] Peter Earl, Markets and Organisations as common Pool Resources" (2013). https://shredecon.files.wordpress.com/2013/01/earl-ostrom-memorial.pdf. Accessed September 20, 2018

[14] Becky Mansfield, "Neoliberalism in the oceans: "rationalization," property rights, and the commons question," *Geoforum* 35 (2004): 313–326.

[15] Not helped by the fact that the meaning of the commons concept has altered between the 1950s and the present. For example, what are currently referred to today as "open access" resources (i.e., resources that were not owned or

focused on small scale common pool resources (such as fisheries, irrigation systems, and grazing pastures), under some form of community ownership (neither state governed or privately controlled) and therefore considered to be outside of the formal market economy and associated property rights regime. In another strand of work, scholars coming from legal disciplines have explored infrastructure that underpins economic activity (e.g., roads, water supplies, energy supplies, communications) as a form of commons, provided by the state but governed under a rule structure to maximize access and thus social and economic benefits.[16] More recent work has started to explore "knowledge" as a commons, along with the rule structures that try to enhance its development, or restrict access, in order to capture the economic benefits (e.g., laws and regulations relating to copyright, patents, control of intellectual property, and development of the internet). See also, for example, in this volume, Chapter 6 by Iaione and De Nictolis on the city as a commons, and Chapter 16, by Hudson, who examines the complex issue of the rights of future generations in relation to "temporal commons").

Managing resources "in common" is also put forward as an alternative[17] to the restrictions of the opposing choices from privatization, or state control of resources. The different approaches and proliferation of terminology, including multiple ways in which the term "commons" itself has been used have created some confusion over the meaning of the concept. The aims of this section are: first, to explain the range of activity around commons by presenting three alternative approaches to the way in which commons are conceptualized; second, to demonstrate how commons are thoroughly integrated into our economic systems; and third, to suggest there may be opportunities for developing alternative governance regimes over a wider range of economic activities that might start to address issues of inefficient resource use and inequality.

First, in relation to the concept itself, three broad approaches to conceptualizing commons resources have developed, which are summarized in the following bullet points and described in more detail below:

- Commons as defined through the natural characteristics of the resource itself (i.e. the ease with which others can be excluded from access and use of the resources; and the extent to which consumption of the resource is subtractable)
- Commons as shared benefits arising from provision of specific services and infrastructure that reduces transaction costs of economic activity (usually by the state, for example a road which enhances trade)
- "Commoning," which involves sharing of the product or outcomes of social processes. Commoning[18] as a perspective focuses on the nature of the outcomes from social interaction, an understanding that some outcomes/benefits belong to all of those in a group or community that have contributed to their creation.

---

regulated and thus open to uncontrolled use and consumption) were identified as "commons" in literature from the 1950s and '60s.

[16] Examples include: Carol Rose (2003), "Romans, roads, and romantic creators: traditions of public property in the information age," *Law and Contemporary Problems* 66, (2003): 89–110; and, Brett Frischmann, *Infrastructure: The Social Value of Shared Resources* (Oxford University Press, 2012).

[17] Ugo Mattei, *The State, the Market, and some Preliminary Question about the Commons* (2011), https://works.bepress.com/ugo_mattei/40/

[18] David Bollier describes commoning as "social practice … acts of mutual support, conflict, negotiation, communication and experimentation that are needed to create systems to manage shared resources. This process blends production (self-provisioning), governance, culture, and personal interests into one integrated system." David Bollier (2015), "Commoning as a Transformative Social Paradigm," www.operationkindness.net/wp-content/uploads/David-Bollier.pdf. Accessed August 27, 2020.

The first of these perspectives includes concepts of common pool resources and common property: usually managed through a formal or informal property regime that allocate a bundle of rights to a group or community. There are many variations and Hess has outlined the difficulties arising from the wide range of meanings for the term commons, where different types of resource may be shared and the rights regime may include ownership, management, use, and the ability to both access and exclude others from accessing a resource.[19] Under this perspective a resource (such as a pasture, or a forest) might be owned by a community or an individual but managed through a system of rights, or it may be a shared resource easily accessible to all (such as the atmosphere) but where certain rights of use are allocated to individuals (e.g., rights to emit pollutants) under a regulatory regime.

The second approach focuses on shared infrastructure, sometimes referred to as "public goods" – certain goods which by their nature provide wider public benefits (roads, urban space, water supply systems) and can be provided in multiple ways (private/public/community). The "public trust doctrine" suggests a category of goods and services that are neither entirely private nor entirely public.[20] Examples go back to the beginnings of settled economic activity and include roads, navigable waterways, and other services and supporting structures that underpin commerce and trade. By their nature, making these services and structures easily accessible to all created a wider range of benefits than the costs required in their provision and upkeep. In essence, this category of "goods" becomes a "productive commons,"[21] where the greater the access and use, the greater the benefits generated (up to a certain point, where congestion may limit the level of benefits that can be generated).

Economic analysis has been undertaken to demonstrate the social and economic values that flow from a wide range of infrastructure managed as commons rather than allowing privatization; although it is important to note that the local context has been identified as crucial in understanding the level of economic efficiency and social equity outcomes achieved.[22] Benkler, for example, identifies the core claims made by Frischmann as relating to a set of resources "whose use creates large positive externalities ... through facilitating downstream production activities of public and social goods," thus providing the basis of the argument for managing such resources as commons rather than as private property.[23] Benkler goes on to suggest that managing infrastructure as a commons resource can provide "a flexibility of use that allows for ease of adaptation under conditions of uncertainty and positive transaction costs, a characteristic that is lost when those resources are appropriated by private interests." On the other hand he also raises questions about the nature of "commons governance" regimes that effectively enclose a resource (e.g. a fishery, or a grazing pasture), limiting access to a specific community of users, (as is the case with most forms of natural resource commons) in order to ensure long-term sustainable use (but in effect creating a closed market and monopoly conditions, which can result in inefficiencies). This is a complex arena and, in some instances, such as

[19] Charlotte Hess, "Mapping the New Commons". Paper presented at "Governing Shared Resources: Connecting Local Experience to Global Challenges"; the 12th Biennial Conference of the International Association for the Study of the Commons, University of Gloucestershire, Cheltenham, England, July 14–18, 2008. https://surface.syr.edu/cgi/viewcontent.cgi?article=1023&context=sul accessed August 27, 2020.

[20] Carol Rose (2003), "Romans, roads, and romantic creators: traditions of public property in the information age," *Law and Contemporary Problems* 66 (2003): 89–110.

[21] Carol Rose "The Comedy of the Commons: Custom, Commerce, and Inherently Public Property", The University of Chicago Law Review, 53, no. 3 (1986): 711–781.

[22] Brett Frischmann, *Infrastructure: The Social Value of Shared Resources*. (Oxford University Press, 2012).

[23] Yochai Benkler, "Commons and growth: the essential role of open commons in Market economies," *University of Chicago Law Review* 80 (2013): 1499–1555, https://chicagounbound.uchicago.edu/uclrev/vol80/iss3/12/

provision of a water supply, a wide range of property rights regimes with public, private, and community involvement in governance can be found (e.g., in this Volume see Bratspies' exploration of the 'urban canopy' as a commons, made up of individual trees under different ownership, management, and legal regimes).

The concept of "productive commons," or shared resources capable of generating benefits for numerous users (as long as they are given rights of access), has more recently been extended to the notion of knowledge as a commons and the role of the internet in the modern economy.[24] Examples of the outcomes from these more recent "productive commons" (which can be considered as a form of "commoning"), include organized knowledge systems such as Wikipedia, open-source software, peer-to-peer activities, and a wide range of other applications, including cryptocurrencies, and the potential for creating new and secure forms of accounting and recording through blockchain technology.[25]

Extending the notion of infrastructure as a commons, a recent strand of literature on the subject of "knowledge commons" explores a range of activities referred to variously as "generative," "production commons," or "commons-based peer production" resulting from interaction between large numbers of people working in the digital economy[26] to produce ". . .information, knowledge, or cultural goods without relying on either market pricing or managerial hierarchies." Wikipedia is an interesting example of such a "social" production system that operates through the joint efforts of large numbers of volunteers who provide information, edit content, perform quality control, and self-manage disagreements and conflict. Although often identified as a good example of a 'peer-produced commons[27] Wikipedia nevertheless suffers from some of the same issues facing any unregulated open access resource; in particular, its vulnerability to free riders who do not contribute to its production or upkeep but nevertheless utilise its benefits. The difference between a common-pool resource and a "knowledge commons," is that knowledge is non-subtractable (one person's use of that knowledge does not prevent others from accessing or using it) so that the presence of free riders does not exhaust the resource, and may even lead to adding value (e.g., through spreading validated, rather than incorrect, information, and increasing the number of users who benefit). More difficult to ascertain are the supply-side impacts and the actual costs (and benefits) to volunteers that provide their time and expertise, the amounts and sources of funding that support the production process, and the capacity of volunteers to remain committed to production over time.

Shared commons resources, although produced through collaborative 'commoning' activities, are not without costs. Financial support is essential to underpin continuation of the activities, to ensure quality of the product and to pay certain key 'agents' in the production process, and must come either from economic value generated by the activity, or from some external source of funding. One example is the Wikimedia Movement, which currently consists of 118 affiliated communities. Just one of these communities (the second largest) has 120 employees and 65,000 members, with donations (from one country alone) approximating nine million US dollars coming from over 400,000 individuals.[28] The Wikimedia Foundation (set up to fund

---

[24] Yochai Benkler and Helen Nissenbaum, (2006) "Commons-based peer production and virtue," *Journal of Political Philosophy* 14, no. 4 (2003): 394–419.

[25] Joseph Abadi and Markus Brunnermeier, "Blockchain Economics," (2018). Accessed November 20, 2019. https://scholar.princeton.edu/sites/default/files/markus/files/blockchain_paper_v3g.pdf

[26] Yochai Benkler and Helen Nissenbaum, "Commons-based peer production and virtue," *Journal of Political Philosophy* 14, no. 4 (2006): 394–419.

[27] Yochai Benkler and Helen Nissenbaum, "Commons-based peer production and virtue," *Journal of Political Philosophy* 14, no. 4 (2006): 394–419.

[28] Wikimedia Deutchland, Personal communication, June 6, 2018.

Wikipedia and other activities) makes reference to 220,000 members and operating expenditures in 2016–2017 in the region of 70 million dollars.[29] Despite this level of funding, there have been complaints of high turnover among editors and volunteer burn-out. The organization and delivery of a 'free access resource' is never wholly costless.[30]

DISCUSSION

Application of these three broad conceptual perspectives demonstrates that 'commons' are deeply embedded in both socio economic and ecological systems in the form of rule structures that create governance regimes around natural resources (such as, oceans, air quality, biodiversity, climatic patterns), infrastructure (roads, urban open spaces, communications, utilities), in the institutional arrangements that structure economic activity itself, and in terms of outcomes from those working together to generate shared benefits. In addition, the socio-economic and ecological production system as a whole exhibits some characteristics of a public good: it is essential to the effective functioning of society, it is difficult to exclude people from accessing it (although access to specific areas can be restricted, for example, credit and banking services), one person's use does not detract from the ability of others to use it or share in the benefits, it provides essential services to society, and in some cases increased use can enhance benefits to all.

The vast majority of users within an economic system, however, have no control over the rules that structure its operation and although the state and the "market" are often described as though they operate in opposition to each other, they are closely intertwined; the state works together with private sector organisations in creating and implementing the rule structures that regulate markets controlling the means of production (land, labor, capital), and the goods and services that are produced. In addition, while everyone may potentially benefit from the services provided through the workings of the system, in practice they do not have equal access to these services, or equal shares in the benefits that are generated. Moreover, the "system" itself generates negative impacts, which are also unequally distributed, and often incompletely or not addressed.

Commons resources do not sit outside of the economic system, they are part of it. The notion has been put forward that governance of more of our resources as 'commons' offers an alternative to the "market-state binary" system (i.e., an alternative to either privatization or state control).[31] This paper has tried to show that commons are not an aberration limited to a few instances where goods and services, or natural resources, are shared by a community or group of individuals, but are intimately wrapped up in the economic system, accounting for some of its efficiencies and, where rule structures fail, can cause problems that result in negative impacts throughout a socio-economic and ecological system.

Evidence for the idea that commons are integral elements of the economic system includes the fact that some of the essential infrastructure that underpins the operation of economic

[29] Wikimedia Foundation. Accessed September 28, 2019. https://wikimediafoundation.org/our-work/ and https://meta .wikimedia.org/wiki/Wikimedia_Foundation_Annual_Plan/2017-2018/Final

[30] A recent report in the Guardian notes ". . . almost half of the entries on the Scots language version of Wikipedia' have been written by a teenager based in the USA, who does not speak Scots." www.theguardian.com/uk-news/2020/aug/26/ shock-an-aw-us-teenager-wrote-huge-slice-of-scots-wikipedia#:~:text=Now%20an%20American%20teenager%20%E2% 80%93%20who,Scots%20language%20version%20of%20Wikipedia Accessed August 27, 2020.

[31] Ugo Mattei, The State, the Market, and some Preliminary Question about the Commons (2011) https://works.bepress .com/ugo_mattei/40/

activity are widely shared and can be viewed as a form of public good (or commons). In addition, all economic activity takes place within large-scale ecological systems that we all share, and which underpin our existence (such as stable climate and nutrient cycles, clean air, and water). Damaging such shared resources can have significant economic impacts through, for example, sea level rise, the spread of pests and diseases, decreased health or quality of life, and increased food production costs. Governing shared ecological systems as commons requires the creation of rule structures that control damaging economic activities (e.g., those that result in greenhouse gas emissions), and a polycentric system for enforcement on a global scale, all arguments that have been made elsewhere.

Part of the solution might be to conceptualize markets themselves, and market operations as a form of commons, and focus on the rule structures controlling activities, which can then shed light on the reasons for market failure and offer alternative approaches to finding solutions. If the institutional arrangements that enable efficient functioning of the market can be considered as rule structures produced through forms of "commoning" activity, and the outcomes shared by specific communities of those involved, then altering the rule structures (or the conditions under which rules are made) may result in more beneficial outcomes, or outcomes that are more equitably shared.

CONCLUSION

Taking commons "out of the system" as a means of dealing with market and/or state failure may provide temporary solutions for some limited resource management problems, but in the long run everyone relies on, and is constrained by, the rule structures created through various forms of "commoning" arising from the institutional arrangements governing economic activity. A multitude of studies exist exploring the impact of rule structures on the management of different types of commons.[32] Many of these studies are at the micro or local level, looking at the impact of variations in common pool resource management schemes at the community level. When it comes to large-scale commons we have only recently started to think about global issues in terms of "socio-economic ecological systems" (SEES), and to understand the interdependencies between political, economic, social, and ecological processes that link cause and effect both spatially and chronologically. Ostrom pointed one way forward in her Nobel prize lecture, suggesting the answer lay in the application of context-specific rule structures developed through cooperation and trust between the people involved, not in government intervention.[33] For Ostrom, the general type of governance was not as important as how specific rules are developed and adapted, and whether users consider the system to be legitimate and equitable.

Work on knowledge, generative, and productive commons illustrates that not all commons are subtractable and excludable, some rely on maximizing the number of users to increase the benefits generated, and some rely on a continual renewal of trust and cooperation for their continued effectiveness and provision. To effectively manage the multitude of resources society

---

[32] Management of marine fisheries, for example, includes studies from the 1950s to the present. See, for example, the following: Scott H. Gordon, The Economic Theory of a Common-Property Resource: The Fishery, 62 *Journal of Political Economy* 124 (1954); Fikret Berkes (1986) "Local-level management and the commons problem: A comparative study of Turkish coastal fisheries," *Marine Policy*, 10, no. 3, 215–229; Jentoft, S., Onyango, P., and Mahmudul Islam, M. (2010). "Freedom and poverty in the fishery commons," *International Journal of the Commons*, Vol. 10, issue 3 4, no. 1, 345–366; Burns, T. R., and Stöhr, C. (2011). "Power, knowledge, and conflict in the shaping of commons governance: The case of EU Baltic fisheries," *International Journal of the Commons*, 5, no. 2, 233–258.

[33] Elinor Ostrom, "Beyond Markets and States: Polycentric Governance of Complex Economic Systems," *Nobel Prize Lecture*, December 8, 2009. Accessed November 29, 2019.

shares "in common" there is a need to look at the economic system in a different way. First, exploration of the elements of the economic system that currently operate as commons is needed in order to improve understanding, and second, analysis of the rule structures that control the existence and operation of those commons and how they change over time is required. Only then will we be in a position to ensure a more sustainable future through improving the governance of shared resources from within the economic system, rather than treating commons as some form of externality that needs to be controlled by the state or private interests.

PART IV

Urban Landscape and Infrastructure as a Commons

10

Seeing New York City's Urban Canopy as a Commons

A *View from the Street*

Rebecca Bratspies

CENTER FOR URBAN ENVIRONMENTAL REFORM

Urban forestry has long been recognized as a key to healthy and beautiful cities.[1] President Theodore Roosevelt championed forests, founding the Forest Service, creating national forests,[2] and embracing Arbor Day.[3] The Progressive Era advocated planting urban trees to improve the physical, mental, and spiritual well-being of city dwellers.[4] The City Beautiful and Garden City movements promoted green spaces as a way to mitigate unhealthy conditions in cities. Modern urban forestry continues this tradition, but has broadened the focus to include maximizing social, economic and ecological benefits.[5]

Who owns the city's forest? Of the trees that make up the urban forest, some are park trees, some are street trees, some are privately-owned and some are outlaws.[6] Together, these trees form an urban forest ecosystem. Yet, for management purposes, urban trees are rigidly divided into categories, subject to different (or no) legal regimes, under the aegis of different, if any, regulators. Bridging these bureaucratic divisions is essential for managing the urban forest as a forest, rather than as a collection of individual trees. Urban commons theory helps cities "see" their urban canopy as a commons – a shared resource in which all urban residents have a common stake or interest.

---

[1] Jill Jonnes, *Urban Forests* (New York: Viking Press, 2016) xviii, 22–35

[2] President, Roosevelt established 150 national forests, as well as 51 federal bird reserves, four national game preserves, five national parks and 18 national monuments. U.S. Dept of Interior, "The Conservation Legacy of Theodore Roosevelt" (October 27, 2016).

[3] In 1907, President Roosevelt wrote an Arbor Day letter to U.S. schoolchildren cautioning "forests which are so used that they cannot renew themselves will soon vanish, and with them all their benefits. A true forest is not merely a storehouse full of wood, but, as it were, a factory of wood, and at the same time a reservoir of water. When you help to preserve our forests or to plant new ones you are acting the part of good citizens." Theodore Roosevelt, "Letter: To the school children of the United States" (April 15, 1907).

[4] E. Gregory McPherson, et al., "Chicago's Evolving Urban Forest: An Initial Report of the Chicago Urban Forest Climate Project," *USDA General Technical Report* NE-169 (1993): 14–16.

[5] Jana Dilley and Kathleen L. Wolf, "Homeowner Interactions with Residential Trees in Urban Areas," *Aboriculture & Urban Forestry* 39 (2013): 267. Eli Goldman, "Seeing Community Through the Trees: Characterizing Resident Response to Urban-Tree Planting Initiatives" (2017) https://commons.clarku.edu/idce_masters_papers/121/.

[6] Occasionally an unauthorized tree will grow without permission under a bridge, against a fence or along the street. Scholars are increasingly suggesting that tree agency, as well as the human-tree interactions that create "place" need to be part of urban forest governance. Cecil C. Konijnendijk van den Bosch, "Tree Agency and Urban Forest Governance," *Smart and Sustainable Built Environment* 5 (2016): 176.

The United States Department of Agriculture (USDA) already defines the urban forest broadly to include "all publicly and privately-owned trees within an urban area."[7] Unfortunately, this definition has little impact on real world management of urban forests. Rather, for management purposes, the urban forest typically consists of three distinct classes of trees: street trees, park trees, and privately-owned trees. This approach makes visible the problems that predominant ways of "owning" property create for managing and enhancing common urban interests.

In a bid to treat public trees as a publicly owned forest, New York City (NYC) unified the management of its street and park trees under the jurisdiction of the Department of Parks and Recreation. That is a big step toward managing the city's urban forest as an ecosystem. However, New York City needs to do even more. First, the City must manage the entire urban canopy – both its public and private trees – as a single urban forest. Second, the city must create an inclusive management regime that respects and includes residents. Reconstituting urban forest management in line with commons theory might open a path for these next steps.

BENEFITS OF THE URBAN FOREST

The United States' urban populations grew by more than twelve percent over the last decade, and currently well over three-quarters of all Americans live in urban areas.[8] Nearly 85 percent of the United States' GDP is generated by the nation's largest cities.[9] Besides economic opportunity, people increasingly move to cities for the lifestyle and the cultural diversity. However, increasing urbanization degrades air and water quality, and promotes heat islands. Thriving urban forests can help mitigate these negative externalities. There are roughly 4 billion urban trees, and an additional 70 billion growing in wider metropolitan areas.[10] Sustaining and expanding the urban canopy to match the expanding urban footprint is a public welfare imperative.

Urban trees beautify neighborhoods, improve vistas and increase property values.[11] The Forest Service estimates that the aesthetic value of NYC's street trees increases property values by roughly $52.5 million annually.[12] However, trees are far more than scenery. Former Forest Service Chief Tom Tidwell put it best when he called urban forests "the linchpin" of green infrastructure, providing ecosystem services "right where most people live."[13]

Urban trees provide a multitude of ecosystem services. They regulate stormwater flow,[14] protect soils, and purify air and water. Planting trees improves local air quality by filtering out particulates, nitrous and sulfur oxides and ozone.[15] Perhaps most importantly from an environmental justice perspective, children living on tree lined streets are less likely to develop asthma.[16] Trees are also critical partners for combatting climate change. Not only do urban trees sequester

---

[7] David J. Nowak, et al., "Sustaining America's Urban Trees and Forests" General Technical Report NRS-62 (2010): 3.
[8] Press Release, "U.S. Census Bureau, Growth in Urban Populations Outpaces Rest of Nation," *Census Bureau Reports* (Mar. 26, 2012).
[9] James Manyika et al., "Urban America: US Cities in the Global Economy," *McKinsey Global Institute* (Apr. 2012): 2.
[10] Steve Bratkovich and Katheryn Fernholz, "Using Industrial Clusters to Build an Urban Wood Utilization Program: A Twin Cities Case Study" (2010): 4.
[11] Kathleen L. Wolf, "City Trees and Property Values," *Arborist News* 16 (2007): 34–36.
[12] Paula J. Peper, et al, "New York City, New York Municipal Forest Resource Analysis" 2 (2007)
[13] Tom Tidwell, "Speech: The Forest Service Role in Urban Forestry," *Partners in Community Forestry National Conference* (November 10, 2009).
[14] "Trees Tackle Clean Water Regulations," *American Forests Magazine* 106 (Summer 2000): 18–20.
[15] David J. Nowak, "The Effect of Urban Trees on Air Quality" (2002).
[16] Gina S. Lovasi, et al., "Children Living in Areas with More Street Trees Have Lower Prevalence of Asthma," *Journal of Epidemiology & Community Health* 62 (May 2008).

carbon directly, but they also provide shade and cooling – reducing energy consumption while simultaneously mitigating the urban heat island effect.[17]

There are also a host of more intangible wellness benefits associated with trees,[18] including reduced childhood obesity rates,[19] reduced stress,[20] and a wide array of other health benefits.[21] Being within sight of a green tree canopy correlates with increased learning outcomes for urban students.[22] Indeed, the Japanese practice of *Shinrin Yoku*, or forest bathing, has spawned an entire wellness industry touting exposure to forests as a cure for many ills of modern society.

As the monetary, ecological, and intangible value of urban trees have become clearer, cities across the country have initiated tree-planting campaigns.[23] Unfortunately, these tree planting campaigns too often reinforce pre-existing inequalities in the urban canopy; inequalities that mirror other social inequities.[24] The map of tree canopy in virtually every American city doubles as a map of income and frequently as a map of race and ethnicity.[25] In Louisville, for example, researchers found that whiter and higher-income areas had twice the canopy coverage of lower income, minority areas.[26] In Baltimore, wealthier, whiter neighborhoods had up to ten times more tree canopy,[27] making those neighborhoods significantly cooler and more aesthetically pleasing.[28] This pattern repeats itself in major cities across the country, including in NYC.[29] Indeed, NYC now recognizes access to trees and greenspace as an environmental justice issue of profound importance.[30] Urban forestry must therefore offer a path toward more equitable allocation of the City's tree canopy.

Embracing urban commons theory can help transform these tree planting efforts into a more comprehensive forest equity plan. In particular, Sheila Foster and Christian Iaione have articulated the value of conceiving the city as a commons in order "to provide a framework and set of tools to open up the possibility of more inclusive and equitable forms of city-

---

[17] "Urban Heat Island Effect," *National Geographic Encyclopedia*, www.nationalgeographic.org/encyclopedia/urban-heat-island/

[18] Warwick District Council, "The Benefit of Urban Trees," date?

[19] Janice F. Bell, Jeffrey S Wilson and Gilbert C. Liu, "Neighborhood Greenness and 2-Year Changes in Body Mass Index of Children and Youth." *American Journal of Preventive Medicine* 35 (2008): 547–553.

[20] Kathleen L. Wolf, "Metro nature, environmental health, and economic value," *Environmental Health Perspectives* 123 (2015): 390–398.

[21] For a partial list of the astonishing array of human health benefits, *see* Pia Hanson and Matt Frank, "The Human Health and Social Benefits of Urban Forests" (2016): 3–5.

[22] Rodney Matsuoka, "Student Performance and high school landscapes: Examining the link," *Landscape and Urban Planning* 97 (2010): 273–282.

[23] Philadelphia adopted the Greenworks Plan, which has a goal of increasing the tree canopy in the entire city to 30% by 2025, with the short-term goals of planting 300,000 trees by 2015. "GreenWorks Philadelphia Plan," *Mayor's Office of Sustainability* (2009). Los Angeles, Denver, Baltimore and Shanghai have engaged in similar campaigns in recent years. Dexter H. Locke and J. Morgan Grove, "Doing the Hard Work Where It's Easiest? Examining the Relationships Between Urban Greening Programs and Social and Ecological Characteristics," *Applied Spatial Analysis and Policy* 9 (2016) 78.

[24] Theresa Machemer, "Which American Cities Have the Most Trees," *The Hill.com* (November 12, 2019).

[25] Ibid. (quoting American Forests CEO Jad Daley).

[26] "Louisville Urban Tree Canopy Assessment" (2015): 22,

[27] Roxanne Ready, et al., "No trees, no shade, no relief as climate heats up," *Code Red: Baltimore's Climate Divide* (2019).

[28] Meg Anderson and Sean McMinn, "As Rising Heat Bakes U.S. Cities, the Poor Often Feel It Most," *NPR* (September 3, 2019).

[29] Kirsten Schwartz, et al., "Trees Grow on Money: Urban Tree Canopy Cover and Environmental Justice." *PLoS ONE* 10 (2015):

[30] Tim Arango, "Turn off the Sunshine: Why Shade is a Mark of Privilege in Los Angeles," *The New York Times* (December 1, 2019).

making."[31] This idea gives some teeth to Lefebvre's "the right to the city"[32] by reconceptualizing questions of management and control as decisions that affect the shared resource of the city itself. By emphasizing the common stake or interest that all urban dwellers share in their city and its collective urban resources, Foster and Iaione offer a way past the increasing tendency to privatize or enclose urban resources for the benefit of economic elites.[33] Moreover, their vision of the city as a shared resource co-created by all its inhabitants lays the groundwork for the claim that those inhabitants have the right to participate meaningfully in the decision-making processes that shape this collective resource.

This thinking could be very useful for devising a way to manage the urban forest. Much as the urban commons is socially produced, creating value through the interactions of its residents, so too the urban forest ecosystem is similarly co-produced through the interactions between trees, plants, and animals with the City's human population. Urban commons theory can help foreground the social, ecological, and economic value created by this interaction, a necessary first step in claiming that value as a commons accessible to the city as a whole. By highlighting the role of interaction between trees in constituting the urban forest, such an approach can help ensure that the value created by the urban forest accrues to the public rather than being captured by private interests, either in the form of gentrification or exclusion.

NEW YORK CITY'S TREES

NYC's urban forest includes 5.2 million trees[34] covering nearly a quarter of the city. To mitigate pollution-related air-quality issues, experts recommend that NYC increase its urban tree canopy to at least 30 percent.[35] That would put tree coverage on par with impervious surfaces like roads and sidewalks, which cover roughly a third of the city.[36]

Street trees[37] are the most visible and most regulated component of NYC's urban canopy. However, they comprise a relatively small portion of the overall urban canopy. Only one in ten of NYC's trees are street trees,[38] and they collectively provide just 5.9 percent of the City's tree canopy.[39] For perspective, private trees, living on privately-owned land, make up 18 percent.[40]

Historically, street trees were viewed as city inventory to be rationed out based on complex, bureaucratic formulas. They were treated no differently than other City-provided goods and services. Each tree was plopped down amidst a sea of concrete, and generally left to fend for itself. This view still holds significant sway. For example, the Parks' Department website announces "if you are a property owner, you can have a tree planted on your street for free!"[41]

---

[31] Foster and Iaione, "City as Commons" 283.
[32] Henri Lefebvre, "The Right to City," *Writings on Cities* (1996).
[33] *Ibid.*, 284.
[34] J. Morgan Grove, et al., "A Report on New York City's Present and Possible Tree Canopy" (2006): 1, 7.
[35] Christopher J. Lulely and Jerry Bond, "A Report to Integrate Management of Urban Trees into Air Quality Planning" (2002): 70. New York City remains an ozone nonattainment zone.
[36] David J. Nowak, et al., "Assessing Urban Forest Effects and Values: New York City's Urban Forests" (2007): 6. www.milliontreesnyc.org/downloads/pdf/ufore_study.pdf.
[37] The term "street tree" means trees growing within the public right of way along the roads of the city. "Million Trees NYC, Street Tree Census," www.milliontreesnyc.org/downloads/pdf/street_tree_fact_sheet.pdf.
[38] Paula J. Peper, et al, "New York City, New York Municipal Forest Resource Analysis" (March 2007): 1. As of 2018, there were 666,124 street trees Statement of Nelson Villarrubia, Executive Director, Trees NYC, Caring for NYC's Forest: A Story of Research, Community and Inspiration (June 17, 2019).
[39] Peper, ""New York City, New York Municipal Forest Resource Analysis," 1.
[40] Grove, "A Report on New York City's Present and Possible Tree Canopy," 4.
[41] NYC Parks, "Request a Street Tree," www.nycgovparks.org/trees/street-tree-planting/request.

Nothing suggests that renters can request trees; the privilege seemingly rests only with landowners. This process thus resonates with the ongoing critique of contemporary urban development as a privatizing of the public domain to accommodate the preferences of powerful economic interests.[42] Wendell Pritchett and Shitong Qiao's recent work highlights the limitations inherent in this kind of property-based urban governance.[43] They document the way that NYC's property-oriented urban governance structures drives gentrification and housing scarcity.[44]

Suspicion that tree-planting is part of a broader gentrification agenda has sometimes translated into resistance to tree street planting, a position Melissa Checker has termed a "pernicious paradox" for environmental justice advocates.[45] For example, research found that certain low–income communities of color in Detroit did not use their city's analogous process to request a single tree.[46]

Commons thinking makes visible the way that the current tree planting process privileges property-owner voices at the expense of residents, and how it functionally privatizes decision-making about the urban canopy. By creating official space for the voices of non-property owners in urban governance discourse, commons theory could drive wider sharing of this resource across a broader class of the city's inhabitants.[47] Something as simple as explicitly inviting a block's *residents* rather than property owners to request trees would embed local priorities and amplify community participation in decision-making about the urban forest. Such an approach could use street tree planting to promote and protect neighborhood vitality and alleviate some of the perceptions that tree planting is about gentrification.

Aside from the gentrification concerns raised by who has the status to request a tree, this *ad hoc* method of tree allocation embodies a transactional, piecemeal vision that treats urban trees as individual units of state property. Successfully managing a unified urban forest requires at a minimum that the decisionmaker actually "see" the urban forest as a single entity and to value the inputs of all stakeholders, not just property owners.

RECONCEPTUALIZING CITY TREES AS A UNIFIED FOREST

Experts have long identified three primary components for urban forest sustainability: enough trees, a strong community framework, and an appropriate governance structure.[48] Planting enough trees is the easiest of the three for government actors to achieve. The City's Department of Parks and Recreation is well-equipped to select and plant a diverse array of trees. These are technocratic decisions that lend themselves to conventional public management strategies.

In 2007, NYC embraced this first component when it launched the Million Trees NYC (MTNYC)[49] campaign as part of PlaNYC.[50] Claiming that it would "re-imagine the public

[42] Saskia Sassen, "Who Owns our Cities and Why this Urban Takeover Should Concern Us All," *Guardian* (November 24, 2015); Sheila Foster and Christian Iaione, "The City as a Commons," *Yale L. & Pol'y Rev.* 34 (2016): 281.

[43] Wendell Pritchett and Shitong Quiao, "Exlusionary Megacities," *Southern Calif. L. Rev.* 91 (2018): 467.

[44] Ibid., 495–499.

[45] Melissa Checker, "Wiped Out by the Green Wave: Environmental Gentrification and the Paradoxical Politics of Urban Sustainability," *City & Society* 23 (2011): 211.

[46] Christine E. Carmichael and Maureen H. McDonough, "The Trouble with Trees? Social and Political Dynamics of Street Tree-Planting Efforts in Detroit, Michigan," *Urban Forestry & Urban Greening* 31 (2018): 221

[47] *See* David Bollier, *Think Like a Commoner: A Short Introduction to the Life of the Commons* (2014); Nicholas Blomley, "Enclosure, Common Right and the Property of the Poor," *Social & Legal Studies* 17 (2008): 311, 315–326.

[48] James R. Clark, et al., "A Model of Urban Forest Sustainability," *Journal of Arboriculture* 23 (1997): 17–19.

[49] www.milliontreesnyc.org/

[50] PlaNYC, 38. www.nyc.gov/html/planyc/downloads/pdf/publications/full_report_2007.pdf.

realm,[51] MTNYC aimed to expand the City's urban forest by roughly twenty percent.[52] This campaign did re-imagine the public realm in two critical ways. First, the campaign announced an intention to plant a significant number of trees in historically underserved communities. Second, using an approach that Dexter Locke and Morgan Grove dubbed *All Lands, All People*,[53] the City provided trees for planting on private as well as public land. Indeed, of the million trees, nearly a quarter were planted on private land.[54] Although this was largely a function of cost (tree planting was more expensive than tree give-aways) blurring the public/private tree line could have been the start of a more inclusive, collaborative management strategy.

Unfortunately, MTNYC's actions aligned more closely with gentrification, rather than with improving neighborhood quality for the existing community.[55] Specifically, MTNYC failed on the other two components for urban forest sustainability: community framework and appropriate governance fronts. Specifically, MTNYC suffered from top-down decision-making[56] that failed to include residents in the decision-making process.[57] It had little room for communities to voice their own aspirations and desires vis-à-vis the urban canopy. To avoid "having to spend a significant amount of time debating the options in public meetings,"[58] no draft plan was ever released. Public outreach instead focused on generating "buy in" for a plan that had already been written.[59] From start to finish there was virtually no opportunity for the public to influence the goals or priorities of the tree planting campaign.[60]

Moreover, MTNYC was inextricably tied to other community investments that exacerbated, rather than ameliorated social inequity.[61] The campaign routinely touted the economic return on NYC's investment in trees, even though much of that value was tied to increased real estate value – the problematic yardstick associated with gentrification.[62] This criticism was particularly salient because MTNYC took place in an era of rezoning that allowed high-end residential developments to radically transform and gentrify many neighborhoods, particularly those along the waterfront with ready access to mass transit.[63] It is

---

[51] Ibid., 36.

[52] Ibid.

[53] Dexter H. Locke et al., "Prioritizing Preferable Locations for Increasing Urban Tree Canopy in New York City," *Cities and the Environment* 3 (2010): 1

[54] Lisa W. Foderaro, "Bronx Planting Caps Off a Drive to Add a Million Trees," *New York Times* (October 20, 2015).

[55] Sarah Fox, "Environmental Gentrification," *University of Colorado Law Review* 90 (2018): 803.

[56] Lindsay K. Campbell, *City of Forests, City of Farms: Sustainability Planning for New York City's Nature* (2017) 186–205 (contrasting Million Trees NYC with the City's grass roots community gardening movement that was led predominantly led by low-income people of color.)

[57] Tom Angotti, "PlaNYC at Three: Time to Include Neighborhoods," *Gotham Gazette* (Apr. 12, 2010).

[58] ICLEI, "The Process Behind PlaNYC," 25 (April 2010) http://s-media.nyc.gov/agencies/planyc2030/pdf/iclei_planyc_case_study_201004.pdf.

[59] Ibid. 19, 24–26.

[60] American Planning Association NY Metro Chapter. "Response to the Bloomberg Administration's PlaNYC 2030 Long Term Sustainability Planning Process And Proposed Goals," 3 (Mar. 14, 2007) www.nyplanning.org/wordpress/wp-content/uploads/2016/05/PlaNYC_2030_response_final_3-14-07.pdf.

[61] New York City's High Line is the poster child for the kind of urban greening that reinforces social inequality and allows property owners to accrue private benefits at the expense of the existing community. Kevin Loughran, "Parks for Profit: The High Line, Growth Machines, and the Uneven Development of Urban Public Spaces," *City & Community* 13 (2014): 49.

[62] Geoffrey H. Donovan and David Butry, "Trees in the City: Valuing Street Trees in Portland, Oregon," *Landscape and Urban Planning* 94 (2010): 77; Greg McPherson, et al., "Municipal Forest Benefits and Costs in Five US Cities," *Journal of Forestry* (2005): 415.

[63] Heather Rogers, "How Michael Bloomberg Greenwashed New York City," *Tablet* (Jan. 5, 2015).

partly in response to this kind of inequity-promoting public–private partnership that the urban as commons movement has emerged.

LIMITS OF NEW YORK CITY'S EXISTING VISION OF THE URBAN FOREST

Merely planting more trees[64] will not allow the Parks Department to successfully "protect, restore, expand, and manage NYC's green spaces and natural areas to maximize the benefits for environmental and community health and resilience."[65]Achieving that goal requires the collaboration and cooperation of a wide range of stakeholders. Forest managers around the world have learned that sustainable forest management is about more than the trees. To be sustainable, forest management must be contextual; it must focus on the setting in which trees and humans interact. This insight is even more true in the urban forest context. Urban forest sustainability means navigating the complex social claims about place that various communities bring to the urban forest.

If NYC embraced the perspective that the entire urban forest is a common resource shared by all urban inhabitants, it would lead to very different management choices. Unfortunately, the Parks Department still limits its management vision to NYC's public trees. Just as the street trees separate the public street from the (mostly) privately owned property that lines the street, so too the Parks Department segments the urban canopy into public trees and private trees. The otherwise innovative *TreesCount!* initiative highlights the limitations of this approach.

In 2015, under the banner of *TreesCount!*, NYC conducted a year-long tree census across the entire city, recording details about every public tree in the city.[66] Based on this tree census, NYC created a detailed map of street trees.[67] This fascinating map offers users a view of the street trees near any NYC address, with sidebars providing details about each such tree. Consistent with the trend toward using the economic utility of trees to justify investment in urban forestry,[68] the map estimated the monetary value of the services each tree provides.[69] Thus, according to the map, NYC has 678,688 street trees that collectively provide $109,809,184.28 in annual functional benefits to the City by diverting stormwater runoff, conserving energy, removing air pollution, and sequestering carbon.[70] *TreeCount!* breaks down this monetary assessment on a tree-by-tree basis. While it purported to use this individual tree "value" to spark an appreciation for the canopy as a whole, *TreeCount!* embraced the neo liberal vision of the environment as a bundle of goods and services. This approach obscured other, less tangible goods provided by trees, things like beauty, aesthetics, or a sense of place, which do not lend themselves to quantification or commodification.

Moreover, even accepting the paradigm of commodification and quantification, this project vastly understated the value of the urban forest because it miscounted the trees. According to *TreesCount!* there are five Pin Oak trees (*Quercus palustris*) lining the sidewalk in front of my co-operative building. The *TreesCount!* map reports that these five trees have collectively

---

[64] Michael Battaglia, et al., "It's Not Easy Going Green: Obstacles to Tree-Planting Programs in Baltimore," *Cites and the Environment* 7 (2014): 4.

[65] NYC Parks, "Tree Planting Standards" (2016): 5

[66] Laura Bliss, "Every Tree in New York City, Mapped," *CityLab* (November 4, 2016). Roughly 55 percent of those trees are native species. Nowak, "Assessing Urban Forest Effects and Values," 5.

[67] NYC Parks, *TreesCount! 2-15-2016 Street Tree Census*, www.nycgovparks.org/trees/treescount

[68] P. J. Peper, et al., "New York City, New York Municipal Forest Resource Analysis," 3 (concluding that New Yorkers receive well over $5.00 in benefits for every dollar spent on street tree planting and care.)

[69] *Id.*

[70] NYC's Street Trees: Citywide Statistics, https://tree-map.nycgovparks.org/.

intercepted 12,000 gallons of stormwater; conserved 6328 kW energy from heating and cooling; removed thirteen pounds of air pollutants (particulates, nitrous and sulfur oxides, and ozone), and sequestered 16,500 lb. of carbon each year.[71] However, this *TreesCount!* map paints a false picture of lived reality – there are not five trees on this block, there are ten. Completely left off the map are the five privately-owned Sycamore trees lining the other side of the sidewalk. They too intercept stormwater, purify the air, and sequester carbon.

On this one short block, there are two lines of mature trees separated by a regulation-width sidewalk. Surely their roots intermingle – their branches and leaves certainly do. These trees are deeply interrelated – they share the same soil, the same air, they drop their leaves at the same time in the fall, and team up to provide much-needed shade in the summer. Ecologically, these trees function together as part of a single unit, but legally they are wholly unconnected. For City purposes, the private trees are simply not there – they are invisible on the map, their contribution to ecosystem services remains uncalculated, and they are not considered in planning. This pattern of practical tree interaction bracketed by the legal fiction of separation is repeated on block after block across the City. The Parks Department simply does not "see" private trees, not even the ones the Department itself planted on private land at the behest of private owners.[72] That is no way to manage a forest.

TreesCount! invites the public to "explore our city's urban forest" without mentioning that it excludes important components of that forest. These unacknowledged gaps mean that the *TreesCount!* map distorts public perceptions in ways that limit the possibilities of social trans-formation around urban forestry. For example, *TreesCount!* proclaimed Hillyer St. between 51st Ave and Kneeland Ave in Elmhurst as "the leafiest block in Queens."[73] What it really meant was that this relatively modest block in Queens had the most mature street trees, not that it was actually the greenest or the leafiest. Nearby, wealthier Forest Hills Gardens was factually much more leafy, with many more mature trees overall. Yet because many of those trees were private trees, the *TreesCount!* initiative obscured this reality, offering instead a distorted egalitarianism that touted public bounty by erasing private abundance.

TreesCount! is not invidious, or even intentionally deceptive. The project is in many ways an admirable attempt to spark interest and pride in the City's trees. And from a budgeting and planning perspective, it is not unreasonable to focus limited public resources on publicly owned and managed trees. If the *Trees Count!* map explicitly acknowledged this gap, it might matter less. But the map gives the public no reminders that it it represents only a slice of the City's tree reality. Because its blinders remain unacknowledged, and uninterrogated, this initiative ultimately reinforces a cramped, narrow conception of the urban forest that inhibits its successful management.

Much like Christian Borch and Martin Kornberger's notion that the networks and relations of the urban commons create much of the value ascribed to private goods,[74] it is the ecosystem that emerges from the confluence of public and private urban trees that creates significant environ-mental and public health goods. Yet if private trees and private tree owners can opt out of joint

---

[71] The specific information is reported tree by tree. Collectively, the City estimates the trees provide $890 in total annual benefits. Just who receives those benefits is left unstated. https://tree-map.nycgovparks.org/#treeinfo-3367153; https://tree-map.nycgovparks.org/#treeinfo-3654742; https://tree-map.nycgovparks.org/#treeinfo-3342614; https://tree-map.nycgovparks.org/#treeinfo-3657536; https://tree-map.nycgovparks.org/#treeinfo-3362841.
[72] Statement of Nelson Villarrubia, Executive Director, Trees NYC, Caring for NYC's Forest: A Story of Research, Community and Inspiration (June 17, 2019).
[73] TreesCount 2015, www.nycgovparks.org/trees/treescount.
[74] Christian Borch and Martin Kornberger (2015). "The Urban Commons: Rethinking the City," 6–7.

management of their trees, they can both capture the "unearned increment" from the urban forest while potentially making choices that undermine the continued vitality of the resource. Re-imagining all the urban trees as one urban commons is a way to move beyond this incomplete framework for urban governance that amplifies the voices of property owners while muting those of renters and other city residents who own no property.

WHAT A COMMONS PERSPECTIVE ADDS

In light of the complex jurisdictional issues, it is not surprising that the Department "sees" the part of the ecosystem it can directly control.[75] Making decisions about street or park trees entails persuading only a few key officials with clear mandates. Managing the whole urban forest, by contrast, means including the diverse motivations, capacities, and interests of all the city's residents into forestry decisions. Many if not most residents will be unfamiliar with ecology, forestry, and other key technical disciplines. Forestry experts are therefore tempted to assume that they know best, and that the public has little value to contribute to their decisions. However, since one of the main goals of urban forestry is to optimize societal benefits, it is critical that urban foresters hear from the communities in which these public trees reside, and that public concerns influence the management of private trees. This requires building an inclusive framework for coordination and collaboration.

A reimagined version of the *All Lands, All People* approach might offer a way to achieve this.[76] *All Lands, All People* already prompted NYC to step beyond conventional urban forestry practices and assess the tree-growing potential of all urban lands – both public and private.[77] However, *All Lands, All People* is an assessment tool rather than a management philosophy. It uses statistics about quantifiable net benefits to identify and prioritize areas for tree planting.[78] It did not address the management of public trees once they were planted, let alone private trees.

All Lands, All People positioned forestry experts as knowledge creators. The public's role was to receive information, not to create it.[79] Foresters ranked neighborhoods and assigned priority levels based wholly on technocratic criteria. The meaning that residents and communities might attach to tree planting was not one of the variables fed into the calculation.[80] Equally problematic, *All Lands, All People* paid little attention to the distribution of the quantifiable benefits of tree planting among a neighborhood's residents,[81] and even less to non- quantifiable considerations like the aspirations and self-images of the communities.[82] Relegated to the status of bystanders, communities were informed about a pre-determined course of action, and were expected to be grateful for largess dispensed to them based on choices made elsewhere.[83] The power dynamics inherent in this framing remained unstated and unexplored.[84] This approach

[75] Nowak, "Sustaining America's Urban Forests and Trees," 6.

[76] Ibid, 126.

[77] Ibid.

[78] Ibid., 10.

[79] Michael T. Rains, "A Forest Service Vision during the Anthropocene," *Forests* 8 (2017): 209, 221.

[80] Christine E. Carmichael and Maureen H. McDonough, "The Trouble with Trees? Social and Political Dynamics of Street Tree-Planting Efforts in Detroit, Michigan," *Urban Forestry & Urban Greening* 31 (2018): 221

[81] Jessica Garrison, "Seeing the park for the trees: NY's million trees campaign vs the deep roots of environmental inequality," *Environment & Planning* 46 (2019): 924.

[82] Ibid.

[83] Lindsay K Campbell, "Constructing New York City's Urban Forest: The Politics and Governance of the MillionTrees NYC campaign," in *Urban Forests, Trees and Greenspace: A Political Ecology Perspective* (Routledge 2015) 255.

[84] Lindsay K. Campbell and Nate Gabriel, "Power in Urban Social-Ecological Systems: Processes and Practices of Governance and Marginalization," *Urban Forestry & Urban Greening* 19 (2016): 253.

reinforced rather than confronted the social structures, property rules, and administrative practices that produce and distribute inequality in NYC.

Resistance to tree planting campaigns is often rooted in objection to precisely this power dynamic.[85] A commons perspective might interrogate the role of power by drawing on the long tradition of community forestry to bring the voices of residents into urban forest management. Arun Agrawal's work highlights "the capacity of [commons] users to self-organize, work with government officials, and take advantage of opportunities to govern their resources sustainably."[86] By challenging top-down management and empowering communities, a commons-informed *All Lands, All People* approach might initiate a broader and deeper collaboration, one that views residents and neighborhoods as important stakeholders with local ecological knowledge vital to the expert discourse. Such an approach might build participatory processes for more collective and more just management of the urban forest – a path that ultimately means more sustainable urban forest management.

Truly sustainable urban forestry requires a re-visioning of governance, rather than merely layering new projects onto existing institutions, practices, and mandates. This is where commons thinking truly adds value. As Elinor Ostrom pointed out, appropriate scale is key to effective governance institutions. Participation at the neighborhood level, where residents are most likely to act, must therefore be central to urban forest management. However, local decision-making is still inherently power-laden. Avoiding capture by gentrifying forces requires explicit attention to low-income and minority community voices.

CONCLUSION

Robust and equitable urban forest management policies can ensure widespread access to the many benefits urban forests provide. Such policies need broad collaborations[87] that not only function ecologically but also truly include the whole urban population. Collaborations among urban elites will not suffice. With some commons-oriented retooling, *All Lands, All People* can facilitate this wider participation necessary to build more transparent, more equitable, more ecological city. Rather than selecting goals and priorities through technocratic expertise and then selling them to the public, this retooled *All Lands, All People* approach would use an inclusive participatory process to identify goals and priorities. Governance of the shared urban forest would be the province of all actors with a stake in the commons.[88] Forestry experts would then implement the goals identified through that process.

Foster and Iaione urban commons analysis offer a normative basis for looking beyond who owns which city trees.[89] A commons perspective reveals the community stake in managing urban forests, and highlights the need for participatory decision-making about management, use, and allocation.[90] This creates space for an urban forest management regime that is not based on private ownership, nor public ownership, nor even a patchwork

[85] Carmichael and McDonough, "Community Stories," 12–13.

[86] Krister Andersson, Arun Agrawal, "Inequalities, institutions, and Forest Commons," *Global Environmental Change* 21 (2011): 866.

[87] Erika S. Svendsen and Lindsay K. Campbell, "Urban Ecological Stewardship: Understanding the Structure, Function and Network of Community-Based Urban Land Management," *Cities and the Environment* 1 (2008): 31.

[88] Foster and Iaione, "City as Commons," 290.

[89] Foster and Iaione, "The City as a Commons," 301–306.

[90] Ibid., 324–334.

of both. Under an urban commons framing, the City's trees emerge as forest dwellers and not merely as private or public resources.[91] That identity opens the possibility of subordinating formal tree ownership to the common management necessary to realize the broader value of the urban forest.[92]

NYC recently enacted two environmental justice ordinances to ensure that vulnerable communities have a voice in the City's environmental decision-making, and that environmental burdens and benefits are shared more equitably and widely. A commons-informed *All Land, All People* approach will further these goals and ensure that NYC's next tree planting campaigns[93] produce a truly sustainable urban canopy.

---

[91] Ibid., 306–311.

[92] Foster and Iaione, "City as Commons," 306–311.

[93] New York City Environmental Justice Alliance, NYC *Climate Justice Agenda* 6 (April 2017); "Press Release: Mayor Announces Program to Help Curb Effects of Extreme Summer Heat," (June 14, 2017).

11

The City as a Commons Reloaded

From the Urban Commons to Co-Cities
Empirical Evidence on the Bologna Regulation

Christian Iaione and Elena De Nictolis*

Over the last decade or so, there has been an emerging interest in the topic of the urban commons, representing a form of collective sharing, management, production, and ownership of critical urban resources, services, and infrastructures (e.g., spaces, buildings and other underused assets). Much of the literature in this area has focused on institutional approaches through which city governments can govern urban commons with city residents and various other social and economic stakeholders. This literature is inter- and transdisciplinary and contains many different intellectual or conceptual strands. This chapter proposes to ground this theoretical focus by attempting to forge an empirical methodology and apply it to a policy experiment run by the City of Bologna to create and support urban commons throughout the city.

The empirical evaluation of Bologna's historic experiment shows that if little effort is put into building city inhabitants' resource management capacity or stimulating the diversity of social and economic actors participating in urban commons governance schemes, particularly for complex or large-scale resources, the urban commons framework will not be able to be a transformative force in the social and economic functioning of cities. As such, this empirical evaluation suggests that legal recognition of the urban commons is not sufficient if not coupled with an integrated policy program and more political and financial investment in urban commons as neighborhood collective economic units. Neighborhood-scale investments that aim to seed collective or community economic ventures emerge as a possible way to overcome the shortcomings of the first urban commons policy experiments. They also suggest the need for more in-depth analysis and investigation by scholars.

TOWARD AN EMPIRICAL ANALYSIS OF LAW AND POLICY ON THE URBAN COMMONS

Academic literature on the urban commons tends indeed to be normative, either heavily theoretical or explicitly ideological. Many scholars writing about the urban commons are devoted to understanding the processes that result in collective action, or cooperation, in the governance of shared urban resources by NGOs or unorganized city residents[1]. Some scholars define the commons not merely as shared resources but also as a process of social cooperation

---

[1] *Article note: This Article is the result of a collaborative work, although Introduction, Parts 1, 2, and the Conclusion are to be attributed to Christian Iaione; Parts 3 and 4 is to be attributed to Elena De Nictolis. The authors wish to express

that reconfigures the relationship between city residents and city administrations.[2] Within the literature on institutional approaches to the urban commons Sheila Foster and Christian Iaione have argued that urban commons are goods – squares, parks, dismissed buildings, vacant lots, roads – that are part of the collective resources of cities and require a more open governance regime than currently exists in most cities.[3] Others conceive of the commons as an institutional arrangement defined by three different elements:[4] a resource critical for the existence, survival or well-being, of a community, a collective governance resource management scheme,[5] and the active role of users in this collective governance schemes.

Apart from notable exceptions such as the work of Harini Nagendra and Elinor Ostrom and that of Amanda Huron, the scholarship on the urban commons is almost completely conceptual, lacking an empirical focus and failing to place under empirical investigation the many applied experiments conducted to date by policymakers. The scholarship on the urban commons also lacks a focus on the role of the commons as a means to achieve stronger urban economies and more inclusive urban prosperity. An economic democracy perspective, that we embrace here, advocates for expanding the access to power in economic institutions such as firms and corporations to employees also through the diffusion of workers-owned enterprises or self-governed enterprises,[6] within an economic system based on solidarity and reciprocity.[7]

An urban economic democracy approach implies a more intense or direct role for city inhabitants in the production and redistribution of the value produced by a vibrant and successful city economy. Urban policies that are directed toward achieving such an economic democracy approach should aspire to uplift not just individuals, but entire urban communities, as argued by Richard Schragger,[8] and focus on stimulating the creation of community-based development institutions and enterprises that are interdependent and networked at the urban level.[9] As scholars who have studied the preservation of urban lakes in Bangalore[10] and the housing commons in

their gratitude to the civil servants from the City of Bologna and the Fondazione per l'Innovazione Urbana for inspiring this work as well as contributing to its concrete realization.

A special thanks goes to Matteo Lepore; Michele D'Alena; Giovanni Ginocchini; Ilaria Daolio; Anna Rita Iannucci; Donato di Memmo; Giacomo Capuzzimati; Antonio Carastro; Chiara Manaresi.

We are also thankful to all civic signatories of the pacts of collaboration and urban commoners from the City of Bologna for being so generous with their time and for sharing their experience with us. We hope their work will keep inspiring future generations of scholars and activists.

Finally, we owe a special dept of gratitude to all mentors and colleagues that contributed with their comments, feedbacks and suggestions to our work. Without their precious collaboration, this chapter would have never reached completion. We are indebted, among others, to Sheila Foster; Marco Cammelli; Leonardo Morlino; Giuseppe Piperata; Paola Chirulli; Giacinto della Cananea; Ivana Pais and Michela Bolis. We finally thank Chiara de Angelis, Benedetta Gillio and Alessandro Antonelli, who provided invaluable and thorough assistance.

Melissa Garcia Lamarca, "Insurgent Acts of Being-In-Common and Housing in Spain: Making Urban Commons?" In *Urban Commons Moving Beyond State and Market* 165, edited by Mary Dellenbaugh et al., Basel: Birkhäuser, 2015. See also Alexandros Kioupkiolis, *The Common and The Political. Commons, Communities and Counter-Hegemonic Politics for The Common Good: Rethinking Social Change* (Edinburgh: Edinburgh University Press, 2019).

[2] Christian Borch & Martin Kornberger, *Urban Commons: Rethinking the City* 169 (New York: Routledge, 2015).

[3] Sheila Foster and Christian Iaione, "The City as a Commons," *Yale Law and Policy Review* (2016) 34.281.6

[4] Tine De Moor, "Avoiding Tragedies: A Flemish Common and its Commoners under the Pressure of Social and Economic Change during the Eighteen Century," *Economic History Review* 62 (2009).

[5] Brett Frischmann et al, *Governing Knowledge Commons*, (Cambridge University Press, 2014).

[6] Robert Dahl, *A Preface to Economic Democracy* (Berkeley and Los Angeles: University of California Press, 1985); Tom Malleson, *After Occupy_ Economic democracy for the 21st Century* (Oxford: Oxford University Press, 2014): 23.

[7] Karl Polanyi, *The great transformation* (Boston: Beacon Press, 2010).

[8] Richard C. Schragger, "The Political Economy of City Power," *Fordham Urban Law Journal* 44, 91 (2017).

[9] David Imbroscio, "Urban Policy as Meritocracy: A Critique," *Journal of Urban Affairs*, 38, 79 (2015).

[10] Harini Nagendra and Elinor Ostrom, "Applying the Social-Ecological System Framework to the Diagnosis of Urban Lake Commons in Bangalore, India," *Ecology and Society*, 19 (2) 67 (2014).

Washington, DC,[11] have shown, the city and the residents in cities can work together. When they do, they generate better economic and social outcomes for local communities.

We define urban commons to mean tangible or intangible socially constructed[12] resources, assets, services, and infrastructure in cities. These can be publicly or privately owned. Either way, urban commons can provide access to critical goods and services and therefore guarantee the fundamental rights – housing, food, etc. – to urban residents and generate added value for the local community. We argue that the governance of urban commons can be enabled by city policies that stimulate collaboration and cooperation between several urban actors in order to enable or improve the enjoyment of benefits that flow from these efforts for a wider range of city inhabitants. However, we argue that city enabled solutions are valuable only when they generate public-community partnerships[13] that recognize community stewardship rights (i.e., rights of use, co-management, co-production, co-ownership)[14] and enable their economic self-sustainability. We define these collaborative and cooperative schemes as forms of "co-govern-ance"[15] of the urban commons.

To more closely examine the ability of the urban commons to realize these goals, we focus in this chapter on the blossoming of urban commons– oriented policies in cities around the world. Italian cities have been the front-runners in the regulatory race to adopt local policies. The "Regulation for Collaboration between Citizens and the City in the Care and Regeneration of the Urban Commons," adopted in 2014 by the City of Bologna ("Bologna Regulation"), pioneered the effort to institutionalize collaboration between government and city residents for the management and governance of urban resources, services, and urban infrastructure as commons. This is especially crucial now that other cities are experimenting with similar regulation and policies, following the Bologna example and model. The city of Naples, for example, recognizes informal management by city residents of city owned buildings as urban commons through its "civic and collective urban uses" policy.[16] The City of Turin has recently approved a regulation that blends the two approaches and introduces further developments.[17] Previously, the City of Seoul issued two ordinances on the promotion of sharing city and the

[11] Amanda Huron "Conclusion: Keep Practicing." In *Carving Out the Commons: Tenant Organizing and Housing Cooperatives in Washington, D.C.*, Minneapolis, London: University of Minnesota Press, 2018, 166.

[12] Michael J. Madison, Brett M. Frischmann and Katherine J. Strandburg, "Constructing Commons in the cultural environment," *Cornell Law Review* 95: 657 (2010); Massimo De Angelis, *Omnia Sunt Communia: On the Commons and the Transformation to Postcapitalism* (London: Zed Books, 2017).

[13] Christian Iaione, "Governing the Urban Commons", *Italian Journal of Public Law*, 7, 1, (2015) 170; Christian Iaione and Elena De Nictolis, "The Role of law in relation to the New Urban Agenda and the European Urban Agenda: a multi-stakeholder perspective," in *Law and the New Urban Agenda: A Comparative Perspective*, edited by Nestor Davidson and Geeta Tewari New York: Routledge, 2020.

[14] Dan Wu and Sheila R. Foster, "From Smart Cities to Co-Cities: Emerging Legal and Policy Responses to Urban Vacancy," *Fordham Urban Law Journal*, 47, 909 (2020).

[15] Jan Kooiman, *Governing as governance*, London: Sage, 2003; Christian Iaione and Paola Cannavò, "The collaborative and polycentric governance of the urban and local commons," *Urban pamphleteer*, 5 (2015); Sheila Foster and Christian Iaione, "The City as a Commons," *Yale Law and Policy Review* (2016): 34.281.6; Christian Iaione, "The Right to the Co-City," *The Italian Journal of Public Law*, 15, 1, 80 (2017); Christian Iaione, Elena De Nictolis, Anna Berti Suman, "The Internet of Humans (IoH): Human Rights and Co-Governance to Achieve Tech Justice in the City, *Law and Ethics of Human Rights*, 2 (2019).

[16] Giuseppe Micciarelli, "Introduction to urban and collective civic use: the 'direct management' of urban emerging commons in Naples", *Draft Heteropolitics International Workshop Proceedings*, 92 (2017), http://heteropolitics.net/wp-content/uploads/2017/09/Conference_Proceedings_Website.pdf; Nicola Capone, "The concrete Utopia of the Commons.* The right of Civic and collective use of public (and private) goods," *Law & (dis)order*, 7 (2017).

[17] Christian Iaione, "The Pacts of Collaboration as public-people partnerships", *Zoom in 1, UIA*, 2018, www.uia-initiative.eu/sites/default/files/2018-07/Turin%20-%2001-051%20Co-City%20-%20Christian%20Iaione%20-%20Zoom-in%201-%20July%202018.pdf.

opening and use of dormant spaces at public facilities, which inspired much of the work in Bologna. Similarly, Madrid passed an ordinance on social cooperation for the urban commons and Barcelona is implementing a "Citizen Asset program for community use and management." Finally, cities in northern and eastern Europe, like Gent, Amsterdam, Gdansk, Presov and Iasi are working alongside Naples and Barcelona on a common regulatory under the auspices of the Civic eState Urbact Transfer Network.[18]

These policies enable city residents to collectively, manage or govern a host of urban resources, from open spaces to buildings to cultural assets. In some cases, these policies promote a shift in the democratic engagement of city residents by promoting new schemes of use, management and ownership of urban critical resources and thereby a possibly new path towards social inclusion and justice. In this chapter, we focus our analysis on the most widely celebrated urban commons regulatory policy, the Bologna Regulation. The legislation was the first of its kind to mention the urban commons as a subject of legislation and has since been copied or mirrored in by many other cities in their policies, resulting to date in more than 200 Italian cities that have adopted the Bologna Regulation in one form or another.

The Bologna Regulation, and its widespread adoption, has sparked a debate within the urban commons literature about whether these kinds of policies are an effective way to enable the creation and economic sustainability of true urban commons. Critics argue that, by themselves, these laws are unable to foster and sustain the kind of collective action required to establish urban commons.[19] For some, the Bologna Regulation represented a way to create a space for urban commons within the city administration.[20] For others, the regulation was depicted as a tool that waters down the antagonistic nature of the commons or more generally that it tries to opportunistically leverage the social capital produced by the commons.[21] This argument echoes what scholars Ugo Mattei and Alessandra Quarta have argued,[22] namely that this type of regulation, by failing to include strict rules that enable communities to self-organize and failing to ensure devolution of decision-making power, is essentially a paternalistic law or policy.[23]

To address these critiques, we empirically evaluate the Bologna regulation through an assessment of the 280 pacts of collaborations signed between 2014 and 2016. The analysis is based on a conceptual and methodological approach rooted in the literature on political economy,[24] especially on the political economy analysis of the city from both a legal and a policy perspective[25] and

[18] Christian Iaione, "Pooling urban commons: the Civic eState," *Urbact* (2019), https://urbact.eu/urban-commons-civic-estate.

[19] Ugo Mattei and Alessandra Quarta, "Right to the City or Urban Commoning? Thoughts on the Generative Transformation of Property Law," *The Italian Law Journal*, 1, 2, (2015): 320; Ioanni Delsante, Serena Orlandi "Mapping Uses, People and Places: Towards a Counter-Cartography of Commoning Practices and Spaces for Commons. A Case Study in Pavia, Italy", *European Journal of Creative Practices in Cities and Landscapes*, 2, 2, (2020): 121–150.

[20] Pierre Sauvêtre, "Foucault and the democratic conflict: the government of the common against the neoliberal government," *Astérion Online* 13 (2015).

[21] Iolanda Bianchi, The post-political meaning of the concept of commons: the regulation of the urban commons in Bologna," (2018): 290.

[22] Ugo Mattei and Alessandra Quarta, "Right to the City or Urban Commoning? Thoughts on the Generative Transformation of Property Law," *The Italian Law Journal*, 1, 2, (2015): 320.

[23] Mattei and Quarta, "Right to the City or Urban Commoning? Thoughts on the Generative Transformation of Property Law," 320.

[24] Paul. D. Aligica, *Institutional Diversity and Political Economy: the Ostroms and Beyond"* (New York: Oxford University Press, 2014)

[25] Vincent Ostrom, Charles M. Tiebout and Robert Warren, "The Organization of Government in Metropolitan Areas: A Theoretical Inquiry"; *The American Political Science Review*, 55, 4 (1961): 831–842; Vincent Ostrom, 'Policentricity' in M. McGinnis (ed.) *Policentricity and Local Public Economies: Readings from the Workshop in Political Theory and*

the quality of democracy.[26] It analyzes the implementation of the Bologna Regulation as empirical evidence of the challenges faced by a city regulation designed to seed urban commons throughout the city. Finally, on the basis of the results of the evaluation this chapter discusses how the cooperation between city government, city residents and other city actors can contribute to the development of an institutional architecture truly enabling urban co-governance which is the core dimension of the city as a commons approach. This implies that different actors (i.e., unorganized city residents or their informal aggregations, local NGOs, knowledge institutions such as universities, schools, research, creative and cultural centers, local businesses or professionals such as architects – see the chapter by Sofia Croso Mazzuco in this book, showing the role of creative architects in developing collaborative urbanisms practices in Brazilian cities) constantly engage in collaborative practices and public authorities become or act as an enabling platform for these practices.

If the goal is to conserve a diversity of urban resources and to create a more equitable urban economic system, a more complex and integrated policy approach is required. Namely, one that includes digital, learning, financial, and institutional tools to create urban commons that preserve the diversity of urban resources and city life and ensure the survival and sustainable financial security of community commons. To accomplish these goals, a more complex and integrated policy program of digital, learning, financial, institutional, and legal tools is necessary.[27] This chapter thus argues that to effectively enable collective action, it is necessary to move beyond legal tools and laws that enable it. Cities should couple them with integrated forms of capacity building at the local level – including digital platforms, mentoring paths to organize and technically equip the urban commons which are chaotic by nature and, as mentioned earlier, resource integration to ensure their financial sustainability. The chapter hypothesizes that the city as a commons approach, in order to be successful, requires the establishment of an economic democracy, rather than political democracy, oriented approach that empowers local communities in the most distressed neighborhoods to incorporate collective economic units that produce collective economic wealth, and thereby economic opportunities, for the many living in the given neighborhood, not just for the few.

DESIGNING THROUGH EXPERIMENTATION: THE GENESIS OF THE BOLOGNA REGULATION

Starting in 2011, the City of Bologna began to put in place a set of policies that would reshape the social, economic, political systems in the city consistent with the idea of the urban commons.[28] The Regulation was the cornerstone of this urban economic transformation and deliberative democracy process.[29] The City of Bologna drafted the Regulation to recognize and facilitate the

Policy Analysis (Ann Arbor, MI: University of Michigan Press, 1999), 52–74; Elinor Ostrom "Unlocking Public Entrepreneurship and Public Economies," Discussion paper Np. 2005/01, study was presented at the EGDI–WIDER Conference on Unlocking Human Potential – Linking the Informal and Formal Sectors in Helsinki, September 17–18, 2004, www.wider.unu.edu/publication/unlocking-public-entrepreneurship-and-public-economies. Richard Schragger, "The Political Economy of City power," *Fordham Urban Law Journal*, 44 (2017): 91.

[26] Leonardo Morlino, *Changes for Democracy: Actors, Structures, Processes* (Oxford University Press, 2012).

[27] LabGov.City, *The Co-Cities Open Book*, 2019, http://commoning.city/the-co-cities-open-book/.

[28] *Iperbole* digital platform dedicated to the Urban Commons, Accessed June 30, 2020, http://partecipa.comune.bologna .it/beni-comuni; *Incredibol*, Accessed June 30, 2020, *Collaborare è Bologna*, Accessed June 30, 2020, www.incredibol .net/tag/bando/; www.comune.bologna.it/collaborarebologna/; *Pilastro 2016 neighbourhood development program*, Accessed June 30, 2020, www.fondazioneinnovazioneurbana.it/64-urbancenter/pilastro-2016; Plan for urban innovation, Accessed June 30, 2020, www.comune.bologna.it/pianoinnovazioneurbana/info/.

[29] These policies must be positioned within the participatory tradition of Bologna. Putnam, Leonardi and Nanetti highlighted the case of Emilia Romagna in their prominent research demonstrating the presence of civic community

right to collective action by residents, and others, to generate and care for shared urban resources. The regulation was designed to rely on neighborhood experimental projects as its starting point. This process of experimentation, called the "cities as a commons" project, was carried out by the City with the support of a local not-for-profit Foundation, the "Fondazione del Monte di Bologna and Ravenna" and realized in partnership with the research center *Labsus* led at the time by Gregorio Arena and Christian Iaione and a local NGO, *Centro Antartide*, selected for their experience in civic engagement, coordination of networking local NGOs and participatory sustainable development projects.[30]

Fieldwork activities that preceded the drafting of the Regulation consisted of three "governance labs," a mentoring and co-design program where local officials worked together with local NGOs and neighborhood residents with the support of experts and scholars. In these governance labs, they were able to identify and co-design projects that would revitalize or regenerate three types of urban commons – cultural assets, green spaces, and city-owned buildings – in order to identify the legal and procedural obstacles or administrative "bottlenecks" that would hinder meaningful cooperation with local officials, more cooperative engagement of neighborhoods inhabitants, ultimately hampering the possibility to establish a public-community collaboration. These three types of projects paved the way for the drafting of the Regulation by a working group composed of three city officers (i.e., one from the Active Citizenship Office, one from the Legal Service and one from the Urban Planning Department) and external legal experts.[31]

The Regulation[32] sets forth a policy toolbox,[33] including general principles (e.g., the principle of civic autonomy), the policy goals (e.g., promotion of social and digital innovation, collaborative economy, urban creativity), collaborative decision – making and administrative procedures through co-design methodologies to promote open and non-exclusive cooperation between the city and the community, and typologies of "interventions" describing the kind of projects to be realized (which, according to the Regulation, are "...").

It defined urban commons as "the tangible, intangible and digital goods that citizens and the City Administration also through participatory and deliberative procedures, recognize as functional for the individual and collective wellbeing, activating consequently towards them, pursuant to the art. 118, par. 4 of the Italian Constitution to share with the Administration the responsibility of their care or regeneration, to improve their collective enjoyment." (art. 2).

The central legal tool foreseen to establish public-community partnerships is the "pact of collaboration," entered into by local administration and some mix of city inhabitants, representative civic groups, local NGOs or foundations, and local businesses. The pacts are created through a co-design process, including public participation, contain a detailed description of the targeted project to co-manage or regenerate an urban resource, and define the project scope (including the duration and the respective roles and commitments of the actors involved). Finally, the Regulation also sets forth a liability and risk-sharing regime between the city and the community, as well as the forms of possible support from the city such as organizational and logistic support, fiscal incentives and direct funding, training and communication activities.

as a crucial condition for the development of responsive representative institutions. Robert D. Putnam, Robert Leonardi and Raffaella Nanetti, *Making democracy work: Civic traditions in modern Italy* (Princeton: Princeton University Press, 1993).

[30] "Per un'amministrazione condivisa dei beni comuni," Accessed July 14, 2020, www.fondazioneinnovazioneurbana.it/en/45-uncategorised/777-per-un-amministrazione-condivisa-dei-beni-comuni.

[31] Gregorio Arena and Christian Iaione, *L'Italia dei Beni Comuni* (Roma: Carocci, 2012).

[32] The English version of the Regulation is available at www.comune.bologna.it/media/files/bolognaregulation.pdf.

[33] Charles E. Lindblom, "Tinberg on Policy-Making," *Journal of Political Economy*, 66, 6 (1958): 531–538.

CODING THE PACTS OF COLLABORATION

The research presented here brings to light some of the challenges that cities might face in adopting and implementing a regulation like the one put in place by Bologna. We analyze the pacts according to four metrics: (1) the institutional "catchment area": the urban institutional level at which the pact is issued (neighborhood-level administration vs city-level administration); (2) implementation of public community partnerships; (3) type of activities undertaken as part of the pacts: ranging from acts of basic care of a resource to co-management to complex regeneration of spaces or buildings; and (4) whether the pact is aimed at generating economic revenues for its signatories or to re-distribute resources.

The empirical analysis was conducted in two phases. First, an analysis of the text of the pacts of collaborations (n. 280) plus other information about the pacts obtained from the *Iperbole* platform and through institutional reports and meetings.[34] Second, a survey (response rate to the questionnaire sent to the pacts' signatories via email of 28%) and group interview with a subset of signatories.

URBAN INSTITUTIONAL CATCHMENT AREA AND NEIGHBORHOODS AS KEY INSTITUTIONS

Overall, the majority of pacts were signed by a neighborhood level representative (i.e., the President of the Neighborhood) versus a municipal level representative (i.e., the Mayor) as figure 11.1 shows. The survey results show that 59% of Pacts signatories do not live in the neighborhood that is the subject of the Pact. This could suggest that the goal of the Pact is also to generate new professional relations and networking opportunities rather than improve or regenerate neighborhood assets.

IDENTIFYING PUBLIC COMMUNITY PARTNERSHIPS

One of the goals of the Regulation was to promote urban commons through multi-stakeholder partnerships. This goal is enshrined in articles 14 and 17 of the Regulation which addresses the

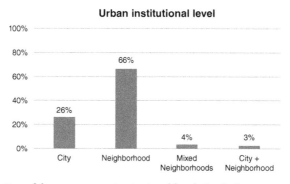

FIGURE 11.1 Distribution of the pacts across institutional levels (code frequency calculated on AV 280)

---

[34] Comune di Bologna, "Operational Manual for the implementation of the Regulation, 2015; Comune di Bologna, "Active Citizenship Report 2012-2016", Accessed June 30, 2020; www.comune.bologna.it/media/files/sintesi_20122016_delle_attivit_di_cittadinanza_attiva_.pdf; "Collaboration as a Method. Two Years of Collaboration Pact," November 30, 2016, https://issuu.com/comunedibologna/docs/report_patti_scenari_comunebologna; "From Ideas to Choices. Towards the Urban Innovation Plan," www.comune.bologna.it/news/dalle-idee-alle-scelte-il-piano-linnovazione-urbana-di-bologna.

co-governance of privately-owned buildings that could serve a "social function" or city-owned buildings. The regulation provides that the governance of these resources shall be multi-stakeholder and shall be institutionalized through the creation of NGOs, Neighborhood Foundations, cooperatives, or other legal entities.

To measure the implementation of co-governance we coded each pact using three categories: (a) bilateral pact (the partnership is composed by the city and only one of the following civic actors: an NGO, a local business); (b) multi-lateral pact (the partnership is composed of the city and different actors belonging to the same category: a group of residents, a group of NGOs); (c) multi-lateral and multi-stakeholder (the partnership is composed by the city and different actors, belonging to different categories, i.e. NGOs and businesses).

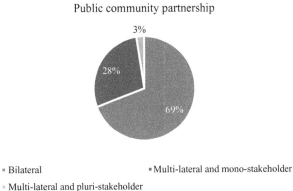

FIGURE 11.2 Public Community Partnership (percentage on AV 280)

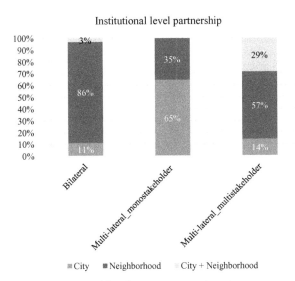

FIGURE 11.3 Institutional level across partnership (percentage on AV 280)

Our analysis of the survey results[35] gives rise to additional observations about implementation of the pacts. The Pact signatories are predominantly men (62%) who work with NGOs and – to a lesser extent – small private companies. Women constitute fewer signatories but represent a wider variety of organizations: informal groups, private companies, NGOs, Universities. Middle age individuals are much more likely to be signatories and represent a prevalence of women in their forties and men in their fifties. Pact signatories were born almost exclusively in Italy (95%, the remaining 5% comes from Germany and Hungary), including 62% in Bologna.

The analysis of the pacts reveals that most of the pacts involved a bilateral partnership, followed by multi-lateral, mono-stakeholder and public–private–civic partnerships (see figure 11.2). These results might be connected to the city's limited capacity or willingness to foster multi-stakeholder-cooperation at the time.

The chart included in figure 11.3 shows the relationship between the institutional level having signed the pact of collaboration and the type of partnership consequently formed.

OBJECT OF THE PACTS

The coding of type of intervention, included in figure 11.4, revealed that 56% of pacts involve activities of resource care, such as the removal of graffiti from a wall or the clean-up of a public street or park, or public events to raise awareness on environmental or civic issues. We also found that 22% of the pacts involve the co-management of spaces or buildings (long term – 1–3 years average,) to realize cultural and social activities such as artistic exhibitions, book sharing, the realization of a mural painting on a school's wall; workshops and laboratories to transfer creative, digital skills to neighborhood residents. Complex interventions of public space and/or building regeneration that include renovation works made up 22% of the pacts.

The majority of pacts were directed urban public spaces (i.e., squares) while only a minority (7%) were to regenerate buildings (see figure 11.5). Among the pacts that were directed towards urban regeneration projects, the majority were for the regeneration of a specific structure. The one exception of an urban regeneration project *not* involving a building was the *Bella Fuori* 3

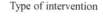

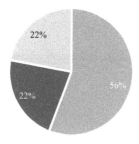

▪ Basic cure   ▪ CO-management   Urban Regeneration

FIGURE 11.4 Type of intervention (percentage AV 280)

---

[35] A detailed account of the Survey methodology and results is available in Ivana Pais and Elena De Nictolis, "Valutare una politica pubblica urbana sui beni comuni" in *La Co-Città*, edited by Paola Chirulli and Christian Iaione (Napoli: Jovene, 2018), 217.

Object of Intervention

· Urban Public Space   · Buildings

FIGURE 11.5 Object of Intervention (percentage on AV 280)

Interventions object/type

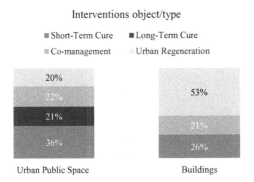

FIGURE 11.6 Interventions' object across type of intervention (percentage calculated on AV)

Partnership intervention

Multilateral Pluristakeholder (AV 7)

Multilateral Monostakeholder (AV 79)

Bilateral Pacts (AV 194)

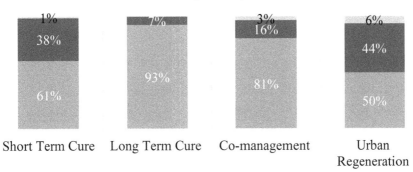

FIGURE 11.7 Partnership across type of intervention (AV 194, AV 79, AV 7)

pact, under which a not-for-profit Foundation promised to provide resources for an extensive renovation of an open square, *Piazza dei Colori*.

Multilateral and multi-stakeholder partnerships occurred more frequently in pacts for urban regeneration projects and less frequently in the pacts for care or co-management of an existing resource like a park or square (see figures 11.6, 11.7). This could be due to the fact that urban regeneration projects are more complex and challenging as they require the pooling of resources from different actors.

Economic Empowerment and Redistribution Goals.

To measure the objectives of economic empowerment and resources re-distribution, we coded pacts according to the goals defined by the Regulation: (1) *Urban quality*, defined as activities that improve the city's livability (art. 6); (2) *Urban creativity*, defined as the urban arts, creative experimentations (including mural art or street art; music; theatre) and artistic education carried out in urban public spaces as a tool to promote regeneration of blighted areas. (art. 8 of the Regulation); (3) *Social innovations and collaborative economy*, including the provision of neighborhood services that integrate local public services or meet critical community needs through legal tools such as housing or worker cooperatives (art. 7 of the Regulation) and which reinvest revenues in the community; (4) digital innovation, defined as the design and implementation of open digital infrastructures by city residents. (art. 9 of the Regulation).

We observe a high concentration of pacts (see figure 11.8) aimed at improving the quality of urban public space as described below.

As a means of improving public space, some pacts involved residents' efforts to restore green areas, streets or squares and organize cultural and social activities (see figure 11.8). An example is the *Paint Your Pumpkin* Pact, which involved participants cleaning up a park and creating a children's laboratory in collaboration with an environmental NGO. Similar pacts involve local businesses or city inhabitants committing to financially support the expansion of a sidewalk or the removal of architectural barriers by building a wheelchair ramp to facilitate access to a sidewalk.

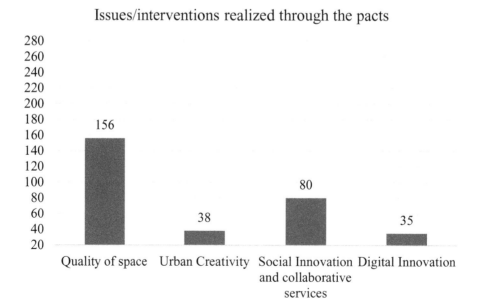

FIGURE 11.8 Issues analysis interventions realized through the pacts (code frequency, multiple codes)

In contrast, a smaller number of pacts (see figure 11.8) involved the promotion of social innovation and collaborative economy through collaborative economies (n.8). Collaborative economy pacts generate forms of collaborative economy through education, training for youth and migrants, coordination. The pacts signed, for instance, with the organization "Social streets" involve resident networks composed of neighbors who live on the same block and that help coordinate maintenance of their streets. The pact *Shared management of the Ex Serre Giardino Margherita* involved the cooperative Kilowatt's creation of a community garden inside of a neighborhood park that was designed to include an affordable co-working space. In the pact *Forever Ultras*, an NGO agreed to use its own resources to renovate and manage a city-owned building that offers socialization opportunities for elderly people through sports or artistic exhibitions as well as an archive of football-related materials. Another example is the pact *Piantala*, that created a circuit of circular economy, where an NGO collects unsold plants from hatcheries and distributes them to city residents that are willing to turn a dismissed green area into a community garden.

Areas Lacking in Implementation

We identify three key areas of potential activity for the collaborative care and management of shared urban resources that are lacking from signed pacts: (1) co-governance of the urban commons as a multi-stakeholder (public–private-community) partnership; (2) urban culture and creativity projects; (3) digital innovation, or community-based digital projects. The prevalence of bilateral partnerships, where the pact was signed by the City and a single actor, indicate a lack of true co-governance and the absences disintermediated peer to peer collaboration among communities, economic and knowledge actors in the city's ecosystem. As such, enabling collective action by promoting the creation of a polycentric system seems to be an ongoing challenge in the implementation of the pacts.

The majority of pacts for urban creativity are short term projects. They were not constructing new goods and services, although they were attempting at meeting the unmet needs of disadvantaged populations through arts. Examples are street art days organized in a public space (*Street Art Pact at the Zaccarelli Center*).

Finally, we note the failure of the Bologna regulatory implementation to promote the collaborative economy and digital innovation, important goals of the original policy from its inception. Few of the pacts are directed to bridge the digital divide or to empower marginal populations. Two notable exceptions are *Reducing digital divide*, a pact for a digital skills lab to serve local residents, and *OUTakes archive*, a pact to collect and digitize material linked to the LGBTQ movement's history.

Another missed opportunity in the implementation of the Bologna regulation is the absence of pacts to stimulate "pooling economies," which is an important aspect of collective and collaborative governance of urban resources.[36] The pacts in theory allow the city and city residents to pool resources: time, skills, communication and financial resources. Yet, we found that the total amount of financial resources invested by the pacts' civic signatories (including foundations and businesses) to be 480.180,27 € over a two-year period of time. The amount of financial resources invested by the City across the whole amount of pacts is 195.558,84 €. Although a deeper analysis is required to fully understand and evaluate the allocation of resources pursuant to this policy, there are some initial takeaways we can offer. On the one hand, the amounts demonstrate that the Regulation was able to stimulate private investment in

---

[36] Christian Iaione and Elena De Nictolis, "Urban Pooling," *Fordham Urban Law Journal*, 44, 665 (2017): 666–701.

urban commons. One the other hand, while the city's contribution was significant, it was distributed across many different pacts in small amounts, suggesting the lack of a transformative investment in any particular urban regeneration project.

Having examined the universe of signed pacts, we observe that there is a smaller group of pacts aimed at reducing economic inequality and promoting social and economic mobility through civic collaboration for urban commons. A particular group of pacts have as their aim to pursue social innovation and collaborative economies (i.e., *Bella Fuori 3 pact, HUB Underground base pact*). These pacts demonstrate a tendency toward complex regeneration projects involving land and buildings but predominantly they are not involving the kind of mix of actors that are likely to be able to support and sustain transformative urban commons.

Finally, although the large number of pacts is certainly a positive outcome of the Regulation, they lack a diversity of actors. Although there are some pacts signed by not-for-profit foundations, social enterprises, startups and businesses, the vast majority of pact signatories consist of NGOs or informal groups and are bilateral partnerships. This seems to bode well for strengthening *bonding social capital*, or relationships among community residents. However, the lack of actor diversity bodes poorly for strengthening bridging *social capital*, which can help pull disadvantaged populations from the social and economic margins into the core of the urban economy. In light of this analysis, implementation of the regulation has not been able to realize one of its aims; to reduce asymmetries in the concentration of power through enabling the construction and sustainability of governance devices for the urban commons.

CONCLUSION: NEIGHBORHOODS AS INSTITUTIONAL SPACES FOR CIVIC ENGAGEMENT AND SOCIAL/SOLIDARITY ECONOMIC UNITS.

Elinor Ostrom's research proved that the high dependence of local communities on community resources[37] is critical in activating collective action, including for urban commons. In cities where the community value of urban assets, spaces, services, infrastructures is based on knowledge, culture, recreation, data production, innovation, technology and growth, however, this is not enough to allow the flourishing of communities depending on such resources. It is a change in the political economy that is needed at the city level, including through the aggregation of social and economic partnerships and the creation of economic units that are cooperating rather than competing. These partnerships can promote forms of mutualism and community cooperation at the neighborhood level in order to reduce the impact of the transition from the industrial and knowledge economy to the data-based urban economy might have on its vulnerable inhabitants.

Our analysis of the historic Bologna regulation suggests that Bologna may have missed an opportunity to create multi-stakeholder partnerships and collective economic institutions at the neighborhood level and throughout the city, that are aimed at promoting sustainable and inclusive economic development in distressed areas of the city. These areas suffer from chronically insufficient funding or access to basic urban services and infrastructure and could benefit from robust urban commons. One of the lessons to be learned from the Bologna "experiment" is the importance of channeling public and private support toward neighborhood-level collective economic units and that grant collective rights of access, use, management and ownership to "social purpose vehicles" collectively incorporated, controlled, managed, and owned by city inhabitants.

---

[37] Nagendra and Ostrom, "Applying the social-ecological system framework to the diagnosis of urban lake commons in Bangalore, India," 9.

An important lesson from the Bologna experiment is that smaller-scale, sub-local (neighborhood/block) level urban commons implementation, coupled with an integrated city-wide policy dedicated to supporting urban commons, can scale-up to the city as a commons[38] if the City invests efforts in developing sustainability plans and capacity building. Other cities in Italy are working in this direction, such as for example Reggio Emilia (Emilia Romagna) with the policy "Neighborhood as a commons". Alessandro Antonelli, Elena De Nictolis and Christian Iaione, Neighborhood as a commons. Citizen participation in Neighborhood planning, Urbanmaestro. org, Accessed August 12, 2021, https://urbanmaestro.org/example/quartiere-bene-comune/.

The City of Turin (Piemonte) recently updated its "Regulation for Governing the urban commons", issued as a result of the experimentation carried out through an EU-funded Urban Innovative Actions project "Co-Cities". UIA.eu, Turin Co-City. The collaborative management of urban commons to counteract poverty and socio-spatial polarization, 2016, Accessed August 12 2021, https://uia-initiative.eu/en/uia-cities/turin.

Our analysis demonstrates that cities cannot create urban commons without significant action and collective efforts occurring at the neighborhood level. This entails the need for a city to invest on a policy strategy that targets neighborhoods, not only as spaces for civic engagement,[39] but as productive units of inclusive collective economic development. This investment must be implemented using design principles that ensure inclusiveness and that avoid the risks that commons institutions develop in exclusionary ways that serve the needs of narrow interests linked to the property value instead of linked to the urban quality of life of groups of inhabitants. As the chapter by Alexandra Flynn in this book shows, this is a risk present in some Business Improvement Districts (BIDs). This involves conceiving of and treating the city as an engine of inclusive economic development in which neighborhoods are spaces or platforms on which communities can identify common interests and begin to co-produce or co-manage services with centralized coordination.

---

[38] Christian Iaione, "The Tragedy of Urban Roads," *Fordham Urban Law Journal*, 37, 889 (2011); Sheila Foster, Sheila R. Foster, "Collective Action and the Urban Commons," *Notre Dame Law Review*, 87, 57 (2011).
[39] Robert. A. Dahl, "The City in the Future of Democracy." *American Political Science Review* 61, 4 (1967): 953–70.

12

Urban Commons Architecture

Collaboration Spaces Innovating Learning within Cities

Sofia Croso Mazzuco

INTRODUCTION

Traditionally, the culture of collaboration reflected on the hands-on practice of bottom-up architecture has always been a valuable part of the Brazilian culture. Its highest form of expression is defined as *mutirão*, which is a Brazilian term referring to collective work done in solidarity between community members. Nonetheless, during the last few decades, community collaboration in urban contexts has been largely associated with poverty. Due to the Brazilian government's inability for equitable provision, collaboration between community dwellers has been a matter of survival for those lacking access to the goods and services that are essential for human development (such as housing, education and healthcare), as in the context of informal settlements – some characterized as *favelas*. These are communities keen to engage in self-organized collaborative efforts to co-produce local services and architectural spaces but, sadly, their collective action is widely devalued as an informal response to gaps in urban welfare provision. Government inaction stimulating inner community collaboration as a means of survival is clearly not to be celebrated, and the admirable ability of citizens to engage in networked cooperation for the common good is lamentably being overlooked. Ideally, communities, governments and different sectors should work together in establishing collaborative urban governance – regardless of the economic context and across all social classes – to articulate collaboration at its best: one that leads to inclusive equitable prosperity and supported by legal/political frameworks that enable citizens' right and ability to co-create the city.

  In Brazil, urban dwellers' widespread misconception that collaboration can only result from, or equates to, scarcity and informality frustrates active citizenship[1] and participatory city-making. In this way, citizens leave the development of *their* cities to centralized control. In fact, Jane Jacobs was right: "[c]ities have the capability of providing something for everybody, only because, and only when, they are created by everybody".[2] Surely, deep urban inequalities persist partly as a consequence of the failure to robustly enact and enforce the "right to the city,"[3]

---

[1] *Active citizens* are city co-creators. They collaborate to enact the *right* and *responsibility* in making their city, by co-shaping spaces, services and interrelationships minding equitable prosperity.

[2] Jane Jacobs, *The Death and Life of Great American Cities* (New York: Random House, 1961) 238.

[3] The "right to the city," a concept by Henri Lefebvre, reclaims the city as a co-created space. Further developed, "[t]he right to the city is far more than the individual liberty to access urban resources: it is a right to change ourselves by changing the city. It is, moreover, a common rather than an individual right since this transformation inevitably depends upon the exercise of a collective power to reshape the processes of urbanization. The freedom to make and

which, as defined by Henry Lefebvre and articulated by David Harvey, entails citizens' *right* to actively "make and remake the city" in a way that ensures inclusion and equity.

At the international level, many citizens are asserting the *right* to participate in making their cities while innovative legal instruments, incentivized by enabling governments, encourage collaborative and collective urban governance,[4] and active citizenship. Supporting this movement is the advancement of "co-cities",[5] a concept developed by Sheila Foster and Christian Iaione that fosters innovative equitable urban development through collaboration including the following actors: (i) social innovators, (ii) public authorities, (iii) private companies, (iv) civil society organizations/ the third sector, and (v) knowledge institutions. They define this multi-sectoral approach as the *quintuple helix* of innovative urban governance of the *co-city*, in support of the "urban commons": spaces and resources co-created and co-governed through networked collaborative nuclei of active citizens engaged in the common good.[6]

The author's experience working on collaborative architecture in Brazil suggests that shifting the cultural perception of collaboration from a scarcity to an empowerment perspective is critical to encourage co-cities. Challengingly, the (not many) architects locally practicing collaborative city-making help shape and enlighten an architecture of the common good. Architectural landmarks, such as the Museum of Art of São Paulo (MASP) and SESC Pompeia, both designed by Lina Bo Bardi, in addition to the School of Architecture and Urbanism of the University of São Paulo (FAU-USP) by João Batista Vilanova Artigas, are spaces that resist undemocratic political authority whilst inspiring citizens to connect to each other. While Bardi valued architecture as "collective service and poetry"[7] and Artigas pursued "the capacity to reorganize society",[8] both have shaped collective mindsets through the strategic design of sheltered architectural spaces rendered empty in order to foster the spontaneous social interaction and knowledge co-production that occupy their voids; spaces that give voice and visibility to citizens.

Given that the lack of public space in Brazilian cities hinders qualities of citizenship and social connection and feeds individualism, architectures stimulating public life instigate exactly the opposite processes – being of immense social and political value. More particularly, architectural design can be tailored towards social interaction and collectivism for quality of life: "[f]irst we shape cities – then they shape us",[9] a crucial interrelationship, noted by Jan Gehl, which must be well harnessed for/within collaborative cities. Cities shaped *for* and *with* people shape citizens' belonging and awareness about their right to the city, instigating active citizenship and civic action. Thus, humane architecture compares to the common pool spaces in

---

remake our cities and ourselves is, I want to argue, one of the most precious yet most neglected of our human rights." David Harvey, in *The Right to the city* (2008) *New Left Review*, **II** (53): 23–40.

[4] Bologna, Barcelona, Seoul and Medellin exemplify innovative co-governance approaches.

[5] There are two types of urban governance rooted in sharing and collaboration. The "Sharing City", promoting sharing practices supported by local legal frameworks and The "Collaborative City", based on Ostrom's *commons* and on worldwide *urban commons* projects, is defined under five design principles: (i) collective governance, (ii) enabling state, (iii) social and economic pooling, (iv) experimentalism, and (v) tech justice. The Collaborative City differs with its methodological "co-city protocol": initially developed and experimented in Italy, it follows an iterative approach where "every field of experimentation has its unique aspects due to the specific characteristic of the city itself." *See* Sheila R. Foster & Christian Iaione, *The City as a Commons* (2016) 343, 345.

[6] Sheila R. Foster & Christian Iaione, 'Ostrom in the City: design principles and practices for the urban commons'. In *Routledge Handbook of the Study of the Commons*, ed. Blake Hudson, Jonathan Rosenbloom, Dan Cole (New York: Routledge, 2019) 235–255.

[7] *Lina Bo Bardi*. Directed by Aurélio Michiles. São Paulo: Instituto Lina Bo e P.M. Bardi, 1993.

[8] Richard J. Williams, *Brazil: Modern Architecture in History* (London: Reaktion books, 2012), 140.

[9] Jan Gehl, *Cities for People* (Washington, DC: Island Press, 2010), 9.

Ostrom's *commons*: abundant with beneficial resources (both tangible and relational/goods), they instigate collectivities to mold their ways of living, propelling the co-design of co-governance structures that enable equitable access to those resources that can foster prosperity.

Merging the virtuous principles and motivations animating the *urban commons* (the cornerstone of the *co-city*) and humane collaborative architecture, in this chapter I propose a definition of an architecture that serves the common good: *Urban Commons Architecture*. To be sure, this is an invaluable but complexly applied concept in need of a clear-cut definition which this chapter hopes to elucidate.

To start with, *urban commons architecture* involves a constellation of actors in line with the quintuple-helix approach to collaborative governance. The *urban commons architecture* projects presented in this chapter were initiated through an alliance between architects and NGOs that engage in the holistic (social-ecological-economic) restoration of urban environments. These two actors *facilitate* co-creation within communities and help tailor co-design strategies that enable local actors, processes and resources to instigate and support collective prosperity; they both also liaise with local municipalities to obtain approval and licenses for co-creation, stimulating the adoption of collaborative legal instruments. Project *facilitators* mutually learn with communities; in particular, architects and NGOs impart scientific knowledge about collaboration in order to stimulate communities to recognize and harness the richness of local knowledge and assets which can lead to enacting local co-governance. In this win-win process, all project actors exchange invaluable knowledge from site-specific planned or serendipitous interactions, thereby collectively generating even more knowledge to co-create innovative solutions to complex multidisciplinary urban matters. How well these site-specific interrelationships are cultivated, and how *active* citizens actually become throughout co-creation, can influence or even determine the evolution of each project and whether it furthers efforts towards a collaborative environment, or *co-city*.

To make tangible the central role that architecture's co-design plays in the creation of co-cities, this chapter presents two *urban commons architecture* projects at different scales. The first project, a public school, reflects the co-design of a single building; whilst the second contemplates co-designing across interconnected streets. Respectively, these projects are: *Escola dos Sonhos/Escola da Pedra Furada* ("School of Dreams"), co-designed by Sofia Croso Mazzuco and "Coletivo de Arquitetos", and *Caminhos da Escola* ("Paths for Education") by "Acupuntura Urbana". Both projects advance our understanding of how collaborative architecture (which, scaled up, includes urban-design) shapes active citizens – who are in fact the vital architects of *co-cities*.

This chapter will merge my experience on collaborative architecture and the urban commons with extensive literature on both, as well as community-based expertise, in order to create an informative framework for *urban commons architecture*. This framework encourages a process of experimentation with co-design, which includes: Engagement of Communities, Program Co-Design, Architecture Co-Design, Architecture Co-Crafting, and Creative Co-Governance. It is important that all steps in this process are tailored to local context, and never the result of a centralized actor. This is a process distinct from mainstream architectural practice where architects centralize project knowledge and design decisions; in contrast, the *urban commons architecture* framework dynamically encourages architects, communities and additional actors to *learn* from each other whilst co-producing innovative local solutions by means of collective knowledge. In this way, project actors *learn* active citizenship whilst engaging in invaluable *active* learning-produce, to directly enhance the quality of life of action spaces.

Given that they are experimental, the projects presented herein develop as *living-labs*. They are people-centered, site-specific innovation ecosystems providing fertile ground for the co-creation and shaping of co-design methodologies. Both projects fit the *co-city protocol*, which itself is based on a cycle/process consisting of: *cheap talking* (activating local actors), *mapping* (local networks and available resources), *practicing* (realizing co-generated ideas), *prototyping* (co-creating local polycentric governance), *testing* (evaluating the co-governance schemes prototyped), and *modeling* (feeding local and collaborative policy-making with iterated knowledge). Due to the lack of an "enabling" state in Brazil (considering that centralized governments are not yet aware of the great value of collaboration, sharing, and participation to urban governance and community development) the *testing* and *modeling* steps in both the projects discussed herein were fragile – but could, nonetheless, plant a seed for further development

The referenced projects raise awareness that the power of transforming cities and developing communities lies with *active* citizens; as such, they democratize architectural and educational practices by engaging citizens to learn civic action by practicing co-design. For that matter, citizens engagement in *urban commons architecture* requires tailored strategies to specific age groups: whilst adults must replace their possibly distorted vision of collaboration with a positive one to be active citizens, children may develop natural inclinations to collaborate through a sense of belonging and responsibility by participating in cities co-design since childhood. As educator Francesco Tonucci argues, children's early participation allows them to appreciate their *right to making and remaking the city* and, as a result, encourage collaboration among future generations: "[t]hey will feel they are citizens today and will get ready to change and look after their city".[10]

Project 1: Escola dos Sonhos ("School of Dreams")

Escola dos Sonhos/Escola da Pedra Furada is an *urban commons architecture* project that has been awarded by the Instituto de Arquitetos do Brasil[11] for harnessing co-design to serve a village affected by one of the lowest human-development indexes in Brazil (namely, a place characterized by strikingly low education, health, and per capita income indicators). The project, initially intended as a small extension of a municipal primary school, evolved into a broader intergenerational process of architectural co-creation through active learning.

Started in May 2018, and still ongoing, the project is set in the small village of Pedra Furada, in the city of Santa Luzia do Itanhy, in the state of Sergipe – on the warm and beautiful northeastern coast of Brazil. A couple of hours away from the capital Aracajú, it is a remote and quiet area next to a mangrove forest. Local inhabitants' lifestyle combines features of both rural and urban environments, embracing a gentle rural pace that facilitates social interaction and community building. Humble homes of *adobe* bricks and *taipa-de-mão*, both made with the village's red clay and with knowledge emanating from the vernacular/local architectural style, rise with beauty above raw streets of the same organic material (see Figure 12.1). These architectural features tell the story of the traditional community-driven effort *"mutirão"*, in which locals gather to collaboratively *craft* homes and to then celebrate with music, dancing and *churrasco*. This solidary tradition of collective action combined with the prescribed use of locally-sourced materials and construction knowledge is the backbone of the approach to the architectural co-design of *Escola dos Sonhos*.

[10] Francesco Tonucci and Antonella Rissotto, *Why do we Need Children's Participation* (Journal of Community and Applied Social Psychology:11, 2001) 8. www.researchgate.net/publication/227725316_Why_Do_We_Need_Children's_ Participation_The_Importance_of_Children's_Participation_in_Changing_the_City

[11] *Escola dos Sonhos/Escola da Pedra Furada* won the prize of best project by the *Instituto de Arquitetos do Brasil (IAB)*, under the architectural category "institutional building - project" of the award ceremony *iabsp 2018 "especial 75 anos"*.

FIGURE 12.1 *Urban Commons Architecture* steps

FIGURE 12.2 Traditionally, the local red earth defines the village's architecture

Escola dos Sonhos' co-design vision was originally conceived by the architecture team[12] in a partnership with a local NGO that, on behalf of the local community, signaled to the municipality the need for an improved school. This collaboration network then gradually expanded to involve a quintuple helix of sectors. The NGO's experience engaging local actors for innovative learning projects was an advantage to the project team; it helped liaise between the local community and the municipality, while influencing, in addition to the project's approval, the municipality granting the land to *Escola dos Sonhos* by proposing a "Collaboration Pact".[13] The Collaboration Pact is a legal instrument that supports collaboration between municipalities and communities in social service provision, most likely inspired by embrace of those pacts in the innovative "Bologna Regulation for the care and regeneration of Urban Commons"[14] – which inspired the development of the *co-cities* framework. Like the Bologna pacts, the project also received public grants and financing from private institutions to support multi-stakeholder collaboration.

The *urban commons architecture* framework guiding the school's architecture co-design embodies the international discourse on "[h]ow can individual practitioners start to describe new territories of knowledge from which to branch off into new fields of practice?"[15] Specifically, the framework's steps transform the mainstream architectural practice of top-down design centralization into an investigative/iterative bottom-up creation process – where collaboration sources knowledge co-production whilst innovating (with) networked solutions, and reaffirming that "ontological practice as a mode of knowledge production stresses the importance of learning and questioning rather than knowing and presupposing".[16]

The collaborative architecture stages of *Escola dos Sonhos* ensure that the school's learning agenda goes beyond the static classroom space and permeates all its active co-design and co-construction processes, creating sharing opportunities grounded on hands-on peer-to-peer knowledge, which also foster locals in creating a new and collaborative economy[17].

The first stage of the school's architectural co-design process occurred during three multi-sector stakeholders workshops that provided a common ground for co-creation, facilitated by the architecture team with support of architecture students. Stakeholders involved members of the locally active NGO, local municipality representatives, directors of an innovative anthroposophical school, and the local community. Adults and children from the community actively participated both as clients and as *joint-architects*, playing a dual role characteristic of communities in *urban commons architecture*, whilst contributing to the creative design process with invaluable local knowledge. The community given name, *Escola dos Sonhos* (e.g., "School of Dreams"), alludes to the dream of building a school based on the community's needs for flourishing – finally coming true.

---

[12] Sofia Croso Mazzuco, Rodrigo Carvalho Lacerda and Guile Canhisares Amadeu envisioned and structured the school's co-design approach. Later on, Gustavo Fontes and other architects joined the architectural project development.

[13] "Art. 1st This Law institutes the legal regime for partnerships between public administration and civil society organizations under the regime of mutual cooperation, for the consecution of finalities of public and reciprocal interest, by the execution of activities or projects previously set forth in work plans agreed upon in terms of collaboration, terms of support or cooperation agreements ..." Law 13, 204 / 2015.

[14] See www.comune.bologna.it/media/files/bolognaregulation.pdf

[15] Markus Miessen. *Crossbenching: Toward Participation as Critical Spatial Practice.* (Berlin: Sternberg Press, 2016), 59.

[16] Miessen, *Crossbenching*, 58.

[17] The school's architecture co-design minds that "shared amenities can be a way to foster social inclusion if they are used as places or means for people to learn skills, obtain access to jobs opportunities, socialize, and to access social services that increase economic inclusion and urban livability." *See* Sheila R. Foster & Christian Iaione, *The City as a Commons* (2016), 340.

The Co-Design Workshops unfolded as follows:

- Workshop 1: *Curriculum Co-Design*. By mapping local learning needs and long-term goals of the community, project actors co-designed a tailored curriculum including: *integrated learning* (mind, body, and soul), *social cohesion and ecological ethics*. Considering *active learning-produce* linked to economic development, an insightful possibility was co-envisioned: having the community establish a co-operative business honoring the traditional local architecture – thus harnessing available resources (raw material and knowledge) to maximize local development and capture value, while minimizing architecture's ecological footprint. The new school building will be the co-operative's first client – absorbing local construction know-how, including locally-crafted *adobe* bricks and *taipa de mão* – in effect, supporting a *pooling economy*: "(...) practices of 'collaborative economy' that foster peer-to-peer approaches and/or involve users in the design of the productive process or transform users into a community".[18]
- Workshop 2: *Architecture Co-Design*. The architecture team led an architecture class emphasizing how the place based co-creation of spaces and learning opportunities stimulates communities to flourish. During the next step the community prototyped the co-design of their dream school, conceiving the relationship between school curriculum and spaces into three different architectural models; the architecture team was supportive without interfering in the design decisions.

Assimilating the output from Workshops 1 and 2, the architecture team integrated the community's collectively produced ideas as the cornerstone of the detailed architecture project,

FIGURE 12.3 Children co-designing their *School of Dreams*

---

[18] Foster & Iaione, *The City as a Commons*, 342.

FIGURE 12.4 The local community prototyping the school's architecture with
support of the project's architects

which was then carried out reliably in the architects' office space by combining community
empirical wisdom and architectural *scientific know-how*, a knowledge combination which gives
power and strength to collaborative projects.

- Workshop 3: *Detailed architecture presentation & design of Creative Co-Governance*. The
  architects presented the further developed architectural project for community review – depicted
  in illustrations, technical drawings and a cardboard model. Feeling that their vision had been
  well incorporated, the community expressed, with emotion, great pride in the outcome. Next,
  community members were invited to gather into discussion groups in order to address key topics
  in which they were either interested or had experience, to begin planning for the school's co-
  construction and co-governance through the application of local knowledge. This proposed co-
  design/co-creation exercise innovates architectural practice whilst honoring the local tradition of
  mutirão. Putting it into practice for the school co-construction, workshops with experts on
  different construction techniques were then planned to be guided be guided by community
  members (and by external experts who bring additional knowledge), thus collectively producing
  the materials and structures contemplated in the co-designed architecture project.

"It relies upon its different members".

Escola dos Sonhos' architectural project (also referred to as *Escola da Pedra Furada)* having won
an important prize by Brazil's leading architecture institution (IAB), affirms that the architecture
of collaboration is openly being valued and will, hopefully, bring about a significant shift in
mainstream architectural practice towards human flourishing.

FIGURE 12.5 Community art-piece comparing collaboration to a healthy body: it relies upon its different members

ENGAGEMENT STRATEGIES FOR *ESCOLA DOS SONHOS*

The engagement tactics applied in the co-design workshops by the architecture team combine tailored group dynamics and different collaborative methodologies adapted to the project.[19] The children were notably fascinated by the playful engagement activities – and so were the adults.

A key obstacle to engagement, however, was the mistrust of the community arising from past municipal development projects; reflecting on previous experience, many felt strongly that community-based projects might not be prioritized. Another obstacle that arose, this time in communication during the workshops facilitation, was the distinctive accent spoken by the architects originating from São Paulo; the difference in accents inhibited deeper engagement of some community members who worried about possible misinterpretation given their local Brazilian-Portuguese accent. Understanding this obstacle prompted the architecture team to encourage the local architects to guide the discussions in order to ensure an easier connection, free of language barriers, was being made with the community.

To further refine communication strategies for the project, the architecture team thought it important to confirm whether the community had fully understood the further developed architectural design in the way it was depicted in workshop 3 – namely, via traditional illustrations, technical drawings and a cardboard model. We realized that, although the community was satisfied with the project approach and look, they could not read the technical architectural drawings with ease. The architecture team has since come to the realization that *urban commons architecture* must be supported by innovative and easy to grasp project representation, which

---

[19] The collaborative methodologies collaged include: *Design Thinking, U Theory, Cooperative Games, Dragon Dreaming, Elos Methodology,* and *Pedagogy of Cooperation.*

FIGURE 12.6 Illustration of *Escola dos Sonhos'* lively patio

means being capable of better engaging communities in project co-creation. Such innovative means of representation can include emergent tools, including virtual reality programs that take viewers into designed spaces, together with multiple alternative illustrations that allow non-architects to grasp space easily. The challenges in communication have demonstrated the importance of aligning the spoken/verbal language and the architectural language with the local language of communities for co-design practices.

Another impediment to project flow was a financing delay that has slowed down the school's co-construction workshops, intended to follow the co-design workshops, and thus negatively impacting the community engagement process. This process unfolds best when part of a continuous dynamic process – one that is central to collaborative projects. Although slower than intended, and with a few adaptations, the dreamed project is inching towards its realization.

Project 2: *Caminhos da Escola* ("Paths for Education")

Caminhos da Escola is a project based on the Educating City and the Educating Neighborhood initiatives. Their founding document, *The Charter of Educating Cities*, developed in 1990 in Barcelona is intended to defend "equality for all, social justice, and territorial balance." It encourages multi-sector collaboration and citizens' "civic co-responsibility," regarding children also as citizens with "full civic and political rights." Moreover, the document articulates how "[t]he educating city constantly recommits to the lifelong education of its inhabitants in its most varied ways,"[20] including through its architecture and urban design elements and the ways that they impact how individuals and communities develop.

[20] In www.edcities.org/en/charter-of-educating-cities/

Following these principles, the project "Paths for Education" fosters collaboration as an educational urban development strategy, operating on multiple social and architectural levels whilst having children's participation at its core. Tailored for a neighborhood in the city of Campinas (state of São Paulo) with many schools, nurseries and civic associations, the project encourages locals to: (i) co-create a collaborative network that attends to children's sense of belonging and educational urban experience, and (ii) co-transform the neighborhood's urban and social environments into an ecosystem of mentors and guardians to cultivate active citizenship and public life.

The project was born from a partnership between a local NGO and the social impact enterprise *Acupuntura Urbana*, which has brought together a multidisciplinary architecture-facilitation team including myself (the chapter's author), two additional architects and an educator, all engaged in project co-design and implementation. We have tailored and further developed the existing *"Educate and Transform"* hands-on methodology (by the same enterprise), collaboratively applying it with local learning institutions and community members.

An existing self-organized group of local institutions has proven advantageous for project development. The architecture-facilitation team helped clarify possible roles and social dynamics for strengthening collaborative local development, at first facilitating constructive conversations with players expressing genuine visions of neighborhood improvement and, next, stimulating these visions to become united around a *common* vision. After initial community engagement, the project followed five collaborative/collective phases: co-mapping, open-air workshops, public space co-design, hands-on transformation, and co-governance agreements.

The *co-mapping* phase involved four different layers. First, the architecture team mapped the neighborhood's urban interaction patterns, identifying public spaces located in or near learning institutions, where open-air educational activities and spontaneous community interaction

FIGURE 12.7 Children co-mapping by their enriching gaze, familiarizing the architects-facilitators with the neighborhood. Image: *Acupuntura Urbana* archive

could be ignited or intensified. The second layer included mapping the paths walked daily by children from their homes to their respective learning institutions. For the third layer, children guided the architecture-facilitation team along these routes whilst indicating unique aspects of them and ways in which the neighborhood open spaces could be redesigned to contemplate children's basic right to walk in safety – and, by addressing children's urban inclusion, also support their belonging, civic participation and learning opportunities.

The fourth mapping layer involved the local institutions' representatives playing a card game designed by the architecture-facilitation team. The "Game of Local Knowledge"[21] features cards with questions triggering urban social interactions to reveal something about a place, and to stimulate players to chat with local businesses owners and long-term community dwellers who have abundant knowledge of the locality. This card game addresses specific themes including: cultural values, traditional children's games, culinary preferences, urban mobility, local narratives, patrimony, technology, and natural environment.[22] Those playing the game discovered a myriad of stories during empathic conversations that nurtured *affection* – a bonding element vital to humane places. The game was later adopted as part of the institutions' pedagogical curriculum to embrace community building and local knowledge as essential learning.

The "Festival of Local Knowledge," a learning event co-created with local institutions (also to stimulate social cohesion), involved open-air workshops led by community members. Workshops on cooking, plant cultivation, magic tricks, recycling processes, and wall painting were hosted in different homes and throughout the neighborhood's public spaces, supporting collective acknowledgement of the wide array of local resources, skills, and sharing spaces. Ultimately, learning beyond the school grounds proved to exponentially enrich the institutions' curriculum and empower community members, particularly for those leading the workshops who recognized their skills worth sharing for the common good.

Public spaces were co-designed by way of the "Meeting of Dreams" = firstly, the institutions' students, among others, co-designed ten public spaces whilst depicting them into architectural models; and secondly, they have listed the availability of skills and resources in the neighborhood to co-build these spaces.

To secure legal approval for the resulting co-designed plaza, green wall, artistic murals, sidewalks with floor games (such as hopscotch), and music walls, the architecture-facilitation team submitted technical architectural drawings to the local municipality. After a series of challenging meetings, the municipality finally granted approval and offered part of the needed construction materials, in addition to hands-on support.

Community skills were made more evident in the hands-on "Transform Festival". Given that festivals are effective in engaging communities for strengthening socializing and learning opportunities, this event encouraged high intergenerational participation in the playful and emotional co-transformation of the co-designed public spaces. The pure action of painting a wall or a sidewalk through collective action paid off in the shine that children's eyes displayed from a deep sense of "*right*" and belonging. Given the chance to act and become part of the change, these children understood that that was *their city*. Confidently, we can predict that when all children are granted such an opportunity, there will be widespread active citizenship in the upcoming generations.

---

[21] *Game of Local Knowledge* available in Portuguese at: https://issuu.com/sofiacrosomazzuco/docs/baralho_saberes_locais_by_smazzuco_au_ce

[22] The mapping themes were inspired by Alana Institute, a non-profit civil society organization that seeks to safeguard the conditions necessary for the integral experience of childhood.

FIGURE 12.8 Children practicing active citizenship and belonging. Image: *Acupuntura Urbana* archive

Besides the children, local businesses particularly benefited from the lively, colorful, and playful public spaces and urban paths which inspired more locals to contribute to the collaborative transformation of these places. A wider network of local businesses and institutions united to support children in their roundabouts with water, food, or simply attention to different needs; on their walls they now display a sticker that reads *Ponto Amigo* ("a Friendly Spot"), designed as part of the project so that the children could easily identify this support.

To sustain this collaborative energy flow, local co-governance agreements were initially co-created with support of the architecture-facilitation team. "*Paths for Education*" kept evolving beyond the formal project's conclusion with the community tackling new challenges while sensitively cultivating the *educating neighborhood* as a common good.

ENGAGEMENT STRATEGIES FOR *CAMINHOS DA ESCOLA*

Connecting the project agenda to the institutions' curriculum without requiring many additional work or study hours resulted in high and intergenerational community engagement. In addition, allying the project with trusted institutions in the community helped to reinforce the importance of local collective action. A big lesson learned is that community engagement in collaborative transformation follows (and mirrors) the establishment of *trust* between project actors.

ENGAGEMENT INSIGHTS FROM *ESCOLA DOS SONHOS AND CAMINHOS DA ESCOLA*

The above case studies reveal that, in *urban commons architecture*, community engagement strategies are correlated with healthy doses of trust and *affection*. Although *affection* might sound misplaced within scientific urban discourse, in Brazil affection is regarded as a central element in methodologies for urban collaboration. To be specific, empirical research from a Brazilian institute (IPCCIC) aimed at mapping principles for a humane city, affection, or "love," has been identified by citizens as a needed "pedagogical attitude" – that is, held essential to learn, co-create, and nurture humane cities – whilst also regarded as the foundation of ethical concern and transformative decision-making: "[t]he human being will only be placed first, if Love, as a pedagogical attitude, permeates all political spheres".[23] As such, affection (in its purest form) supports fraternity, solidarity and positive shifts, promoting environments able to foster sharing and collaboration. From this perspective, *affection* is one of the seven steps of the hands-on Elos Methodology,[24] which encourages individuals and communities to actively enact collaboration.

Cultivating affection is simple and powerful: it can start from nurturing empathic conversations and may lead to harvesting collaboration.

The *urban commons architecture framework* is sensible to place-based differences and local knowledge, and so must always be tailored to each action community (honoring Ostrom's finding of *commons'* governance adapting to local context – principle 2). Throughout this process, the cultivation of affection within communities is essential for all project actors and by all means, since it has the capability of connecting people and spur collaborative engagement.

Regarding engagement beyond community space on both the projects discussed herein, the responsible architecture-facilitation teams and NGOs proved well placed to bridge the wide gap between communities and local governments, partly dissolving the mistrust-disregard dynamic that characterized the relationship between them. Although the interaction with government officials has proven as complex as anticipated, the resulting presence and legal approval for collaborative interventions on local public spaces hopefully indicates a step forward towards the *co-city* agenda while encouraging public officials to engage with polycentric co-governance.[25]

CONCLUSION

With the goal of creating equitable and prosperous cities, this chapter described an architecture rooted in the principles of the urban commons: *Urban Commons Architecture*. This framework encourages multi-sector collaboration and active citizenship, both via its co-design process and resulting (collective and co-governed) architectural spaces.

Urban Commons Architecture is complex and multidisciplinary. It encourages citizens to simultaneously collaborate on spatial/architectural, social, political, economic, and ecological solutions to guide an *active learning-produce* process and fuel the shift towards collaborative or *co-cities*. This shift requires citizens to learn a new language together with its innovative

---

[23] Instituto Paulista de Cidades Criativas e Identidades Culturais, *6 Passos Para a Cidade Humana*, ed. Kathia Castilho e Solange Pelinson (Barueri, SP: Estação das Letras e Cores, 2019), 32.

[24] By Brazilian NGO Instituto Elos, *Elos Methodology* steps are: Gaze, *Affection*, Dream, Care, Miracle, Celebration, Re-evolution.

[25] It is crucial to clarify that polycentric co-governance is not intended to "(. . .) supplant the local government's role over that resource. We might understand these groups as supplementing, not supplanting, the goods and services that local government traditionally provides." Sheila Foster, *Collective action and the urban commons*, 87 Notre Dame L. Rev.57 (2013), 109.

vocabulary: the language of collaboration and (to voice it playfully) its accompanying *collabolary* – as I define herein, *collaboration's vocabulary*. Collectively mastering this language requires both on-the-ground/empirical and scientific knowledge, and utmost, the affection that supports its humanity. Ideally, we would learn these attributes beginning in childhood, and through playful experiences, that would facilitate the natural flow of collaboration to the creation of flourishing communities.

Honoring the fact that collaboration at best is playful and dynamic, *urban commons architecture* only prospers by means of lively urban social interactions; it cannot be learned in a centralized classroom/office setting. This clearly challenges static and concentrated knowledge systems whilst aligning to the infinite creative possibilities sprouting from serendipitous interactions in every community. Namely, *urban commons architecture* asks architects and communities to embark upon a peer-to-peer pedagogical journey that inspires the emergence of *active* citizens who seize the *right* to shape innovative spaces and multiple polycentric collaborations that create, genuinely, *comum-unidades*[26] – precisely, "common-unities" in the Brazilian-Portuguese *collabolary*.

---

[26] Fábio Brotto, founder of *Projeto Cooperação*. See www.projetocooperacao.com.br/

PART V

Reassessing Old and New Institutions for Collective Action

13

Business Improvement Districts and the Urban Commons

Alexandra Flynn

The word 'city' comes from the Latin *cīvitās*, meaning a highly organized community – something that has existed almost as long as human history.[1] Many of these urbanized communities make critical decisions for the vast numbers of people living within their boundaries through city councils that serve as the 'legislatures' of city decision-making. In addition to city councils, residents and businesses are also represented by associations that seek a decision-making role in local matters. One example is a Business Improvement District (BID). These neighbourhood-based bodies, which are most commonly located in downtown areas and otherwise scattered unevenly across cities, are formed through a city bylaw that permits the levying of a tax on member businesses and property owners, which can amount to millions of dollars per year. BIDs also have a powerful voice in planning and politics as a representative organization of local businesses. There is wide debate in the academic literature as to whether BIDs should be considered lobbyists for businesses, enablers of local action, or an arm of the city government. The existence and oversight of BIDs raise important questions about whose interests are given priority in city governance. Delegating power to localized bodies, generally speaking, has negative effects for racial and ethnic minorities, as well as low-income populations. BIDs are specifically critiqued as exacerbating space-based tensions in relation to historically disadvantaged residents.[2]

The term "urban commons" has no uniform definition or agreed upon principles, and is used in a wide range of disciplines.[3] The city is an especially interesting setting for commons debates, as it is "not a frictionless agglomeration of commoners, but rather a site for ongoing contestation about what counts as a common and who counts as commoners."[4] The notion of the urban commons suggests that, regardless of whether spaces are privately or publicly owned, the city is a territorial space in which citizens claim to have a role or stake, a norm that is reinforced in law. The conversation about the urban commons is relevant where multiple bodies claim to have rights to govern within an urban context, and centers on discussions pertaining to how such claims are mediated and by whom.

---

[1] René Maunier, "The Definition of the City," *American Journal of Sociology*, 15, no. 4 (1910): 536.
[2] Gabriella Schaller & Susanna Modan, "Contesting Public Space and Citizenship Implications for Neighborhood Business Improvement Districts," *Journal of Planning Education and Research*, 24, no. 4 (2005): 394.
[3] Maja Hojer Braun, "Communities and the commons" in Christian Borch and Martin Kornberger, eds., *Urban Commons: Rethinking the City* (Routledge, 2015): 154.
[4] Christian Borch & Martin Kornberger, *Urban Commons: Rethinking the City* (Routledge, 2015): 15.

This chapter contributes to existing work that bridges two rich scholarly conversations by examining the role that BIDs play in city governance and their relationship to the urban commons.[5] The first section summarizes the existing literature on the scope and meaning of the urban commons: what do we mean by the governance of the "urban commons," and how do BIDs fit into this scheme? Section two contends that decision-making, representation, and accountability should be used as factors in evaluating urban commons institutions. Third, the chapter concludes that, instead of framing BIDs as singular bodies capable of managing a common pool resource within the city, scholars should insist on inclusive decision-making, representation, and accountability as necessary elements of the urban commons, including BIDs.

CONCEPTUALIZING THE URBAN COMMONS

Scholars exploring the meaning of the commons and its implications for urban centres generally reference the works of Garrett Hardin and Elinor Ostrom, the grandparents of contemporary notions of the commons. Hardin, a biologist, claimed that coercive, centralized government regulation is necessary to avoid the overuse and exploitation of commons resources as individual parties do not have a vested interest to conserve or sustainably use the resource, which inevitably leads to depletion and destruction.[6] Hardin ominously called this the "tragedy of the commons." Free-riders will take advantage of the unrestricted nature of the good or land and, because there are no consequences to this abuse, the common property will ultimately fall into disrepair.

Elinor Ostrom critiqued Hardin's claims among other reasons on the basis of governance.[7] She asserted that a commons is not solely a single resource, as Hardin saw it. She argued that it is a resource *plus* the social community and its corresponding values, rules, and norms that are used to manage or govern the resource. In her book, *Governing the Commons*, for which she won the Nobel Prize in 1999, Ostrom offered real-world examples of the management of common goods such as fisheries, land irrigation systems, and farmlands.[8] Identifying a number of factors conducive to successful resource management using a mix of private and public instruments, she argued that the tragedy of the commons could be avoided.

Three characteristics of the urban commons are especially relevant to the role of BIDs in local governance: scale, ownership, and governance. First, the urban commons may represent the city as a whole, but also micro-spaces within a municipality, e.g., public streets, public parks, and any public and neighbourhood amenities. Boavetura de Sousa Santos offered an analogy between maps and law by distinguishing between "large scale" and "small scale." A large-scale map shows less land but far more detail ("a miniaturized version of reality") and small-scale land, showing relative positions, but ultimately less detail.[9] To Santos, the specific scale to be studied results in

[5] Sheila R. Foster, *Collective Action and the Urban Commons*, 87 *Notre Dame Law Review* 57 (2013); and Garnett, Nicole Stelle, Managing the Urban Commons (November 14, 2011). Essay for the November 2011 University of Pennsylvania Law Review Symposium on "New Dimensions in Property Theory" 160 University of Pennsylvania Law Review 1995 (2012); Notre Dame Legal Studies Paper No. 11–44.

[6] Garrett Hardin, "The Tragedy of the Commons," *Science*, 162, no. 3859 (1968): 1243–1248.

[7] Elinor Ostrom, *Governing the Commons: The Evolution of Institutions for Collective Action* (Cambridge University Press, 1990). See also Lee Anne Fennell, "Ostrom's Law: Property Rights in the Commons," *International Journal of the Commons*, 5, no. 1 (2011): 9.

[8] Elinor Ostrom, James Walker, & Roy Gardner, "Covenants With and Without a Sword: Self-Governance Is Possible," *American Political Science Review*, 86, no. 2 (1992): 404.

[9] Boaventura de Sousa Santos, "Law: A Map of Misreading – Toward a Postmodern Conception of Law" (1987) 14 J.L. & Soc'y 281 at 458.

a different kind of analysis. The urban commons, too, exists at different scales. Sheila Foster and Christian Iaione asserted that, regardless of whether spaces are privately or publicly owned, the city is a territorial space in which citizens have a role or stake. Nicholas Blomley argued that an urban commons may include specific and discrete buildings within which squatting occurs.[10] BIDs lie within micro spaces of a city; in some cases, only a few city blocks and in others larger geographies, but in all cases smaller than the city itself. A focus on BIDs allows for an analysis of the very specific effects of these bodies on urban governance and an understanding of how they fit within notions of the urban commons.

Second, ownership is not the only type of property interest in a resource, whether public or private. While the language of the urban commons is also linked to categorizations within property law, the urban commons challenges the four traditional property categories: private, common, public, and non-property or open access. In particular, common property complicates the idea of private interest in land and, in so doing, recognizes shared uses among many users without necessarily having divided lines, hierarchical interests, or the capacity to exclude. Urban commons scholars echo critiques that "black letter" notions of property law are overly simplistic, omit notions of belonging, disregard obligations to third-party non-interest holders, and undermine Indigenous conceptions of property, to name just a few challenges. BIDs do not have any of the management tools that accompany private ownership, the right to exclude outsiders and establish formal governance rules yet play a central role in administering the common pool resource.[11]

A third characteristic of the urban commons especially relevant to BIDs concerns the governance of the urban commons. Foster and Iaione equate urban commons with particular urban spaces that are collaboratively managed or governed. The city as commons is thus a system of governance over particular urban spaces, which incorporates *subsidiarity*, or delegated authority, and *polycentrism*, which refers to multiple parties working together. Institutions are meant to protect and enhance shared resources in a city, and land use regulations are seen as a way to improve utility or value within an urban landscape. If a local government does not manage urban spaces appropriately for whatever reason, regulatory slippage can occur, whereby the resource is degraded in value or attractiveness for other types of users and uses.[12] Put simply, the common pool resource of the city may be overseen by a variety of actors, with the resulting governance and involvement of multiple actors as the core characteristic in a commons analysis. This is sometimes called "bottom-up governance" – making room for co-partners or co-collaborators who use and have a stake in the commons.[13] BIDs, as explored in the next section, have been described as bodies that manage or govern common urban resources. I argue that they should be understood as one of many stakeholders in a multisector, multi-actor governance approach.[14]

EVALUATING BIDS: RELATIONSHIP TO CITY GOVERNMENT, INCLUSIVITY, AND REPRESENTATION

BIDs play a pivotal and often positive role in local public realm management, through their financing and coordinating of public improvements, as well as the provision of other local services.

---

[10] Nicholas Blomley, "Enclosure, common right, and the property of the poor," *Social and Legal Studies*, 17 (2008): 318.
[11] Garnett, 2016.
[12] Tara Lynne Clapp & Peter B Meyer, "Managing the Urban Commons: Applying Common Property Frameworks to Urban Environmental Quality," *Constituting the Commons: Crafting Sustainable Commons in the New Millennium, the Eighth Biennial Conference of the International Association for the Study of Common Property* (May 31–June 4, 2000): 1–2.
[13] Sheila Foster, 57.
[14] Foster & Iaione, 289.

BIDs benefit from these actions by increasing business activity and, in some cases, revitalizing deteriorated neighbourhoods. BIDs can also bring together multiple stakeholders and broker partnerships, particularly in mid-sized cities.[15] At the same time, BIDs are not always transparent or inclusive, and represent only the narrow interests of their members, not the wider public, thus undermining democratic values.

The first BID was designed in Toronto in 1970. In the late 1960s, a small group of business leaders wanted to create a form of business association that would circumvent the "free-rider problem," whereby improvements by a small set of business owners would also advantage those who did not pay or otherwise contribute. Local business leaders believed that a stable and effective funding source would help a group of businesses with beautification and improvement, promote urban business areas, and ultimately allow them to regain market share. Now exported to thousands of cities across the world, the organizational form has not changed substantially in the five decades that followed.[16] BIDs provide a specific set of powers to business and property owners to achieve their mandate, most notably an organizational structure and direct access to the local councillors who serve on their boards.[17] Funding is collected through a levy against local property owners or businesses, which functions as a form of taxation. BIDs differ in size and budget depending on their locations and members.

RELATIONSHIP TO CITY GOVERNMENT

BIDs exacerbate the tension in the line between "public" or "private" governance. They are not simply private actors seeking additional power and do not fit easily within particular descriptions as exclusionary or inequality-enhancing: they are complex organizations that resist simple categorization. BIDs are uneasily classified as private and public because city taxation schemes secure funding and tie the organizations to the city, although some BIDs do not consider themselves governmental institutions, but rather part of the private sector.

Many BIDs provide useful services and programs that would ordinarily be the responsibility of municipal governments, like security, sanitation, physical improvements, beautification, social services, and business-oriented programs, although services vary significantly depending on the urban area in question. Some BIDs also play a substantially more proactive role in local governance and administration by establishing policy partnerships with local governments. Nathaniel Lewis found that as BIDs become service providers, development brokers and place makers, there is a corresponding retreat of municipal government.[18] Functions may also differ based on BID size: in New York, smaller BIDs focus on physical maintenance, mid-sized ones focus on marketing and promotional activities, and the large ones take care of a massive range of activities, including capital improvements.[19] At the same time, BIDs do not own the common property (e.g., city sidewalks) and must act within the scope of the enabling legislation, although it is unclear how much oversight occurs in practice.[20]

[15] Audrey Jamal, "From Operational to Aspirational? Business Improvement Areas (BIAs) in Mid-Sized Cities," *Planning Practice & Research*, 33:5 (2018), 506–522; Randy Lippert & Mark Sleiman, "Ambassadors, Business Improvement District Governance and Knowledge of the Urban," *Urban Studies* 49:1 (2012): 61–76, 62.
[16] City of Toronto, *City of Toronto Municipal Code*, s. 170–70.
[17] Gerald E. Frug, "The Seduction of Form," *Drexel Law Review*, 3, n. 1 (2010).
[18] Nathaniel M Lewis, "Grappling with Governance: The Emergence of Business Improvement Districts in a National Capital," *Urban Affairs Review*, 46, no. 2 (2010): 180.
[19] Lorlene Hoyt & Devika Gopal-Agge. "The Business Improvement District Model: A Balanced Review of Contemporary Debates," *Geography Compass*, 1, no. 4 (2007): 946, 949.
[20] Foster, 124.

In Toronto, BIDs are embedded within the city's bureaucratic structure, which offers professional, operational and administrative support, as well as partnership opportunities for streetscape improvements and street beautification initiatives. Through this enhanced institutional voice, BIDs can have an enormous impact on the built form within a neighbourhood. For example, in his study of the development of the "creative city" within Toronto's Entertainment BID, Sébastien Darchen found that the BID had a strong voice in community deliberations and that its interests were specific to advantages for the member businesses.[21] While the city council ultimately supported a mixed-use neighbourhood with a more diverse range of economic activities than those proposed by the BID, Darchen concluded that the promotion of arts and culture as imagined by the BID led to the area's revitalization.[22]

REPRESENTATION

BIDs advance an "us" versus "them" within particular communities, with economically and ethnically mixed neighbourhoods especially vulnerable. Susanna Schaller and Gabriella Modan concluded that BIDs fundamentally increase space-related tensions.[23] Representation is a major element of these space-based tensions, specifically in relation to the composition and mandates of BID boards. At present, residents have few, if any, representative votes on BID boards. The board composition concentrates power among property and business owners, restricting the scope of representation. This framework reinforces political dynamics that exclude marginalized and low-income residents, as well as small businesses. BIDs insulate development decisions from communities and neighbourhoods by focusing on entertainment and high-rent housing, with minimal attention to the interests of existing residents and with "profound implications for notions of spatial and social justice."[24]

An especially poignant illustration of BIDs and vulnerable populations is in the area of homelessness. In 2014, actions for injunctive relief and damages were brought against the City of Los Angeles and the Los Angeles Downtown Industrial District Business Improvement District for confiscating the property of homeless people, despite clear jurisprudence that precludes such activity. The plaintiffs alleged that the City of Los Angeles "acts in concert with the BID to identify property to be removed and to ensure that the removals were not stopped or hindered."[25] These seizures appeared to be random occurrences taking place while homeless people were at shelters getting food and services, with items like tents, bedding, identification, and medications being seized.[26] The court enjoined the City and the bid from seizing a homeless person's property that is not abandoned, or seizing abandoned property without notice or due process and, in 2017, the case settled for close to $500,000. Similarly, in 2015, Toronto's Chinatown BID objected to a plan to introduce a youth homeless shelter within the boundaries of the BID.[27] The BID noted a lack of consultation on the proposal and possible negative effects on the area, stating: "the BID had worked hard for a decade to "clean up"

---

[21] Sébastien Darchen, "The Creative City and the Redevelopment of the Toronto Entertainment District: A BID-Led Regeneration Process," *International Planning Studies*, 18, no. 2 (2011): 188.

[22] Darchen, 201.

[23] Schaller & Modan.

[24] Lewis, 208.

[25] Schonburn Seplow Harris & Hoffman, LLP, "Skid Row Residents/Organizations Sue Downtown Business Improvement District and the City of Los Angeles for Unlawful Seizure of Property" (2016): 1.

[26] *Los Angeles Catholic Worker et al v. Los Angeles Downtown Industrial District BID*, 2:14-cv-07344 1 (2014).

[27] Kendra Mangione, "'We don't need any more grit': Chinatown BID on street youth centre," CTV News Toronto (December 30, 2015).

the area, and business owners are worried the facility will turn Spadina into a "centre of homelessness". To support their objection member businesses placed placards in their premises and demonstrated at City Hall. While some BIDs hope to harness their considerable influence to address homelessness, as a study done in Washington, DC suggests, the organizations must work collaboratively with other stakeholders, including local advocates, although this is at the discretion of BIDs themselves.[28]

ACCOUNTABILITY

Accountability refers to the degree to which BIDs operate with openness and fairness, and especially the degree to which they are subject to the same transparency and accountability requirements as other public bodies. Richard Briffault declared that BIDs are "autonomous, even though subjected to municipal oversight in theory."[29] He defined accountability in terms of reporting requirements to public officials, making a BID accountable to its board, the business community that it represents, city council, and the public. City governments may implement measures such as annual reports, outside audits, and sunset and reauthorization requirements. The rationale for these mechanisms is to ensure continuous evaluation of BID performance and to give power to municipal governments if BIDs are overstepping their authority, although others argue that they are pro forma and after the fact.[30]

For example, the City of Toronto manages accountability issues through various laws and policies, principally the *Code of Conduct for Members of Local Boards*, which sets out the requirements of BIDs and other local boards in the city.[31] In Toronto, BID directors and board members, including the local city councillor, must conduct their affairs in compliance with all applicable law and City policies, which include privacy legislation, conflict of interest requirements, and the public appointments policy. Many other cities have similar accountability measures.[32]

Despite these requirements, some scholars have argued that the design of BIDs limits the degree to which they can ever be held accountable. Ian Cook stated that BIDs may claim accountability to the public through their links to city council, but "ultimately BIDs are not really accountable to the public in general and are more focused on being accountable – of sorts – to businesses."[33] The increasing number of BIDs and their important role in local governance has been linked to municipal fragmentation and privatization in North American cities.[34] BIDs, which are led by and accountable to business owners, add a layer between urban citizens and elected councillors. The price of this process is to allow what has been conceived as "public" to become incrementally more "private."

One example is the accountability of BIDs in relation to public safety. A study in New York revealed the extent to which BIDs use strategies such as public realm design (e.g., planters),

[28] Wonhyong Lee, "Downtown management and homelessness: the versatile roles of business improvement districts," *Journal of Place Management and Development*, 11:4 (2018): 411–427.
[29] Richard Briffault, "A Government for Our Time? Business Improvement Districts and Urban Governance," *Columbia Law Review*, 99, no. 2 (1999): 414.
[30] Hoyt & Gopal-Agge, 952.
[31] City of Toronto, *Code of Conduct for Members of Council City of Toronto Annotated Version* (2011): 1.
[32] Wayne Batchis, "Business Improvement Districts and the Constitution: The Troubling Necessity of Privatized Government for Urban Revitalization," *Hastings Constitutional Law Quarterly*, 38 (2010): 91.
[33] Paul Gallagher, "Business Improvement Districts: Local firms charged with funding BIDs say they are unaccountable - and are fighting back," *The Independent* (October 11, 2014).
[34] Meghan Joy & Ronald K. Vogel, "Toronto's governance crisis: A global city under pressure" 49 (2015).

collaboration with police, surveillance techniques, and even harassment to limit street vending (which is largely illegal) within their boundaries.[35] These techniques are highly successful, and the landscape of street vending reflects the "decentralized, privatized and informalized vending management" of BIDs, rather than formal laws.

This brief review of the relevant literature on BIDs and their relationship to city government, inclusivity, and representation substantiates that, in their existing design, BIDs have significant decision-making power in local geographies and represent BID members rather than the broader local public. Accountability provisions may not safeguard the effects of BID activities on the public, particularly the most vulnerable. The next section applies this knowledge to the urban commons.

BIDS AND THE URBAN COMMONS FRAMEWORK

The legal and social problems identified in BID governance – representation, accountability, and relationship with city government – reflect the challenges of BIDs within a broader system of local governance. They also complicate the role of BIDs as an example of the urban commons, as the devolution of responsibility and power to BIDs may undermine the very sense of belonging that advocates of the urban commons seek to foster.

According to Ostrom, the commons is a matter of collective governance. However, urban governance arrangements are generally voluntary and bind only those actually involved in the governance scheme. Such arrangements can have effects for many, beyond the actors that are specifically involved: "[I]n the case of urban commons governance institutions the governance arrangement may affect the everyday life of all city inhabitants that fall within the boundaries of the governance scheme (think of the BIDs, the decisions of which can have an impact also on those who are not part of the BID governance)."[36] Bodies that are sharing governance authority may further inequality amongst residents, stressing the need for questions of accountability and legitimacy to be "raised and constantly invoked" when querying collaborative governance in the urban commons."[37] Parker and Schmidt put it this way: "The urban commons perspective may also underplay the role of government in deliberately creating shared urban resources and in selecting and enabling particular groups."[38]

BIDs deserve particular scrutiny as to how they bolster or frustrate the urban commons framework. On one hand, BIDs are woven into city administration through the existence of a dedicated office, an approved budget, and accessible information on how they may be contacted. This suggests that they are like any other local board of the city, with oversight by the city in regard to their expenditures and in their delegated service delivery role. On the other hand, they have significant power in public realm management. This dual role creates confusion as to what role they serve (local boards or independent actors?) and to whom they are accountable (to the public or their members?).

The "common pool resource" engaged in BIDs is the spatial area defined by city bylaws. The spaces are not simply those that belong to business and property owners, but include "public" areas like sidewalks and street furniture, and may include residential areas above or

---

[35] Ryan Thomas Devlin, "'An area that governs itself' Informality, uncertainty and the management of street vending in New York City," *Planning Theory*, 10, no. 1 (2011): 53, 59.

[36] Foster & Iaione, 339.

[37] Foster & Iaione, 340.

[38] Peter Parker & Staffan Schmidt, "Commons-based Governance in Public Space: User Participation and Inclusion," *Nordic Journal of Architectural Research*, 28, no. 3 (2016): 114–139, 118.

adjacent to storefronts.[39] Thus, the resource interest is shared among a diverse set of property holders. BID members, but also a broader range of residents and the public. Non-property owners have a stake in the area in question, however, these broader interests are not reflected in the BID governance model.[40] Moreover, this common pool resource is also subject to many city policies and bylaws, with numerous other parties asserting interest in the same spaces, including elected officials and organizations such as neighbourhood associations.[41] Ultimately, BIDs are but one entity operating within a larger, polycentric governance constellation, and can be reimagined as more representative, accountable, and collaborative entities within the common pool resource, or urban space.

There may be no evidence that regulatory slippage has occurred where, for example, sidewalks are well-maintained by the BID. The regulatory slipping in question may not be the degradation of the resource (e.g., the city street) as identified by Hardin, where the resource becomes prone to destruction. Instead, the regulatory slippage is reflected in the erosion of openness, participation, and representation in city-making, caused by a focus on narrow interests to the detriment of a broader population. Rather than balancing the competing interests of the space and those in it, the BID may be solely focusing on the profitability of member businesses. In short, BIDs advance a particular notion of the commons despite other competing conceptions.[42]

Looking solely at BID management of the resource impairs the strength and importance of the urban commons as a conceptual tool in reimagining city governance. Reframing the BID as one player among many in local city management acknowledges that the multiplicity of interests at the smaller-than-city scale. BIDs serve an important function, yet have narrow interests and little accountability, thus reducing the extent to which they should exert decision-making power in city spaces. Instead, city governments should mediate BID power within a thoughtful, inclusive, and representative local governance framework that balances the roles of other local bodies, like resident associations, but also public involvement through mechanisms such as charrettes and opportunities for deliberative participation.

The acknowledgement of BIDs as just one entity in local decision-making is evident in some local planning and infrastructure decisions in Toronto, where BIDs, resident associations, and the public are consulted as representative community voices.[43] The city consults each of these associations and residents with the understanding that no single one of these stakeholders can speak on behalf of the neighbourhood. When it comes to local resource management by BIDs, however, there is no corresponding acknowledgement that multiple entities should be reflected in the local governance model. While this chapter does not have the space to delve into the breadth of possibilities, there are lessons to draw from other jurisdictions. For instance, some cities have mandated that residents serve on BID boards or hold open meetings, thus bringing community voices to bear in BID deliberations.[44] Other jurisdictions have provided for "horizontal" governance in the management of public space, where multiple actors including BIDs have discrete roles and similar levels of power, as well as opportunities to come together and

---

[39] Vinay Gidwani & Amita Baviskar, "Urban Commons," *Economic and Political Weekly*, 46 (2011): 1, 2.

[40] Sarah Hamill, "Private Rights to Common Property: The Evolution of Common Property in Canada," *McGill Law Journal*, 58, no. 2 (2012): 365.

[41] Clapp & Meyer, 1–2; Foster & Iaione, 298.

[42] Richard Schragger, "The Limits of Localism," Georgetown Public Law Research Paper No. 298003 (2001).

[43] Alexandra Flynn, "The Role of Business. Improvement Areas and Neighbourhood Associations in the City of Toronto," *Institute of Municipal Finance and Governance* 45 (2019).

[44] Mark Steel, & M. Symes, "The Privatisation of Public Space? The American Experience of Business Improvement Districts and their Relationship to Local Governance," *Local Government Studies*, 31:3 (2005): 321–334, 326.

collaborate.[45] At the end of the day, BIDs are legislated creatures, with governments holding the cards in the power and authority – and corresponding obligations – held by these smaller-than-city entities, and in the way that their roles are legally defined alongside other local stakeholders.

The urban commons recognizes the polycentric set of interests that legitimize a shared authority to govern, regardless of formal property rights. Put another way, the urban commons speaks to the relationships at the core of a governance model. Contextualizing BIDs as one of many actors in local governance offers an opportunity to reframe decision-making that avoids narrow interests.

CONCLUSION

The urban commons is less preoccupied with property rights and who has what interest in the standard "bundle" language that property law asserts, and instead theorizes the city as a territorial space in which citizens claim to have a role or stake, regardless of ownership, with law playing an enabling role. The urban commons is a helpful framework in considering local actors that claim to have rights to govern or be heard within an urban context, and how such claims are mediated and by whom. The strength of the urban commons framework is the room left for polycentric, bottom-up decision-making outside of formal governments.

BIDs have a long history as helpful partners in urban management through their financing and coordinating of public realm improvements, as well as the provision of other local services, especially in distressed neighborhoods. However, BIDs are not always transparent or inclusive, with countless examples of having narrow interests corresponding to their members' prosperity, rather than those of the wider public, especially the most marginalized.

This paper argues against framing BIDs as a singular body capable of managing a common pool resource within the city. Instead, local spaces within the city include residents, businesses, and other key stakeholders, of which BIDs may be one. This conceptualization allows for a broader notion of local governance that incorporates multiple voices, including but not solely BIDs, and centers smaller-than-city spaces as the site of urban commons analysis. Such spaces can then be analysed with attention to accountability, representation, and relationships to city governments, for a richer understanding of how common pool resources are claimed, managed, and meditated, and by whom.

---

[45] Claudio de Magalhães & Sonia Freire Trigo, "'Clubification' of urban public spaces? The withdrawal or the re-definition of the role of local government in the management of public spaces," *Journal of Urban Design*, 22:6 (2017): 738–756, 754.

14

To Have and To Hold? Community Land Trust as Commons

Barbara L. Bezdek

Community land trust practice in the United States maps onto the commons institutions frame developed through the pioneering work of Elinor Ostrom and her colleagues; but not all CLTs function as commons institutions. Some CLTs have been reported to function as do other affordable-housing providers that deliver homes and housing services, rather than engage the CLT's residents as community member-managers in a commons. This paper seeks to distinguish CLTs that function as a commons from CLTs that function as housing providers, a critical distinction that often gets lost in the literature and in the analyses of CLTs. The CLT-as-Commons analysis here emphasizes two characteristics of enduring commons institutions in Ostrom's canon: self-governance, and rules for the transgenerational resource-preservation in commons 'management.'

The CLT-as-Commons inquiry is prompted by the ubiquity of CLTs in fair development movements, metaphorically reclaiming commons for the commoners in the context of vacant disinvested housing that would otherwise be claimed by the private sector or the State. This analysis is particularly salient in cities of neighborhoods pockmarked by longstanding vacancy and disinvestment. Community Land Trusts (CLTs) are part of nearly every progressive response to today's affordable housing crisis because they offer an alternative ownership structure to disrupt market forces of development by displacement, and to secure land for permanently affordable housing. The CLT offers an intermediate form of land ownership and control between the speculative market and the State; yet its distinct tenure and shared-equity legal structure are not a sufficient basis to categorize every CLT as a commons institution, at least as scholars have defined it. This is because, while CLTs increasingly are promoted in housing policy circles as an economically efficient form of affordable housing,[1] insufficient attention is given to its operational and cultural dimensions, particularly with respect to sustaining community control of the land and housing.[2] Overemphasizing access to an opportunity for affordable

---

[1] CLTs maintain long-term housing affordability using a shared-equity model designed to prevent CLT residents from selling these low-cost homes and the land on which they stand to speculative developers. First, dividing ownership (the Trust owns the land, the resident buys or rents the home) and a resale price restriction to a certain percentage over the initial sale price, these keep the homes affordable through multiple sale cycles. These are managed through stewardship practices directed by an elected board comprised of residents of the CLT, residents of the broader community, and public- and not-for-profit board members.

[2] Robust framing of CLTs as a civil rights strategy for preserving communities of color exist, see for example Policy Link, "Preserving Neighborhoods with Community Land Trusts," June 2019, www.youtube.com/watch?v=A5n-3_fUtlk. The dominant purveyor of CLT support in the US is Grounded Solutions Network, which more mutedly, prioritizes long-term-affordable housing and the creation of strong, lasting, and inclusive communities. GS resulted from the merger of the National Community Land Trust Network and Cornerstone Partners, https://groundedsolutions.org/.

home ownership tends to suppress the central features of classic-form CLTs, which are based on collective governance by an elected group of CLT-land residents, CLT members who are non-resident neighbors, and supportive stakeholders, who manage and govern the CLT land to assure its transgenerational and multi-stakeholder purposes.

This paper contributes to the contemporary turn of commons literature beyond natural common pool resources, toward the influence of commons models in additional areas of policy-making and resource management all along a spectrum of ownership ideas between Marx and markets.[3]

To succeed as a self-governing CLT-Commons requires constructing that commons through robust practices of stewardship, which build the CLT knowledge commons within the CLT membership in order to elevate and sustain the corresponding community interests on par with the member interest as CLT "homeowner." A CLT-as-Commons must do more than hold a portfolio of housing units in trust across generations at below-market sales prices. It must construct the cultural commons – that essential CLT knowledge, its reproduction and distribution, and the commons members' capacity for efficacious self-management – necessary to steward the land as the community of members determines for generations.

This paper draws on an ongoing case study of a campaign in Baltimore, Maryland for multiple community land trusts (CLTs) to take back empty homes after decades of private disinvestment and public demolition plans.[4] Starting in 2014, the Baltimore Housing Roundtable began spearheading grassroots activism that resulted in local legislation for an Affordable Housing Trust Fund, millions of dollars dedicated to non-speculative affordable housing models including CLTs, and by 2018, a broadly representative Affordable Housing Commission to determine the allocation of municipal housing resources.[5] After years of campaigning for annual investment in neighborhood-driven permanently affordable housing developments, an agreement was forged by six Baltimore CLT-forming communities acting together as the entity SHARE Baltimore, and the City of Baltimore for the rehab of the first 50 properties in a CLT-led vision.[6]

This analysis applies Ostrom's understanding that a property right is a "social relationship between a resource user and other potential users, with respect to a particular object, place, or feature of the land."[7] Common property occupies the middle ground between open access and private ownership, in that common property is owned by an identified group of people together, who are invested with the right to exclude non-owners and with the duty of maintaining the property and protecting it against exploitation or deterioration. Commonly held property is distinguishable from Hardin's fabled open-access grazing commons where no one has the legal right to exclude anyone from using the shared pasture, leading to the "tragedy of the commons": the overuse, ineffective management and degradation of the resource. Ostrom's profound achievement in institutions analysis and in property theory has been to reinforce the point that

[3] The phrase is from Michael A. Heller, "The Tragedy of the Anticommons: Property in the Transition from Marx to Markets." *Harvard Law Review* 111: 3 (1998): 621–688, referring to shifts in property rules for transitional economies.

[4] Also see "The Revolution of the New Commons," – www.inmotionmagazine.com/global/gest_int_4.html. This rise of new commons activity and claiming "signals alarmed reactions to increasing commodification, privatization, and corporatization, untamed globalization, and unresponsive governments."

[5] Jared Brey, "Baltimore Advocates Keep Up the Housing Demands," *Next City*, August 1, 2019, https://nextcity.org/daily/entry/baltimore-advocates-keep-up-the-housing-demands; Peter Sabonis, "Rebellion Spurs Opportunity and a New Housing Movement," *Shelterforce* May 7, 2018, https://shelterforce.org/2018/05/07/rebellion-spurs-opportunity-and-a-new-housing-movement/.

[6] "We envision a new model of housing and community development, where outside real estate developers and speculators are not in control," www.baltimorehousingroundtable.org/

[7] Elinor Ostrom & Edella Schlager, The Formation of Property Rights, in *Rights to Nature: Ecological, Economic, Cultural, And Political Principles of Institutions for The Environment* (Washington, DC: Island Press 1996) 127–156.

the "tragedy of the commons" is not a necessity in human communities or property systems.[8] Ostrom's work detailed innumerable successful institutions for the collective management of significant resources,[9] illuminating within property-institutions theory the category of limited-commons management as viable alternatives to both hyper-private property and government ownership. It is this conceptual and legal space where CLTs reside.

COMMONS AS METAPHOR AND PRAXIS

As the commons literature amply demonstrates, a commons is not a singular concept. The commons idea provides a metaphor for virtually any environment in which an identified resource is contested by some population of human creators and consumers over rights to contribute and appropriate resources.[10] Natural resources and many public spaces, such as groundwater aquifers, beaches, air and food sheds, and the polar ice caps, as well as parking spots and sidewalk vending,[11] are all examples of traditional commons. "New Commons" candidates include knowledge, silence, government budgets, and e-mail inboxes.[12]

Functionally, a commons is a resource shared by a group where the resource is vulnerable to enclosure, overuse and social dilemmas and thus, requires management and protection to sustain its common character.[13] Considering scarce urban resources, "neighborhood commons" have been claimed in contests between neighborhoods and city officials over gardens, the effect on homeless populations by certain types of urban enclosures, art or gig work on shared public space, 'predatory planning' after disasters, and disposition of development rights. The conceptual framework of a commons rejects the framing of the city as essentially an aggregation of private property rights;[14] instead, the ideal city is a place where collaborative governance strategies and structures that preserve existing social networks and manage collectively "owned" city resources are in place.[15] Hess also includes playgrounds, sidewalk and street vending, local streets, parking, public spaces, and street trees as commons. Bolliers adds that a commons is a self-organized social system for long-term stewardship of that resource, so as to preserve the resource and community identity with minimal reliance on the market or the state.[16]

CLT-MOVEMENT FROM COMMONS-CLAIMING TO COMMONS-MAKING

The CLT movement in Baltimore incorporates commons practices at two junctures, the *commons-claiming* that framed its popular education and political campaigns, and since 2018, its advance into *commons institution-building* through practices intended to facilitate the creation and sustainability of actual CLTs-as-Commons across the geo-political city.

---

[8] Carol M Rose, "Ostrom and the Lawyers," 8.

[9] Ostrom "Private and Common Property"; Carol M Rose, "Ostrom and the Lawyers: The Impact of Governing the Commons on the American Legal Academy" (2010). *International Journal of the Commons* 5(1), 28–49.

[10] Michael J. Madison, Brett M. Frischmann & Katherine J. Strandburg, "The University as Constructed Cultural Commons," *Washington University Journal of La. & Policy* 30: 365, 372–373 (2009).

[11] Brigham Daniels,"Governing the Presidential Nomination Commons," *Tulane Law Review* 84: 899, 906–907 (2010).

[12] Id.

[13] Charlotte Hess, "Mapping the New Commons", (Presented *at Governing Shared Resources: Connecting Local Experience to Global Challenges*, the 12th Biennial Conference of the International Association for the Study of the Commons, University of Gloucestershire, Cheltenham, England, July 14–18, 2008), 37.

[14] Hess, Mapping, at 16

[15] Sheila Foster, "The City as an Ecological Space: Social Capital and Urban Land Use." *Notre Dame Law Review* 82 (2):527–582. 2006.

[16] David Bollier, *Think Like a Commoner* (New Society Publishers, 2014), 175.

The Baltimore campaign to reclaim land and redirect municipal policy, initiated in 2014, asserts a moral claim on the City's distribution of disinvested properties and development dollars, and seeks major shifts in development norms toward democratic stewardship of urban spaces and land-trust housing. The CLT movement in Baltimore asserts the "right to *not* be excluded"[17] from land parcels that harm communities and yet are withheld from productive reuse.

The scarcity of urban land available for the housing needs of low-wealth households and the high entry barriers to formal housing markets,[18] present conditions that beset other resources classified as commons. As such, the same questions and challenges facing other commons arise here, with respect to affordable housing and disinvested properties. Inherent in fair-development campaigns is the idea that now-vacant urban land calls for revisiting the means of acquisition and management because the existing rules exclude millions from the potential benefits attached to that land. Assertions of human rights to the minimum necessities for wellbeing, and of distributive justice, underpin utilitarian and moral arguments against societally harmful speculation in real estate.[19] Vacant lands scourge US cities on a startling scale. A recent inventory of vacant land and structural abandonment in the urban United States revealed that roughly 16.7% of the land mass is vacant in large US cities.[20] This equals the land area of New York City, Los Angeles, Chicago, Houston, Philadelphia, and San Diego combined.[21] Housing activists argue this is immoral, a result of the ideological dominance of, and priority for, private property embedded within American planning practices and property law.[22]

CLT activists call to address unmet housing needs intersects with commons analysis in the assertion that municipal land distribution practices revisit the harms of enclosure on those who gain the least from government's attention to the general welfare. The fact that land is finite, and that its privatization has extracted much land from availability to meet critical human needs such as housing, invokes the enclosure element of commons analysis. Land originates as a commonwealth, a non-renewable resource passed down from previous generations. Enclosure and the subsequent evolution of property laws allow that resource to be appropriated and held by some as commodified rights in real property, to have exchange value, to be accumulated, and held in order to extract profits from the land's use. The existing legal rules benefit land financiers and neglect or harm others. Municipal policy that relies on for-profit housing production perpetuates the land-grabbing displacement of historical enclosure. There are thousands of square miles of vacant real estate across US cities, permitted to sit unused, its desolate condition protected by the valorization of private ownership that privileges speculation while denying human need.

The commons framework helps activists, practitioners and policymakers conceptualize the need to focus on values and goals that go beyond the marketplace. As the scholar-activist David Bollier puts it, "[t]he idea of the commons helps us restore to the center stage a whole range of

[17] Nicholas Blomley, "Enclosure, Common Right and the Property of the Poor," *Social & Legal Studies* 17, 311, 320 (2008).
[18] Meehan, J. "Reinventing Real Estate: The Community Land Trust and the Social Market in Land," *Journal of Applied Social Science* 8 (2): 113–133 (2014), doi:10.1177/1936724413497480.
[19] *Frank S. Alexander,* Land Banks and Land Banking (PDF). *Center for Community Progress (June 2011).*
[20] Galen D. Newman, Ann O'M. Bowman, Ryun Jung Lee & Boah Kim, "A current inventory of vacant urban land in America," *Journal of Urban Design,* 21:3, 302–319 (2016); Pagano, M.A.; Bowman, A.O.M. "*Vacant Land in Cities: An Urban Resource,*"(Brookings Institution, Center on Urban and Metropolitan Policy: Washington, DC, 2000) 10.
[21] Paul Brophy, Jennifer Vey, *Seizing City Assets* (Brookings, 2002).
[22] Matthew Thompson, "Between Boundaries: From Commoning and Guerrilla Gardening to Community Land Trust Development in Liverpool," *Antipode* 47:4 (2015).

social and ecological phenomena that market economics regards as sideshows – externalities – to the marquee events of the marketplace, economic exchange."[23] CLTs – in political argument and in praxis – promise to carve out commons as restoration of a prior-state common-wealth, and preserve such lands into the future for use values beyond market values.

CLTS AS COMMONS INSTITUTIONS: STRUCTURE FOR FUNCTION

As the Baltimore CLT movement advances into *commons institution-building* to facilitate the creation and sustainability of actual CLTs-as-Commons across the geo-political city, the details of the institutional structures are important.[24] CLTs put into practice an alternative vision of what development and land value can look like, unlike most advocates for housing policy to center use-value goals over land-value. Those practices of self-governance transform CLTs into a type of *commons institution*.

Commons are not found, they are constructed by purposeful human activity, distinguishable from the environment around them, and managed according to a set of shared rules. CLTs, like the commons studied by Ostrom et. al., have membership criteria and specific rules specifying who may contribute to, use and appropriate resources from the commons. Likewise, commons typically establish standards and rules for resource contribution and appropriation, decision-making, conflict resolution, and sanctions for noncompliance. As Ostrom's field studies revealed, the rules that govern a commons tend to persist over many generations.

CLTs emerged in the last 50 years and must interact with a complex regime of long-established legal rules and cultural meanings of land title that are framed by a dominant neoliberal ideology of individualized property ownership, which presumes that social needs are best met by private market forces left unfettered to pursue capital accumulation. As CLTs have taken root in cities, offering an alternative vision of what development and land value can look like,[25] they may collide with the manifesto of neoliberal private property, i.e. the idea that individual property owners reserve the right to sell their property to the highest bidder, even to the point of foreclosure, homelessness and denial of human dignity. It is an uphill challenge to take on this long-dominant and deeply entrenched ideology and to convince others to appreciate the CLT model, which combines private home ownership with shared community investment in the land's use and the housing's perpetual affordability. CLTs, however, have been designed to provide an alternative value-frame, with the land held in trust for the benefit of the community's long-term use-value, which is determined through communal decision-making mechanisms and residents' engagement.

CLT proponents are not radicals; they are not insisting that 'property is theft,' nor rejecting the property claims of existing title-holders. They are, after all, aiming to secure land for the community's long-term needs within an existing legal framework of title, and the protection of the full bundle of property rights that the law and legal institutions provide to individual owners. The community trust entity holds title to the land, and leases it to land users under detailed agreements enforceable according to the community's internal terms and procedures, intended to operate through mutuality and primacy over express contract provisions necessary to protect

---

[23] David Bollier, *Silent Theft: The Private Plunder of our Common Wealth*, 12.

[24] Elinor Ostrom, *Governing the Commons* 39 (Because all organizational arrangements are subject to stress, weakness, and failure).

[25] Harvey Molotch, "The City as a Growth Machine: Toward a Political Economy of Place," *American Journal of Sociology*, 82 (2): 309–332 (September, 1976)

the land-based interests of the trust and its members and leaseholders within the traditional system of property law, title protection and real estate lending.

Like more familiar forms of urban commoning, as when residents of disinvested neighborhoods build gardens, parks, and farms, CLTs adopt institutional features to balance collective efforts and household appropriation of commons resources.[26] These depend on agreement, commitment and mutuality for success over time. Managing commons resources requires establishing a set of working rules or contracts that define the legal relationships between the involved actors. The CLT form of governance comports with Ostrom's definition of commons institutions as the set of working rules that are used to determine who is eligible to make decisions about the resource held in common, what actions are allowed or constrained, what procedures must be followed, what information must or must not be provided, and what payoffs will be assigned to individuals dependent on their actions.[27] Sustaining the commons requires operation, monitoring and enforcement of an agreed plan of governance.[28]

According to Ostrom's design principles, the CLT promotes and preserves access to land users now and in the future, who (homebuyers or renters, in the case of housing CLTS) would otherwise be priced out by rising exchange values. In separating land ownership from homeownership, the CLT model isolates land's use value from its exchange value via the ground lease mechanism. The lease between the Trust and the unit owner assures that the use value of the land remains subject to the management and stewardship decisions of the identified community of multiple stakeholders. The 99-year ground lease works two ways to secure against displacement: it both establishes a strong relationship between the CLT and the homeowner, and it provides the CLT with long-term legal power over the disposal and development of the land. It emphasizes the social benefits (i.e., the use value) of providing affordable housing, retaining long–term affordability, and reducing subsidy loss by restricting the resale price increase (i.e., the exchange value).

Ostrom's life work gives evidence that community-based resource management can in fact accomplish patterns of commitment, sustainability, and stability. It is this interior life that distinguishes a CLT-as-Commons from a CLT as housing provider. The CLT holds land for housing, in a form designed to preserve its availability as housing for generations. Its internal rules allocate housing units to qualifying householders in tandem with governance rights in the CLT. Key aspects of the CLT structure include: (1) the provision of resale-restricted homes that remain affordable in perpetuity, which ensures that affordable assets are preserved and thus available for successive lower-income households to acquire; and (2) distinctive governance rules. The classic CLT requires commitments by all CLT members to sustain the resource (community land and the housing contained thereon) – while allowing for exit (sale of the housing unit) according to the prescribed terms for sustaining the CLT. The CLT governance regime, through its formal bylaws, connects residents of the CLT housing units with residents of the broader neighborhood and additional stakeholders in the success of the mutual commitments of the Trust, the residents and the community. While in a narrow property-holding sense, a CLT is similar to other existing forms of dual ownership that combine collective ownership of the land and individuated rights in homes on the shared real property, such as condominiums,

---

[26] Sheila R. Foster & Christian Iaione, "The City as A Commons," *Yale Law & Policy Review* 34, 281, 296 (2016) (categorizing such endeavors as urban commons institutions, in that they are ways of managing a common resource, without privatizing).

[27] Ostrom, *Governing the Commons*, 51 (1990); Ostrom, "An Agenda for the Study of Institutions," *Public Choice* 48:3–25 (1986)

[28] Ostrom, *Governing the Commons* (1990).

co-operatives, or mutual housing,[29] the CLT is distinct in its design purpose, governance theory and structure of community control to secure transgenerational resource benefits. From the governance process perspective, this entails communication in a democratically controlled organization of co-equal trustees, which are not confined to the legal title holders of CLT residences, all jointly focused on the CLT's success within a broader community.

In property theory terms, CLTs re-arrange the familiar property rights of access, use, exclusion, and alienation, and unite them with governance responsibilities of commons management.[30] *Dual ownership places the land under community control, subject to the trust's purpose to steward the land to meet community use needs*, more broadly conceived than gain in real estate value. By separating the ownership of the land from the ownership of the buildings on it, CLTs effectively remove the land value from the market's ups and downs. Purchasers or renters of the buildings on the CLT's land gain rights in land use and in the CLT governance that preserves community control. Specific management practices include supportive stewardship programs to aid CLT residents to weather economic stressors, as well as legal rights to transfer the housing by sale, will or inheritance and to a portion of the appreciation in value, under terms stated in the ground lease at the time of purchase. *Access to the homeownership opportunities of the land so held is determined by the CLT's qualitative purpose in holding land, which also directs the terms of use and of alienation, as stated in the governing ground lease.* A CLT's formation documents commit the Trust to hold the land forever in trust to serve its charter purpose, usually to preserve affordability for low-wealth home buyers or renters, and it holds the housing subsidies and rising land values to that purpose.[31]

A core goal of most urban CLTs is to promote long-term housing affordability. The Trust leases land to the residents, and the extensive CLT ground lease constructs the relationship between the home and the Trust land, typically for a 99-year renewable term. The lease incorporates a resale formula developed by each CLT to keep the housing affordable over the long term for successive buyers. This arrangement differentiates the land retained by the CLT for community use in perpetuity from the stipulated equity share an owner-occupant takes with her upon sale of their housing unit. The resale formula may be tailored to specific goals that each CLT determines, for example to promote home occupants' mobility or longevity, or to limit capital improvements that decrease the affordability of CLT homes.[32] Regardless, the CLT reserves a pre-emptive right to purchase when housing units are resold, and residents leaving a CLT have a contractual obligation to sell back their housing to the CLT at the price set by the resale formula in the lease.

A CLT's governance structure is designed to ensure that the community remains invested in the CLT's broader mission.[33] Importantly, CLT membership, while place-based, is not restricted

---

[29] Why some institutions are stable, and some are not, is a key theme of the commons institutions literature. Ostrom *Governing the Commons* 90-102 (design principles for enduring success); Arun Agrawal, "Common Resources and Institutional Stability", in *The Drama of the Commons* at 41–85 (Elinor Ostrom et al., eds., 2002) (providing a comprehensive review).

[30] Ostrom, "Design Principles of Robust Property-Rights Institutions: What Have We Learned?" *Property Rights and Land Policies*, 3–4

[31] Planners sometimes assume that this means a neighborhood will be forever poor or comparatively low-income, and that this will impede public policies of economic integration. In fact, like any legally constituted trust, a CLT does have the legal power to buy and sell properties, engage in land swaps, change its footprint. The Md statute enacted 2010 specifies what will happen to land trust property if the not-for-profit were to fail. Affordable Housing Land Trust Act, Maryland Annotated Code, Real Property § 14–501.

[32] Burlington Associates in Community Development LLC, "Choosing a Resale Formula," www.burlingtonassociates .com/clt-resources/choosing-a-resale-formula/.

[33] Davis, "Origins and Evolution of the Community Land Trust," 10–12.

to resident homeowners nor persons with direct capital stakes in the CLT. In this way, CLTs differ from all other home-owner associations with respect to their constituencies and in terms of the character of their social welfare purposes, which "cannot be reduced to the aggregation of their members' individual interests as owners of houses."[34] The governing board of the 'classic' CLT is tripartite, with three classes of stakeholders. Two-thirds of a CLT's board of directors are nominated and elected by voting members who either live on the CLT's land or members who reside within the CLT's broader service community but do not live directly on CLT-owned land.[35] The final third are appointed by the CLT to represent the local public interest and may include public sector officials, non-profit service providers, and local funders.[36]

Specifically, through its site acquisition decisions and its organizational documents, a CLT may bind itself to focus on the long-term collective needs of those whose needs are most likely to be neglected by the private market. The governance structure reflects this broadened notion of the relevant community in that it recognizes the interests of non-owners in the management and use of the CLT land and CLT residents' property although their stake does not extend to property rights of use, exclusion or alienation.

The *community* idea in the CLT is potentially a site for commons construction. The CLT's formal structure is designed to preserve the land resource, its use, character and alienability across time as owner-occupants change, and its unique inclusion of non-owners in its governance system gives voice to individuals who have stakes in the success of the community. As Lowe and Thaden report, successful fully-dimensioned CLTs operationalize community control of land as much through relationships as by rules – that is, not solely by the bylaws or through its constitution, but through "[r]esident engagement activities [that] supplement governance and corporate membership structures in order for meaningful community control to be actualized in a way that may counter traditional tenure arrangements."[37]

GOVERNING THE CLT-COMMONS: PRESERVING THE ME-NESS AND WE-NESS OF COMMONS PROPERTY

How do you develop confidence in a community and individuals to speak, to stand up for, to strive, to fight and to have hope. I think those are the key challenges. It's not so much what building are you gonna build or what social program are you gonna change, but it's the people part of it, the part that has people investing themselves to make a difference, to make a change and to see that hope. That's the challenge.[38]

A principal aspect of collective action capability by the members of a commons inheres in the social bonds shared by that community. Such bonds include the need for trust, cooperation and human relationships. Ostrom asserted that commoners must have "shared a past and expect to a future,"[39] so that they are capable of not just "short-term maximization" or the "me-ness" of the

---

[34] James J. Kelly, Jr.,"Land Trusts That Conserve Communities," *DePaul Law Review* 59: 69, 89 (2009).

[35] "Key Features of the 'Classic' Community Land Trust, Burlington Community Development Associates (2006) 2; CLT Network

[36] John Emmeus Davis, "Origins and Evolution of the Community Land Trust in the United States," *The Community Land Trust Reader* (Cambridge, MA, 2010), 9–10.

[37] Jeffrey S. Lowe & Emily Thaden (2016) "Deepening stewardship: resident engagement in community land trusts," *Urban Geography*, 37:4, 611–628

[38] Che Madyun, in *Holding Ground: The Rebirth of Dudley Street*.(video by Leah Mahan and Mark Lipman, Holding Ground Productions, 1996).

[39] Ostrom, Governing the Commons

resource asset, but also be able to engage in "long-term reflection about joint outcomes" that anchors the 'we-ness' of the resource that they share.[40] To the extent that "we-ness" is foreign to traditional notions of private home ownership, it is a necessary to create a culture and buy-in around this new conceptualization, which lies at the heart of the CLT mission, with its extensive ground lease, limited equity and resale price, and commitments of shared governance.

CLTs have demonstrated their utility in enabling communities to persist through market upheavals. Assessments of CLTs such as Dudley Neighbors, Inc. in Boston, the Figueroa Corridor CLT in Los Angeles, the Time of Jubilee CLT in Syracuse,[41] the Detroit People's Platform in Detroit, and the New Community CLT in DC[42] show that the model is capable of sustaining economically diverse communities with strong social cohesion.[43] Additional case studies will illuminate the extent to which this cohesion is the product of legalistic stewardship – by which the CLT exercises the monitoring and enforcement terms expressed in the ground lease – or an outgrowth of thicker relationships stemming from shared commitments by CLT members, promoted by practices as a community that affirm reciprocal trust and sustain the values that generated the CLT.[44]

A necessary part of the CLT-as-Commons inquiry is internal CLT knowledge and production of its culture of commoning – of collective stewardship of the CLT's assets and social welfare vision. What is known about these specific practices, and do they foster sustainability and stewardship of a CLT as a bulwark against economic forces? What internal practices sustain a membership capable of disciplined self-management, and the requisite forms of knowledge to maintain the CLT as land resource and as reserve of cultural practices of co-stewardship? Commons knowledge plays as central a role as clarity of property rights, in mediating competing and complementary individual and social interests in the CLT. By studying commons applicability in the community land trust, we can explore how the cultural commons metaphor becomes concrete in the practices of community land trusting. While the number of studies is growing, it still remains scant.

COMMUNITY OVER COMMODITY HOUSING

01.03 ParaFirstqualities that attend its formative organizing, which is why organizing remains an important component of CLT sustainability long after the initial struggle to obtain land and launch the CLT. Among the oldest CLTs operating in the US are the Community Land Association of Clairfield, Tennessee (now known as the Woodland CLT), which originated to provide local people with housing and other economic opportunities not provided by absentee land and mine owners, and the Covenant CLT of Hancock County, Maine, which formed after

[40] Ostrom, "Reformulating the Commons," *Swiss Political Science Review* 6 (1 29), at 29–52 (2000) (appropriators who trust one another and use reciprocal relationships with one another face lower costs in monitoring and enforcement of shared maintenance). Id at 38
[41] James J. Kelly, Jr., "Land Trusts That Conserve Communities," *DePaul Law Review* 59: 69, 89 (2009).
[42] "How Community Land Trusts Can Help Address the Affordable Housing Crisis" *Jacobin Magazine*, July 2019
[43] See also Jennifer Le, *"The 'Community' In Community Land Trusts: The Role of Community Control in Pursuing Community Land Trust Activism"* (M. Planning, Ryerson University 2018), 38–60; Lee Dwyer, "Mapping Impact: An Analysis of the Dudley Street Neighborhood Initiative Land Trust" (M.City Planning 2015), 27–28 (contrasting DSNI to three not-for-profit housing developers).
[44] Kimberly Skobba, Andrew T. Carswell, "Community Land Trust Homeowners: Past and Present Housing Experiences," *Family & Consumer Sciences Research Journal* 43:4–17 (2014).

a plant closing left a number of locals unemployed and turned to housing economics after they started craft sales, a school, daycare center, and other projects, and ultimately housing.[45]

A useful body of literature published by several longtime CLT proponents warns that CLTs may be losing "the C in the CLT", abandoning the essential discourse of community control and benefit.[46] CLTs face competitive funding environments and feel intense pressure to promote CLTs as a tool for providing affordable housing, while downplaying their role in empowering poorer people to control land in perpetuity.[47] Where the neoliberal frame of private property rights leads some CLTs into thin stewardship, actualizing community control over CLT land depends upon both the depth and breadth of resident and community participation and leadership within a CLT.[48]

"Community control' is a term used widely in political, theoretical, and community organizing discourses since the 1960s. Although there is no singular consensus on its definition or the actual practices involved, many activists and scholars feature the concern of community control in a variety of efforts to collectively own and govern resources, as alternatives to dominant models of resource distribution that perpetuate and increase inequalities in wealth and well-being. Worker-owned producer cooperatives, community credit unions, housing cooperatives, community land trusts, local currencies, are examples of alternative ways of producing, distributing, consuming, and living that are gaining new visibility within an evolving framework of solidarity economics that center people over profit.[49] Critical studies scholars emphasize the local autonomy that derives from ownership of resources by disadvantaged groups, which can buffer them against the onslaught of discriminatory[50] or global capitalism.[51] These scholars also highlight the potential for community-owned property to carve out exceptions to the credit-based economy and power-laden relationships with landlords, bosses, banks, and corporations.[52]

According to surveys done by the National Community Land Trust Network, the majority of CLTs are implementing stewardship activities that include pre-purchase education, prevention of CLT buyers' use of high-risk loans, ongoing support for homeowners after purchase, and early detection of, and intervention in, delinquencies and foreclosure filings. The high prevalence of comprehensive stewardship practices incorporating education, prevention, and intervention activities, is thought to explain the low rates of delinquencies and foreclosures and high cure

[45] Karen Gray, "Community Land Trusts in the United States," *Journal of Community Practice* 16: 1, 65–78 (2008).

[46] See John Emmeus Davis, "Origins and Evolution of the Community Land Trust in the United States, in *The Community Land Trust Reader* (2010) 3–47; James DeFilippis, Brian Stromberg & Olivia R. Williams (2018) "W(h)ither the community in community land trusts?," *Journal of Urban Affairs*, 40:6, 755–769; Karen Gray, "Keeping 'Community' in a Community Land Trust," *Social Work Research* 35:4, 241–248 (2011).

[47] DeFilippis, Stromberg & Williams, "W(h)ither the Community" (2018); Olivia R. Williams, "Community Control as a Relationship between a Place-based Population and Institution: The Case of a Community Land Trust," *Local Economy* 33:5 (2018) 459–476

[48] Emily Thaden and Jeffrey S. Lowe," Resident and Community Engagement in Community Land Trusts," 2014 Lincoln Institute of Land Policy Working Paper

[49] Emily Kawano, "Crisis and Opportunity: The Emerging Solidarity Economy Movement," *Solidarity Economy I: Building Alternatives for People and Planet* (Center for Popular Economics, Amherst Mass., 2008).

[50] Jessica Gordon Nembhard, *Collective Courage: A History of African-American Economic Thought and Practice* (Penn State University Press, 2014).

[51] James Defillipis, *Unmaking Goliath: Community Control in The Face of Global Capital* 2003; "Community Control and Development: The Long View," *The Community Development Reader* 30–37 (Saegert and DeFillipis eds., 2010).

[52] Olivia R. Williams, "Community control as a relationship between a place-based population and institution: The case of a community land trust," *Local Economy* 33: 459, 460 (July 12, 2018).

rates in CLTs.[53] Thaden depicts methods of robust intervention that some CLTs use in helping residents manage financial stress, cure delinquencies and prevent foreclosures.[54]

CLTs devote substantial resources to the sustainability of homeownership for communitarian reasons. A CLT's success in preventing foreclosures and sustaining homeownership has a social and economic impact that extends well beyond a homeowner's property line. The costs of foreclosure ripple through neighborhoods and municipalities. Foreclosures significantly diminish nearby property values, making proximate properties vulnerable to depreciation and foreclosure. Costs to municipalities mount from the city's demolition of vacant buildings, unpaid utilities and property taxes, increasing crime around vacant buildings, and declining assessments in neighborhoods where foreclosures are clustered. Many CLT homebuyers are first-generation homeowners, who do not have current or transgenerational wealth that could ease the stressors of hard times. While homeownership can be a path to prosperity for low-income families, this is only possible if they remain in their homes for the long-term. One of the most devastating consequences of unsustainable homeownership is that it strips wealth away from low-income and minority communities. Even in the absence of foreclosure, roughly half of all low-income, market-rate homeowners revert to renting within five years of purchase.[55]

CONSTRUCTING THE CLT CULTURAL AND KNOWLEDGE COMMONS IN BALTIMORE

The CLT-as-Commons analysis here emphasizes two characteristics of enduring commons: self-governance and the transgenerational resource-preservation. CLT stewardship activities exceed the homebuyer education typical in the market or in other publicly-subsidized homeownership programs, and are better tailored to address the challenges and risks that may arise over the course of a lower-income household's acquisition and operation of a home.[56] A few CLTs – Dudley Neighbors in Boston, Durham CLT in North Carolina, Champlain Housing Trust in Vermont – have robust practices and rich histories of involving their neighborhood residents in community-based planning and outcomes beyond providing permanent housing.[57]

In an effort to learn from one another synergistically, several nascent CLT communities formed Share Baltimore, an inter-organizational coalition, in 2017 to facilitate resource sharing and capacity-building of members in order to create a sustainable movement of shared-equity, community-led development in Baltimore.[58] The participants knew each other from years of grassroots advocacy for municipal policy to fund housing as a human right.[59] After much informal consulting with CLT movement and capacity builders in Boston, New York City, Oakland, and elsewhere, SHARE formalized its knowledge-building efforts in 2019 and formed

---

[53] Sungu-Eryilmaz, Yesim, and Greenstein, Rosalind. A National Study of Community Land Trusts (Working Paper). Lincoln Institute for Land Policy, 2007. http://cltnetwork.org/wp-content/uploads/2014/01/2007-A-National-Study-of-CLTs.pdf; Emily Thaden, "Outperforming the Market: Making Sense of the Low Rates of Delinquencies and Foreclosures in Community Land Trusts,"2010 Lincoln Institute of Land Policy, 16–25.

[54] Emily Thaden, "Stewardship Works," *Shelterforce* (December 24, 2010).

[55] "Paths to Homeownership for Low-Income and Minority Households," *Evidence Matters*, Fall 2012 www.huduser.gov/portal/periodicals/em/fall12/highlight1.html

[56] The NCLTN study found that 95 percent required a CLT-specific orientation, 85 percent of CLTs required general homebuyer education, and 67 percent required homebuyers to meet with a lawyer before purchase. About half of CLTs offer post-purchase services to build homeowner competency and security, such as financial literacy training, referrals to contractors for improvements and repairs, and mandatory counseling for delinquent homeowners.

[57] Lowe and Thaden, "Deepening Stewardship," 622.

[58] Share Baltimore, *Bylaws* Article II, Purpose.

[59] www.baltimorehousinggroundtable.org/media

the Learning Exchange, which is focused on supporting start-up CLTs. One of their first projects was to launch a joint pilot project to demonstrate the effectiveness of CLTs in creating permanently affordable, community-driven development throughout the city of Baltimore.

SHARE's Learning Exchange is seen as an essential practice to ensure commitment to community control and agency in Baltimore's emergent CLT culture, and to avoid the pitfalls experienced by other CLTs. The Learning Exchange works to share and deepen the knowledge base and capacity of existing and emerging CLTs to effectively participate in the Pilot.[60] SHARE's participants share twin priorities to deliver durably affordable housing units, while organizing and sustaining the engagement of community members in their CLTs and the CLT movement. The first iteration of the Share Baltimore LX, still underway, has instilled in the participants an appreciation for the work ahead, which will include building sustainable CLTs that maintain the affordability of the land long-term, preserving and enhancing the role of the community in making this happen. This process has emphasized the importance of CLT members' personal agency and collective power, and intentionality to sustain the cultural shift from commodity housing to 'keeping the C in the CLT.' The training underway engages participants to connect four skill-and-knowledge sets – community organizing, community development, human service delivery, and public policy advocacy – as ongoing rather than sequential elements in the life of a CLT-as-commons. Share Baltimore members are determining that a deep commitment to each is essential in order to steward a CLT over the long haul. Combined, these can accrue social and political capital, physical and economic capital, and human capital to the CLT over time.

Specific areas of practical training include encouraging the interdependence of residents and institutionalizing community members' power and responsibility by creating a culture of democratic decision-making and transparency. Participants apply their experience and knowledge of community organizing to this new phase of community building and collective action and focus on institutionalizing democratic practices into the CLT's formal governance structure. CLT-forming communities have need early for the empowering knowledge of how to stand together in the role of land owner, with the confidence to hire and direct the services of the physical development of CLT homes, and its subprocesses of strategic planning and resource development for land acquisition, property rehabilitation or construction, and cost factoring, for which CLTs commonly turn to a variety of professionals. Baltimore Share's learning exchange aims to support each emergent CLT in practices of community-based governance and community-wide social welfare purpose.

CONCLUSION

In conclusion, the legal form of community land trust recognized in American law usefully maps onto the common-property regime first analyzed and articulated by Elinor Ostrom and her colleagues. While CLTs face resource pressures to devolve into not-for-profit housing providers, Ostrom's work reveals how a robust form of CLT-as-Commons is possible, both theoretically and in reality. A CLT-as-Commons must do more than hold a portfolio of housing units in trust across generations at below-market sales prices. It must construct a cultural commons — the essential knowledge production and distribution, and capacity for efficacious self-management by the members – necessary for its members' to remain committed to the CLT mission and vision.

[60] Real estate development services for the pilot project, to develop the first 50 CLT homes in five neighborhood-based CLTs, are being provided through the Govans Ecumencial Development Corporation.

15

Ostromian Logic Applied to Civil Society Organizations and the Rules That Shape Them

Anthony J. DeMattee and Chrystie Swiney

This chapter applies the Institutional Analysis and Development (IAD) Framework, conceived by Nobel Laureate Elinor Ostrom in 1990, to the institutional arrangements that structure and organize the operating environments for civil society organizations (CSOs). We begin by defining what is meant by "civil society" and "CSOs," highlighting their essential attributes, followed by a discussion of the importance of the legal and regulatory frameworks that underlie the existence and operation of CSOs. We then briefly review Garett Hardin's "Tragedy of the Commons" thesis before discussing the role that CSOs can play in preventing such "tragedies" from emerging in the first place. After presenting the types of rules that inform every IAD action situation and applying them to the existing research on CSOs, we conclude by reconceptualizing CSO regulatory regimes through the lens of Ostrom's IAD framework and analysis.

DEFINING CIVIL SOCIETY & CSOS

"Civil society," considered the "invisible subcontinent on the landscape of contemporary society,"[1] is an amorphous term defined in a dizzying number of ways by a multitude of organizations, scholars, lawyers, and civil society practitioners.[2] It is used to refer to individual activists, broad social movements, non-governmental organizations, religious organizations, cultural and sports clubs, philanthropic foundations, political parties, the media, and community groups. We define CSOs as nongovernmental, voluntarily formed, organizational entities that exist for purposes other than political control, economic profit, or crime.[3] This definition situates CSOs as entities within civil society but differentiates them from other actors such as amorphous social movements, political parties, or terrorist groups. CSOs, under our definition, include both formal organizations that have officially registered with the state, and therefore receive certain tax privileges and are held to certain legal obligations, as well as informal groups of individuals who have no formal relationship with, or recognition by, the state. CSOs include established transnational organizations with well-known names, multi-million-dollar budgets,

---

[1] L. M. Salamon & H. K. Anheier, "The Civil Society Sector," *Society*, 34, 2 (1997), 60–65, 60–61.

[2] A. C. Vakil, "Confronting the Classification Problem: Toward a Taxonomy of NGOs," *World Development*, 25, 12 (1997), 2057–2070; J. N. Brass et al., "NGOs and International Development: A Review of Thirty-five Years of Scholarship," *World Development*, 112 (2018), 136–149.

[3] J. Wolff & A. E. Poppe, *From Closing Space to Contested Spaces: Re-assessing Current Conflicts over International Civil Society Support* (Frankfurt, 2015); N. Ferguson, *The Great Degeneration: How Institutions Decay and Economies Die* (London: Penguin Books, 2012), 15–16.

and satellite offices spread throughout the globe, such as the International Committee of the Red Cross, the Open Society Foundations, and Doctors Without Borders. But they also include neighborhood book clubs, local gardening groups, and other "amateurs without borders,"[4] or no-name groups consisting of a few individuals working on shoestring budgets with the help of volunteers to advance their particular agenda. CSOs include "do-good" organizations, such as Human Rights Watch, Amnesty International, Save the Children, and the Girls Scouts, as well as organizations with what many would consider malicious agendas, such as the Ku Klux Klan, the Alt-Right, and the United Aryan Front.[5] Perhaps the only thing that unites this exceedingly diverse array of organizations is, at least according to our definition, what they are not: *nongovernmental* and *not-for-profit*.[6]

Conventional approaches lead us to believe that all CSOs are non-exclusive, open to all, and non-discriminatory in their distribution of goods and services. But this does not accurately reflect reality, which is more nuanced and complicated than that kind of dichotomous thinking. CSOs vary considerably, with many having exclusive or status-based membership requirements and others being open to a broader, albeit still defined, swath of the population. The current literature on CSOs does not lend itself to this type of nuanced conceptualization of CSOs. However, the Ostromian paradigm, which has never been applied to CSOs, usefully provides a framework to differentiate among the multitude of CSOs that exist. More specifically, Ostromian logic allows us to differentiate goods, in this case CSOs, according to their varying levels of excludability and subtractability. Excludability refers to the ability to restrict which individuals can use and enjoy a particular good,[7] while subtractability is the extent to which an individual's use of a collectively shared good subtracts from the availability of that good for consumption by others.[8]

Combinations of excludability and subtractability, according to Ostrom and her colleagues, produce four well-known types of goods: public, private, toll, and common pool.[9] Public and toll goods have characteristically low subtractability: one person's use of the good doesn't reduce or limit another's enjoyment of that good. Private goods and common-pool resources (CPRs), on the other hand, have high subtractability: one individual's use of the good takes away from others' enjoyment and use of that good. Toll goods (such as country clubs) and private goods (like consumer products) are easily excludable. In contrast, CPRs (like forests and water basins) and public goods (like community parks) are generally nonexcludable and accessible to all.

[4] A. Schnable, *Amateurs Without Borders: The Aspirations and Limits of Global Compassion* (Oakland: University of California Press, 2021).

[5] S. Chambers & J. Kopstein, "Bad Civil Society," *Political Theory*, 29, 6 (2001), 837–865, 842. state that "vibrant and well-organized civil society … gave birth to and nurtured the Nazi movement."

[6] A. Klotz, "Transnational Activism and Global Transformations: The Anti-Apartheid and Abolitionist Experiences," *European Journal of International Relations*, 8, 1 (2002), 49–76; T. Risse-Kappen, *Bringing Transnational Relations Back In: Non-state Actors, Domestic Structures, and International Institutions* (Cambridge: Cambridge University Press, 1995), 3.

[7] V. Ostrom & E. Ostrom, "Public Goods and Public Choices," in M. D. McGinnis (ed.), *Polycentricity and Local Public Economies: Readings from the Workshop in Political Theory and Policy Analysis* (Originally printed in *In Alternatives for Delivering Public Services. Toward Improved Performance*, ed. E. S. Savas. Boulder, CO: Westview Press, 7–49 edition., Ann Arbor: University of Michigan Press, 1977 [1999]), 76–77; E. Ostrom, *Understanding Institutional Diversity* (Princeton: Princeton University Press, 2005), 23.

[8] M. D. McGinnis, "An Introduction to IAD and the Language of the Ostrom Workshop: A Simple Guide to a Complex Framework," *Policy Studies Journal*, 39, 1 (2011), 169–183, 174; Ostrom, *Understanding Institutional Diversity*, 23.

[9] E. Ostrom, *Governing the Commons: The Evolution of Institutions for Collective Action* (Cambridge: Cambridge University Press, 1990).

While Ostromian logic is useful for classifying specific types of CSOs, none of its categories captures the experiential good that many individuals enjoy simply by participating in CSOs. For this, we develop a new concept, which we refer to simply as an *associational good*. Individuals use and enjoy "associational goods" when they voluntarily assemble, in the absence of profit-motivations or governmental coercion, to engage in a shared activity, cause, or agenda. Examples of associational goods, which are in part tangible and in part intangible, and which are rooted in practices and behaviors rather than discrete resources or physical property, include: celebrating a shared faith, enjoying shared activities, joining a professional society or association, protesting against social injustice, and advocating for a particular policy proposal. For most CSOs, the associational good they offer has low subtractability, and enjoyment by one generally does not subtract from the enjoyment of another. Excludability, by contrast, can and does vary.

Using Ostromian logic, we can differentiate CSOs according to who can participate in them. Some CSOs are like public goods or CPRs because it is difficult to exclude individuals from associating with them. Animal welfare societies, human rights groups, religious congregations, and museums all have a limited ability or interest in restricting which individuals can and cannot participate in them. Of course, excludability is not a discrete category but rather a continuum. Museums may suggest a "recommended donation" or require a purchased ticket, but they cannot easily exclude who chooses to purchase a ticket; the same with religious groups and many advocacy organizations, which are motivated to have as many congregants or participants as possible but who implicitly exclude those who don't believe in their cause. Like goods, CSOs can be differentiated on the basis of how easily and to what extent they exclude certain groups; CSOs vary wildly on this front. CSOs with high levels of excludability are exclusive associations, which typically use a variety of means to exclude individuals from associating, including membership dues (e.g., private clubs and fraternal societies), educational degrees (e.g., the American Bar Association), aptitude tests (e.g., MENSA), or public service (e.g., Veterans of Foreign Wars).

We can further differentiate CSOs based on what they produce and for whom (Figure 15.1). We begin with inclusive CSOs that have little ability to restrict access to which individuals receive their services, which we refer to as *Public Goods CSOs* ("*PG CSOs*"). This kind of CSO is open to an expansive portion of the population and produces goods or offers services with low subtractability, or goods and services that, when consumed or utilized, do not exclude from the enjoyment or use by others. Examples of *PG CSOs* include legal clinics that collect and publish free online repositories of legal information, environmental organizations that voluntarily build rain gardens in parks, and democracy-promoting groups that host voter education booths at farmers markets. The services and goods produced by *PG CSOs* are offered freely to all without exclusion.

Common Pool Resources CSOs (*CPR CSOs*) organize staff, volunteers, and resources to produce nonexcludable, but subtractable goods, such as meals or health services. They share all but one key element with *PG CSOs*: these organizations produce goods or offer services that are in limited supply. When one individual consumes the good they offer or accepts their services, that consumption subtracts from the use of that good or service by others. *CPR CSOs* include food banks that offer a limited number of meals each week, battered women shelters that offer safe housing on a first come, first serve basis, and clinics that voluntarily provide free medical screenings until their supplies run out.

CSOs that produce goods and services that are excludable but non-subtractable can be categorized as *Toll Goods CSOs* (*TG CSOs*). This kind of CSO can easily limit access to their goods or services through membership requirements, such as employment status, education level, membership dues, or residency in a particular neighborhood. Once a member, however,

Source: Adapted from V. Ostrom and E. Ostrom 1977 [1999] (p. 12) and E. Ostrom 2005 (p. 24)

FIGURE 15.1 Conceptualizing CSOs using an Ostromian Framework[10]

all members have exclusive and generally equal access to the goods or services offered by the CSO. Examples of *TG CSOs* include trade unions that negotiate better conditions for their workers, professional associations that conduct membership trainings, and organizations serving economically marginalized groups.

Private Goods CSOs, by contrast, produce organizational outputs that are excludable and subtractable. Funding intermediaries and foundations are one example. Although these CSOs may have a public or charitable mission, they provide grants to specific recipients. Village savings and loan associations are additional examples. These small, self-governed groups collectively save their money so members can access small loans and emergency insurance. Both examples feature limited financial resources that are highly subtractable. We conceptualize private goods CSOs as private and self-governed groups that exist for purposes other than political control or economic profit and produce goods that are both easily excludable and highly subtractable.

Ostrom's pioneering research allows us to conceptualize CSOs in a more nuanced, complex way, and in a way that better reflects reality. It's critical that we understand CSOs as the enormously complex and varied array of organizations that they comprise, and resist encapsulating them all in the same altruistic, black and white ways. The typology introduced above can help to break down this conventional and overly simplistic way of understanding CSOs and, more specifically, assist civil society scholars and practitioners to better understand the various ways that CSOs operate and serve their communities.

THE TRAGEDY OF THE COMMONS APPLIED TO CSOS

It was not until the efforts of a team of determined researchers at the Workshop in Political Theory and Policy Analysis at Indiana University, led by Vincent and Elinor Ostrom, that

---

[10] Figure adapted from Ostrom & Ostrom, "Public Goods and Public Choices," 12; Ostrom, *Understanding Institutional Diversity*, 24. This figure shows the familiar typology of goods with categories for excludability (y-axis) and subtractability (x-axis). Associational goods discussed in terms of who can participate in the CSO. Four CSO types discussed in terms of the goods and services CSOs produce and for whom.

scholars began to understand that there was a third way to avert the tragedy of the commons. Others in this volume, such as William Blomquist, Andrew P. Follet, Brigham Daniels, and Taylor Petersen, have reviewed the particulars of Hardin's seven-page essay from 1968, "the Tragedy of the Commons," so it will not be reviewed here.[11] Elinor Ostrom, whose empirical work on this question led to her becoming the first female noble laureate in economics, closely analyzed hundreds of real-life commons' cases, such as high mountain meadows and forests in Switzerland and Japan, irrigation communities in Spain and the Philippines, fisheries in Turkey, Sri Lanka, and Nova Scotia, and groundwater management systems in California.[12] This bottom-up, evidence-based, globally comparative approach defined and shaped Elinor Ostrom's ground-breaking work, which is outlined in her book, *Governing the Commons*.[13] In this book, Ostrom empirically confirms that a "third way" to solving commons dilemmas is possible, even if not guaranteed. At the heart of the solution are local voluntary associations of individuals who, in the absence of private ownership or governmental oversight, successfully create, oversee, and enforce their governance regimes and prevent the degradation or over-use of their shared resources. This conclusion – that under the right conditions, which Ostrom carefully defines, self-governance is a viable alternative to government regulation or privatization – was revolutionary for its implications for the widely cited and believed "tragedy of the commons" thesis.

Elinor Ostrom emphasized the value of civil society in her research, even if she didn't use that precise term.[14] She understood civil society to be the domain of society organized through voluntary association, which is what teaches us the art and science of self-governance and what builds, according to Vincent Ostrom (her husband), "political capacity."[15] While CSOs are not always virtuous in their aims or means,[16] research from contexts as diverse as Kenya, Haiti, Peru, and North Korea provide examples of the many valuable and indeed essential roles that CSOs play in societies throughout the globe.[17] Overall, without CSOs, the skills, organizational infrastucture, and motivation necessary for self-governance can quickly vanish.

[11] G. Hardin, "The Tragedy of the Commons," *Science*, 162, 3859 (1968), 1243–1248.

[12] E. Ostrom et al., *Rules, Games, and Common-Pool Resources* (Ann Arbor: University of Michigan Press, 1994); E. Ostrom et al., "CPR Coding Manual," Bloomington: Indiana University, Workshop in Political Theory and Policy Analysis (1989).

[13] Ostrom, *Governing the Commons: The Evolution of Institutions for Collective Action*.

[14] "Tocqueville" is the name given to space of highest honor in the Vincent and Elinor Ostrom Workshop in Political Theory and Policy Analysis. The Ostroms' numerous honors and awards adorn the walls of The Tocqueville Room in which large, artisan wooden tables stage public discussions and facilitate intellectual debate. Moreover, the Ostroms founded and funded the Tocqueville Fund for the Study of Human Institutions.

[15] V. Ostrom, *The Intellectual Crisis in American Public Administration* 3rd ed., (Tuscaloosa: University of Alabama Press, 1973 [2008]), 149.

[16] Chambers & Kopstein, "Bad Civil Society"; C. C. Gibson et al., *The Samaritan's Dilemma: The Political Economy of Development Aid* (Oxford: Oxford University Press, 2005); T. T. Schwartz, *Travesty in Haiti: A True Account of Christian Missions, Orphanages, Fraud, Food Aid and Drug Trafficking* BookSurge Publishing, 2008); D. Moyo, *Dead Aid: Why Aid is Not Working and How there is a Better Way for Africa* (New York: Farrar, Straus and Giroux, 2009); N. Banks et al., "NGOs, States, and Donors Revisited: Still Too Close for Comfort?," *World Development*, 66 (2015), 707–718; M. Edwards & D. Hulme, "Too Close for Comfort? The Impact of Official Aid on Non-governmental Organizations," *World Development*, 24, 6 (1996), 961–974; E. S. Clemens, "The Constitution of Citizens: Political Theories of Nonprofit Organizations," in W. W. Powell & R. Steinberg (eds.), *The Nonprofit Sector: A Research Handbook* (2nd ed., New Haven: Yale University Press, 2006), 207–220; D. H. Smith, "Impact of Voluntary Sector on Society," in D. H. Smith (ed.), *Voluntary Action Research* (Lexington, MA: Lexington Books, 1973).

[17] W. Mutunga, *Constitution-Making from the Middle: Civil Society and Transition Politics in Kenya, 1992-1997* (Nairobi, Kenya: SAREAT, 1999); J. Nelson-Nuñez, "Substitution or Facilitation: Service-Delivery NGOs and Political Engagement in the Peruvian Amazon," *Comparative Political Studies*, 52, 3 (2019), 445–477; J. N. Brass, *Allies or Adversaries? NGOs and the State in Africa* (Cambridge: Cambridge University Press, 2016); A. J. DeMattee, "Was it Worth It? The Effects of ODA, NGOs, and Time on Local Politics in the Haitian State," in S. Haeffele et al. (eds.), *Informing Public Policy: Analyzing Contemporary US and International Policy Issues through the Lens of Market*

APPLYING AN OSTROMIAN LENS TO CSO RESEARCH

Civil society is critical to certain fundamental sociopolitical outcomes, including the emergence, ongoing existence, and robustness of democracy.[18] But civil society is only able to contribute to these outcomes under certain conditions, which are often dictated by their relationship with the state. Scholars have identified a variety of frameworks that describe the state-civil society relationship.[19] The rules contained in a nation's laws, public policies, and regulations are influential, and at times decisive, in determining the nature of the state-CSO relationship. A recent systematic review of over 3,000 peer-reviewed articles shows that for over 35 years, scholars have studied the legal institutions that regulate state-CSO relations.[20] Yet, the existing CSO literature continues to lack a coherent or nuanced theory for explaining the differences between the variety of CSO rules seen throughout the globe, the implications of these different rules on CSOs, and more generally, the ways in which a nation's legal regime shapes the ability of CSOs to emerge, operate and flourish.

Interdependence theory, first articulated by civil society expert Lester Salamon in the 1980s, acknowledges the important synergies between the government and CSOs. It predicts that the legal and regulatory regime is what, in large part, determines state-civil society relations. This theory can, in part, help to explain the frequent rule changes impacting CSOs that we've seen across the globe, particularly over the past two decades. However, this theory assumes a well-meaning state and a virtuous nonprofit sector, which limits its application to legal provisions that grant additional autonomy and opportunities for collaboration with CSOs. The adversarial state-CSO relationship, and rules that limit (rather than enhance) CSOs' independence, are blind spots for this otherwise illuminating theory.

A nascent area of research, which casts doubt on the interdependence theory, examines the widespread use of the law as a tool of state repression and control over civil society actors.[21] Practitioners and scholars call this global trend the "closing" or "shrinking" space phenomenon,

Process Economics (Lanham: Rowman & Littlefield International, 2019), 141–169; S. Snyder, "American Religious NGOs in North Korea: A Paradoxical Relationship," *Ethics & International Affairs*, 21, 4 (2007), 423–430.

[18] A. de Tocqueville, *Democracy in America* English edition, (Indianapolis: Liberty Fund, 1840); R. D. Putnam, *Making Democracy Work: Civic Traditions in Modern Italy* (Princeton: Princeton University Press, 1993); F. Fukuyama, *Trust: The Social Virtues and the Creation of Prosperity* (New York: Free Press, 1995); P. D. Aligica, *Public Entrepreneurship, Citizenship, and Self-Governance* (Cambridge: Cambridge University Press, 2018); T. Skocpol & M. P. Fiorina (eds.), *Civic Engagement in American Democracy* (Washington, DC: Brookings Institution Press and Russell Sage Foundation, 1999); Ostrom, *Governing the Commons: The Evolution of Institutions for Collective Action*; Mutunga, *Constitution-Making from the Middle: Civil Society and Transition Politics in Kenya, 1992-1997*; J. J. Linz & A. C. Stepan, *Problems of Democratic Transition and Consolidation: Southern Europe, South America, and Post-Communist Europe* (Baltimore: Johns Hopkins University Press, 1996).

[19] M. Bratton, "The Politics of Government-NGO Relations in Africa," *World Development*, 17, 4 (1989), 569–587; M. C. Cammett & L. M. MacLean, "The Political Consequences of Non-state Social Welfare: An Analytical Framework," in L. M. MacLean & M. C. Cammett (eds.), *The Politics of Non-state Social Welfare* (Ithaca, NY: Cornell University Press, 2014), 31–56; A. Najam, "The Four C's of Government Third Sector-Government Relations," *Nonprofit Management and Leadership*, 10, 4 (2000), 375–396; D. R. Young, "Alternative Models of Government-Nonprofit Sector Relations: Theoretical and International Perspectives," *Nonprofit and Voluntary Sector Quarterly*, 29, 1 (2000), 49–172.

[20] Brass, J. N., Longhofer, W., Robinson, R. S., & Schnable, A. (2018). NGOs and international development: A review of thirty-five years of scholarship. *World Development*, 112, 136–149.

[21] T. Carothers, "The Backlash Against Democracy Promotion," *Foreign Affairs*, 85, 2 (2006), 55–68; C. Gershman & M. Allen, "The Assault on Democracy Assistance," *Journal of Democracy*, 17, 2 (2006), 36–51; D. Christensen & J. M. Weinstein, "Defunding Dissent: Restrictions on Aid to NGOs," *Journal of Democracy*, 24, 2 (2013), 77–91; C. Swiney, "The Counter-Associational Revolution: The Rise, Spread & Contagion of Restrictive Civil Society Laws in the World's Strongest Democratic States," *Fordham International Law Journal*, 43, 2 (2019), 399–456.

which refers to the attempt by governments to constrain the spaces where civil society can operate freely and autonomously from government control. Unlike the interdependence theory, the closing space theory assumes an adversarial state-CSO relationship and tends to depict the government as the "bad" actor and CSOs as the "good" one. It is, therefore, silent on amicable state-CSO relationships, creating its own set of blind spots.

Neither interdependence theory nor the closing space literature comprehensively explains how and why governments use laws to regulate CSOs and shape different state-CSO relationships. The history, complexity, and dynamism of state-CSO relationships call us to reevaluate existing theories and, perhaps, develop new ones. New theories must consider the nuanced nature of the CSO sector, the goods or services they offer, and the communities or groups they serve (or exclude). In the following section, we attempt to offer a new way to conceive of state-CSO relations, one that is more inclusive, flexible, and agnostic concerning the intentions of the actors involved. This new conceptual framework builds on the Ostromian Institutional Analysis and Development Framework (the IAD Framework) and the new way of conceptualizing CSOs articulated above.

RULES AFFECTING THE IAD ACTION SITUATION

The "action situation" is the centerpiece of the IAD Framework, which explains how self-governance can lead to successful outcomes in the absence of governmental or private sector involvement. The "action situation" represents the arena in which actors interact to produce outcomes.[22] Many interactions occur within a single action situation, including the exchange of goods and services, problem-solving and dispute resolution, the domination of one actor over others, and moments of discord.[23] Table 15.1 revisits the seven types of rules that define the IAD action situation. The left column summarizes these several rule types and provides page numbers to Ostrom's authoritative explanations of each (left column). The right column shows applied examples of exogenous legal rules that affect CSO action situations.

CSOs engage in many "action situations" throughout their existence. One of the earliest is the decision to remain as an informal association or apply for formal registration with the state. The decision to register produces links to another action situation because the registration process generally requires interacting with government actors. The rules of the registration process vary, but the process typically leads to one of two outcomes: a favorable decision that allows the CSO to enjoy the privileges that accompany the legal form or a rejection that the CSO can either accept or appeal. CSO action situations are not limited to interactions with the government. CSOs routinely interact with donors, volunteers, beneficiaries, members, organizational leaders, and other CSOs. These interactions showcase different actors engaging in collective decision-making, problem-solving, and dispute resolution. Each exchange is a unique CSO "action situation," and the only shared characteristic is that exogenous rules affect them. Even then, however, CSOs that are different legal types may be subject to a different set of exogenous rules.

CSO REGULATORY REGIMES

Governments use laws to overtly and explicitly communicate the exogenous legal rules that regulate CSOs. We refer to these legal frameworks as *CSO Regulatory Regimes*, which are defined as the various restrictive and permissive legal provisions that constrain and/or incentivize CSOs' existence

---

[22] McGinnis, "Introduction to IAD," 173; E. Ostrom, "Beyond Markets and States: Polycentric Governance of Complex Economic Systems," *The American Economic Review*, 100, 3 (2010), 641–672, 64.

[23] Ostrom, *Understanding Institutional Diversity*, 14.

TABLE 15.1 *Rules affecting CSOs' action situations*[24]

Type and function of rule	Type and function of CSO rule
1. *Position Rules* (p. 190): specify the required positions, how they are filled and replaced, and how many actors can hold each one.	• Applied Examples: government must *create* an agency to regulate and monitor CSOs; informal associations *must* meet clear legal definition to incorporate as an official CSO legal form.
2. *Boundary Rules* (p. 190; 194–200): how actors are assigned to or leave positions and how one situation links to other situations.	• Applied Examples: CSOs *must* have a minimum number of members and/or possess a certain amount of capital before registering; CSOs *may* appeal regulatory actions to an independent court.
3. *Choice Rules* (p. 200; 301): specify the duties and actions required of each position.	• Applied Examples: CSOs *must* apply for registration with the government; regulator *must* be overseen by a board of civil society representatives and government officials.
4. *Aggregation Rules* (p. 202): specify how decisions are made, such as majority or unanimity rules.	• Applied Examples: CSOs *forbidden to* appeal a registration denial or deregistration order (nonsymmetric aggregation rule); members *must* agree on a governing document, commonly known as bylaws, for CSO self-management (symmetric aggregation rule).
5. *Information Rules* (p. 206): authorize channels of information flow among participants, and obligations, permissions, or prohibition to communicate.	• Applied Examples: agency *may* publish certain information about a CSO or seize a CSO's documents without reasonable cause; the agency *must* have reasonable cause and follow explicit rules when investigating CSOs or conducting inspections of CSO property or premises.
6. *Payoff Rules* (p. 207): assigns external rewards or sanctions to particular actions.	• Applied Examples: CSOs *must* surrender certain organizational assets to the government or its agent upon project completion; taxpayers *may* take a tax deduction for supporting specific CSOs according to their legal type.
7. *Scope Rules* (p. 208): specify the outcomes that could be affected.	• Applied Examples: the government *may* make new rules regulating CSOs on certain matters; CSOs *may* adopt standards for self-regulation through umbrella associations.

and operations. As defined, this concept is neutral concerning the degree to which the existing legal and regulatory frameworks in place help or hinder the flourishing of an independence civil society. A CSO regulatory regime affects CSOs' action situations depending on the legal rules they contain and how the government implements and enforces them. The IAD framework identifies seven rule types that externally affect an action situation at any particular time.[25]

RESTRICTIVE CSO RULES

Though the concerns raised in the "closing space" literature are warranted, this body of work can be unclear regarding how 'restrictions on CSOs,' which include restrictive CSO laws, are

---

[24] The left column contains definitions provided by Ostrom with page numbers identifying relevant sections in *Understanding Institutional Diversity*. Ostrom, "Beyond Markets and States," 652; Ostrom, *Understanding Institutional Diversity*. For other discussions of these rules see Ostrom et al., *Rules, Games, and Common-Pool Resources*, 41–42; McGinnis, "Introduction to IAD," 173–174; D. H. Cole, "Laws, Norms, and the Institutional Analysis and Development Framework," *Journal of Institutional Economics*, 13, 4 (2017), 829–847, 8–10. The right column includes examples of rules that regulate CSOs selected from a review of research studying CSO laws, which uncovered over fifty distinct rules that govern CSO action situations. See A. J. DeMattee, "Toward a Coherent Framework: A Typology and Conceptualization of CSO Regulatory Regimes," *Nonprofit Policy Forum*, 9, 4 (2019), 1–17.

[25] Ostrom, *Understanding Institutional Diversity*, 14, 190; Ostrom, "Beyond Markets and States," 652.

defined. A maximalist definition holds that any conceivable new rule (whether embodied in a law, policy or regulation) imposed on CSOs is, by definition, restrictive (irrespective of the contents of the rule). Such a broad definition overlooks the advantages that might accompany certain rules, such as access to tax advantages in exchange for a rule requiring the filing of annual tax returns. What is more, some rules broadly serve the public's collective interest by preventing CSOs from engaging in fraud or criminal misuse of their legal status, rules that apply to all organizational forms. To classify such rules as "restrictive," as certain closing space researchers have done, seems an overuse of that term.[26]

Restrictive rules, as we define them here, are those that lessen the autonomy of CSOs by imposing restrictions on their ability to form, operate, self-govern, and access resources.[27] Restrictive CSO rules reduce the public's trust in CSOs, decrease demand for their goods and services, and ultimately, can shrink the number and diversity of CSOs in a country. The more restrictive the CSO rules, the more control the government has over their emergence, operations, and resources.[28] Such legal provisions grant government agencies broad discretion to deny CSO registration or renewal applications[29] and empower agencies to interfere with CSOs' internal operations,[30] and limit CSOs' access to vital resources, including funding.[31]

PERMISSIVE CSO RULES

The "closing space" phenomenon is a serious matter, but we urge analysts not to forget that permissive legal rules can empower the work and independence of CSOs. Permissive rules, as defined here, are those that *increase* the autonomy of the civil society sector by making it easier for them to form and operate, enlarging their permissible scope of activities, and lessening or

---

[26] A. J. DeMattee, "Covenants, Constitutions, and Distinct Law Types: Investigating Governments' Restrictions on CSOs Using an Institutional Approach," *VOLUNTAS: International Journal of Voluntary and Nonprofit Organizations*, 30, 6 (2019), 1229–1255; DeMattee, Anthony J. 2020. "Domesticating Civil Society: How and Why Governments Use Laws to Regulate CSOs." Doctoral Dissertation, Department of Political Science and O'Neill School of Public and Environmental Affairs, Indiana University. finds different risk factors predict the adoption of different types of restrictive provisions.

[27] DeMattee, "Toward a Coherent Framework'; Swiney, "The Counter-Associational Revolution."

[28] Wolff & Poppe, *From Closing Space to Contested Spaces*; M. T. Maru, *Legal Frameworks Governing Non-Governmental Organizations in the Horn of Africa* (Kampala, Uganda, 2017); D. Rutzen, "Aid Barriers and the Rise of Philanthropic Protectionism," *International Journal of Not-for-Profit Law*, 17, 1 (2015), 1–42.

[29] S. N. Ndegwa, "NGOs and the State in Kenya," *The Two Faces of Civil Society: NGOs and Politics in Africa* (Kumarian Press Books on International Development; West Hartford, CT: Kumarian Press, 1996), 31–54; P. Kameri-Mbote, *The Operational Environment and Constraints for NGOs in Kenya: Strategies for Good Policy and Practice* (Geneva, Switzerland, 2002); M. Tiwana & N. Belay, *Civil Society: The Clampdown is Real – Global Trends 2009-2010* (Washington, DC, 2010); M. K. Gugerty, "Shifting Patterns of State Regulation and NGO Self-Regulation in Sub-Saharan Africa," in O. B. Breen et al. (eds.), *Regulatory Waves: Comparative Perspectives on State Regulation and Self-Regulation Policies in the Nonprofit Sector* (Cambridge: Cambridge University Press, 2017), 69–91.

[30] Kameri-Mbote, *Operational Environment and Constraints for NGOs in Kenya*; S. H. Mayhew, "Hegemony, Politics and Ideology: The Role of Legislation in NGO–Government Relations in Asia," *The Journal of Development Studies*, 41, 5 (2005), 727–758; Maru, *Legal Frameworks Governing NGOs*.

[31] T. Hodenfield & C.-M. Pegus, *Mounting Restrictions on Civil Society: The Gap Between Rhetoric and Reality* (Washington, DC, 2013); S. Appe & M. Marchesini da Costa, "Waves of Nonprofit Regulation and Self-Regulation in Latin America: Evidence and Trends from Brazil and Ecuador," in O. B. Breen et al. (eds.), *Regulatory Waves: Comparative Perspectives on State Regulation and Self-Regulation Policies in the Nonprofit Sector* (Cambridge: Cambridge University Press, 2017), 154–175; Christensen & Weinstein, "Defunding Dissent'; M. Sidel, "State Regulation and the Emergence of Self-Regulation in the Chinese and Vietnamese Nonprofit and Philanthropic Sectors," in O. B. Breen et al. (eds.), *Regulatory Waves: Comparative Perspectives on State Regulation and Self-Regulation Policies in the Nonprofit Sector* (Cambridge: Cambridge University Press, 2017), 92–112; M. Reddy, "Do Good Fences Make Good Neighbours? Neighbourhood Effects of Foreign Funding Restrictions to NGOs," *St Antony's International Review*, 13, 2 (2018), 109–141.

eliminating restrictions on access to funding, both domestic and foreign. Permissive CSO laws strengthen society's trust in civil society, tend to increase the supply and diversity of CSOs, and in general, lead to a more robust and vibrant CSO ecosystem.[32]

In practice, permissive rules allow CSOs to self-regulate and keep government oversight at an appropriate minimum. These rules require government agencies to make registration and renewal decisions impartially and efficiently and offer appeals in the event of registration rejections or operational obstacles. Permissive rules restrict the involvement of government actors in CSOs' internal affairs to a bare minimum, and place strict limits and apply the full array of due process standards with respect to the government's ability to investigate, inspect, and prosecute CSOs suspected of criminal wrongdoing.

LEGAL VS. WORKING RULES

As many have identified, rules do not enforce themselves, and rules on the books do not always mirror rules in action.[33] Daniel Cole, working in the Ostromian tradition, has offered a three-part typology to explain this important distinction between what he calls "legal rules" (or *de jure* rules) and "working rules" (or *de facto* rules).[34] According to Cole, there are three types of rules: Type 1, which include working rules that closely match formal legal rules; Type 2, which include legal rules that interact with social norms to produce different working rules; and Type 3, which include those legal rules that bear no apparent relation with *de facto* rules. Cole's typology adds analytical clarity to the research program we propose herein.

Figure 15.2 depicts the degree to which civil liberties promised in constitutions diverge from the on-the-ground realities in countries around the world. Instead of a perfect relationship between *de jure* and de facto civil liberties, the scatterplot shows a distribution with just as many countries outperforming their constitutional freedoms as underperforming them. Many countries enjoy similar levels of de facto civil liberties despite enjoying different constitutional protections. New Zealand (NEW, top-left), Finland (FIN, top-middle), and Portugal (POR, top-right), for example, have similarly high levels of *de facto* civil liberties despite differences in *de jure* civil liberties. More interestingly, some cases have similar levels of formal rule protections but experience different working rule realities: North Korea (PRK, bottom-middle), Djibouti (DJI, middle), and Sweden (SWD, top-middle) have a similar *de jure* value (x ≈ 0.4), but each de facto value is different: North Korea underperforms its constitutional liberties (y ≈ 0.0), Djibouti matches its liberties (y ≈ 0.4), and Sweden overperforms (y ≈ 1.0).

Returning to Cole's typology, Djibouti and Portugal portray Type 1, where legal rules resemble working rules. Finland and North Korea represent Type 2, where laws and social norms produce working rules that deviate from legal rules. The result is better for Finland than North Korea. New Zealand, Sweden, and other countries in the off-diagonals exemplify Type 3 working rules that drastically outperform (top-left area) and underperform (bottom-right area) *de jure* legal rules. A key finding to emerge from this illustration is that deviating from

---

[32] DeMattee, "Toward a Coherent Framework'; M. Kiai, *Report of the Special Rapporteur on the Rights to Freedom of Peaceful Assembly and Association* (United Nations General Assembly, 2012); World Bank, *Handbook on Good Practices for Laws Relating to Non-Governmental Organizations* (Washington, DC, 1997).

[33] J. R. Commons, *Legal Foundations of Capitalism* (New York: Macmillan, 1924); M. D. McGinnis, "Networks of Adjacent Action Situations in Polycentric Governance," *Policy Studies Journal*, 39, 1 (2011), 45–72; V. Ostrom, "John R. Commons's Foundations for Policy Analysis," *Journal of Economic Issues*, 10, 4 (1976), 839–857; R. Pound, "Law in Books and Law in Action," *American Law Review*, 1 (1910), 12–36.

[34] Cole, "Laws, Norms, and the IAD," 11–16.

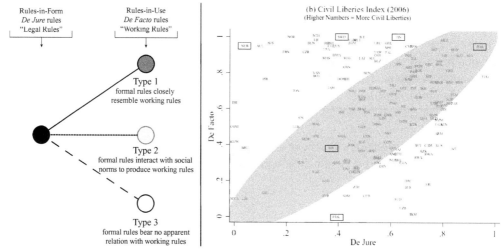

Source: Adapted from Cole 2017 (pp. 11-16) and Elkins, Ginsburg, and Melton 2009 (p. 54)

FIGURE 15.2 Cole's working rules applied to De Jure and De Facto Constitutional Law[35]

legal rules is not necessarily detrimental to the on the ground experience of those who would benefit from those rules.

Rarely have "closing space" scholars seriously discussed the difference between legal and working rules. Applying Cole's typology is relevant to the study of CSO regulatory regimes because while scholars have identified the inconsistent, subnational enforcement of rules in countries such as Ethiopia, North Korea, and Russia,[36] they have failed to explain such variation. Why and to what degree working rules deviate from legal rules is perhaps the most crucial, yet most understudied question among CSO researchers. Yet, understanding formal laws on their own is not enough. If we are to understand the state-CSO relationship in full, a necessary starting point is to know what rules exist and how the government enforces them.

CONCLUSION

Existing research on CSOs shows a strong correlation between civil society and certain desired sociopolitical outcomes, including a country's development status, level of democratization, and interpersonal trust between citizens and their government. These theories, while illuminating, do not address the influence that CSO legal and regulatory regimes have on state-CSO relations or the environment that enables civil society to achieve such desired outcomes. Simplistic assumptions and narrow scope conditions limit the theoretical arguments offered by civil society and closing-space scholars. On the one hand, civil society scholars assume a well-meaning state and virtuous CSOs, which together pursue complementary and supplementary agendas. Their theories tend to predict the existence of permissive rules but cannot explain the rescission of

---

[35] Figure adapted from *The Endurance of National Constitutions*. The scatterplot illustrates 2006 measures for *de jure* civil liberties in constitutions (x-axis) and *de facto* civil liberties experienced by citizens (y-axis). Higher numbers indicate greater civil liberties. Shaded areas arbitrarily demarcate Cole's working rule types. Type 1 show a strong correlation between *de jure* and *de facto* (dark gray area), Type 2 show a weaker correlation (light gray areas), and Type 3 are in the unshaded areas.

[36] S. Toepler et al., "Subnational Variations in Government-Nonprofit Relations: A Comparative Analysis of Regional Differences within Russia," *Journal of Comparative Policy Analysis: Research and Practice* (2019), 1–19; A. Cunningham, "Law as Discourse: The Case of Ethiopia," *International Humanitarian NGOs and State Relations: Politics, Principles and Identity* (Routledge Humanitarian Studies; London: Routledge, 2018); Snyder, "American Religious NGOs in North Korea."

permissive rules or the passage of restrictive ones. Arguments offered by closing-space scholars, on the other hand, assume power-hungry governments and defenseless CSOs that only pursue adversarial activities. Because closing-space analysts focus solely on restrictive rules, while imposing an extremely broad definition of "restrictive," their arguments tend to be narrow and undertheorized concerning the passage of permissive rules.

Adopting an Ostromian lens significantly strengthens and clarifies the research program on CSO regulatory regimes. First, Ostrom's IAD framework is capable of analyzing both permissive and restrictive rules to understand the full variety of action situations. Second, the framework allows us to view CSOs in all their diversity, and to remain agnostic as to their "do-good" status, by categorizing them according to their excludability and subtractability. Third, an appreciation for the important differences between rules-in-form and rules-in-use is built into the IAD framework. Recognizing that incongruencies exist between legal and working rules advances the CSO research agenda by eliminating the overly simplistic assumption of perfect congruence between *de jure* and *de facto* rules. And finally, the IAD framework embraces interdisciplinarity and methodological pluralism, which is essential to understanding something as complex, nuanced, and ever-evolving as state-CSO relations. These characteristics, combined with the framework's inclusive vernacular, offer a promising new way of conceptualizing the relationship between governments and CSOs, as well as the ways in which the CSO legal and regulatory regimes can shape this critical relationship in both positive and negative ways.

16

A Conceptual Model of Polycentric Resource Governance in the 2030 District Energy Program

Erik Nordman

The conventional wisdom on collective action at a large scale suggests that a global problem like climate change must have a global, legally binding solution.[1] Elinor Ostrom, however, wisely noted, "[i]f … we simply wait until the big guys make a decision, we are in deep trouble."[2] Ostrom's work on global commons, and climate change specifically, indicated that a top-down, legally binding approach is not the only approach, and perhaps not even the best one, to manage a global commons. Action can be taken at various levels, from local to national, and by a range of actors such as governments, private companies, and civil society organizations.[3] She called this a polycentric approach to climate governance - a social system that has many centers of decision-making, each acting somewhat independently but under a common set of guiding principles.[4]

With the United States poised to withdraw from the Paris Agreement in 2020, cities, states, and civil society groups are attempting to fill the leadership void in a polycentric manner. One such effort is the 2030 District program created by the American Institute of Architects and managed by the 2030 District Network. Cities participate in the 2030 District program by drawing a downtown district boundary and inviting commercial building owners to make voluntary reductions in energy and water use. The goal, called the "Challenge for Planning," is to reduce by half their building energy use, water use, and transportation-related greenhouse gas emissions by 2030. The 2030 District program is voluntary and led by the private sector – it is not a regulation or government policy, although governmental units can participate. To date, twenty cities across the United States and Canada have established 2030 Districts comprising more than 44.59 million m^2 (480 million feet^2) of commercial building space.[5]

The choice to invest in resource efficiency and decarbonization is ordinarily a firm's private decision. The 2030 Districts, however, encourage building owners to work together to achieve these goals on a district-wide basis. In a 2030 District, the pathway to success lies in collective

[1] Geoffrey Brennan, "Climate Change: A Rational Choice Politics View*," *Australian Journal of Agricultural and Resource Economics* 53, no. 3 (2009): 309–326.

[2] Elinor Ostrom, Big Think Interview With Elinor Ostrom, November 11, 2009, https://bigthink.com/big-think-interview-with-elinor-ostrom.

[3] Elinor Ostrom, *A Polycentric Approach For Coping With Climate Change*, Policy Research Working Papers (The World Bank, 2009); Andrew Jordan et al., *Governing Climate Change: Polycentricity in Action?* (Cambridge University Press, 2018).

[4] Paul D. Aligica and Vlad Tarko, "Polycentricity: From Polanyi to Ostrom, and Beyond," *Governance* 25, no. 2 (2012): 237–262.

[5] 2030 Districts Network, "2030 District Network Charter," 2017, www.2030districts.org/toolkits/district-administration.

action. But, as economist Mancur Olson noted, voluntary collective action often fails. "Indeed, unless the number of individuals in a group is quite small," he wrote, "or unless there is coercion or some other kind of special device to make individuals act in their common interest, rational, self-interested individuals will not act to achieve their common or group interests."[6] It is unclear, therefore, if this form of collective action is an effective method for reaching the resource efficiency goals. This invites several research questions:

- Why would a city voluntarily join the 2030 District program?
- Why would a commercial building owner voluntarily join a 2030 District?
- Do participating building owners reduce resource use and emissions more than non-participants do?
- How do 2030 Districts hold their members accountable for meeting the voluntary goals?
- Are 2030 District cities improving resource efficiency more effectively than non-participating cities?

Voluntary programs like the 2030 Districts are one way that "public entrepreneurs" (as Ostrom called them) can promote the public good outside of either government regulation or the free market. This chapter examines the 2030 District program and the twenty cities that have established such districts. I use the club theory of voluntary programs[7] and the Institutional Analysis and Development framework[8] to develop a conceptual model of the 2030 District program – a polycentric, voluntary environmental agreement. The club theory of voluntary programs shows how organizations can encourage firms to, for example, reduce pollution beyond what is legally required by offering both benefits in return for that action and sanctions for non-compliance. Ostrom's Institutional Analysis and Development (IAD) framework is a tool used to identify the building blocks of all kinds of structured interactions, from markets to legislatures and community groups.[9] Combined, the club theory and the IAD framework will help explain the basic, common structure of all 2030 Districts. In addition, these tools will aid in revealing the diversity of rules and norms found in each 2030 District and how they may contribute to a district's success or failure.

In the first research phase, covered here, I reviewed the Districts' annual reports to obtain information about monitoring, enforcement, and progress toward the 2030 District goals. Only the building energy use commitment was assessed. Additional phases will include data from more in-depth surveys of 2030 District program managers, building owners, and other stakeholders. Although a few authors have described the 2030 Districts, such as Huddleston et al.,[10] Barnes and Parrish,[11] and Johnstone,[12] none has investigated the program from the perspective of the club theory of voluntary programs, the Institutional Analysis and Development framework, or polycentricity. This chapter therefore is a novel contribution to this emerging topic of polycentric climate governance.

---

[6] Mancur Olson, *The Logic of Collective Action* (Harvard University Press, 1965), 2.

[7] Matthew Potoski and Aseem Prakash, *Voluntary Programs: A Club Theory Perspective* (MIT Press, 2009).

[8] Elinor Ostrom, *Understanding Institutional Diversity* (Princeton University Press, 2005).

[9] Ostrom.

[10] "Pittsburgh 2030 District Energy Baseline: Motivation, Creation, and Implications," *Journal of Green Building* 9, no. 4 (January 1, 2014): 79–104.

[11] "Small Buildings, Big Impacts: The Role of Small Commercial Building Energy Efficiency Case Studies in 2030 Districts," *Sustainable Cities and Society* 27 (November 1, 2016): 210–21, https://doi.org/10.1016/j.scs.2016.05.015.

[12] "San Francisco 2030 District: Performance and Implications for Urban Energy Efficiency" (Master of Environmental Management, Durham, North Carolina, Duke University, 2017).

THE 2030 DISTRICT PROGRAM

The American Institute of Architects, one of the nation's leading advocates for buildings and infrastructure, initiated its Architecture 2030 project in 2006. Architecture 2030 seeks to achieve the twin aims of dramatically reducing "energy consumption and greenhouse gas emissions from the built environment"; and advancing "the development of sustainable, resilient, equitable, and carbon-neutral buildings and communities." Architecture 2030 laid out a pathway to achieve these goals and challenged the global architecture and construction industry to meet specific efficiency targets called the Challenge for Planning Targets (Table 16.1).[13] Consequently, Architecture 2030 established the 2030 District program as a means of encouraging cities and building owners to achieve Challenge for Planning targets. 2030 Districts draw boundaries around their downtown cores and invite commercial and other building owners to accept the challenge. Each local 2030 District is an independent private-public partnership that agrees to adopt the Architecture 2030's Challenge for Planning resource reduction targets. The 2030 District Network, a separate organization, links the independent city-based districts. The 2030 District advertises the benefits of a collective, rather than an individualistic, approach to resource efficiency: "Building owners, managers, and developers participating in a 2030 District understand that by working collectively toward shared goals they are improving not only their assets, but also those of their neighbors, and thereby increasing the entire District's value and attraction to tenants, businesses, and patrons."[14] (See also Section III in this volume for further discussion of urban commons.)

A reduction target requires a baseline. Architecture 2030 established its standard building energy baseline as the national average reported in the 2003 Commercial Building Energy Consumption Survey from the US Energy Information Administration. The standard metric is energy use intensity (kBTU/ft²/year).[15],[16] That metric, however, does not distinguish between fossil fuel and renewable sources. The Challenge for Planning goal for new buildings is carbon

TABLE 16.1 *Challenge for planning targets*

	Existing building 2020	Existing building 2030	New building immediate	New building 2030
Building energy	20% below national average	50% below national average	70% below national average	Carbon neutral
Water	20% below District average	50% below District average	50% below District average	50% below District average
Transportation CO$_2$	20% below District average	50% below District average	50% below District average	50% below District average

[13] Architecture 2030, "The 2030 Challenge for Planning," 2019, https://architecture2030.org/2030_challenges/2030_challenge_planning/.

[14] 2030 Districts Network, "2030 Districts and Other District Approaches," 2020, www.2030districts.org/toolkits/learn-about-2030-districts.

[15] One British thermal unit (BTU) is the amount of heat energy required to raise the temperature of one pound of water one degree Fahrenheit. A kilo BTU (kBTU) is 1,000 BTU. A typical home furnace, for example, might be deliver 80,000 BTU (80 kBTU) of heat energy per hour. If it was used to heat a 1,000 square foot house and ran for 250 hours per year, the house would use 20 kBTU/ft²/year of heat energy (80 kBTU/hour * 250 hours/year / 1,000 ft² = 20 kBTU/ft²/year)

[16] "FAQs – Architecture 2030," accessed February 4, 2020, https://architecture2030.org/about/faq/.

neutrality which cannot be measured using EUI as currently defined. Buildings can earn credits toward the energy goal, up to 20%, by using on-site and off-site renewable energy. The Pittsburgh 2030 District developed a methodology that enables buildings that generate more than their renewable allowances to share the extra credits with the entire District.[17] This efficiency-first approach encourages reducing energy needs as much as possible and then using renewable, carbon-free sources for the remainder. Architecture 2030 created the Zero Tool to help 2030 Districts and their members establish the energy baseline and reduction targets. Each 2030 District establishes its own water and transportation baselines instead of having a single, national baseline. The 2030 District members themselves determine whether the water and transportation baselines are established using city, county, or state data. Like energy, 2030 Districts measure progress toward the water goal using an intensity metric (gallons/ft²/year). The districts have not agreed on a single metric for measuring progress toward the transportation goal. Some districts have created their own metrics while others do not have a metric at all yet.

Although the 2030 Districts welcome diverse building owners such as government agencies, schools, and houses of worship, the primary membership is targeted at commercial building owners. The Districts also have membership opportunities for stakeholders, such as construction and technical service providers and community organizations. Stakeholders are usually not building owners within the district (although some are), but they provide information and services that help the participating building owners achieve their goals. Twenty North American cities have established 2030 Districts and several more are in the planning stages. The Districts differ in population and climate, from the snowy college town of Ithaca to sunny San Diego (Figure 16.1).

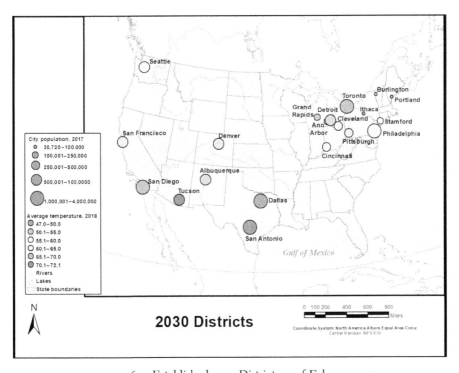

FIGURE 16.1 Established 2030 Districts as of February 2020

---

[17] Green Building Alliance, "Pittsburgh 2030 District Progress Report 2018," 2019, www.2030districts.org/pittsburgh.

To date, few scholars have analyzed the 2030 District program. The Pittsburgh 2030 District, an early adopter, developed a protocol for measuring building energy performance and encouraging cooperation.[18] Barnes and Parrish[19] developed a case study library and template for the 2030 District Network's Small Commercial Toolkit. The authors identified several barriers faced by small building owners seeking to achieve the 2030 District targets. Small business owners lack several key resources, including access to comprehensive and consistent information about how to achieve the targets; tools for measuring building performance; financial incentives; and models for effective collaboration. Their case study library shows how small building owners in the 2030 Districts can overcome these barriers.

As part of her master's degree project, Eleanor Johnstone conducted a complete performance assessment for San Francisco's 2030 District for the 2016 reporting year.[20] Johnstone found that the 31 buildings participating in the 2030 District had already achieved the 50% reduction in building energy use intensity compared to the national baseline. Although this did reflect some commitment on behalf of San Francisco's building owners, it also revealed some quirks in the 2030 District standards. The standard is the CBECS national average energy use intensity. The northeastern United States is the most densely populated region, has the most buildings, and the buildings there tend to be older. Therefore, a national inventory of buildings will have a large number of buildings from the northeast. And because those northeastern buildings tend to be older, they are generally less resource efficient than new buildings especially with regards to heating. Therefore, any national average of building energy use intensity will be affected by the large number of old northeastern buildings. San Francisco's more temperate climate and newer building stock mean that its buildings, including 2030 District participants, already use substantially less energy than the national average. Cold weather cities with older building stocks may find meeting the 2030 District standards more challenging than cities like San Francisco in temperate climates and newer buildings stock. My analysis will show how 2030 Districts can encourage building energy efficiency and reduce pollution, how district members can hold one another accountable for achieving the district's goals, and how districts can establish incentives that align the interests of building owners and the general public.

THEORETICAL FRAMEWORK: CLUB THEORY AND INSTITUTIONAL ANALYSIS

A Club Theory of Voluntary Programs

Many government agencies and non-governmental organizations advocate for green buildings. However, such organizations typically focus on individual buildings. The 2030 District program is distinct in that it establishes a community of building owners and stakeholders that agree to work toward a common goal. The 2030 District can be considered, in the economic sense, a club that provides the public with the benefits (club goods) of reduced pollution and resource efficiency.

[18] M.D. Huddleston et al., "Pittsburgh 2030 District Energy Baseline: Motivation, Creation, and Implications," *Journal of Green Building* 9, no. 4 (January 1, 2014): 79–104; Aurora L. Sharrard, Sean C. Luther, and Anna J. Siefken, "Pittsburgh 2030 District: Collaborating to Develop High-Performance Buildings," *Global Business and Organizational Excellence* 34, no. 1 (2014): 18–31.
[19] Elizabeth Barnes and Kristen Parrish, "Small Buildings, Big Impacts: The Role of Small Commercial Building Energy Efficiency Case Studies in 2030 Districts," *Sustainable Cities and Society* 27 (November 1, 2016): 210–221.
[20] Johnstone, "San Francisco 2030 District: Performance and Implications for Urban Energy Efficiency."

TABLE 16.2 *Rival and exclusive framework for goods and services.*

	Rival (one user at a time, or depletable)	Non-rival (more than one user at a time, or not depletable)
Exclusive (Owners can exclude users)	Private goods	Club goods
Non-exclusive (Owners cannot reasonably exclude users)	Commons or open access	Public goods

Economic clubs produce goods and services that are non-rival and exclusive (Table 16.2). Like a movie theater, the club goods can be enjoyed by multiple users at once (non-rival) but the club owners can exclude people (those that don't pay).[21]

Potoski and Prakash[22] developed a club theory of voluntary programs in the environmental sector. The theory builds on the work of public choice theorists like Olson[23] and Buchanan and Tullock.[24] While some firms may produce club goods to turn a profit, like a movie theater, voluntary programs seek to enhance social welfare. Firms join the voluntary program to gain certain benefits that are only available to members. In return, the firm agrees to reduce some kind of defined social harm, such as pollution or dangerous working conditions. For example, appliance manufacturers who voluntarily produce high-efficiency products that meet the EPA's criteria can display the "Energy Star" label. The manufacturer agrees to make a product that exceeds the minimum efficiency standards and in return gets a valuable branding tool that customers look for. In an unregulated free market, firms would presumably not have an incentive to adopt these measures. For example, the customer is often sensitive to an appliance's upfront costs. The customer may also not have good information about the product's energy usage over its lifetime, which can be another significant cost. Because the manufacturer does not pay the customer's electricity cost, it has less incentive to produce a more expensive, but more efficient, product. The Energy Star label provides a quick and easy signal to the customer that, even though the appliance is more expensive to purchase, it has lower lifetime costs than other models.

Potoski and Prakash[25] identified three types of benefits from voluntary programs:

1. Promotion of positive social externalities (e.g., better working conditions or reduced pollution);
2. Private benefits accessible only to club members (e.g., information, clients); and
3. Branding benefits that come with association in the club (e.g., "dolphin-safe" tuna, Energy Star product labels).

Public entrepreneurs use club goods to solve a social problem. A rational firm would be expected to join the voluntary program if the membership benefits exceed the cost of resolving the social externalities. However, Potoski and Prakash[26] also note several ways such voluntary

[21] Vincent Ostrom and Elinor Ostrom, "Public Goods and Public Choices," in *Alternatives for Delivering Public Services: Toward Improved Performance*, ed. E. S. Savas (Boulder, CO: Westview Press, 1977), 7–49.

[22] Potoski and Prakash, *Voluntary Programs.*

[23] Olson, *The Logic of Collective Action.*

[24] James Buchanan and Gordon Tullock, *The Calculus of Consent: Logical Foundations of Constitutional Democracy* (Ann Arbor: University of Michigan Press, 1962).

[25] Potoski and Prakash, *Voluntary Programs.*

[26] Potoski and Prakash.

TABLE 16.3 *Attributes of voluntary programs (from Potoski and Prakash 2009)*

Club standards		Enforcement and monitoring rules		
		Weak	Medium	Strong
Lenient	Participation cost	Low	Low-Moderate	Low -Moderate
	Shirking	High	Moderate	Low
	Branding	Marginal	Low-Moderate	Low-Moderate
	Social Benefit	Low	Low-Moderate	Moderate
	Name	*Shams*	*Boy Scouts*	*Boot Camps*
Stringent	Participation cost	Moderate-High	Moderate	High
	Shirking	High	Moderate	Low
	Branding	Marginal	Moderate	High
	Social Benefit	Low	Moderate	High
	Name	*Country Clubs*	*Prep Schools*	*Mandarins*

programs could fail. First, the program could cast a "warm glow" of virtue over the entire industry. Firms could enjoy the warm glow benefits whether or not they actually joined the club. These "free riders" would undermine the program and reduce its social benefits. Second, firms may join the club to obtain the membership benefits but shirk their responsibilities. It's critical, therefore, that the voluntary program excludes benefits from those who don't join, monitors their members for adherence to the program's rules, and sanctions noncompliance.

The level of social benefits actually delivered may depend on the program's standards and enforcement. Voluntary programs with lenient standards and lax enforcement have easy entry, but may fail to provide any social benefits. At the other extreme, programs with very high standards and strong enforcement may attract only a few members and provide few aggregate benefits. Therefore, there may be a "Goldilocks" level of standards and enforcement that is strict enough to provide reasonable social benefits without scaring away potential members.

Potoski and Prakash[27] further describe voluntary programs using a number of additional attributes. These include participation costs, likelihood of shirking, branding benefits, and policy implications (how effective it is at addressing social externalities). The authors gave each type of club a label ranging from "sham" to "mandarin" (Table 16.3).

Although sanctioning for non-compliance is important, voluntary clubs also offer an opportunity for a positive "behavioral contagion."[28] Behavioral economists have shown that an individual's choice can be influenced, for better or worse, by the choices of those around them. In one example, home owners who installed solar panels soon saw many of their neighbors also installing panels.[29] Voluntary clubs may form a conducive environment in which positive behavioral contagions can flourish.

THE INSTITUTIONAL ANALYSIS AND DEVELOPMENT FRAMEWORK

Club theory describes the incentives that may encourage a firm to go beyond what's legally required to promote social welfare. But it does not describe the institutional structure of the

---

[27] Potoski and Prakash.

[28] Robert H. Frank, *Under the Influence: Putting Peer Pressure to Work* (Princeton, N J: Princeton University Press, 2020). Make sure your font is consistent throughout

[29] Marcello Graziano and Kenneth Gillingham, "Spatial Patterns of Solar Photovoltaic System Adoption: The Influence of Neighbors and the Built Environment," *Journal of Economic Geography* 15, no. 4 (July 1, 2015): 815–839, https://doi .org/10.1093/jeg/lbu036.

voluntary program or its members. The Institutional Analysis and Development (IAD) framework is a useful tool in this regard (see also Chapter 1 in this volume for a history of the IAD framework).

Ostrom described the IAD framework as "a systematic method for organizing policy analysis activities that is compatible with a wide variety of more specialized analytic techniques used in the physical and social sciences."[30] The IAD framework consists of (1) a set of external variables (biophysical conditions, community attributes, and the set of rules that define the allowable actions); (2) an action situation in which actors use information to assess costs and benefits to obtain potential outcomes; and (3) interactions between the action situation, outcomes, and evaluative criteria. The outcomes can in turn affect the external variables and action situation. The action situation can be considered a dependent variable upon which a set of independent (external) variables act (Figures 16.2 and 16.3).

Taken together, the club theory of voluntary programs and the IAD framework offer a powerful set of tools to examine the structured interactions, like making decisions and enforcing rules, of various types of organizations. In the next section, club theory and the IAD framework are used to examine the decision-making structures of the 2030 District program in general as well as within specific 2030 Districts.

DATA

The first phase of this project focuses on the network and district (city) levels. Only the building energy portion of the 2030 Challenge for Planning was analyzed. The latest progress reports for each 2030 District were obtained from either the official program website (www.2030districts .org/) or directly from the program manager. Each progress report was analyzed for evidence of monitoring (baseline established, building data reported), enforcement (number of buildings reporting), and progress toward the 2020 interim goal of a 20% reduction in building energy use.

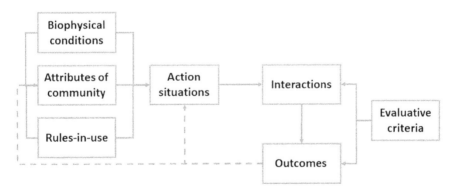

FIGURE 16.2 Institutional Analysis and Development framework[31]

[30] Elinor Ostrom, "Background on the Institutional Analysis and Development Framework," *Policy Studies Journal* 39, no. 1 (February 1, 2011): 7–27; Ostrom, *Understanding Institutional Diversity*; Margaret Polski and Elinor Ostrom, "An Institutional Framework for Policy Analysis and Design," in *Elinor Ostrom and the Bloomington School of Political Economy*, vol. 3: A framework for policy analysis (Lexington Books, 2017), 13–48.
[31] Ostrom, *Understanding Institutional Diversity*.

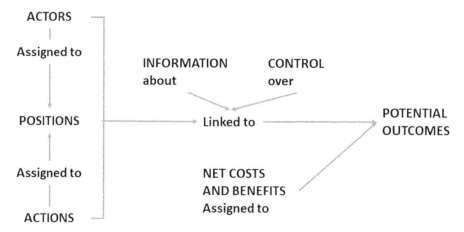

FIGURE 16.3 Action situation within the Institutional Analysis and Development framework[32]

I obtained some additional information about individual districts and the program as a whole from the 2030 District Network program manager.[33]

Club Theory

Club theory helps explain why building owners and other stakeholders would join the 2030 District. All 2030 Districts have the same relatively stringent standard – the 2030 Challenge for Planning goals. Success would involve significant energy and water retrofits for existing buildings, converting fleet vehicles to electric, and reducing single-driver commuting.

The 2030 District provides its members with certain direct and indirect benefits. The primary membership benefit is access to information about energy efficiency and renewable energy practices. The information facilitated by membership in the 2030 District reduces the search costs and may help overcome the energy efficiency gap. Implementing such practices could save the member money over the long run. Members may also receive discounts from contractors associated with the 2030 District. Additionally, members can enjoy the branding benefits from association with the 2030 District. This would be of most benefit to for-profit businesses looking for a marketing edge. The branding benefit may be of less direct benefit to NGO members, such as houses of worship. On the other hand, District membership may align with the NGO's values.

The cost of membership is the commitment to make progress toward achieving the 2030 Challenge for Planning goals. There is no direct financial cost, such as dues, for joining the 2030 District and there is no direct financial cost for a city to establish a district. The cost comes in the form of the commitment to invest in resource efficiency projects. Creating a 2030 District requires considerable bureaucratic costs, which occur across three phases. These bureaucratic costs suggest that the 2030 District is a stringent program.

In Phase 1, the "prospective district" forms an exploratory committee and expresses its intent to the 2030 Districts Network. In Phase 2, the "emerging district," under the leadership of a sponsoring organization, obtains commitments from at least five different property owners and

[32] Ostrom.
[33] David Low, "2030 District Operations," 2020.

TABLE 16.4 *Three of the five 2030 Districts that reported results have achieved the interim energy goal of a 20% reduction*

District	# buildings participating	# buildings reporting	Energy reduction relative to baseline (%)
Cleveland	281	108	24
Dallas	42	35	17
Philadelphia	47	43	29
Pittsburgh	540	371	24
San Antonio	86	44	14

pledges to strive toward the Architecture 2030 Challenge for Planning goals. In Phase 3, the "established district" creates an advisory committee and writes a detailed business plan. The district must have commitments from at least ten building owners or managers or ten million square feet of building space or 10% of the commercial real estate within the district boundary.[34]

Club theory suggests that monitoring and enforcement is critical to prevent shirking and to achieve the voluntary program's goals. Each 2030 District establishes its own methods for monitoring and enforcement. The 2030 District Network does not, as yet, require individual 2030 Districts to submit annual or periodic progress reports. The 2030 District Network is considering making periodic progress reports a requirement in the future.[35] District leaders are expected to participate in regular conference calls with the 2030 District Network and attend the annual meeting. In 2019, two 2030 Districts (Austin and Los Angeles) had their statuses demoted from "established" to only "emerging." In both cases, changes in the sponsoring organization and local leadership left an administrative vacuum. The Districts were unable to actively continue but members may reconstitute the Districts in the future.[36] This suggests that the current level of monitoring at the District level is low to moderate and the Network is able to enforce some degree of compliance among the Districts.

Of the 20 established 2030 Districts, eight published a progress report for 2018. Although San Francisco reported results in 2016, it did not submit one for 2018. Five of the progress reports included quantitative data about the District's progress such as building energy use intensity. Other districts report progress in more general narratives without data. The five 2030 Districts that reported quantitative progress all used the Energy STAR Portfolio Manager[37] to track building energy use intensity. By 2018, three 2030 Districts reported that they already exceeded the 2020 interim goal of a 20% reduction from the baseline. Two others were making significant progress (Table 16.4).

IAD Framework

The 2030 District Network participating cities vary in terms of biophysical conditions and community attributes. Cities differ by climate, size, culture, and economic environment. Although they share the same "rules-in-form" – the 2030 District goals – they may differ in their "rules-in-use." Each individual District has autonomy in deciding how to encourage compliance (Figure 16.4).

[34] 2030 Districts Network, "Become a District," 2020, www.2030districts.org/become-district.
[35] Low, "2030 District Operations," 2020.
[36] Low.
[37] Energy STAR Portfolio Manager is a software program that enables building managers to track energy use and greenhouse gas emissions. It also has a database of average building energy usage for various building types, like warehouses and restaurants. More information is available at: www.energystar.gov/buildings/facility-owners-and-man agers/existing-buildings/use-portfolio-manager.

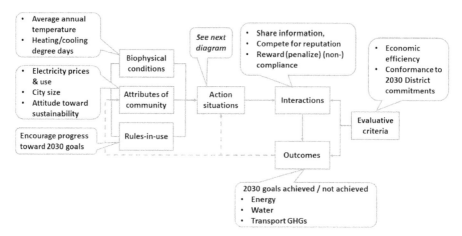

FIGURE 16.4 Institutional Analysis and Development framework annotated with 2030 District elements

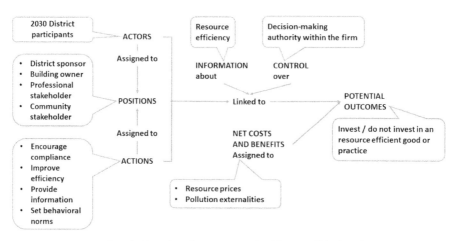

FIGURE 16.5 Action situation annotated with 2030 District elements

These biophysical conditions, community attributes, and rules-in-use affect the action situation where the key decisions are made (Figure 16.5). The IAD framework shows that what was once a private, individual decision whether to invest in efficiency practices is now a socially influenced decision within the 2030 District. The efficiency investment decision is influenced not only by the building owners and market prices, but also by the 2030 District sponsoring organizations, professional stakeholders, and community stakeholders. The stakeholders provide support by facilitating the flow of information, encouraging compliance, and setting behavioral norms (district sponsors); providing audits and other services (professional stakeholders); and providing institutional and policy support (community stakeholders). The annotated IAD and action situation clearly illustrate how the decision-making process within a club, like the 2030 District, differs from that of an individual firm. "Instead of making completely independent or autonomous decisions," Ostrom wrote, "individuals may be embedded in communities where initial norms of fairness and conservation may change the structure of the situation dramatically. Within these situations, participants may adopt a broader range of strategies. Further, they may change their strategies over time as they learn about the results of past actions."[38] As 2030 District members share knowledge and experiences at regular gatherings, they are also building trust that may help encourage action toward the shared goals (see also Chapter 6 in this volume for further considerations of social trust and collective action). The 2030 District gatherings also present an opportunity for a positive "behavioral contagion" to spread among participants.[39]

The standard model of whether to invest in energy efficiency is framed as a onetime decision made by the building owner.[40] By expanding the analysis to include the community, the IAD framework allows us to consider how the other actors within the 2030 District can influence a building owner's decision about efficiency investments. The rules-in-use may influence the decision-making process as well. This may happen through formal rules, such as the defined 2030 District goals, or informal norms and expectations of incremental progress. 2030 District building owners report progress on energy efficiency projects (outcomes), which in turn, inform, in the short term, the decisions of others in similar action situations and, in the long run, the attributes of the community and the rules-in-use.

Criteria can be used to evaluate a set of outcomes. Ostrom lists several commonly used evaluative criteria: economic efficiency, equity through fiscal equivalence, redistributional equity, accountability, conformance to values of local actors, and sustainability.[41] The 2030 District participants are likely to consider the economic efficiency of their investments. But as voluntary adopters of the 2030 District goals, they are also likely to consider those targets as well, which align with "conformance to values of local actors." Sustainability is also likely to be an evaluative criterion at the firm and District levels.

Discussion

Potoski and Prakash's club theory offers a systematic method for evaluating voluntary programs. The documentary evidence, although limited and preliminary, suggests that the 2030 District program, as a whole, can be described as a "Prep School" with stringent standards but low to moderate enforcement (Table 16.1). The expected 50% reduction in building energy use, water use, and transportation emissions is a stringent membership standard. The participation cost is moderate to high. The 2030 District Network established a rigorous three phase process for entry. The degree of shirking is low to moderate. Most 2030 Districts have not filed regular progress reports suggesting that enforcement is relatively weak. On the other hand, the 2030 District Network did sanction districts that failed to meet the basic requirements to maintain their "established district" status. Demoting a district, rather than withdrawing its membership entirely, is an example of a graduated sanction. Ostrom identified graduated sanctions as a key design principle in a well-managed commons.[42]

Of the five 2030 Districts that reported quantitative results in 2018, three have already achieved the interim energy goal of a 20% reduction and done so two years early (Table 16.4). This suggests that many of the participating buildings within these high-achieving 2030 Districts are more energy efficient than the national building stock. However, it is unclear whether this is actually due to participation in the 2030 District program. Participating firms may strategically

[38] Ostrom, "Background on the Institutional Analysis and Development Framework."
[39] Frank, *Under the Influence: Putting Peer Pressure to Work.*
[40] Hunt Allcott and Michael Greenstone, "Is There an Energy Efficiency Gap?," *Journal of Economic Perspectives* 26, no. 1 (February 2012): 3–28.
[41] Ostrom, "Background on the Institutional Analysis and Development Framework."
[42] Elinor Ostrom, *Governing the Commons* (Cambridge University Press, 1990).

enroll their most efficient buildings to obtain branding benefits without investing in additional efficiency improvements. The high-achieving districts are all in the Northeast and did not have the advantage of a mild climate.

The IAD framework offers an opportunity to generate hypotheses that can be tested in future work. For example, the IAD framework suggests that biophysical conditions and community attributes may affect decisions within the action situation. The District's population size and composition may also influence relationships among members. It is possible that Detroit's district, which includes a large number of houses of worship, may behave very differently than office buildings in Dallas. The IAD framework emphasizes the role of interactions among decision-makers and stakeholders. This opens up the possibility of a positive behavioral contagion in which District members follow the lead of early adopters of efficient technologies and practices.

These research questions and hypotheses will be explored in the next phase of the research project. I will use a survey to obtain more detailed information about decision-making at the building and District levels. The results will shed light on how interactions among members of a 2030 District influence additional investments in energy efficiency.

CONCLUSION

The concept of polycentric climate governance suggests that we do not need to wait for strong federal regulations to reduce greenhouse gas emissions. Most Americans live in cities and this is where their energy-using and emissions-generating activities happen. Cities, therefore, can take steps to reduce energy use and emissions. The 2030 District program is one such effort. The 2030 District program itself has polycentric properties with decisions being made at the Network, District, and building levels.

The club theory of voluntary programs suggests that the 2030 Districts must have strong monitoring and enforcement mechanisms if they are to achieve their goals. Documentary evidence shows that the 2030 District Network operates, in the vocabulary of Potoski and Prakash, as a "Prep School" with stringent standards and a moderate level of enforcement. Only about a third of 2030 Districts voluntarily submitted progress reports in 2018, which suggests that shirking could be a problem. Although three of the twenty Districts have already achieved the interim target for building energy efficiency, it is unclear if this is because of the 2030 District's influence or selection bias.

The IAD framework proved to be a useful tool for illustrating the institutional structure of a 2030 District member. The framework suggests that biophysical and community attributes may affect decision-making. The framework's action situation shows how decisions by a participating building owner may be influenced by other members of the 2030 District. These ideas will be explored in upcoming research efforts.

PART VI

Managing and Restoring the Commons

17

Management of Facilitated Common Pool Resources in India

Pradeep Kumar Mishra

Common pool resources (CPR), particularly natural resources like water bodies, pastureland, and forest, are important sources of livelihood for low-income groups throughout rural India; however, these natural resources have seriously degraded over the last few decades. To counter such degradation, the federal government in India as well as the state (provincial) governments have undertaken many programs involving the development of watersheds and pasturelands. These programs were implemented by both governmental and non-governmental organizations (NGOs). Sometimes referred to as "commons" projects, such interventions invariably included promotion and capacity building of community-based institutions.[1] These projects encompassed the development of both biophysical resources (pastures and plantations, for example) and social resources (training and generating awareness, for example), and both types of interventions were considered equally important.[2]

Ostrom was one of the first to recognize the importance of institutions in managing commons effectively. She studied the long-enduring and self-governed commons and provided design principles centered on those institutions. In these design principles, institutions are considered endogenous.[3] The focal point of this body of knowledge is that collective action either occurs on its own or is indifferent to the inputs of an external agency. But, Ostrom recognized, external agencies do play an important role in facilitating collective action.[4] In Indian context also studies have found that institutions facilitated by external agencies have proven both successful and unsuccessful in a variety of situations.[5] In the interventions aimed at developing CPRs, invariably, a facilitating agency provides active support by way of training, funding, and/or handholding. The manager of such interventions faces several inherent constraints including time and funding and often has to make decisions in dynamic and complex situations. Implementing any program focused on developing CPRs (here, developing CPR means reviving the degraded

[1] Saunders, F. P., "The Promise of Common Pool Resource Theory and the Reality of Commons Projects," *International Journal of Commons*, 8, no. 2, 2014: 636–656.

[2] Bromley, D. W., and M. M. Cernea (1989). *Common Property Natural Resources: Some Conceptual and Operational Fallacies* (World Bank Discussion Paper, WDP 57). Washington, DC: World Bank.

[3] Ostrom, E., *Governing the Commons: The Evolution of Institutions for Collective Action* (New York: Cambridge University Press, 1990).

[4] Ostrom, Elinor (1965) *"Public Entrepreneurship: A Case Study in Ground Water Basin Management."* Ph.D. Dissertation. Los Angeles, CA: University of California-Los Angeles.

[5] Mishra, P. K., and M. Kumar (2007). "Institutionalisation of Common Pool Resources Management: Case Studies of Pastureland Management". *Economic and Political Weekly*, 42, 3644–3652; Reddy, V. R. "Getting the Implementation Right: Can the Proposed Watershed Guidelines Help?" *Economic and Political Weekly*, 41, 2006: 4292–4295.

resources and sustaining it) is thus particularly challenging, to which an external agency adds another dimension. Barring a small handful of research papers such as one co-authored by Nagendra and Ostrom,[6] which recognized the importance of the particular governance system and the actors involved in maintaining an urban lake as a commons, these issues have not been adequately addressed in the existing literature, nor do the existing theories based on self-governing institutions adequately explain the successes or failures of these institutions.

This chapter attempts to fill this knowledge gap and, more specifically, seeks to understand the issues involved in developing and managing facilitated CPRs and the process of building the institutions that manage them. Based on a case study of 19 villages and 12 organizations from India engaged in developing CPRs, this chapter elucidates the dynamics and organizational elements of facilitated CPR institutions.

DEVELOPMENT OF COMMON PROPERTY RESOURCES: A LITERATURE REVIEW

Ostrom's design principles marked a breakthrough in the field of commons scholarship, and Wade further highlighted the conditions under which collective action could successfully take root.[7] Agrawal then updated, revised, and synthesized the attributes of collective action required for the management of CPRs.[8] The critical factors listed by these scholars include characteristics of the resource itself (size, cost, and boundaries) and of the group involved in its management, the arrangements for sharing the resource (rules), the stakeholders (and the extent of their dependence on the resource), any sanction regimes, and governance structures. Agrawal and Gupta added more attributes, including the characteristics of the likely participants, their education levels, and their access to officials.[9]

These attributes were largely related to internal dynamics and factors and to their relationships and interactions. However, in CPR development programs, institution building is substantially influenced by external factors, which is not the case for self-generated institutions.[10] Such differences are rarely acknowledged, and this could have complex political ramifications in implementing such projects.[11] Although Ostrom's work highlights the need for self-determined rules and norms, external agencies do not hesitate to impose their own rules while developing CPR programs – rules that become ineffective when new formal institutions clash with the traditional ones. Facilitating agencies, driven by the donor community, usually impose democratic practices that are often very different from the way traditional institutions are governed. But CPR management is invariably embedded in the local context and the intervention of facilitating agency may compromise traditional institutions. This may influence the traditional rights, but a robust CPR management cannot always be separated from the traditional rights of

---

[6] Nagendra, H. and E. Ostrom. 2014. "Applying the Social-ecological System Framework to the Diagnosis of Urban Lake Commons in Bangalore, India," *Ecology and Society*, 19(2): 67.

[7] Wade, R. "The Management of Common Property Resources: Collective Action as an Alternative to Privatization or State Regulation," *Cambridge Journal of Economics*, 11 (1987): 95–106.

[8] Agrawal, A. "Common Property Institutions and Sustainable Governance of Resources," *World Development*, 26 (2001): 1649–1672; Baland, J. and J. Platteau, *Halting Degradation of Natural Resources: Is There A Role for Rural Communities* (Oxford: Clarendon Press, 1996); Kerr, J., "Watershed Management: Lessons from Common Property Theory," *International Journal of the Commons*, 1 (2007): 89–109.

[9] Agrawal, A. K., and K. Gupta, "Decentralization and Participation: The Governance of Common Pool Resources in Nepal's Terai," *World Development*, 33 (2005): 1101–1114.

[10] Saunders, The Promise of Common Pool Resource Theory, 2014.

[11] Ibid. at 649.

local people.[12] Some projects supported by government agencies have weakened traditional systems; for example, in Uttarakhand, the implementation of state-sponsored joint forest management schemes increased bureaucratic control over the forests and disempowered the local community.[13] Imposing simplistic democratic principles that do not meet the complex needs of the local community, placing undue emphasis on economic aspects, and ignoring the local political economy (power relations, the traditional system of using resources, and economic dependence on CPR) also weakens CPR-related institutions.[14]

These observations support the criticism that Ostrom's design principles were drawn from successful cases and ignored certain contextual factors,[15] which could lead to failure. However, the design principles were meant only as guideposts and were never intended to be a blueprint. Subsequent research recognized the dynamic aspects of CPR management. For example, the framework of institutional analysis and development (IAD) includes such elements as action situations and patterns of interaction[16] in which contextual factors are often taken into consideration.

The existing literature is not entirely oblivious to organizational aspects in the context of facilitated institutions. A study in Nepal found that community members with greater access to officials of the facilitating agency were more likely to derive greater benefits from the intervention.[17] Donor-funded projects often proposed target-oriented rather than institutional solutions, which were unsuited to local conditions.[18] This challenges the assumption that facilitating agencies act as catalysts.

The above literature review shows that the influence of facilitating organizations in CPR development has been ignored, a void clearly seen in the statement of Ravnborg, who implemented watershed development projects in Colombia. In this statement, Ravnborg admitted that, in practice, a manager operated under several constraints, and one cannot wait until all criteria of institutional design are fulfilled. She observed that had she followed the design principles, she could not have successfully implemented the project.[19] External agencies typically facilitate projects aimed at developing CPRs and aim to complete the project in three to five years.

CONCEPTUAL FRAMEWORK AND METHODOLOGY

Two bodies of literature – the IAD scholarship and the literature dealing with implementation research (which includes issues like organizational processes[20] and dilemmas at the ground

---

[12] Schnegg, M. and T. Linke. "Living Institutions: Sharing and Sanctioning Water among Pastoralists in Namibia," *World Development* 68 (2015): 205–214.

[13] Sharin, M. "Disempowerment in the Name of 'Participatory' Forestry? – Village Forests Joint Management in Uttarakhand," *Forests, Trees and People Newsletter* 44 (2001).

[14] IDRC. "From Theory to Practice and Back Again: Report on IDRC Workshop on Common Property, 14–15 August 2004, Oaxaca, Mexico," (Ottawa: IDRC, 2004).

[15] Steins, N. A., V. M. Edwards, and N. Röling. "Re-designed Principles for CPR Theory," *The Common Property Resource Digest* 53 (2000): 1–4.

[16] E. Ostrom, "Institutional Rational choice: An Assessment of the Institutional Development Framework," in *Theories of Policy Process* ed. by P. Sabatier, 35–71 (Boulder, CO: Westview Press, 1999).

[17] Agrawal and Gupta, Decentralisation and Participation, 2005.

[18] Morrow, C. E., and T. E. Hull, "Donor-Initiated Common Pool Resource Institutions: The Case of the Yanesha Forestry Cooperative," *World Development*, 24, 10 (1996): 1641–1657.

[19] Ravenborg, H. M. "CPR Research in Practical Application," *Common Property Resource Digest*, 53 (2000): 8–9.

[20] Allison, G. T. *Essence of Decision: Explaining the Cuban Missile Crisis* (Boston, MA: Little, Brown and Company, 1971).

level[21]) – help to clarify and explain the conceptual framework for the study presented in this chapter. The IAD literature[22] recognizes the importance of material conditions, rules in use, attributes of the community, and the dynamics of action situations. The implementation literature highlights the issues like standard operating procedures, dilemma of field level officials, and organizational processes. Drawing on these two bodies of literature, the study examines the following five elements in the context of CPR projects: context, nature of the problem, system of operation, organizational process, and dynamics of implementation.

To understand the complexity of institution building, cases of 19 villages involving CPR management projects (published as well as unpublished) were selected for this study. The cases identified were implemented in Gujarat and Rajasthan, both in western India. To introduce diversity in the observations and variety in experiences, published case studies of two organizations were added; these include Social Action for Rural and Tribal In-Habitants of India (SARTHI) in Gujarat, and the Mysore Resettlement and Development Agency (MYRADA) in Karnataka (located in southern India). These two organizations are involved in implementation of natural resource management projects (including CPRs) and they have pioneered the issue of community-driven management. In particular, MYRADA has played a key role in convincing the policymakers about the importance of the community's role in CPR projects. The distinctive features of these two cases are that it described the organizational experience in CPR development projects, while the other cases were experiences from specific villages. Most of the case studies have been published, although some unpublished reports also provided essential data and background information for the study. To ensure diversity in observations, projects implemented by different types of facilitating agencies (government-run and NGOs), those dealing with different kinds of problems related to CPRs (free grazing *versus* encroachment), and those involving different types of interventions (biophysical, advocacy, or institutional) were chosen. Additional information was collected by means of a questionnaire emailed to the involved organizations or filled out during telephonic conversations. Primary data was received from eight organizations; for the four that did not respond, secondary sources of information were used.

The collected data were then recorded and coded. The first cycle of coding involved descriptive coding, using terms taken directly from the text of the case studies.[23] This exercise yielded eleven generic codes, one for each category (Figure 17.1). The most frequently mentioned points were identified and categorized, keeping in view the emerging patterns and the conceptual framework. Finally, interlinkages between themes were identified through pattern matching,[24] and propositions were built from these observations.

FINDINGS

Before going to the findings, it would be useful to provide a brief background of the case studies. The case studies were related primarily to pastureland management and water bodies. Six case studies in the Rajsamand district of Rajasthan illustrated how under the same conditions (similar community, single government facilitating agency) different villages had different kinds of

[21] Lipsky, M. *Street-level bureaucracy: Dilemma of the Individual in Public Services* (New York: Russell Sage Foundation, 1980).

[22] Ostrom, *Institutional Rational Choice*, 1999.

[23] Saldana, J., *The Coding Manual for Qualitative Researchers* (London, California, New Delhi: Sage Publications, 2009).

[24] Yin, R. K., *Case Study Research: Design and Methods* (Thousand Oaks, London and New Delhi: Sage, 2003).

Primary codes

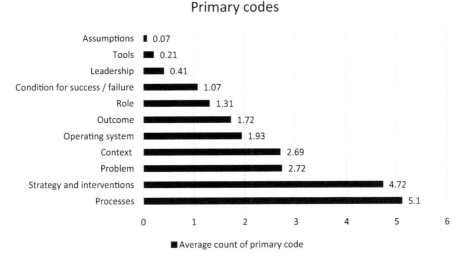

FIGURE 17.1 Primary Code Counts by Average Frequency of Mention

results. Similarly, in Udaipur district of Rajasthan, Seva Mandir implemented common land development projects where the focus was to free these resources from encroachments by dominant groups in the village. One organization, Ubeshwar Vikas Mandal (UVM) considered such projects as social experiments in meeting its ideology of community empowerment. Other organizations implemented CPR development projects in these areas. These projects were either solely focused on CPRs (as in Seva Mandir and UVM), or it was part of integrated development projects such as watershed projects where issues like agriculture, water, animal husbandry, soil conservation were addressed in a holistic manner.

The texts of the above cases were coded, as mentioned in the previous section. The primary code counts are summarized in Figure 17.1. The most frequent codes were those related to processes, strategies, problems, context, systems for operation, and outcomes. These codes became the foundations for further inquiry into the reasons and explanations of various issues and problems to be looked into in this study. Other issues, which received fewer counts, were not highlighted in these findings.

CONTEXTUAL FACTORS OF INSTITUTION BUILDING
IN DEVELOPMENT OF CPRS

Three important contextual factors played key roles in the development of CPR programs: resource adequacy, social relationships, and a history of conflict or cooperation. If everybody derives ample benefits from the resource, it would be something like a public good. However, resources, particularly in the context of CPR projects, were scarce and their use had to be limited – although such scarcity did not result in their judicious use. For example, the pasture was too small to meet the needs of the large cattle population in Sakroda village in Rajasthan, where the Department of Watershed Development and Soil Conservation (WD & SC) of the Government of Rajasthan had undertaken a pastureland development project.[25] If a resource was severely degraded, people believed that the chances of increasing its productivity were high.

---

[25] Mishra and Kumar, Institutionalisation of common pool resources management.

This became the basis for designing the interventions, as was observed in the projects undertaken by the BAIF Development Research Foundation (BAIF is an NGO, which has its headquarters in Pune, Maharashtra) and UVM, based in Udaipur.[26] Thus, resource adequacy was judged not only in terms of its current size, but also in terms of its potential to yield future benefits. The extent of resource adequacy had significant implications for the facilitating organization and influenced the potential for collective action. The greater the resource adequacy, the lower the level of commitment in a community to protect the resource. If resource adequacy was low, the community believed that the resource was unlikely to last and therefore it was not worthwhile to spend money and time to protect a small patch of land with which the resource was associated. Thus, the community responded positively to conserve and protect CPRs if those CPRs offered significant future benefits.

The degree of resource adequacy was embedded in social relationships within a local community. Social relationships, also referred to as the "attributes of a community," can be gauged from the homogeneity or heterogeneity of the community.[27] Generally, a homogenous community responds better to collective management: in the words of a respondent who managed a CPR development project undertaken by BAIF, "There is no formula to ensure that a homogenous community will respond positively. However, it is easier to convince the community if its members are from the same tribe or the same occupation. You convince one person, and others will start listening to you: in a heterogenous community, if you convince one, another will start opposing you."[28]

This observation was not always accurate, as turned out to be the case with WD & SC, and a relatively homogenous community often preferred unrestricted grazing access for its animals rather than protecting the pasture.[29] Sometimes opposing factions can be for or against the protection of a resource, and the facilitating agency can easily find an ally. In the projects undertaken by Aga Khan Rural Support Programme of India [AKRSP (I)] and Seva Mandir, powerful groups had encroached upon the common resource, a feature of the deep-rooted feudal culture that affected decision-making in those localities.[30] A history of conflict between the two groups, each representing different castes, made the community more heterogeneous, making it impossible to arrive at a consensus on the right system for managing the resource. Existing institutions facilitated collective decision-making, whereas existing conflicts made it more difficult.

NATURE OF THE PROBLEM

Contextual factors proved important in defining the nature of the problem confronting the development of CPR management programs. A project to develop CPR primarily addresses the

[26] Ghorpade A., A. K. Chourasia, and S. Naik, "Gudha Gokulpura Pasture Development Case Study." In *Silvipasture Development and Management Case Studies by BAIF Development Research Foundation* edited by A. Ghorpade and S. Naik (BAIF/NRI Goat Research project Report No. 8, NRI Report No. 2684. Udaipur: BAIF/RRIDMA, 2002), pp. 22–38; Saint, K. *Silvipasture Management Case Studies by Ubeshwar Vikas Mandal (Dhar): Jogion-ka-Guda, Keli and Seedh* (BAIF/NRI Goat Research project Report No. 4, NRI Report No. 2535. Udaipur: Ubeshwar Vikas Mandal, 2000).

[27] Ballabh, P. "Profile of the region." In *Land, Community and Governance*. Edited by P. Ballabh (pp. 4–24). (New Delhi: National Foundation of India and Udaipur: Seva Mandir, 2004); Also see Mishra and Kumar, Institutionalisation of Common Pool Resources Management, 2007

[28] Makwana, L. Personal Communication, June 18, 2014.

[29] Mishra and Kumar, Institutionalisation of Common Pool Resources Management, 2007.

[30] Gupta, A. *Common Pool Resources in Semi-arid India. Gujarat regional report.* CRIDA/CWS/AKRSP (I)/WRMLtd/MSU/NRI Common Pool Resources Research Report No. 3 (Ahmedabad: AKRSP (I), 2001); Also see Ballabh "Profile of the region." In *Land, Community and Governance*. Edited by P. Ballabh, 2004.

degradation of resources. However, the way the problem is defined can differ from place to place. In the cases examined herein, the problems ranged from biophysical (soil erosion, land degradation) to economic (poverty, low productivity of land), to social (one dominant group had access to the resource, whereas the less powerful group did not), to institutional (lack of sustainable harvesting mechanisms, encroachment by the state, boundary disputes, lack of access for some groups). These problems were not always perceived the same way by everyone in the community. Even the background and the work culture of the facilitating agency influenced the way the CPR-related problems were defined. A government-run agency such as the Gujarat Land Development Corporation (GLDC) or WD & SC tried to solve land-based physical problems whereas NGOs tended to focus more on institution building and community empowerment. Why did the facilitating agencies follow their own priorities rather than identifying what the community needed? One reason behind it was that the organizations followed their own areas of expertise. The answer, according to one respondent: "We are here to implement a project. Hence, we need to see that project interventions match the local problems. If there is no match, that area is unsuitable for the project—it is that simple."[31]

Even within the category of NGOs, the organizations differed in their roles. In Udaipur, the traditional caste-based structure had created power relations resulting in one group being more dominant; more often, such groups encroached upon the common land. Seva Mandir, which had been working in that locality for several decades, dealt with issues related to local power structure and introduced such interventions as leadership building,[32] whereas BAIF, another NGO, focused more on interventions such as improving the degree of protection and refining the harvesting mechanism.[33] The problems in villages were often diverse, and the priorities set by the facilitating agencies were not always those set by the community. This discrepancy meant that sometimes the designed interventions did not address the needs of the community. Flawed perceptions pertaining to the nature of the problem could lead to negative results, as happened in the village of Jogion ka Guda: UVM officials relied on the self-organizing capabilities of the community and believed that people would protect the pasture. But the sociopolitical realities were far from these assumptions, and, because of the lack of cohesion in the community, the protection mechanism designed by UVM failed.[34]

ORGANIZATIONAL PROCESSES AND THE ROLE OF THE FACILITATING AGENCY

Projects aimed at the development of CPRs are usually based on grants, and the donors invariably provide guidelines on how the project must be implemented. For example, state-run schemes have detailed guidelines that clearly define the role of the facilitating organizations. But the organizations typically have some autonomy in their choice of methods. Broadly, the organization can be a service provider, a catalyst, or a patron. As a service provider (e.g., WD & SC), the role is to provide financial or technical support. BAIF, for example, provided technical support as well as institution-building services. As a catalyst (e.g., MYRADA and UVM), the role is limited only to providing guidance, support, and conflict resolution. As a patron (e.g., Seva Mandir), the role is to provide support in many forms including monitoring, advocacy, and capacity building. However, these categories are seldom mutually exclusive, and all the

---

[31] Choudhary, P. *Personal Communication*, February 15, 2016.
[32] Ballabh, "Profile of the region," In *Land, Community and Governance.* Edited by P. Ballabh., 2007.
[33] Ghorpade and Naik, *Silvipasture Development and Management Case Studies by BAIF*, 2002.
[34] Saint, *Silvipasture Management Case Studies by Ubeshwar Vikas Mandal*, 2000.

facilitating organizations often play overlapping roles. Such roles are also determined by the way organizational processes influence the implementation of projects.

A project for CPR development is of limited duration, usually three to five years. When the project is over, ideally the facilitating agency withdraws from the day to day implementation and the local community takes over. The withdrawal strategy, which is also referred to as the exit policy, may differ from organization to organization. State-run agencies (e.g., WD & SC and GLDC) withdrew immediately, sometimes even abruptly, after a project was completed.[35] MYRADA decreased the intensity of its involvement gradually, and by the end of the project, the involvement was minimal.[36] Most NGOs continued their association with the community institution in some form. For service-providing organizations, CPRs had some instrumental value; for the catalyst organizations, institution building was an end in itself; and patrons continued their support much longer and recognized that some form of support would be necessary in the future as well. However, the roles kept changing, and organizations such as Seva Mandir and AKRSP continued their operations one way or another.[37] As a respondent who worked in GLDC put it, "NGOs continue working in a particular place forever, but we cannot do that. We have to move on once a project is over. We have to hand it over to the local people or the *panchayat* [the local government] and move on; we cannot continue at one place even if we want to."[38]

Flexibility was also a function of discretion. Functionaries of NGOs enjoyed greater discretionary power than their government counterparts, although the latter were not always inflexible; indeed, whenever possible, they did exercise discretion, as happened in Sundarcha village. Here, against the standard protocol, WD & SC officers preferred to hand over the pasture to a local committee rather than to the *panchayat* (the village council).

In principle, the facilitating agencies wanted to keep their processes separate from community affairs, but it was not an easy task. In Patosan village, when a functionary of the implementing agency was transferred and the newcomer could not handle a conflict within the community, the whole system of managing the CPR crumbled.[39] Similarly, a man who had volunteered to work for Seva Mandir was asked to leave when he was elected as a *sarpanch* (elected head of the village council). This was the protocol, but it made him unhappy, and he grudgingly tried to abet a long-standing conflict over the CPR in the village.[40]

One of the objectives of any CPR project is to set up a system for managing the CPR. This involves formulating rules for protection of the relevant resource, and for harvesting and sharing it. Although the donors and the funding agencies emphasized that the community should decide on the details of such a system, the facilitating organizations influenced those decisions significantly. However, they did not operate unilaterally and made it a point to consult with the community every time. The NGOs usually made some effort to build a community-driven system, although that took some time; the government-run agencies, on the other hand, preferred to start immediately and often imposed their system without any community input. Invariably however, the systems kept on changing. The system worked well in the Sundarcha

---

[35] Mishra and Kumar, Institutionalisation of Common Pool Resources Management, 2007.

[36] Armstrong, L., Shashidharan, E. M., & Kumar, P. *Catalysing Village Level Institutions for Natural Resource Management* (Ahmedabad: DSC, 1999).

[37] Ibid.

[38] Musa, M. Personal cCmmunication, August 12, 2017.

[39] Mishra, P.K. and R. Saxena, "Integrated Impact Assessment Model for Explaining Differential Impact of Watershed Development Projects", (*Impact Assessment and Project Appraisal*, 27, 2009): 175–184.

[40] Kashwan, P. (2004). "Kojon ka Guda." *Land, Community and Governance*. Edited by P. Ballabh (New Delhi: National Foundation of India and Udaipur: Seva Mandir, 2004), pp. 45–62

and Kundeli villages, whereas in Sangawas it was not accepted by people until they saw its benefits.[41] An acceptable system was one in which the views of the organization (whether a government agency or a NGO) matched those of the community. Why did some organizations impose their own priorities instead of seeking consensus? After all, they were facilitating organizations and should not exercise undue influence. According to a respondent from WD & SC: "Villagers have diverse viewpoints and also diverse interests. Sometimes, a consensus is impossible. Therefore, the best way is to start somewhere: people would listen to us in the beginning because we had an upper hand. We disburse funds and are also expected to be impartial outsiders; hence our proposals are considered the least controversial."[42]

Those who stood to benefit from the project, namely the users of the CPR who belonged to the local community, were often divided into factions and failed to agree on the desired interventions. In such a situation, the facilitating agency was guided by technical viability, which meant that its opinion was considered neutral. In one village, Jodha ka Kheda, the facilitating agency (BAIF) chose the particular plant species that would be planted on the common land, and people accepted the choice gracefully because they considered their recommendations to be expert opinions based on neutral viewpoints.[43]

Another crucial organizational process involved monitoring. Tools of monitoring differed greatly from one organization to the next. State-run agencies often focused on progress reviews, timelines, and biophysical structures, whereas NGOs tended to focus on strengthening institutions. The nature of monitoring tools reflected the priorities and the orientation of the facilitating organization. For example, AKRSP (I) measured the strength of institutions using a tool referred to as the institutional maturity index. In contrast, the employees of WD & SC often used rules of thumb based on heuristics. The majority of agencies used biophysical indicators (the proportion of plants that had survived, the amount of output, etc.), economic logic, or direct impact (profitability of interventions). Managers often depended on heuristics that were ad hoc and practical. One rule of thumb was that institutions that deal with crises successfully are more sustainable than others.[44] The state-run agencies emphasized the need for biophysical indicators and paid less attention to institutional strength.

Despite having similar programs, why did the organizations follow different monitoring strategies? A respondent from the WD & SC, who stated that survival percentages of plants were monitored rigorously, observed:

> Our actions are determined by some given criteria. Suppose there are two villages. In one, the survival percentage is higher (making the plantation look more pleasing aesthetically); in the other, the community initiative is strong, but survival percentage is low. My supervisor would choose the first village for documentation and highlight it—I know in the long run the second village will have a more sustainable resource, but my hands are tied.[45]

The above statement made sense in the case of Kundeli, where the survival rate was low, but local institutions were robust. However, the facilitating agency did not notice the positive development of institutional strength because the success of the project was measured in terms

---

[41] Mishra and Kumar, Institutionalisation of Common Pool Resources Management, 2007.

[42] Dasora, N. Personal Communication, June 17, 2014.

[43] Conroy, C., A. Ghorpade, B. G. Rathod, and M. Vadher, "Jodha ka Kheda", in Ghorpade and Naik (ed.), *Silvipasture Development and Management Case Studies by BAIF Development Research Foundation*. Edited by Ghorpade and Naik. BAIF/NRI Goat Research project Report No. 8, NRI Report No. 2684 (Udaipur: BAIF/RRIDMA., 2002), pp. 1–21.

[44] Mishra and Kumar, Institutionalisation of Common Pool Resources Management, 2007.

[45] Sharma, R. Personal Communication, June 12, 2017.

of biophysical indicators.[46] The priority for this organization was to ensure that the plantation was a success, the material aspects being more important than the institutional ones.

DYNAMICS OF IMPLEMENTATION

Ideally, all the project villages should receive equal attention from the facilitating agency. Yet the agencies often paid additional attention to those villages in which the community responded positively to their interventions. In Sundarcha and Sangawas, WD & SC officials participated actively in village politics and supported the protection of the common pastureland; in other villages, the agency responded differently, its indifference being quite visible in Dipti and Sakroda.

How did the organizations cope with the village dynamics when things went wrong? The managers working for Seva Mandir used subtle coercion; for example, in Viyal and Kojon Ka Guda, the opposing groups were compelled to come to the negotiation table when the agency stopped all developmental interventions in the village.[47] In one village, UVM stayed away from politics, assuming that the community would solve its own problem; but that approach did not work, rather the different factions in the village got into more conflicts.[48] In Sangawas and Sundarcha, WD & SC supported the groups that were in favor of protecting the resources and encouraged opinion leaders to weigh in.[49] However, it was not clear from the narratives whether, and to what extent, the organizations were involved in litigation or court cases, although in at least three cases this was mentioned as a possibility.

All the organizations engaged in routine follow-up. When the organization initially approached the community for the development of the commons, not everybody agreed to the proposal. But the organization was persistent in its appeals: regular follow-up and iterations were common features of the dynamics of implementation. When the officials in WD & SC found that the existing 22-member committee in Sundarcha was inactive, they changed the form of the institution, and established a new committee with only 8 members. This time, the officials ensured that people supporting the project interventions were part of the committee.

Similarly, respondents from Seva Mandir, BAIF, GVNML, and Shiv Shiksha Samiti all mentioned regular follow-up and dialog as core parts of their strategy. Problem-solving was not a one time phenomenon, rather it was an iterative process. Such iterations can be a short-term process, for example the reconstitution of a committee in Sundarcha, or a long-term process, as happened in Keli, where the pasture developed by UVM was plundered. The villagers requested UVM to help in restoring the pasture, which it did.[50] Similarly, in Jodha ka Kheda, seasonal grazing was prohibited: instead, users could cut the grass and take it away; however, in drought years such restrictions were relaxed. To protect the pasture, parts of it were harvested in rotation, and later a watchman was also employed.[51] The system thus evolved through trial and error, an iterative process of implementation.

---

[46] Mishra and Kumar, Institutionalisation of Common Pool Resources Management, 2007.

[47] Ameta, N. L. and P. Roy, "Viyal" *Land, community and governance*. Edited by Ballabh, P (New Delhi: National Foundation of India and Udaipur: Seva Mandir, 2004), pp. 45–62; Kashwan, Kojon ka guda

[48] Saint, *Silvipasture Management Case Studies by Ubeshwar Vikas Mandal*, 2000

[49] Mishra and Kumar, Institutionalisation of Common Pool Resources Management, 2007.

[50] Saint, *Silvipasture Management Case Studies by Ubeshwar Vikas Mandal*, 2000.

[51] Conroy et al. Jodha ka Kheda, in Ghorpade and Naik (ed.) *Silvipasture Development and Management Case Studies*, 2002.

CONCLUSION

Projects to develop CPRs as facilitated by external agencies need to overcome a range of dynamics and challenges if they are to succeed.[52] They are different from the self-initiated institutions that form the focus of Ostrom's design principles, which were later refined by Agrawal (2003) and others. The findings of our study lead to the following propositions:

- An abundance of resources results in an environment unsupportive of collective action to preserve the common resource.
- Negative social relationships hinder a facilitating agency's efforts to promote collective action to manage CPRs.
- The background of the facilitating agency (whether a service provider, a catalyst, or a patron) and its work culture influence the way it defines the problem of managing a CPR, and this definition becomes the basis for designing project interventions.
- Organizational roles and processes, in addition to the terms of the project and local needs, shape the design of the project and its monitoring.
- Facilitating organizations that align themselves with a particular group, rather than remaining neutral, handle problems more effectively. This happens because in a village with contesting groups it is difficult to bring in everybody to a single platform. It is easier to go with a group whose priority matches with the organization.
- Iterative processes lie at the core of a facilitating organization's effectiveness. The more the managers are acquainted with such processes, the higher their chances of success.

A framework based on these conclusions for explaining the development of facilitated institutions is shown in Figure 17.2.

The success of CPR development projects is determined by contextual factors, the community's priorities, and organizational roles. The nature of the problem that the CPR faces

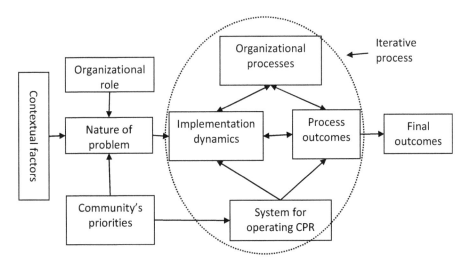

FIGURE 17.2 An iterative model of developing common property resources with the help of an external agency

---

[52] Saunders, The Promise of Common Pool Resource Theory, 2014.

(biophysical or institutional), which is significantly influenced by the facilitating agency's prioritics and the community's perceptions, is determined by this conflicting set of priorities. Based on these inputs, the interventions, including the system for managing a CPR, is formed. However, at this stage, the system is tentative: during its implementation, it is refined through an iterative process of trial and error. The lessons learned from the implementation and the inputs from stakeholders (particularly the community and the facilitating agency) are used for fine-tuning the system along the way, and any inadvertent outcomes, if negative, are eliminated (such as the benefits going to a category that is not intended to benefit from the interventions). After several iterations, the system becomes institutionalized.

These findings propose a dynamic model for the facilitated institutions that differs from the existing static models, which frequently use such criteria as scientific knowledge, sustainability and preservation, the extent of participation, economic efficiency, and equity in evaluating the performance of institutions.[53]

The iterative process of implementation has some practical implications as well. Every funding agency expects its project to succeed: however, if the action situation is dynamic, how does a manager of a CPR project meet the criteria for a sustainable institution? One way is to use certain rules of thumb, and follow a practice termed as "adaptive management," which involves learning by doing.[54] This practice includes iterative and experiential ways of planning and undertaking interventions, and requires that the organization be good at documenting, adapting, and learning. Unless practical knowledge is documented and integrated into existing knowledge, it will remain only tacit knowledge.[55] This may lead to local dynamics being ignored, and this ignorance can lead to failure in institution building.

Institution building is a complex phenomenon, and a deterministic theory cannot explain it: an iterative theory seems more realistic. Literature on implementation research highlights routines, which can be equated with an institutionalized system.[56] In running an iterative process, the discretion of field-level (or street-level) officials is crucial. That is where priorities of the organization affect decision-making[57] and may lead to development actions being diluted at some stage of implementation, a lacuna that can be filled through the iterative process.

Some of the findings are consistent with those reported in the implementation literature. Street-level bureaucrats are often more attentive to the better-performing clients,[58] an observation that supports the findings in the case of WD & SC, in which focusing on better-performing CPRs ultimately led to positive results. It was also observed that a rule of thumb for evaluating success was the ability of the institution to resolve critical cases. These two observations appear to be interrelated: managers focus on institutions that respond positively, and institutions make more significant efforts to resolve a crisis. Thus, it is the initial response of the members of an institution that seems to matter most.

[53] Ostrom, E., and C. Hess, "A framework for Analyzing the Knowledge Commons," In Hess, C. & Ostrom, E. (Eds.), *Understanding Knowledge as a Commons: From Theory to Practice* (pp. 41–82). (Cambridge, MA: MIT Press, 2006)

[54] Blann, K., S. Light, and J. A. Musumeci, "Facing the Adaptive Challenge: Practitioners' Insights from Negotiating Resource Crises in Minnesota", In F. Berkes, J. Colding, & C. Folke (Eds.), *Navigating Socio-ecological Systems: Building Resilience for Complexity and Change* (pp. 210–240). (Cambridge, England: Cambridge University Press, 2008).

[55] Ibid.

[56] Allison, *Essence of Decision*, 1971.

[57] Lipsky, *Street-level Bureaucracy*, 1980.

[58] Ibid.

Institutions that facilitate the management of CPRs not only face complex interactions at the community level but are also influenced by their organizational priorities. Such external agencies are essential to the development of CPRs because they have a significant say in the process. Last, it must be kept in mind that these findings, along with the propositions stated earlier, cannot be extrapolated to the entire population but serve to support a contingency theory that can be usefully applied in limited contexts. Nevertheless, the findings presented herein open up vast opportunities for future research, which I hope this chapter will inspire.

18

Social Environmental Dilemmas and Governing the Commons

The Itanhém River Basin in Southern Bahia, Brazil

Fernando Rios De Souza and Herbert Toledo Martins

Seven years after its official creation in December 2012, the basin committee for the Peruípe, Itanhém and Jucuruçu rivers (*Comitê de Bacias Hidrográficas dos rios Peruípe, Itanhém e Jucuruçu*, or the CBHPIJ), located in the extreme south of the Brazilian state of Bahia, has failed to carry out environmental management actions to ensure the river's preservation, particularly on the Itanhém river basin, which is the focus of this research. This Committee is governed collectively by a body of government officials, ordinary users of resources and representatives of civil society, who together democratically make decisions about the environmental management and sustainability of these rivers. Despite the operating time and the collective represented, we still observe the absence of riparian forests, siltation, water contamination by pesticides, and pollution in various forms.

Using the structure of the Socioecological Systems (SES) model,[1] we argue that the factors and conditions that hinder the management of the Itanhém River reside in a mismatch between its management committee and the community. On the one hand, the community follows its own socio-environmental laws, as if there is no committee, assessing the costs and benefits of its individual actions. On the other hand, the Committee lives in an isolated world, as if there was no community, which is governed by plenaries and meetings where rules and norms are discussed in the abstract, and the actions generally produce little or no useful applicability to the users' daily lives. In the vacuum between these two worlds, the absence of clear and effective collective rules means that users of the river's resources practice their own individual rules, trapped in a vicious cycle that keeps them focused only on individual financial profit.[2]

The research discusses the "environmental tragedy" happening in the Itanhém River, focusing on the actions of users who follow their own practices, on the one hand, and the committee members who propose collective management strategies and rules for this common resource, on the other. In all, ten farmers and fourteen committee members were interviewed, and answered questions elaborated in a specific questionnaire extracted from the SES Framework created and

---

[1] E. Ostrom, "A General Framework for Analyzing Sustainability of Social-Ecological Systems," *Science*, Vol. 325, No. 5939 (2009): 419–22.
[2] M. Olson, *The Logic of Collective Action: Public Goods and the Theory of Groups* (Cambridge, MA: Harvard University Press, 1965).

adapted by Ostrom and Meinzen-Dick.[3] Eight design principles[4] related to robust common resource institutions are formulated from this model. Given the wide variety of ecological problems that individuals face at various scales, design principles are an ideal governance parameter, and an instrument for assessing whether or not the collective arrangement will succeed in implementing its sustainable rules.

This empirical work presents a qualitative interpretation of the research results of our study. The relevance of the research presented below lies in the application of the above-mentioned model in the case of a watershed committee in the Northeast region of Brazil, thus deepening our understanding of the practical problems involved when an external committee attempts to regulate a common resource. Moreover, this chapter adds to our expanding knowledge regarding water management in river basins throughout the country and potentially, the globe.

This paper utilizes the theoretical-methodological framework proposed by Ostrom for Common Pool Resource (CPR) management (the Ostrom's SES framework)[5] an empirical application from here divided into three more parts. The next section discusses the theoretical foundations that illuminate the problem at hand, which focus on Hardin's assumptions in his famous "Tragedy of the Commons" essay,[6] Olson's logic of collective actions,[7] and Ostrom's governance of the commons.[8] After that, in the "Methodology" section, we applied the SES framework of Ostrom[9] to the Committee, focusing on the action arena that involves the relationship between CPR users and the leading actors of the committee, comparing the actual situation found with the eight design principles of Ostrom to understand how close the collective body is to an ideal type considered sustainable. We ended in the last section discussing the challenges and future perspectives for the collective body if you want to take new directions in the face of the urgency of a balanced world.

COLLECTIVE ACTION DILEMMAS AT ITANHÉM RIVER BASIN

The Committee has been in operation since December 2012 but despite more than seven years it still seeks a decentralized and participative collective management among public authorities, users of water resources, civil society and communities. The committee is responsible for an area corresponding to 16,161 km², covering the hydrographic basins of the Jucuruçu, Itanhém and Peruípe rivers, from the interior of the country to the Atlantic Ocean, directly involving 381,983 inhabitants in a total of 15 municipalities. The regional climate is tropical, of Atlantic Forest, with average monthly temperatures above 64° F and rainfall above 720 mm. The committee was approved as a collegiate body, of a consultative, normative and deliberative character, and is part of the State Water Resources Management System, which is linked to the State Water Resources Council (CONERH).

---

[3] E. Ostrom, A General Framework for Analyzing Sustainability of Social-Ecological Systems, *supra* note 1; R. Meinzen-Dick. Beyond panaceas in water institutions. Proceedings of the National Academy of Sciences, Vol. 104, No. 39 (2007), pp. 15200–15205; E. Ostrom. A diagnostic approach for going beyond panaceas. Proceedings of the National Academy of Sciences, Vol. 104, No. 39 (2007), pp. 15181–15187.

[4] E. Ostrom. *Governing the Commons: The Evolution of Institutions for Collective Action* (Cambridge University Press), 1990.

[5] *Id.*

[6] G. Hardin. "The tragedy of the Commons." *Science*, v. 162, n. 3859, 1968, 1243–1248.

[7] M. Olson, *supra* note 2.

[8] E. Ostrom, *supra* note 6.

[9] E. Ostrom, *supra* note 1.

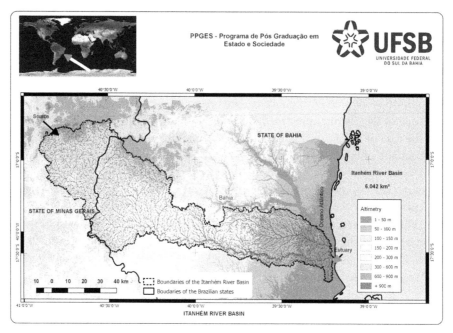

FIGURE 18.1 Hypsometric map of Itanhém River Basin.
Source: Souza and Martins (2019)

The Itanhém River has significant socio-economic value in Southern Bahia. The basin has an area of 6.042 square kilometres and a population of approximately 230,000 inhabitants, draining the better part of the municipalities of Alcobaça, Teixeira de Freitas, and Medeiros Neto in the state of Bahia, and also the municipalities of Bertópolis, Santa Helena de Minas, Machacalis and Fronteira dos Vales, which are in the state of Minas Gerais (see Figure 18.1).

Unfortunately, the river suffers continuously from the actions of interested users who are not yet under the influence of collective rules for sustainable cooperation. Polluting industries, farmers who use pesticides and landowners who deforest water sources and riparian forests, which results in silting, are common. Among the many observable problems, there are also irregular dwellings built along its bed, favouring problems such as urban flooding. All of this represents a sample that illustrates a problem of collective action. Olson analysed the dilemma faced by citizens who wish to use a common resource through collective action. He noticed that collective action is always a problem because, typically, contribution costs are individual and concentrated, while benefits are diffuse and collective. In the absence of cooperation (a trust-based process), individuals tend to maximize their individual interests. In the end, without externally imposed regulations, Olson's theory predicts that collectively used natural resources will be mismanaged.[10]

Individual interests prevail when each user is tempted to withdraw more than one unit from a limited resource. In this context, environmental destruction is a certainty, and for this reason, natural resources exploited in ineffective collective systems will be depleted. Driven by individual rationality, individuals seek to maximize their own preferences, producing a suboptimal and eventually catastrophic result for the collective. Hardin proposes two solutions to this

[10] M. Olson, *supra* note 2.

dilemma.[11] In the first, natural resources (e.g., the river) must be privatized because, under the private regime, the forms of use are strictly controlled by someone interested in sustaining the resource. In the second solution, the government must be the official administrator and apply rules of use, also exercising a type of property system. These two options – privatization or government regulation – in Hardin's view, would guarantee the sustainability of natural resources. Since its formulation, this line of thought has gained both sympathizers and detractors, such as Azevedo, Martins and Drummond.[12] In recent decades, Hardin's reasoning has been criticized as applied to the use and management of natural resources, which have broadened the scope and theoretical understanding of Common Pool Resources (CPR).

The alternatives to "the Tragedy of Commons" concern the identification of factors that lead to the success or failure of collective arrangements, as well as the institutional arrangements – their governance regime, actors, rules of access and exclusion, and mechanisms to guarantee established rules – that contribute to their success. The most influential scholar in this field was the late Elinor Ostrom, whose studies around the world proved that it is possible, through organization and collective participation, to establish rules, which are monitored and enforced, so that collections of individuals, communities and groups can successfully manage a collectively used resource.

Ostrom identified alternative paths that could avert a "tragedy of the commons."[13] She showed that the commons' dilemma can be overcome provided that those involved share the feeling that if they do not adopt new rules of collaboration, they will succumb to the temptations of self-interest. This alternative assumes that humans may not be able to fully analyze all situations, but will put effort into solving complex problems by learning norms of behaviour, particularly reciprocity. Ostrom believed that those who depend on common resources are not forever trapped in a collective action dilemma. In some ways, governance becomes an adaptive and iterative process that involves multiple actors at various social levels.

By locating examples from around the world of communities collectively managing shared resources, Ostrom was able to elaborate principles common to successful, robust and resilient CPR governance in the face of everyday problems.[14] She developed an "ideal type" of practice, consisting of eight principles, which relate to the information that group members' share, and their practical actions with respect to the socioeconomic environment. Briefly, the eight design principles are as follows:

1. *Well-defined Limits*: the limits of a resource must be clearly defined, as well as the set of individuals with rights to it. Enforcing governance rules becomes easier when the limits are well defined.
2. *Proportional Equivalence of Costs and Benefits*: rules should provide benefits in proportion to the costs required for these rules to function. An imbalance in costs and benefits may lead some participants to refuse to obey rules they consider unfair.
3. *Collective Choice Agreements*: most individuals affected by resource regulation should be involved in drafting the applicable rules. Participation increases the likelihood that the rules will be considered fair by participants.

---

[11] G. Hardin, *supra* note 8.

[12] A. I. Azevedo; H. T. Martins; J. A. L. Drummond. A dinâmica institucional de uso comunitário dos produtos nativos do cerrado no município de Japonvar (Minas Gerais). *Sociedade e Estado*, v. 24, n. 1, p. 193–228, 2009.

[13] E. Ostrom, "Coping with tragedies of the commons". *Annual Review of Political Science*, v. 2, n. 1, 1999, 493–535.

[14] E. Ostrom, *supra* note 6.

4. *Monitoring*: reliable monitoring builds confidence among users that they can cooperate without the fear that others are not cooperating.

5. *Graduated Sanctions*: sanctions for violated rules should be graduated because this will encourage people not to break rules by lightly penalizing them (at first) and allowing them to return to the cycle of continuous trust.

6. *Conflict Resolution Mechanisms*: there must be affordable, efficient, and impartial arenas where conflicts between users, or between users and employees, can be quickly resolved.

7. *Minimum Rights Recognition*: the government must recognize users' rights to make their own rules.

8. *Cooperative Efforts*: when common resources are part of a larger system, any required activities should be organized in a cooperative manner among the various social entities.

In essence, the Ostrominian theories have for decades been trying to understand common goods from the perspective of how people can overcome social dilemmas, and create, maintain and adapt ways of living and working together, even in difficult circumstances. As Blomquist interestingly said in Chapter 1 of this volume, the rules (even by the Ostrom principles) that govern the rights to a natural resource are more than on-off, can-cannot or inside-outside dichotomies. Logically, in the socio-ecological atmosphere there are human beings and institutions interacting with social choices and actions within humanly created sets of rules, and therefore, subject to fallibility. Fortunately, and on the other hand, people are not "condemned" or imprisoned in tragic immutable conditions, it ends up bringing the beauty of the phenomenon of choice, enabling resilience and robustness in this incredible evolutionary learning process.

With due respect for this appropriation, applying Ostrom's design principles we seek to understand why the Committee's attempt to manage the Itanhém river has largely failed to achieve its objectives.

METHODOLOGY

After presenting the problem and the theoretical assumptions underlying our analysis, we now evaluate the practical reality of the physical and psychological disjunction between the committee and the river's users. We seek to understand the pieces of information that are relevant to the users of the resource system, and the ways in which information motivates them, or fails to motivate them, to choose the sustainable option. We use Ostrom's SES Framework to perform this analysis.[15] This model consists of an interpretation of the relations between society, economy and the environment. The institutional development analysis considers several factors in the management of a commonly used resource or socio-ecological system (see Table 18.1). Ostrom suggests that consideration be given to social, economic, and political configurations as well. From there, the resource is analysed through four sublevels, namely: Resources System (RS), Resources Unit (RU), Governance System (GS), and Users (U). Each one of these four aspects can easily be disaggregated into smaller units of study, as shown in Table 18.1.

According to Ostrom, these are the variables that every study on governance of commonly used resources should take into account.[16] Based on these variables, we view the Ostrom's SES framework through the lens of the Meinzen-Dick's framework for water management systems

---

[15] E. Ostrom, *supra* note 1.
[16] E. Ostrom, *supra* note 3.

TABLE 18.1 *Factors hypothesized to affect irrigation system management*

Social, Economic and Political Settings (S)
S1 – Economic development S2 – Demographic trends (density, settlement pattern)
S4 – Government water policies and commitment to reform S5 – Market incentives (distance to Market)

Resource System (RS)	*Governance System (GS)*
RS1 – Sector: Water	GS1 – Government organizations
RS2 – Clarity of System boundaries	GS2 – Nongovernment organizations
RS3 – Size of irrigation system	GS3 – Structure of user groups
RS4 – Water infrastructure	GS4 – Property Rights
RS4-a Headworks	GS4 – a Property rights to infrastructure
RS4-b Channels	GS4 – b Property rights to water
RS4-c Control structures	GS5 – Operational rules
RS4-d Roads	GS6 – Collective choice rules
RS4-e Communications	GS7 – Constitutional rules
RS5 – Scarcity: relative water supply	GS8 – Monitoring & sanctioning processes
RS6 – Equilibrium properties	*Users (U)*
RS7 – Predictability of supply	U1 – Number of users (total and in local units)
RS7 – a Seasonal	U1 – a Number of users in whole system
RS7 – b Inter-annual	U1 – b Number of users in local units
RS8 – Storage characteristics	U2 – Socioeconomic attributes of users
RS9 – Location	U2a Wealth
Resource Units (RU)	U2b Heterogeneity
RU1 – Resource unit mobility	U2c Land tenure
RU2 – Water availability, by season	U2d Stability of group
RU3 –Hydrologic interaction among irrigation units	U3 – History of irrigation
RU3-a Interaction within a system	U4 – Location (residence relative to canals)
RU4-b Interaction between systems	U5 – Leadership
RU4 – Economic value of output	U6 – Shared norms/social capital
RU7 – Spatial & temporal distribution of water	U7 – Knowledge of irrigation
	U8 – Dependence of irrigation
	U9 – Technology used
Interactions (I) ←——→	Outcomes (O)
I1- Water use by diverse users	O1- Socioeconomic performance
I2- Information sharing	O1-a Equity of water distribution
I2-a Information on resource use	O1-b Water use efficiency
I2-b Information on conditions of resource	O1-c Cropping intensity
I3- Deliberation processes	O1-d Yields
I4- Conflicts among users	O1-e Value of output
I5- Investment in maintenance	O2- Ecological performance measures
I6- Lobbying activities	O2-a Waterlogging
	O2-b Salinity
	O3- Externalities to other systems

Related Ecosystems (ECO)
ECO1-Climate patterns ECO2-Pollution patterns ECO3-Flows into and out of focal irrigation systems

Source: Adapted from R. Meinzen-Dick. Beyond panaceas in water institutions. *Proceedings of the National Academy of Sciences*, vol. 104, no. 39 (2007), pp. 15200–15205.

(see Table 18.1);[17] this adaptation served as a parameter for the development of our questionnaire in order to produce data that could be compared to our ideal type.

Our data focused on the daily practices of water users, in addition to the leading actors who are members of that Committee. Based on the SES Structure and the Table 18.2, we prepared a

[17] R. Meinzen-Dick, *supra* note 5.

TABLE 18.2 *Design principles, user reality, and the CBHPIJ committee board reality*

Design principles	User reality	The CBHPIJ committee board reality
Principle 1: Clarity in Biophysical and Social limits	Users see the basin only on the horizon of their individual properties, their farms. The rules they follow are diverse. They do not know what the theoretical rules are, and they do not know data on the attributes of the watershed.	They do not have proper knowledge of the river basin in its biophysical and social aspects. They do not know the communities, their wants or needs. They do not know the biophysical attributes of the river because they do not have accurate and reliable data.
Principle 2: Proportional Equivalence between Costs and Benefits	Users do not trust the government's environmental management and conservation bodies. The costs to comply with the imposed rules are not proportional to the consideration given. The preservation rules are unfair, and there is no penalty.	Government employees who participate in CBHPIJ receive daily rates and have a vehicle structure at their disposal. Representatives of organized civil society do not have any resources to participate. Users are not interested because they find the plenary sessions a waste of time and money.
Principle 3: Collective Choice Agreements	Users do not participate in the elaboration and fair preservation of rules as they are distant from the bureaucratic reality of this system.	The collective organization CBHPIJ has a deficient participation of users. Those who participate are from large companies that use water and therefore defend their interests and have no class vision.
Principle 4: Monitoring	Users feel free to use environmental resources as they see fit, and only when complaints arise and they feel exposed to inspection. In the general daily routine, they are not inspected on compliance with the rules.	The committee and the monitoring bodies do not have the physical and financial structure to monitor the use of water resources effectively. They have only two inspectors who are seen as enemies of the population.
Principle 5: Grading Sanctions	Gradual sanctions have no influence on users because there is no monitoring, therefore, there is no sanction and, therefore, users prefer to follow their own rules since they are more financially advantageous.	Due to the problems mentioned in principle 4, the environmental management structure is deficient in the application of sanctions because it does not comply with the monitoring of misconduct. The standards are developed, but their faithful practical effect is not required.
Principle 6: Conflict Resolution Mechanisms	Conflicts between neighbours are rare. The dissatisfied make complaints to the management bodies and when they accumulate, penalties are applied. There is also no arena that promotes ease and agility for resolving conflicts.	The committee's structure does not have simplified conflict resolution mechanisms. When resolved, the environmental damage has already occurred and is irreparable.
Principle 7: Minimum Rights Recognition	Users do not trust that they can help to make their own rules for a collective purpose. Thus, they believe that they have no recognition of their rights.	Management members are not heard by the government. If the government disagrees with the collectively agreed deals, the actors believe that their wishes will not be believed.
Principle 8: Cooperative Efforts	Users do not notice the existence of a network of entities that can promote adequate environmental management. For them, they are all the same, and defend their own interests.	Actors recognize a structure of networked entities, but they believe it is ephemeral, disconnected and temporary.

Source: Drawn from information gleaned from the research questionnaires administered by the authors.

questionnaire that was addressed to 10 farmers and 14 members of the committee. For the interviews with users, the sample of ten farmers reached saturation, when the data obtained began to show redundancy or repetition. For the sample of the Committee's leading actors, the interviews were directed to all those available. The interviews produced data that could be compared with Ostrom's design principles. Between the everyday reality (that is captured by empirical research) and our ideal standard (the design principles), we discuss how the collective approaches or departs from success in implementing sustainable rules. The results were combined according to Table 18.2.

As shown in the qualitative interpretation of research results presented above, all principles have proven fragile, either from the user's perspective or from the Committee management agent's perspective. Management members are unaware of the geophysical limits of the basin that they manage. Users do not understand the costs and benefits of choosing to follow collective rules, and do not feel they belong to a system that respects their beliefs, values and culture in collective choices.

The comparison with principles of analysis shows a disjunction between categories. For example, Users see conservation investments as unnecessary and costly and they do not trust government-run environmental management organizations to do this. They feel the costs of complying with government-imposed rules are not proportional to the benefits they would receive in return. Also, Users find preservation rules implicitly unfair, and do not follow them because there is no penalty for noncompliance.

From the Committee's perspective, the collective structure isn't entirely active because, in a way, those absent see no advantage in participating. With some exceptions, Users see no advantage in being interested in the subject, as they find that time and resources are lost in bureaucratic and lengthy plenary sessions. The organization that represents the government participates because there are civil servants specifically designated for this purpose; they receive compensation for their participation and have vehicles and other facilities at their disposal. A third part of the committee includes representatives of organized civil society, who also have few financial and material resources and, as a result, have low rates of participation and attendance at collective meetings.

As if the problems of collective action were not enough, in the region of this study, external solutions appear almost always out of step with internal perceptions, causing a mismatch between the theoretical solutions projected (by these same external solutions) and those daily practices carried out by the community (the reality experienced by small farmers, for example), one question similar as in India described by Mishra in Chapter 3 of this volume. It is when the government and other entities supported by it often try (and assume) the role of leaders, imposing external rules based on prefabricated theories brought in from afar.

At the end, this analysis reveals that the committee is fragile and unable to prevent or deter individual selfish action; as such, the common resource is vulnerable to degradation. This is the end result of poor interaction between government officials and users, which negatively affects forms of ownership, rule composition, monitoring, and conflict resolution. With this antagonistic relationship in mind, we conclude with some thoughts on what this represents for social and environmental balance and for the "health" of the collective governance system represented by the Committee.

CONCLUSION

Why has the CBHPIJ river basin committee failed to implement proposed actions seven years into its operation? Results reveal two parallel and distant worlds. A world involves the practical and lived reality of real users of the common resource, cultivation, livestock, direct relations with land and water extraction. Another, entirely separate world, involves plenaries and bureaucratic meetings at Committee, where rules and theories are discussed in the abstract. Our research reveals that the Committee members, users, and other members of organized civil society alike, need to better understand themselves as complementary and belonging to a multi-layered polycentric management system that includes, fundamentally, the actual users of the resource. They also need to understand that this system needs to be dynamic, adaptive, and effective in the short, medium and long terms.

Within the heterogeneity of the Users' category, the data show a differentiation in relation to participation in Committee meetings. Large agricultural companies actively participate in Committee meetings, while small farmers have low participation rates. This is because these large companies are the main users of the Itanhém river and therefore invest financial and material resources, such as vehicles, computers, and human resources, to attend meetings and defend their private interests. Meanwhile, less affluent small farmers do not attend meetings because they do not feel part of the bureaucratic reality of the system, and also because they do not have the financial and material resources to invest in participating in these meetings.

CBHPIJ Committee faces the challenge of improving its communication and decision-making process, since preservation requires, first and foremost, knowledge of the biophysical and social limits of the relevant system. Information should be shared and discussed collectively, taking into account that it is a large watershed with multiple requirements and many rich and poor communities interacting dynamically. Distances must be shortened through technologies and easily accessible educational channels that reach the most remote places, so that everyone knows their rights and duties as well as the particularities of the region in which they operate.

CBHPIJ was created to help improve the rules governing river use, as practices have not proved sufficient to meet local needs and conditions. A sense of justice, which could make rule enforcement more natural and self-motivated, has not been equally embraced by all relevant users. To make matters worse, users believe that the State does not offer an adequate counter-benefit in the way of improving life and that the CBHPIJ Committee is just another bureau-cratic and disorganized government entity that wastes taxpayers' money. Users do not believe that the government is really interested in balancing the pillars of sustainability, only in generating more tax revenue.

Another issue to be improved, if the Committee wants to fulfil its duty as a management leader, is the incentive for the collective re-education of individuals. The organization should encourage individuals to actively participate in the deliberative meetings and the drafting of their own rules, freeing themselves from the influence of external agents. The environmental management system needs to improve its monitoring and inspection measures in the use of environmental resources, as well as compliance with the rules for natural preservation and restoration. It is also necessary to invest financial and human resources by expanding monitor-ing, not only by government agents, but also by citizens and users themselves. When citizens become part of the CPR and are motivated to help and preserve by participating in the monitoring of rules and conduct in their community, they exercise their citizenship, helping to denounce new deviations, and to keep the system stable.

As for the process of sanctioning noncompliance with the rules, crucial for tackling selfish actions, the committee has shown a well-developed system in theory only. Due to previous shortcomings, local and regional coercion mechanisms have not ensured proper compliance with management rules, which weakens the organization. Although there is a multi-level collaboration system, with societal and government agencies involved, the rules are out of line with social needs. Users work to pursue their unique interests and do not collaborate together, and therefore do not increase their resilience, information exchange, knowledge, and learning of each other's mistakes.

For everything, our analysis showed that the Committee does not have good connectivity with users in the watershed; and without advancing the management proposals it leads, it has so far proved to be yet another ineffective state intervention. The Committee fails because it has an unbalanced management structure, which feeds into a vicious cycle of feedback on poor socio-environmental relations. All this because the biophysical characteristics, the rules in use, and the attributes of the community are not in line with the Committee. Not understanding the characteristics that support its arena of action, the Committee becomes one of the gears of a dismantled body of environmental management, preserving the status quo towards the environmental tragedy. Do we point a way?

Criticism of the Committee's operation from the perspective of Ostrom's legacy can illuminate a resilient path. Exercising this vision throughout this work, we can say, in general, that for future perspectives the CBHPIJ Committee needs to produce satisfactory practical results to the point of ignoring a process of trust between the real users of the hydrographic basin. It needs to reflect a management model that is conducive to regional development, seeking collective solidarity with issues that motivate individuals to act in cooperation. On the other hand, knowing that it is a process of trial and error, and that there is no single path, until the satisfactory resilience process is reached, the watershed will remain in a state of exposure, where degradation and unsustainable exploitation will always be the rule practiced as it is the most advantageous for individual rationality.

However, at the end of this study, the authors hope that the analysis carried out here on the factors and conditions that prevent the Committee from guaranteeing the sustainability of rivers serves as a practical element for errors to be corrected, the management structure to be realigned and that trust between members be strengthened and, in this way, we can reverse the tragedy announced.

19

Social Trust, Informal Institutions and Community-Based Wildlife Management in Namibia and Tanzania

Daniel Ogbaharya

Community-based conservation (CBC) projects have been proliferating in sub-Saharan Africa since the end of the Cold War. Conceived and executed in conjunction with international conservation actors,[1] community-based conservation aims to transfer resource management rights, benefits and responsibilities to locally and communally governed entities. New user rights, along with government enforced injunctions, are granted to local communities to benefit from nature-derived enterprises such as hunting concessions and eco-tourism fees, the operation of lodging facilities, and the sale of endemic plants and traditional crafts. The most lucrative of these ventures is trophy hunting where communities are entitled to charge fees for certain wild animals according to a quota specified by the respective government agency based on periodic counts and the availability of wildlife species and numbers.[2] The underlying premise behind these initiatives is that communities are incentivized to cooperate to protect natural resources in their vicinity including endangered species of fauna and flora. A distinct attribute of communal conservation in sub-Saharan Africa has therefore been the emphasis on tying ecological out-comes to the alleviation of poverty and improvements in local livelihoods.

The specific form of community-based conservation that is most common in sub-Saharan Africa is *community-based wildlife management* (CBWM), which entails the transfer of the rights and responsibilities pertaining to wildlife conservation to local and communal actors. However, transfer of resource ownership from the state to a community has also involved other natural resources, such as forests, grazing lands, water, and, while less common, fisheries. The earliest and relatively more successful CBWM programs are found in Eastern and Southern Africa mainly in Kenya, Tanzania, Zambia, and Zimbabwe. Prior to these programs' decline due to a

---

[1] Such as the International Union for Conservation of Nature (IUCN) and the World Wildlife Fund (WWF).

  However, other organizations whose traditional mandate does not necessarily encompass conservation have also been actively involved. These include international financial institutions mainly the World Bank and the International Monetary Fund (IMF), which as part of their conditions of economic restructuring, imposed policies of privatization and decentralization on cash-strapped African countries. Privatization and decentralization were attached to the restructuring package, particularly in the form of Poverty Reduction Strategy Papers (PRSPs) that were required of highly indebted countries seeking debt forgiveness and other forms of economic and financial assistance. In the 1990s, for example, the World Bank staked its programming in the idea that the state was less effective than "local non-state actors" in planning and executing conservation projects. N. Kabiri (2007). *Global environmental governance and community-based conservation* in Kenya *and Tanzania.* Retrieved from ProQuest Digital Dissertations. (UMI Number: 3289080), at 5.

[2] Richard D. Kiaka, "Subsidized Elephants: Community-based Resource Governance and Environmental (in)justice in Namibia," *Geoforum* 93 (May 2018), 109, https://doi.org/10.1016/j.geoforum.2018.05.010.

combination of corruption, cumbersome bureaucracy, and duplication of efforts,[3] Zimbabwe's Communal Areas Management Program for Indigenous Resources (CAMPFIRE) was "one of Africa's earliest and most successful wildlife and natural resource management programs."[4] Some of these signature programs would later face a recentralization of decision making both at the local and national levels, thereby eroding the initial gains in collaborative management of wildlife.[5] Other CBWM programs have evolved with varying degrees of success in diverse institutional and political contexts, such as Namibia, Senegal, South Africa, Zambia, and Tanzania, to name just a few.

Transferring ownership and management of "nature" from the state to local entities has been met with some resistance both from within the host communities as well as external stakeholders, including animal rights groups and conservation organizations from the Global North. Northern conservation groups, which are primarily concerned with "wilderness preservation," see these initiatives as providing cover and license for accelerated "consumption of nature" by removing state control. Local communities fear that such initiatives erode their autonomy and tenure security, further exposing them to rapid loss of ancestral land and cultural heritage sites, which are transferred to profit-driven ventures. Critics liken these schemes to backhanded privatization, commodification, and the monetization of nature.[6] Given their universalizing and "depoliticizing metaphors," such as local "ownership, capacity building and good governance," community-based conservation efforts have been demonized as ideological and discursive covers for neo liberal policies that are doomed to fail.[7]

Devolution of natural resource governance in Africa also has to contend with the competing objectives, visions, and diverse institutional actors that impinge on the efficacy of CBC schemes. For example, there is the delicate tradeoff between ecological protection, on the one hand, and rural development – the creation of viable livelihoods for marginalized populations – on the other. Nor is there consensus on the metrics used to define and evaluate the effectiveness of these programs. Early on, success in community-based conservation was measured by looking at ecological outcomes as well as the material and economic benefits accruing to local communities as a result of the decentralization of natural resource management. Multidimensional indicators, such as level of participation in the planning and governance of CBC initiatives, evidence of "upward and downward" accountability,[8] the presence of well-defined mechanisms

---

[3] Regis Musavengane and Danny Simatele, "Significance of Social Capital in Collaborative Management of Natural Resources in Sub-Saharan African Rural Communities: A Qualitative Meta-analysis," *South African Geographical Journal*, Vol. 99, No. 3 (2017): 275.

[4] Brain Child, "Zimbabwe's CAMPFIRE Program: Using the High Value of Wildlife Recreation to Revolutionize Natural Resource Management in Communal Areas," *The Commonwealth Forestry Review*, Vol. 72, No. 4 (1993): 284.

[5] Regis and Simatele, "Significance of Social Capital in Collaborative Management of Natural Resources in Sub-Saharan African Rural Communities," 268.

[6] As a result, "today CBNRM is facing a crisis of identity and purpose." Proponents and institutional supporters of CBNRM have thus not only to grapple with "... complex administrative and policy structures," but also have to engage in a discursive struggle to ward off "... a resurgent protectionist conservation" and to salvage CBNRM from being "perversely hybridized with wider neo-liberal structuring." W. Dressler et al., "From Hope to Crisis and Back Again? A Critical History of the Global CBNRM Narrative," *Environmental Conservation*, Vol. 37, No. 1 (March 2010) at 10.

[7] B. Buscher, "Anti-Politics as Political Strategy: Neoliberalism and Transfrontier Conservation in Southern Africa," *Development and Change* Vol. 41, No. 1 (2010): 29.

[8] Accountability here refers to the ability of actors in an equal or unequal relationship to interact and engage with one another in an open and transparent manner. It can take two forms. Downward accountability is also sometimes referred to as horizontal accountability. Horizontal accountability, unlike vertical accountability, is a relationship among actors that command more or less equal powers. Examples include: Conservancy management and traditional authorities; conservancy staff and conservancy members, etc. Vertical accountability refers to unequal and hierarchical relationships. J. C. Ribot, J. F. Lund, and T. Treue, "Democratic Decentralization in sub-Saharan Africa: Its Contribution to

for conflict resolution, and mitigation of human-wildlife conflicts are now widely accepted as
more holistic indicators of long-term success in community-based conservation.[9]

Community buy-in of these programs – the sense that host communities have greater
ownership over the goals and benefits of the programs – is also increasingly viewed as an
important indicator of long-term success. Community members are more likely to support
and sustain these programs through greater participation when rules of management and
decision making are perceived to be fair, transparent, and accessible. It is also thought that
there is likely to be greater solidarity among community members when they are empowered to
contribute to the formulation of rules, as well as if they are significantly involved in conflict
resolution. Conversely, CBC initiatives tend to falter when community members and stakeholders perceive that governmental bodies monopolize the decision making process, and when the
rules adjudicating disputes are not clearly enunciated.[10]

In this chapter, we examine the institutional factors that undermine social cohesion in
archetypically mature cases of community-based governance of natural resources in sub-
Saharan Africa. We do so through a comparative study of community-based conservation
(CBC) programs pertaining to a homogenous resource base (wildlife) in Namibia and
Tanzania. Specifically, the chapter examines whether and how social differentiation arising
from the unequal distribution of benefits from the use of nature is upending the long-term
viability of community conservation efforts in sub-Saharan Africa, which if true, would lend
support for "a resurgent protectionist conservation" movement.[11]

The chapter also sheds light on the relationship between the formal institutional processes
governing community conservation and the informal or de facto institutions that govern long-
standing claims to collective rights to water and land, and the adjudication of disputes pertaining
to those resources. Our examination goes beyond the usual material and ecological metrics of
evaluating success in community-based conservation and instead, focuses on how CBC schemes
integrate and adapt to existing intra-communal institutions. Additionally, we seek to identify
ways in which greater degrees of "institutional synergy[12]" can be cultivated between the state and
local communities as well as a cornucopia of new organizations created for community-based
conservation. This institutional approach allows us to gauge success of CBC initiatives in terms
of greater autonomy and involvement of local communities in local governance. A consolidated
CBC program is one where communities are acquiring greater roles in various crucial aspects of
natural resource governance, including the ability to hold external actors – relevant governmental bodies as well as investors – accountable as well as adjudicating disputes over the use of
natural resources.

Forest Management, Livelihoods, and Local Enfranchisement," *Environmental Conservation* Vol. 37, No. 1 (March
2010), 35–44, https://doi.org/10.1017/S0376892910000329.

[9] Musavengane and Simatele, "Significance of Social Capital in Collaborative Management of Natural Resources in
Sub-Saharan African Rural Communities," 274–75.

[10] Ibid., 275.

[11] W. Dressler et al., "From Hope to Crisis and Back Again? A Critical History of the Global CBNRM Narrative,"
Environmental Conservation, Vol. 37, No.1 (March 2010), at 10.

[12] Institutional synergy refers to greater complimentarity and integration between formal and informal rules governing
wildlife management. Formal rules are codified into the law, hence they are "visible," whereas informal (and
customary) rules can be understood as "invisible" social norms and cultural beliefs including "gods, traditional
priesthood [elders] and local taboo" that significantly impinge upon communal governance of wildlife. Emmanuel
Yeboah-Assiamah, Kobus Muller, and Kwame Ameyaw Domfeh, "Two Sides of the Same Coin: Formal and Informal
Institutional Synergy in a Case Study of Wildlife Governance in Ghana," *Society and Natural Resources* Vol. 32, No.
12 (August 2019): 1365.

By comparing Namibia and Tanzania, we intentionally limit our analysis to a homogenous resource base – wildlife – because institutions evolve in contexts unique and specific to the specific resource being managed. This allows us to account for the variation across cases that could arise from the dynamic of the "biophysical element" inherent in the resource being managed.[13] The management of roaming wildlife, for example, entails a different institutional milieu than the governance of communal forests; the former presents unique transaction costs and threats to human safety that are not present in the latter, and these differences are key to successfully devising appropriate management and enforcement institutions.[14]

Both Tanzania and Namibia are also widely hailed as sponsoring successful models of community-based wildlife conservation programs. Tanzania's Wildlife Management Areas (WMA) and Namibia's Communal Conservancies have transformed rural populations both economically and socially. There have also been significant positive ecological outcomes as a result of the implementation of community-based wildlife management in both countries. In Namibia, for example, both the number and species of wildlife have improved considerably. There has been a doubling of wildlife numbers nationally from 10,000 prior to the advent of communal conservancies to 20,000 in 2012, a decade and a half into the Communal Conservancy Program.[15] As a result, Namibia is witnessing the rebounding of numerous wildlife species, including rare species, and is now considered to have "the world's largest free-roaming population of black rhino."[16] As community-based conservation (CBC) schemes, Tanzania's Wildlife Policy and Namibia's Communal Conservancy Program (CCP), which both came into effect in 1998, share the core features of a community-based system of wildlife management. These include: the setting aside of land for conservation; the placing of trust in communities to determine for themselves how to best benefit from consumptive and non consumptive uses of wildlife; and the creation of joint business ventures between communities and tourist/lodge operators.[17] In both cases, the rights transferred to communities primarily take the form of a usufruct, as the state retains ultimate dominion over the ownership of wildlife.[18]

SOCIAL TRUST, SOCIOECONOMIC HETEROGENEITY, AND THE GOVERNANCE OF THE COMMONS

The scholarship on the impact of social inequality on commons management has evolved to include a new conception of communities as "delocalized," or internally differentiated entities

[13] Yeboah-Assiamah, Muller, and Ameyaw Domfeh, "Two Sides of the Same Coin," 1366.

[14] Management institutions and the benefits accruing from resource rights could also significantly vary even across a homogenous resource base as the distribution and endowment of the resource geographically and temporally determines social and ecological outcomes. For example, in the case of Namibia, conservancies in the northwest are able to accrue significantly higher income and tangible benefits from wildlife because of greater endowment of wildlife found there, whereas conservancies in the south have not had much luck in deriving lucrative benefits from being constituted as conservancies due to the fact that they are less endowed in number and diversity of wildlife.

[15] Schnegg and Kiaka, "Subsidized Elephants," 109.

[16] World Resources Institute, "Nature in local hands: the case for Namibia's conservancies," in *World Resources 2005– The Wealth of the Poor: Managing Ecosystems to Fight Poverty* (Washington DC: World Resource Institute) Chapter 5). Retrieved from http://pdf.wri.org/wrr05_full_hires.pdf, 116.

[17] Rose P. Kicheleri, et al., "Institutional Rhetoric Versus Local Reality: A Case Study of Wildlife Management Area, Tanzania," *Journal of Environment and Development*, Vol. 8, No. 2 (May 2018), at 1.

[18] Jevgenity Bluwstein, Francis Moyo, and Rose P. Kicheleri, "Austere Conservation: Understanding Conflicts over Resource Governance in Tanzanian Wildlife Management Areas," *Conservation and Society*, Vol. 14, No. 3 (2016): 218.

with ties that go well beyond a specific locale.[19] As opposed to traditional theories of communities as place-bound entities, more recent studies by critical institutionalists treat the "community as embedded in a wider social system," which involves "interactions among actors within and between spatial scales and levels of political organization."[20] The "delocalization" of communities has wide-ranging implications for understanding how inequality impacts socio-ecological outcomes in community-based governance of natural resources.

Social trust is a main ingredient of collective action, dialogue, and negotiation. The level of trust and/or distrust that resource users, stakeholders, and participants perceive affects the overall effectiveness of a resource management regime. Greater socio economic inequality is likely to be detrimental to overall trust especially when resource users perceive the rules and procedures about participation, decision-making, revenue sharing, and governance to be either ambiguous, poorly communicated or exclusionary. Top-down and exclusionary resource management regimes create a climate of uncertainty and generalized sense of risk that could hamper cooperation, thereby resulting in poor socio ecological outcomes. Among the many forms and dimensions of trust, Stern & Coleman identify "procedural trust[21]" to be "the most actionable for process managers." Procedural trust can be improved through "joint development of procedures, transparency in decision making processes, responsiveness, and the equitable distribution of benefits and risks where possible."[22]

Social trust in commons management can be cultivated through measures that enhance procedural equity, which include but are not limited to "representation of marginal groups in resource management bodies and opportunities for marginal groups to influence decision-making through deliberation, membership, authority, power, leadership, rules and regulations, customs and laws."[23] Equally important in shaping trust in the governance of commons is "distributive equity," which refers to the principle that benefits are fairly and equitably shared among resource users and members. A generalized sense of fairness contributes to overall participation of members in a resource management regime.[24] Community members are more likely to participate and cooperate in community-based conservation if they believe that benefits are being distributed equitably. Even more crucially, the amount of benefits that communities receive is less important for intra-community cohesion and trust than whether or not such benefits are distributed fairly and equitably. Equally detrimental to the viability of community-based conservation is the perception that some in the community receive disproportionately more benefits because they have close access and proximity to "external agents" such as government representatives and non-governmental organizations (NGOs).[25]

Socio-economic inequality co-determines natural resource governance because of its potential to trigger deep-rooted conflicts, which can be detrimental to effective management and conservation without proper institutional arrangements that could diffuse the outbreak of

[19] H. Ojha et al., "Delocalizing Communities. Changing Forms of Community Engagement in Natural Resource Governance," *World Development*, Vol. 87 (November 2016): 274–290.
[20] Ibid., 276.
[21] Procedural trust refers to whether or not rules governing the commons are perceived to be fair or not. Procedural trust is high when all actors, participants, and entities involved in a resource management regime deem the rules and procedures of participation and decision making to be clear, fair and equitable. Marc J. Stern and Kimberly J. Coleman, "Multidimensionality of Trust: Applications in Collaborative Natural Resources Management," *Society and Natural Resources: An International Journal*, Vol. 28, No. 2 (November 2015): 129.
[22] Ibid., 129.
[23] Ibid., 229.
[24] Ibid.
[25] Enrique Calfucura, "Governance, Land and Distribution: A Discussion on the Political Economy of Community-based Conservation," *Ecological Economics*, Vol. 145 (March 2018): 18–26.

violence.[26] Community-based initiatives focused on governing natural resources are vulnerable to potential conflict due to both endogenous and exogenous factors. Common Pool Resources (CPRs), such as forests, grazing land, water, and agricultural land, require the specification of fixed communal boundaries including geographic, spatial, legal, and social boundaries.[27] The process of demarcating community lands may be complex in some cases. Conflicts will arise, particularly if resources are, or become, valuable over time."[28] Furthermore, membership in a homogenous community that is socially distinct and legally incorporated is a pre-requisite to benefiting from programs that seek to devolve rights to access, use, and benefit from natural resources. Transfer of rights from central governments to local users often involve the creation of special entities or delineated zones such as "village commons, [community] forests, nature reserves [and conservancies] and fishing grounds, or plots of property demarcated in a cadastral registration system."[29]

Governance of collectively held resources can be derailed by two types of public disputes. The first, referred to as "tradeoff conflicts," involve competing uses of natural resources, as in economic development versus conservation, for example.[30] Such conflicts erupt "when two or more parties have strongly held views and one of those parties is attempting to assert its interests at the expense of the other."[31]

Intra-communal conflicts could also result from new institutions that are created in the process of transferring resource management rights and roles from central authorities to local entities. This is because new, formally codified rules for using resources run the risk of sidelining existing informal arrangements – social norms, roles, and networks – that govern multiple domains beyond natural resources. Community-based management institutions tend to treat governance of natural resources as disjointed and insulated from other social domains. Natural resources are embedded within multiple social relations in communities that share ethnic and cultural ties. Social norms mediating the use of water, for example, are embedded in normative structures and traditions that affect many other domains. Communities using water collectively tend to also be genetic relatives who "share land for grazing as common property, help each other in everyday life, and belong to the same church. In short, they are linked in multiple different ways."[32] In both ecological and socio economic terms, locally governing natural resources is more successful when designed to take into account the preexisting social relations that underlie access to, use, and management of natural resources. On the contrary, if designed to subsume all relations into the singular goals of economic

---

[26] Francine Madden and Brian McQuinn, "Conservation's Blind Spot: The Case for Conflict Transformation in Wildlife Conservation," *Biological Conservation* Vol. 178 (October 2014): 97–106.

[27] That communities have to have "well-defined boundaries" in order to manage a resource collectively is one of the eight design principles discussed in Elinor Ostrom's groundbreaking work on the commons. A community of users need to define rules for membership in the community, including the right of benefiting from the use of the resource as well as sharing the cost of managing the resource. Elinor Ostrom, *Governing the Commons: The Evolution of Institutions for Collective Action* (Cambridge: Cambridge University Press, 1990).

[28] Arnoldo Contreras-Hermosilla and Chris Fay, *Strengthening Forest Management in Indonesia through Land Tenure Reform: Issues and Framework for Action* (Washington DC: Forest Trends, 2008).

[29] Franz von Benda-Beckmann, keebet von Benda-Beckmann, and Anne Griffiths, "Space and Legal Pluralism: An Introduction," in *Spatializing Law: An Anthropological Geography of Law in Society*, ed. Franz von Benda-Beckmann, keebet von Benda-Beckmann, and Anne Griffiths (New York: Routledge, 2009), 5.

[30] Brain C. Chaffin, Hannah Gosnell, and Barbara A. Cosens, "A Decade of Adaptive Governance Scholarship: Synthesis and Future Directions," *Ecology and Society*, Vol. 19, No. 3 (2014).

[31] Stephen M. Redpath, Saloni Bhatia, and Juliette Young, "Tilting at Wildlife: Reconsidering Human-Wildlife Conflict," *Oryx*, Vol. 49, No. 2 (November 2014), 222–223.

[32] Michael Schnegg, "Institutional Multiplexity: Social Networks and Community-based Natural Resource Management," *Sustainability Science* Vol. 13, No. 4 (July 2018), 1023.

livelihoods and ecological sustainability, such initiatives are not only unlikely to be fully realized, but they could also put in motion processes that undermine intra-communal social trust, thereby laying the foundation for conflict.

UNEQUAL BENEFITS AND SOCIAL CONFLICT IN COMMUNITY-BASED WILDLIFE MANAGEMENT: NAMIBIA AND TANZANIA COMPARED

More than two decades after local communities gained limited rights to manage wildlife in Namibia and Tanzania, community-based conservation is facing a crisis of legitimacy in both countries. There is a growing perception among community members that the economic and social benefits of wildlife are not being distributed fairly and equitably, which has threatened to upend the significant success that was achieved early on in terms of ecological and social outcomes.

In Namibia, the mandate for community-based conservation emanates from the 1996 Nature Conservation Amendment Act. As a result of the post-Apartheid reform, local communities were granted rights to nature that were hitherto only confined to private and white commercial interests. In order to exercise these rights to benefit from wildlife-related ventures, communities must register as Communal Conservancies. The first conservancies were established in 1998. As of 2020, the number of conservancies has reached 86 and the total number of people living in conservancies is estimated at 227,941.[33] Communal conservancies now account for close to a quarter of Namibia's total land mass.[34] The business model behind communal conservancies is a joint venture between the community registered as a conservancy and a tourist/lodge operator. Currently, some 42 joint venture lodges have created a stream of income for communal conservancies, and revenues from eco-tourism are outstripping those from trophy hunting.[35]

In Tanzania, Wildlife Management Areas (WMAs) are the formal entities that allow local communities to reap the economic benefits of wildlife derived from launching joint businesses with eco-tourist companies and lodge operators. The 1998 Wildlife Policy (revised in 2007) defines WMAs as rural land designated for conservation. Participating villages that designate land to form a WMA usually establish a Community-based Organization (CBO) known as Authorized Association, which represents their interests as members of that WMA. The incentive for villages to set aside land to form WMAs include the financial and economic benefits that flow from using and managing wildlife. WMAs allow participating villages to enter into lucrative investment and commercial partnerships with eco-tourism businesses. In exchange for these benefits, communities agree to set aside land for wildlife conservation with limits on the use of their land for farming, grazing, and domicile.[36]

There are currently some thirty eight WMAs at different levels of operational growth extending over 13% of Tanzania's total land area.[37] In 2014, a portion of Tanzania's WMAs, the Burunge villages, generated $218,000 (USD) in revenue. This breaks down to around seven dollars per person when distributed among the total population of 36,000.[38] Concerns among

---

[33] Namibian Association of CBNRM Support Organizations (NACSO), Registered Communal Conservancies, www .nacso.org.na/conservancies#statistics.

[34] Schnegg and Kiaka, "Subsidized Elephants," 109.

[35] Ibid.

[36] Kicheleri et al., "Institutional Rhetoric Versus Local Reality," 1.

[37] Ibid., 2.

[38] Jevgenity Bluwstein, Francis Moyo, and Rose P. Kicheleri, "Austere Conservation: Understanding Conflicts over Resource Governance in Tanzanian Wildlife Management Areas," *Conservation and Society*, Vol. 14, No. 3 (2016): 220.

villagers over the distribution of benefits from eco-tourism have resulted in increasing tensions and social mistrust. Lack of openness and transparency regarding how benefits are distributed and how the WMAs are run has pitted disparate actors – the central government, local government representatives, and village elders – against one another in an increasingly frequent dispute over who owns and benefits from eco-tourism. On the part of community members and villagers writ large, there is a sense of an increasingly tenuous hold, if not an outright loss, of ownership over their ancestral land to outsiders.

For villagers, complaints about the WMAs range from frustration over not receiving significant and tangible benefits, to the perception that community members are not fully consulted in the planning and management of the WMAs and the associated eco-tourist operations. For example, one villager saw no significant improvement in the lives of fellow community members as a result of benefits and revenues derived from WMAs. In the words of one informant: "How can that policy improve peoples' lives if we are living in mud houses while we are deprived of grasses for roofing, poles for building, firewood for cooking and we have no electricity for lighting? We wonder how the government can care more for the wild animals and forget about us."[39]

Villagers also complain about token participation where crucial decisions are made outside the wildlife management area and they are only consulted in enforcing rules that are decided upon elsewhere.[40]

Community conservancies in Namibia are also experiencing a similar sense of injustice arising from intra-community disparity in the distribution of benefits. Conservancy members in Namibia are, however, not just increasingly concerned about unequal distribution of benefits. Actual benefits distributed to community members have also declined over time. Currently, the cash benefits that community members receive amounts to on average twenty percent of overall income that a conservancy collects.[41] However, some non-cash and in-kind benefits such as distributions of game meat fluctuate greatly depending on drought conditions and availability of wildlife. Community members experience a shortfall in this direct benefit more acutely than other benefits such as investments that the conservancy makes in community projects namely the construction of new schools and the provision of electricity through generators.[42]

Declining benefits are a threat to the overall viability of Namibia's conservancy program in that community members can be reluctant to support such programs if they believe that they are not receiving substantial benefits from the use of wildlife. This is especially so when the costs of running a conservancy and the liability arising from rebounding wildlife outweigh the benefits that community members receive. The return of big game such as the desert elephant (*Loxodonta Africana*) in both actual numbers and diversity is lauded as one of the major indicators of ecological success in Namibia's community-based conservation. However, for community members, the costs to their livelihood that these resurgent wild animals inflict outweigh the economic and social benefits they receive from their commercial and economic uses. For example, conservancies in the arid region of northwest Namibia (Kunene) could

---

[39] Kicheleri, et al., "Institutional Rhetoric Versus Local Reality," 5.

[40] Ibid., 223.

[41] The Ministry of Tourism and Environment (MET) and Namibia Association of CBNRM Support Organizations (NACSO), *The State of Community Conservation in Namibia: A Review of Communal Conservancies, Community Forests and Other CBNRM Initiatives (Annual Report 2017)*. (Windhoek, Namibia, MET/NACSO), 2018. Accessed from www.nacso.org.na/sites/default/files/State%20of%20Community%20Conservation%20book%20web_0.pdf, 12.

[42] The Ministry of Tourism and Environment (MET) and Namibia Association of CBNRM Support Organizations (NACSO), *The State of Community Conservation in Namibia*, 12.

receive on average US$13,296 for an elephant from international trophy hunters and US$ 274 for an oryx.[43] However, elephants also inflict significant damage to crops and compete with domestic animals and humans for limited and scarce resources, such as water.[44]

Similarly, unequal distribution of benefits as well as differential costs associated with managing wildlife is increasingly a cause of discontent and conflict within community conservancies. For example, community members in the ǂKhoadi ǁHôas conservancy – widely cited as a model conservancy and considered to be a "success story" for being the first to run a tourist lodge operated entirely by the community – are experiencing "immense distributional discrepancy."[45] Some community members saw very little benefits accruing to their community. With echoes of Apartheid and South Africa's colonial rule in Namibia, community members felt that the conservancy was largely serving the needs of "white tourists":

> The elephant is only useful to the white tourist and maybe those who work in the lodge. Maybe they are happy and enjoy the benefits. For us, we suffer so that they can enjoy. We are a slave of the conservancy; our progress is held hostage in our land.[46]

> The conservancy is ours and not ours at the same time. It is ours because this is our land, our traditional land for |Gaiodaman [traditional] authority. We have our chief, Max Haraseb. So it is our land. But the office in ǁKai-|uis [Grootberg] is not ours. It is for tourists and those who want elephants to be here and destroy our things. They don't listen to us however much we struggle to tell them our problems with elephants and lions that destroy and eat our things. When you speak in meetings, they say 'we will look into that'. But they don't do anything to help. I struggle to get a little money which I add to my pension, and then I use it to buy diesel. But then the elephants come to drink the water. Then the conservancy does not give diesel for that. And they know it is their elephants. Can I praise the conservancy? Let the tourists who come in cars to see the elephant praise the elephants.[47]

The marginalization that community members express regarding the benefits and governance of conservancies is a far cry from rectifying the "injustice of the past," which the Conservation Amendment Act was designed to address. Namibia's conservancy program was in part intended to ameliorate the vast inequality in land ownership and economic fortune that existed between white minorities and the majority of black Namibians, which was the legacy of South Africa's racist colonial rule in Namibia. Conservancies as legal entities extended certain rights to rural communities in the colonially designated "native homelands," allowing historically marginalized populations to reap the economic and social benefits of wildlife. As noted above, during South Africa's apartheid rule in Namibia, the commercial use of wildlife was a right only reserved to propertied white leaseholders. Paradoxically, the conservancy program has simultaneously made rural communities more vulnerable for further marginalization and economic exploitation by allowing white-owned for-profit enterprises to expand into the hitherto unreachable frontiers of the ancestral homeland. Reminiscent of white colonial rule, wealth is being extracted from communally governed areas, and community members are so embittered that they have begun to compare their situation to being "slaves of the conservancy."[48]

---

[43] Schnegg and Kiaka, "Subsidized Elephants," 109.
[44] Ibid., 107.
[45] Ibid., 110.
[46] Ibid.
[47] Ibid.
[48] Ibid.

RISING DISENCHANTMENT AND DECLINING PARTICIPATION

Unequal distribution of benefits threatens the feasibility, performance, and sustainability of community-based conservation. Unequal benefits also raise the specter of conflict, thereby eroding overall trust and cooperation among community members. The perception that some community members, powerful elites, and external actors disproportionately benefit from the program can also weaken cooperation. Sometimes the nature of the benefit received is material to the level of participation and solidarity for one another that community members demonstrate in the context of community-based conservation. For example, communities who receive non-cash benefits in the form of improvements in the well-being of the community as a whole tend to have a higher level of trust, cooperation, and participation than those who mainly receive household level cash benefits.[49]

However, as witnessed in Tanzania, community participation can still be low even when wildlife revenues produce tangible community-level benefits such as the construction of schools and health clinics. The economic benefits of wildlife are unlikely to induce a higher degree of participation if communities perceive that the governance of wildlife is undergirded by unfair, unclear, and unaccountable rules and regulations.[50] Local communities in Tanzania are increasingly disillusioned with the new rules of wildlife management enforced through WMAs. Villages that have formed WMAs experience these rules and organizations as highly bureaucratic, top-down and unaccountable, resulting in their alienation and exclusion from key decisions concerning access to and use of local resources. Formally constituted organizations created as part of the establishment of WMAs are assuming a more intrusive role in managing use and access to not only wildlife, but other natural resources critical to rural livelihoods.

Furthermore, the 1998 Wildlife Policy that promulgated rights to form WMAs was developed with very little consultation with local communities. When community members were involved, they participated in a "listening only" capacity making little or no contribution to key decisions at the different phases of policy development and establishment of WMAs. Prior to the establishment of WMAs, Village Councils enjoyed a degree of autonomy in writing rules concerning access to and use of village land for "agriculture, grazing, settlement, firewood collection, watershed management, extraction of building materials and other non-timber forest products."[51] However, once incorporated into a WMA, villagers face restricted access to "land for cultivation, wildlife hunting, grazing, fishing, collection of firewood, building poles, roofing grasses, and Doum palm (*Hyphaene compressa*)."[52] Loss of access to these livelihood resources is a major setback for rural communities with limited economic opportunities. The new restrictions on accessing Doum palm, for example, could prevent women in rural areas from earning a living by selling various handicrafts – baskets, mats, etc. – made from this material.[53]

As a result of new actors that have proliferated in the aftermath of WMAs, a contentious institutional terrain has emerged in which community members find themselves ironically in a somewhat disempowered position. The locus of decision-making is rapidly shifting away from them toward the formal and external organizations created to run nature-derived ventures in the

---

[49] Enrique Calfucura, "Governance, Land and Distribution: A Discussion on the Political Economy of Community-based Conservation," *Ecological Economics*, Vol. 145 (2018), 21.

[50] Musavengane and Simatele, "Significance of Social Capital in Collaborative Management of Natural Resources in Sub-Saharan African Rural Communities," 9.

[51] Kicheleri, et al., "Institutional Rhetoric Versus Local Reality," 9.

[52] Ibid., 9.

[53] Ibid., 10.

wake of the WMAs.[54] Local communities have to operate in a contested resource management regime in which they have no exclusive authority over "devising, revising, and enforcing of resource management rules," the core principles of a robust common property regime as pioneered in the groundbreaking work of Elinor Ostrom. For example, without much deliberation with the community and village-level councils, Authorized Associations can now negotiate with outside investors such as eco-tourist operators over not just wildlife but also over the use and allocation of rural land.

The erosion of local control and autonomy at the hands of newly formed entities has created a level of discontent that has led some participating villages to leave WMAs, and those considering joining WMAs to reconsider their move because doing so entails a loss of authority over their land and resources. WMAs, therefore, have created new unaccountable organizations that are recentralizing decisions over wildlife and associated resources under the guise of decentralization. By undermining local authority in decisions over livelihood resources including wildlife, WMAs endanger the legitimacy and continuity of community-based conservation in Tanzania. CBC initiatives that threaten to encroach upon the authority of local communities are likely to fail in the long run, even if they provide some economic relief and social benefits in the short term.

THE ROLE OF TRADITIONAL COUNCILS IN NAMIBIA AND VILLAGE COUNCILS IN TANZANIA

In both Tanzania and Namibia, devolution of wildlife management has resulted in a cornucopia of new organizations that are supplanting and interfering with the traditional roles of village-level authorities: Traditional Councils (Namibia) and Village Councils (Tanzania). For example, new community organizations compete with village authorities over land tenure. Another important area where such interference and competition occurs is in conflict resolution, which becomes increasingly important with the advent of community-based conservation.

In Tanzania, Authorized Associations are interfering with the customary role of Village Councils in local conflict resolution. While in the past village-level conflicts over land and associated resources were adjudicated by Village Councils, now juridical authority over local conflicts remains fluid and diffused. Due to this lack of "specific participatory and transparent mechanisms to manage and resolve conflicts," external interests are engaged in manipulation of local disputes, which has further exacerbated conflicts in WMAs:

> ...actors use different means and ways to push their agendas. For example, villagers report conflicts to the Village Councils or the Village Executive Secretary. The Village Councils report conflicts to the Authorized Association or the Babati District Council. The Authorized Association reports conflicts to the Babati District Police and Wildlife Division, while the investors report conflicts to the Authorized Association, District Council and the Police. Also, some villagers deal with problems simply by extracting products in contravention of the WMA rules, that is, through everyday forms of resistance.[55]

[54] Paul Hebinck, Richard Dimba Kiaka, Rodgers Lubilo, "Navigating communal conservancies and institutional complexities in Namibia," in *Natural Resources, Tourism, and Community Livelihoods in Southern Africa*, ed. Moren T. Stone, Monkgogi Lenao, Naomi Moswete (New York: Routledge, 2019).

[55] Rose P. Kicheleri, Thorsten Treue, George C. Kajembe, Felister M. Mombo and Martin R. Nielsen (November 5, 2018). "Power Struggles in the Management of Wildlife Resources: The Case of Burunge Wildlife Management Area, Tanzania," In *Wildlife Management: Failures, Successes and Prospects*, ed. Jafari R. Kideghesho and Alfan A. Rija

In Namibia, Communal Conservancies are by law required to "operate in a transparent and accountable way and enable people to make informed decisions."[56] The 1996 Nature Conservation Amendment Act (CAA) necessitates "the formation of a management institution that is composed of local membership, a committee representing the membership, and a constitution that sets out how the institution will be governed."[57] The CAA mandates that these institutions must be elected, accountable, transparent and participatory in running conservancies. Elected Conservancy Management Committees (hereafter CMC) are expected to govern conservancies based on customary law, a legitimate constitution, and an amalgam of locally conceived policies, procedures, and game management plans.[58]

What sets the CCP apart from Tanzania's WMAs is the fact that Conservancy Committees are explicitly mandated to work in close partnership with customary authorities in developing and managing the conservancies. The requirement emanates not only from the CAA but also from the Traditional Authorities Act, which explicitly recognizes the role of customary institutions in natural resources management and local dispute resolution. Traditional leaders are responsible for determining the boundaries of their respective conservancies and qualifications for membership.

CMCs, which have both male and female representatives, serve as an important institutional linkage between government representatives and communal conservancies in two important bottom-up and top-bottom functions. First, CMC members play an important accountability function since they conduct periodic meetings whereby they report to, and consult with, their respective communities regarding the use of revenues, wildlife management and other conservancy matters. In this intermediary role, CMCs also facilitate direct meetings between local government representatives and community members. Traditional leaders in the more agricultural areas of north-central and north-eastern Namibia have historically played a greater role in allocation of land and adjudication of land disputes, while those in the more arid and nomadic pastoralist areas in the South have had a more diminished role in land tenure. As a result, there is regional variation in the preferences of communities for a customary system of land tenure in which traditional leaders assume a significant role both in overseeing allocation of land but also adjudicating land-related disputes. Communities in the north-east and north-central regions generally favor a land tenure system that empowers traditional authorities to allocate land, while those in the arid areas of the South prefer the government to allocate land.[59]

The relationship between Traditional Authorities (TAs) and CMCs has at times been contentious in the area of land use within the boundaries of the Conservancies.[60] For example, Traditional Authorities have used their legal status within the Commercial Land Reform Act (CLRA)[61] to allocate land leases for commercial ranches and farmers within the confines of conservancies. Moreover:

(IntechOpen, 2018), 119. Accessed from: www.intechopen.com/books/wildlife-management-failures-successes-and-pro spects/power-struggles-in-the-management-of-wildlife-resources-the-case-of-burunge-wildlife-management-area

[56] Namibian Association of CBNRM Support Organizations (NACSO), *Namibia's Communal Conservancies: A Review of Progress and Challenges in 2009* (Windhoek: NACSO), www.nacso.org.na/sites/default/files/SOC_2009.pdf, 12.

[57] Ibid., 12.

[58] J. G. E. Collomb et al., "Integrating Governance and Socioeconomic Indicators to Assess the Performance of Community-based Natural Resources Management in Caprivi (Namibia)," *Environmental Conservation*, Vol. 37, No. 3 (September 2010): 303–309.

[59] Wolfgang Werner, "Land Tenure and Governance on Communal Land" (paper presented at the Second National Land Conference, Windhoek 1–5 October 2018).

[60] Ibid., 45.

[61] While land is designated in Article 100 of the 1990 Constitution of Namibia as state property, the Communal Land Reform Act (CLRA), which was enacted in 2002, grants Traditional Authorities the right to allocate land for different

TAs have been wary of conservancies, fearing a loss of power over land and natural resources. Beyond powers officially recognized in the Traditional Authorities Act and the CLRA, there is a widespread belief among chiefs—and at least some of their subjects—that land is "owned by them." They have, therefore, often tried to control the Conservancy Management Committees or to secure a share of conservation related benefits.

Additionally, the government through the Ministry of Land and Resettlement (MLR) has contributed to the contested nature of land management by distributing land grants for farming and ranching to settlers from outside the Communal Conservancies, an unpopular move that has alienated many groups including conservation organizations. The root cause of this schism seems to be located in the ambiguous and bifurcated land tenure regime that Namibia has, in which the state commands *de jure* ownership of all natural resources including land, but apportions some of its prerogatives to subnational entities such as the TAs as de facto user rights.[62]

Conflict over land tenure has, however, not foreclosed the possibility of cooperative partnership between CMCs and Traditional or Customary Authorities in operating the activities of the Conservancy. There are crucial areas in managing the conservancy such as information sharing and awareness campaigns in which TAs and CMCs continue to work together. This partnership is stronger in some conservancies, and less effective in others. Except for some cases such as the Wuparo and Mayuni conservancies in the Caprivi region in the northwest of Namibia, most conservancies have been lackluster in informing members about the state of their finances and utilization of their natural resources.[63] Generally, "information transfer of financial data[64] was higher than reporting on the state of wildlife, indicating that conservancies are less accountable on the latter than the former."[65] Although almost all conservancies in Caprivi have a subpar record with respect to being transparent and accountable to their members, some conservancies were more capable in "information transfers" than others. This disparity in transparency and accountability is due to the fact that conservancies at different stages of development have different technical and material capacities to regularly and adequately inform their members. Other issues such as membership size and geographic diversity also make "information transfer" difficult for some conservancies.

The ability to work closely with traditional authorities is particularly crucial in north and northeast Namibia where traditional leaders exercise a greater role in the allocation and management of land, resolution of disputes, and decision-making involving many aspects of communal livelihoods. In the north where customary institutions remain strong, conservancy leaders have to learn to co-govern along with customary authorities, which requires that everyone's roles and responsibilities be clearly defined. For instance, when a conservancy is

---

purposes. TA can, therefore, approve commercial land leases up to 50 hectares (about 124 acres) in the original legislation and up to 100 hectares today, all subject to oversight of regional Land Boards (LBs). Large commercial land leases must be approved by the Ministry of Land and Resettlement. Eduard Gargallo, "Community Conservation and Land Use in Namibia: Visions, Expectations and Realities," *Journal of Southern African Studies* Vol. 46, No. 1 (2020): 121, https://doi.org/10.1080/03057070.2020.1705617, 134.

[62] Eduard Gargallo, "Community Conservation and Land Use in Namibia," 134.

[63] Collomb et al., "Integrating Governance and Socioeconomic Indicators to Assess the Performance of Community based Natural Resources Management in Caprivi (Namibia)," 306.

[64] Measured by asking respondents whether or not they have received information conservancy budget and expenditure, hunting fees, income from joint ventures and lodges. Collomb et al., "Integrating Governance and Socioeconomic Indicators to Assess the Performance of Community-based Natural Resources Management in Caprivi (Namibia)," 306.

[65] Ibid., 306.

negotiating a joint venture with a tourism company in order to take advantage of eco-tourism dollars, they have to consult with the appropriate customary authority in the area so that the latter lends support for the project. Joint ventures usually require a land lease, and customary leaders have a say in land-related matters. Revenue sharing need also be open and transparent where the portion of the income paid to traditional authorities is clearly conveyed, and its use openly justified.[66] In the northwestern and southern regions where traditional leaders command a more diminished and dispersed authority, conservancies may not necessarily need to co-govern alongside customary authorities. These conservancies instead often need to achieve some degree of representation and revenue sharing with the various local leaders known as *local headmen*.

The regional variation in customary authority has unsurprisingly resulted in marked differences in the way conservancy management and customary authorities interact. Traditional leaders in northern and northeastern Namibia have been pro active in founding and running communal conservancies, but their counterparts in the Northwest and the South have not benefited equally from the conservancy program. In the northeast in the Caprivi Province, for example, the Basubia people and their customary court, Khuta, had a substantial role in launching the Salambala Conservancy. The Khuta was particularly instrumental in drawing the boundaries of the conservancy and adjudicating intra-conservancy disputes.[67] Nearby in the Kongola region, Chief Mayuni contributed significantly to the success of the Mayuni conservancy by, among other things, providing seed money from communal funds, which were used to defray the costs of forming the conservancy's Anti- Poaching Unit (APU). In the northwest where customary authority is less centralized and dispersed into disparate local headmen, traditional leaders have only had an indirect role in the formation of conservancies, and virtually no part in their daily management and operation. Moreover, tensions among the local headmen have in some cases resulted in the delay of conservancy registration.[68]

In sum, the interaction between customary authorities and conservancy management is characterized by regional variation. Customary leaders enjoy a high degree of local legitimacy in northeast Namibia, and thus have a good deal of leverage and power "over natural resource management and their delegation of authority over natural resources to conservancies."[69] Thus, it is important to resist the temptation to centralize decision-making in conservancy committees in the north. Rather, governance of conservancies should be anchored in co-existence, coordination, and mutual respect between conservancy management and customary authorities.

CONCLUSION

Tanzania's Wildlife Management Areas and Namibia's Communal Conservancies are relatively advanced institutional schemes of community-based conservation in sub-Saharan Africa. Local communities in both schemes have benefited from wildlife. However, perceptions among community members that economic and social benefits from wildlife use are being distributed unequally is resulting in declining trust in these programs. There is also a general sense of disengagement among some community members who perceive that influential individuals within the community, as well as tourists and lodge operators, disproportionately benefit from their local conservation program.

---

[66] Jones and Luipert, *Best Practices for the CBNRM Program*, 45.
[67] Ibid., 13.
[68] Ibid., 23.
[69] Ibid., 43.

In the case of Tanzania, the inequitable distribution of benefits from wildlife conservation programs among the community is eroding the confidence and trust of community members in the overall program. In Namibia, similar perceptions of inequality in benefits accruing from consumptive and non consumptive uses also exist, but they tend to be much more pronounced across geographic zones: conservancies in the northeast tend to earn more income by virtue of richer wildlife numbers and diversity than in the South. However, unlike in Tanzania, the laws and policies governing Namibia's Communal Conservancy Program seem to be better geared toward fostering greater partnership and synergy between Conservancy Committees and customary or traditional authorities.

Ultimately, as demonstrated in these two cases, the fact that communities receive economic gains and social benefits from the commercial use of wildlife is a necessary but not a sufficient condition for continued success of community-based conservation. The further consolidation of these programs also depends on whether or not community members have a greater role and participation in devising, changing, and implementing the rules governing access to and use of wildlife and associated resources. Sustaining trust in conservation requires that community members are actively involved in planning, running, and restructuring community-based conservation programs, initiatives, and management areas. Equally important is the need to align the roles of newly formed conservation organizations with pre-existing institutions that are embedded in socio cultural norms.

A common loophole in many of these initiatives emanates from the failure to reconcile community-based conservation with other livelihood strategies such as farming and livestock. Local communities face an institutional conundrum: while decentralization of conservation provides unprecedented opportunities for social and economic development for hitherto marginalized communities, the entitlement to benefit from wildlife could come at the expense of other rights such as loss of land tenure security, which further restricts their ability to pursue diverse livelihood strategies.[70] The inherent bias toward conservation, along with de facto privatization and individualization of land that used to be held as a collective resource entrusted in the community, can potentially restrict other livelihood strategies that local communities have historically relied on to cope in times of social and environmental shocks.[71] This is especially crucial now in the wake of the global pandemic due to COVID-19 whereby dependence on eco-tourism and trophy hunting has been amply shown to be not a wholly viable livelihood strategy for local communities. Mitigation efforts against COVID-19 such as mandatory national lockdowns and global restrictions on travel are beginning to inflict severe economic damages on communities in the Global South that rely on international tourism revenues in general, and eco-tourism in particular. In Namibia, COVID-19 has already impacted Communal Conservancies in multiple ways including incurring "losses of revenues and cash flow, disruption to management and regular operations, and disruption to donor-funded projects and programs."[72] Revenues from hunting and tourism are drying up, which is expected to deal a major blow to not only communal conservancies, but also to the national economy as a whole as eco-tourism is a significant economic sector in Namibia. Conservancies in other parts of sub-Saharan Africa are also bound to suffer from similar shocks from the

[70] Brian E. Robinson et al., "Incorporating Land Tenure Security into Conservation," *Conservation Letters* Vol. 11, no. 2 (April 2018): 2.

[71] Eduard Gargallo, "Community Conservation and Land Use in Namibia," 121.

[72] S. Lendelvo, M. Pinto, & S. Sullivan, "A Perfect Storm? The Impact of COVID-19 on Community-Based Conservation in Namibia," *Namibian Journal of Environment*, Vol. 4 (2020), 2.

pandemic as they are joined at the hip with the travel-sensitive joint ventures of trophy hunting and ecotourism.[73]

Coping with the multifaceted shocks of COVID-19, similar outbreaks and other unprecedented shocks in the future would require that local communities have a basket of livelihood resources and strategies that they can draw sustenance from. It is therefore imperative that policies and programs promoting community-based wildlife ensure that community members have a degree of security over the use and ownership of various resources including vitally land – e.g., for grazing and farming – at the same time they are being empowered to benefit from wildlife. Similarly, new rules and organizations governing conservation initiatives need to be formally and properly aligned with and integrated into informal and traditional mechanisms of dispute resolution. For example, when formal conflict resolution mechanisms supplant and overrule customary practices by among others bypassing and sidelining their judicial jurisdiction over local disputes, conflict due to competition over increasingly scarce livelihood resources is likely to turn violent at a scale and frequency that would be devastating for peace and social harmony within and beyond conservation areas.

The multifaceted impact of the global pandemic on community-based conservation will undoubtedly preoccupy researchers of community-based conservation in the near future. The fate of the Global Commons under Covid-19 has already rightly garnered significant interest among scholars of the commons. In July and August 2020, for example, the International Association for the Study of Commons (IASC) organized a series of Zoom Webinars on "Covid-19 and the future of Commons Research," including a panel exclusively devoted to "Africa, Covid-19, and the Commons."[74] Institutional analysis will provide some crucial insights into the challenges and opportunities that the global pandemic creates for devising effective and scalable programs of community-based conservation in Africa and elsewhere. Another area of potentially innovative research and policy making in community-based conservation lie in the political and socio-economic dynamic arising from the need to safeguard the autonomy of local communities by securing their rights to local livelihood resources as well as creating avenues for their active participation. Specifically, we need greater understanding of how institutional synergy – the extent to which social norms mediated by customary law are integrated and cross-fertilized with formal rules and organizations created in the aftermath of the decentralization of wildlife management – co determines the success and consolidation of community-based conservation in sub-Saharan Africa and elsewhere, both intra-nationally as well as comparatively.

---

[73] Ibid., 2.
[74] IASC Commons. "Africa, Covid-19, and the Commons." Panel Discussion, July 13, 2020. www.youtube.com/watch?v=pvRUfxUcwS4&list=PLAAFvhxfMjvfv5sZoxuIof9Yw6_bvx1h-&index=7

20

Restoring the Commons

Itzchak E. Kornfeld

The loss of biological diversity and habitats are usually due to the extension of the urban core, by the construction of housing, shopping malls, highways, and commercial centers.[1] This growth may also include the destruction of older parks and other commons used by people.[2] In confronting this Pac-Man mentality of gobbling up every piece of open space, some municipalities have developed a new paradigm of what the urban environment should look like. They have begun to stem the losses to development and to previously polluted or degraded spaces, by designing and constructing a variety of new sites, thereby creating numerous benefits, including the expansion of social capital. These sites include artificial wetlands, stormwater retention ponds, and the reclamation of previously polluted streams.

Two examples of this phenomenon are presented below. The first, is the revitalization of a heavily polluted stream near Tel Aviv, Israel, and the second describes the conversion of a pasture into a thriving wetland in Orlando, Florida. Finally, I investigate whether these sites fit within Ostrom's common pool resource archetype.

COMMON POOL RESOURCES VS. PUBLIC GOODS

As this volume focuses on "commons," I begin with the question of what type of resource or good is a newly constructed or revitalized "commons"? Does it fall within the sphere of Elinor Ostrom's common pool resources (CPR), or is it another type of resource? Ostrom defined CPR's as non excludable but rivalrous goods.[3] That is, a CPR is a natural or man-made resource from which it is difficult to exclude or limit users once the resource is provided, and where one person's consumption of resource units makes those units unavailable to others.[4] She explained that they include fisheries and forests, where numerous actors – i.e., rival harvesters, such as fishermen or lumberjacks, possess a non excludable access to these resources.[5] Consequently,

---

[1] *See generally*, Thomas Elmqvist *et al.*, *Urbanization, Habitat Loss and Biodiversity Decline: Solution Pathways to Break the Cycle*, in The Routledge Handbook of Urbanization and Global Environmental Change 139 (Karen C. Seto et al. ed. 2015). ("Urbanization impacts biodiversity and ecosystem services both directly and indirectly.").

[2] Dennis D. Murphy, *Challenges to Biological Diversity in Urban Areas* in Biodiversity 71, 72 (E. O. Wilson & Frances M. Peter eds. 1988).

[3] Elinor Ostrom, *Coping with Tragedies of the Commons*, 2 Ann. Rev. Pol. Sci. 493, 494 (1999), available at www.annualreviews.org/doi/pdf/10.1146/annurev.polisci.2.1.493.

[4] *Id.* at 497.

[5] *Id.* at 494.

the resource can be over harvested leading to a depletion of the stocks.[6] Therefore, in order to limit over-consumption of a resource by one or more parties, CPR consumption may be regulated by government regulation or via agreements by the harvesters themselves.[7]

There also exists another type of good: public goods, or resources. In contrast to CPR, the public good is both non excludable and non rivalrous.[8] That is, individuals cannot be prevented from using or benefiting from the resource without paying for it, and its consumption by one party will not decrease its accessibility to others – i.e., the resource may be utilized simultaneously by multiple users. A common example of a public good is a streetlight,[9] where A's use of the light does not diminish B's use. Thus, streetlights are non rival – i.e., my use does not interfere with your use.[10] Likewise, my benefit from the streetlight does not limit, or exclude your benefit from it, so this good is non-excludable.

CASE STUDIES

I will, in due course, address the classification of a good or resource that these newly created commons are. However, before doing so, I want to introduce the two types of localities under review here, where both nature and leisure were designed in conjunction as urban commons. The first addresses the reclamation of the Alexander Stream in central Israel, where the Israeli government undertook the clean-up of an intermittent stream fouled by human waste and agricultural runoff. The second examines the Orlando, Florida Easterly Wetlands Reclamation Project, a 1,200-acre constructed wetland, built in lieu of a large, expensive concrete wastewater treatment plant to filter the city's wastewater.

COMMONS AS SPACES FOR PEOPLE AND NATURE

Commons, as used herein, include large urban parks, walkways and other public spaces. Unlike the two examples presented here, their faunal assemblage is limited to pigeons, squirrels, mice, rats, crows, and raptors.[11] Additionally, many large urban parks were both envisaged and established during the nineteenth century, exclusively for human leisure and not for the enhancement of faunal or floral biodiversity.

For example, in the United States, the nineteenth century landscape architect Frederick Law Olmsted, Sr., generally deemed to be the father of American landscape architecture,[12] envisaged parks "as places of harmony; places where people would go to escape life and regain their sanity. He wanted these parks to be [public locales] available to all people no matter what walk of life the person followed."[13] Olmsted is best known for conceiving and designing Central and

---

[6] *Id.* ("External authorities are presumably needed to impose rules and regulations on local users, since they will not do this themselves.")
[7] *Id.* at 503.
[8] *See generally*, HAL R. VARIAN, MICROECONOMIC ANALYSIS 414–415 (3rd ed. 1992).
[9] *Id.* at 414.
[10] *Id.*
[11] Murphy *supra.* ("In patches of eastern deciduous forest near Washington, D.C., migrant bird species restricted as breeders to forest interiors also survive in only the largest natural habitat remnants … These are merely obvious examples of an accelerating decline in the global diversity of living things. The term biological diversity has been used to describe 'the variety of life forms, the ecological roles they perform, and the genetic diversity they contain'").
[12] *See generally*, *Olmstead's Philosophy* (2011), FredrickLawOlmstead.com/philos.html.
[13] FredrickLawOlmstead.com, *A Celebration of the Life and Work of Frederick Law Olmsted, Founder of American Landscape Architecture* (2011), www.fredricklawolmsted.com/philos.html.

Prospect Parks in New York City, the grounds of the U.S. Capitol in Washington, D.C., and North Carolina's Biltmore Estate, among others.

Similarly, under the post – World War II Marshall Plan, the conception of United States Secretary of State George C. Marshall, had a series of parks built in many European cities, destroyed during World War II.[14] For example, in the capitol of the Nazi regime, Nuremberg, Germany, a number of green parks were constructed as part of the city's rebuilding. One of the many parks that was created, Stadtpark Nürnberg, known in English as Nuremberg's Garden Paradise, is "a nineteen-hectare [46.95 acre] city park. Under the established trees are fields of flowers there is the park lake, the popular Park Café, kiosks and ice cream parlours along with an adventure playground."[15]

This type of green infrastructure establishes cities as places that also enrich the regional ecology.[16] Indeed, some years ago, the City of Edmonton in Alberta, Canada, observed in its Urban Parks Management Plan that:

> Residents enjoy a lush diversity of parks, natural areas, trees, trails and recreation facilities that help shape individuals, neighbourhoods and the city as a whole …

> Parks are complex elements of a city. Well-planned, well-maintained parks benefit a community in many, many ways. Quite often people view parks as simply "play" places. While play remains important, parks offer many other benefits.[17]

These community benefits include *social capital*, healthier citizens and natural beauty, as well as habitats for birds and other animals. When speaking about social capital, one refers to the connections or relationships that people establish when they interact or network with one another, thereby building trust, shared goals, and social communities.[18] The concept was first introduced in 1916 by Lyda Johnson Hanifan, the State Supervisor for West Virginia's rural schools. He conceived of social capital as "those tangible assets [that] count for most in the daily lives of people: namely goodwill, fellowship, sympathy, and social intercourse among the individuals and families who make up a social unit."[19] Open commons, such as parks, foster increased social capital by providing places for people to meet and interact with each other in communal settings, benefit from their free time, while enjoying the company of family and friends.[20] They also build "a sense of community and improve quality of life, [which is exceedingly crucial] as we become a more culturally, economically and socially diverse community."[21]

[14] *See generally*, The George C. Marshall Foundation, George C. Marshall, *History of the Marshall Plan* (undated), www.marshallfoundation.org/marshall/the-marshall-plan/history-marshall-plan.

[15] Stadtpark Nürnberg (2020), https://tourismus.nuernberg.de/en/experience/leisure-sports-the-surrounding-areas/parks-green-areas/location/stadtpark-nuernberg.

[16] The City of Edmonton [Alberta, Canada] Asset Management and Public Works, *Edmonton's 2006 – 2016 Urban Parks Management* (Mar. 2006) www.edmonton.ca/documents/PDF/UPMP_2006–2016_Final.pdf.

[17] *Id.*

[18] Sheila Foster, *The City as an Ecological Space: Social Capital and Urban Land Use*, 82 Notre Dame L. Rev. 527, 529 (2006). ("Scholars from various disciplines have long recognized the centrality of social capital to, and the resources it purchases for, the governance, health, and sustainability of urban communities.").

[19] L. J. Hanifan, *The Rural School Community Center*, 67 The Ann. Amer. Academy of Pol. & and Soc. Sci. 130, 130 (1916).

[20] The COVID19/Corona Virus pandemic, which ostensibly began on December 31, 2019, in Wuhan, China, with a reported "cluster of cases of pneumonia in Wuhan, Hubei Province. A novel coronavirus was eventually identified." World Health Organization, WHO Timeline - COVID-19 (Apr. 27, 2020), www.who.int/news-room/detail/27-04-2020-who-timeline—covid-19.

[21] The City of Edmonton *supra* note 17 at 8.

Moreover, open commons, including parks, further the well-being and health of citizens, as they can walk, run and play, ride bikes, etc., in fresh air and green spaces. Indeed, "a well-planned park and public open space system ... preserve[s] a lasting natural legacy that enhances a community's awareness and appreciation of the natural world. They give people a place to connect with nature and provide respite from busy lives."[22]

RESTORING AND CONSTRUCTING A NEW COMMONS

Natural spaces are developed as part of the construction of new commons in and around urban areas, thereby increasing peoples' well-being, social interactions, and the ecosystem. "Nearly all environmental issues have aspects of the commons in them. [Indeed] ... [a]t the heart of all social theory is the contrast between humans as motivated almost exclusively by narrow self-interest and humans as motivated by concern for others or for society as a whole."[23] Research has also revealed that spending time in the outdoor environment provides pleasant feelings and reduces peoples' stress levels.[24] Other benefits of spending time in nature, "or even viewing scenes of nature, reduces anger, fear, and stress and increases pleasant feelings. Exposure to nature not only makes you feel better emotionally, it contributes to physical wellbeing, reducing blood pressure, heart rate, muscle tension, and the production of stress hormones."[25]

Spending time in nature also provides "people with multiple benefits to health and well-being ... Interest in nature as a therapeutic resource has ancient foundations. Hippocrates extolled the necessity of 'airs, waters, and places', for physical and mental well-being ... and ancient Roman texts suggest that there are health benefits to countryside and greenspaces."[26] Alternatively, a person's stress levels increase in unpleasant or poor inner-city urban environments, where there are often few natural or open spaces for commoning together safely.[27]

DEAD AREAS: THE ALEXANDER STREAM, ISRAEL

The Alexander Stream is located north of the City of Netanya, which is part of the Tel Aviv Metropolitan area. Its watershed originates in the upper portion of Wadi[28] Zeimar in Palestine, east of the City of Nablus[29] and flows westward for 22 kilometers. The stream then crosses into Israel, where it flows for another 32 kilometers along Israel's coastal plain, discharging into the Mediterranean Sea (see Figure 20.1).[30]

---

[22] *Id.*
[23] Elinor Ostrom et al. The Drama of the Commons 4 (2002), www.nap.edu/catalo/10287.htm
[24] *See e.g.*, University of Minnesota, Earl E. Bakken Center for Spirituality & Healing, *Taking Charge of Your Health & Wellbeing, How Does Nature Impact Our Well Being* (2016), www.takingcharge.csh.umn.edu/how-does-nature-impact-our-wellbeing.
[25] University of Minnesota, *Taking Charge of Your Health & Wellbeing: The Summer of Wellbeing, Part VI* (2016), www.takingcharge.csh.umn.edu/summer-wellbeing-part-vi
[26] Lara S. Franco, et al., *A Review of the Benefits of Nature Experiences: More Than Meets the Eye*, 14 Int'l J. Environ. Res. Pub. Health 864, 864 (2017).
[27] Leo Benedictus, *Sick Cities: Why Urban Living Can be Bad for Your Mental Health*, The Guardian (UK), Feb. 25, 2014, www.theguardian.com/cities/2014/feb/25/city-stress-mental-health-rural-kind.
[28] A Wadi is a dry riverbed equivalent to an arroyo in the southwestern United States.
[29] Nir Becker, Eran Friedler & Marwan Haddad, *Case Study Final Report The Alexander River – Wadi Zeimar Basin Palestinian Israeli Case Study II* (2006), http://nir-becker.telhai.ac.il/uploaded_files/Alexander%20river%20report%20.pdf.
[30] *Id.*

FIGURE 20.1 Map of Israel and the Alexander Stream (and its Sister Streams)

The Alexander Stream has been ravaged by acute pollution, which has posed significant health and other hazards to nearby communities, to biodiversity and to natural resources.[31] A number of factors have contributed to the pollution of the streams.[32] For decades, sewage and industrial pollutants have poured into the Alexander from Israel's Emek Hefer Industrial Zone and from the Nablus River in Palestine.

Moreover, the stream has been used as a conduit for the year-round flow of raw sewage, agricultural runoff, stormwater runoff, or low-quality effluent.[33] Indeed, in 2011, the managing director of the Alexander Stream Rehabilitation Authority, declared that the river was contaminated with saltwater and "a lot of raw sewage and other waste enters the river from the West Bank ... whose residents don't seem to mind that their waste is being sent in our direction."[34] He also noted that:

> ...a sewage treatment plant built by Israel near Tulkarem before it became part of the Palestinian Authority is not being properly maintained even though the Israeli government pays money towards its upkeep. [The Palestinians] receive the money to take care of the facility but do not use these funds to maintain it. Because of this, their sewage finds its way into the Alexander ... I have no idea how much money is involved, but whatever it is, it is obviously being used for something else.[35]

---

[31] Lior Asaf et al., *Transboundary Stream Restoration Rain Israel and the Palestinian Authority*, in INTEGRATED WATER RESOURCES MANAGEMENT AND SECURITY IN THE MIDDLE EAST 285, 285 (Clive Lipchin et al. eds. 2007).

[32] *Id.*

[33] *Id.* at 285. "These transboundary streams of Israel and Palestine are plagued by severe pollution, posing a serious health hazard to humans and devastating the natural ecosystems."

[34] Maurice Picow, *Israel's Rivers: Back from the Dead*, JERUSALEM POST, June 11, 2011, www.jpost.com/Health-and-Sci-Tech/Science-And-Environment/Israels-rivers-Back-from-the-dead.

[35] *Id.*

Moreover, in January 2016, Israel's Nature and Parks Authority ("INPA") observed that the continuing pollution caused by the discharge of untreated sewage from Palestinian cities and some Israeli settlements, have led to severe damage being inflicted on Israel's nature reserves, streams and groundwater aquifers, despite assurances made by the government to solve these problems.[36] The pollution was so severe that it caused the partial extinction of the rare Nile soft-shell turtle (*Trionyx triunguis*).[37] *According to Israel's Ministry of the Environment:*

To stop the discharge of pollution from the Palestinian Authority, the Emek Hefer Regional Council has undertaken to implement an emergency solution until such time that a joint treatment plant, which will treat wastewater from both the Palestinian side and the Israeli side, can be established ... A demonstration project that involves scenic, ecological and drainage restoration along a 750-meter [2,462 feet] stretch of the river was launched in 1999.[38]

REHABILITATION

As part of its pre-1999 plan, the Israeli government undertook a series of projects for the rehabilitation of the area where the Nile softshell turtles previously made their home. That effort included the construction of a variety of parks along the Alexander's banks. For instance, in 1994, the environment ministry established a River Restoration Administration, to coordinate the work of various agencies and nongovernmental bodies in their efforts to restore the Alexander and other impaired streams.[39] Subsequently, in 2002, the Ministry created a regional river administration for the Alexander Stream, charged with developing a masterplan for the preservation and enhancement of the area.[40] Thereafter, the Ministry began landscaping and developing a park along the Alexander's banks.

Then, in 2011 and 2012, the Ministry's Bureau of Rivers and Lakes excavated two multi-acre oxidation/settling ponds, into which waste from Palestinian sources is channeled for preliminary treatment.[41] Additionally, the Bureau constructed a secondary treatment plant, which discharges the treated water into the Alexander Stream. Subsequently, in 2015, the Ministry finally produced a masterplan for the development of the Alexander Stream. Today, the Nile turtles have returned and made their home along the stream's banks and a bridge was built over their habitat, so that people can watch them. The bridge is part of a larger recreational area or commons that includes picnic tables, bike and hiking trails, bird watching sites, a river walk and an observation tower that allows the park's sightseers to view a panoramic scene of the area.[42] Furthermore, the Alexander's corridor was widened, replacing abandoned farmland.[43]

---

[36] Zafrir Rinat, *West Bank Sewage Inflicting Environmental Damage, Israeli Nature Authority Warns*, HAARETZ Feb 21, 2016, www.haaretz.com/israel-news/.premium-nature-authority-asks-yaalon-to-act-on-west-bank-sewage-1.5407035. (Emphasis added).

[37] Özgür Güçlü, *et al.*, *Genetic Variation of the Nile Soft-Shelled Turtle (Trionyx triunguis)*, 12 INTER. J. MOLEC. SCI. 6418 (2011).

[38] State of Israel Ministry of the Environment, *The Environment in Israel* (Compiled and written by Shoshana Gabbay (Jerusalem 2002)), www.sviva.gov.il/English/ResourcesandServices/Publications/Documents/ TheEnvironmentInIsrael2002 .pdf.

[39] *Id.*

[40] *Id.*

[41] Zafrir Rinat, *West Bank Sewage Inflicting Environmental Damage, Israeli Nature Authority Warns*, HAARETZ Feb 21, 2016, www.haaretz.com/israel-news/.premium-nature-authority-asks-yaalon-to-act-on-west-bank-sewage- 1.5407035.

[42] The Society for the Protection of the Environment, *The Alexander River from the Turtle Bridge to the Sea* (undated) (In Hebrew), www.teva.org.il/?CategoryID=1677&ArticleID=175.

[43] *Id.*

In addition to the turtles, other wildlife has made its home along the Alexander and its banks, including waterfowl, plovers, jungle cats, indigenous fish, river eels, and the brackish water mullet.[44] Moreover, in an attempt to plant more indigenous trees the Ministry planted a large number of trees mentioned in the Bible. These include the Tamarix, mentioned in Genesis 21:33; the Mastic tree, discussed in Daniel 13: 54–55;[45] and the holy bramble, noted in Numbers 33:55.[46] These trees help promote cleaner, healthier air for humans and animals alike. The government also launched a program to eradicate various invasive species.[47]

Clearly, clean streams and rivers are the main cradles of terrestrial life in Israel and elsewhere, as they provide habitats, esthetic and recreational sites and water, a vital resource for the existence of diverse ecosystems.[48] A stream's, or river's health is measured by how polluted it is.[49]

CONSTRUCTED WETLANDS: THE ORLANDO EASTERLY WETLANDS RECLAMATION PROJECT

Wetlands serve as one of the principal habitats for numerous wildlife species – from waterfowl to small mammals, and to insects.[50] They also form an ecosystem connection between water and land. What's more, wetlands also perform an important role in sustaining water quality, by acting as the "earth' s kidneys," they filter out agricultural and other nutrients and absorb sediments.[51] Moreover, wetlands provide natural buffers, guarding against storm surges and rising floodwaters.[52]

Nevertheless, wetlands have been the victim of progress in America and elsewhere in the world.[53] Research has shown that less than half of the million acres of wetlands originally present in the United States prior to settlement by Europeans, has been lost due to infilling and the conversion of wetlands into farmland.[54]

Constructed wetlands mimic natural ones; they essentially work the same way. When water enters the wetland its rate of flow slows, and the solids suspended in the water settle out either due to the sluggish flow or by becoming trapped by the marsh grasses and reeds. In both cases, other nutrients – including nitrogen and phosphorus from fertilizers and manure or septic tank discharges – and pollutants are either taken up by the vegetation or settle into the soil. Wetland

---

[44] *Id.* Picow, *Israel's Rivers* note 34.
[45] Daniel 13:54–55, "Now then, if you saw her, tell me under what tree you saw them together. He said: Under the mastic tree …." The Bible: The Pentateuch and Haftorahs (J. H. Hertz, ed. 2nd, 1980).
[46] *Id.*
[47] Ministry of Environmental Protection, The Alexander Stream (In Hebrew) *supra* note 31.
[48] American Rivers, *Protecting Small Streams and Wetlands* (2019), www.americanrivers.org/threats-solutions/clean-water/streams-wetlands.
[49] Dashiell Bennett, *Half of All U.S. Rivers Are Too Polluted for Our Health*, THE ATLANTIC, Mar. 27, 2013, www.theatlantic.com/national/archive/2013/03/half-all-us-rivers-are-too-polluted-our-health/316027.
[50] Scientific American, *Wetlands Update–Has Preservation Had an Impact?* (July 9, 2008), www. scientificamerican.com/article/wetlands-update.
[51] *Id.*
[52] *Id.*
[53] *Id.* ("The eradication of wetlands in the so-called New World began when white settlers, intent on taming the land, started developing homesteads and town sites throughout what was to become the United States and Canada.")
[54] EPA, Office of Water, Orlando, FL - Wetland Treatment Systems: A Case History - The Orlando Easterly Wetlands Reclamation Project (1993), https://floridadep.gov/water/domestic-wastewater/documents/case-history-orlando-easterly-wetlands-reclamation-project-then click on Document: EPA_Case_History_OEW.pdf.

vegetation also promotes conditions where bacteria and other microbes can neutralize these wastes.[55] Consequently these wetlands are used to treat human and other waste, and reuse of treated water for crop irrigation, and for wildlife habitat.

CONSTRUCTED WETLANDS: ORIGINS AND BENEFITS

Given the many benefits that natural wetlands provide it isn't surprising that scientists have sought to replicate them. One such effort occurred during the 1950s when a German limnologist, Käthe Seidel, was researching lakeshore bulrushes, and found that they are exceptionally absorptive.[56] Using them as her foundational species, she designed and constructed an artificial marsh, finding that the plants in the marsh were able to treat or purify wastewater by absorbing the polluted substances.[57] Seidel's initial project inspired many others to construct artificial wetlands using her model.

Constructed wetlands provide people with an esthetically pleasing environment, enhance water quality and sustain wildlife habitat.[58] They have also been shown to be a cost-effective and successful way of filtering wastewater.[59] Moreover, these wetlands are much less expensive to construct than conventional steel and concrete wastewater treatment plants. They also have much lower operating and maintenance costs.[60] Finally, constructed wetlands are both aesthetically pleasing and capable of diminishing or completely removing the odors associated with polluted wastewater.[61] We now move to our case study.

THE ORLANDO EASTERLY WETLANDS RECLAMATION PROJECT

The Orlando Easterly Wetlands Reclamation Project[62] occupies approximately 1,640 acres, in Orange County, Florida,[63] previously used as a cow pasture.[64] Operational since 1987, it is located in the eastern portion of the county, in an area known as the Seminole Ranch, and is about two miles west of the main channel of the St. John's River.[65] The wetlands themselves cover 1,220 acres and are divided into 12 cells that are 3–6 feet deep. The project relies on discharged wastewater, which is funneled into the wetland from Orlando's Iron Bridge Regional Water Pollution Control Facility ("WPCF"),[66] where it is cleansed of all of its contaminants; the purified water is then discharged into the St. Johns River.[67]

---

[55] *See generally*, Qaisar Mahmood *et al.*, *Natural Treatment Systems as Sustainable Ecotechnologies for the Developing Countries*, 2013 BIOMED RES. INT'L 1 (June 6, 2013).

[56] Revathi Devaraj, et al., *Reed Bed Systems for Treatment of Poultry Pre-Treated Wastewater*, 7 INT. J. RES. PHARM. SCI. 245 (2016), www.pharmascope.org/index.php/ijrps/ article/view/8/1.

[57] Davor Stanković, *Constructed Wetlands for Wastewater Treatment*, 69 GRAĐEVINAR 639 (2017).

[58] U.S. Environmental Protection Agency, *Constructed Treatment Wetlands*, at Why Build Them?, https://nepis.epa.gov/ Exe/ZyPDF.cgi/ 30005UPS.PDF?Dockey=30005UPS. PDF.

[59] *Id.*

[60] *Id.*

[61] *Id.*

[62] Wetland Treatment Systems: A Case History *supra* note 54.

[63] *Id.*

[64] *Id.*

[65] *Id.*

[66] *Id.*

[67] *Id*

REJUVENATION

Variable water levels are vital for the maintenance of preferred plant communities of wetland treatment systems. The key objective in creating the wetlands reclamation project was to filter effluent originating in the WCPF wastewater treatment plant by planting aquatic plants, such as water lilies or eelgrasses. These plants accelerate nutrient removal for up to 20 million gallons/day of effluent from the WPCF. However, due to uncertainty about how well the system would work at its inception, the facility's original operating permit limited water flow to eight million gallons/day.[68] Once the Easterly Wetlands proved to be effective, the flow rate was increased.[69] During the 1990s the U.S. Environmental Agency reported that the Easterly Wetlands Reclamation Project could receive thirteen million gallons/day of effluent for treatment from the Iron Bridge Regional Water Pollution Control Facility.[70] Then in 2012, a study found that the Easterly wetlands could successfully treat in excess of 40 million gallons/day.[71]

The impacts of the Orlando Easterly Wetlands Reclamation Project are dramatic. First, Over 2,000,000 aquatic plants and over 200,000 trees were planted in order to create the wetlands.[72] In the pre-wetlands era the pasture had very little fauna or flora, as cows trampled the land. However, by 1993, after operating for only five years, scientists observed 145 bird species, of which, ten were listed as endangered under both state and federal laws.[73] Today, over 30 threatened or endangered species have been observed at the site.[74] Other benefits include a reversal in the levels of various nutrients, which leads to a healthier ecosystem.[75]

Finally, the project's 1985 original cost was $21,525,000, which included the cost of land acquisition.[76] Even assuming that the standard wastewater concrete and steel treatment plant costs less to build, its benefits are nowhere near what constructed wetlands offer: creating a new commons, which *produce* new life, in the form of flora and fauna, as well as amenities such as parks and hiking trails for people. Additionally, the Easterly Wetlands are open as a City of Orlando park 365 days a year and over 44,000 people visit the park annually.[77] The number of visitors has increased by 165% over the past decade.[78] The park also offers numerous recreational opportunities including bicycle, equestrian and hiking trails; nature photography; observing wildlife in a natural habitat; birding organized by the Orange Audubon Society; educational opportunities for scouts and school groups that include field trips; as well as the City of Orlando's Orlando Wetlands Festival, which began in 1999 and has since grown into a large community event drawing thousands of people,[79] and increasing social capital.

---

[68] *Id.* at Project Background.

[69] *Id.*

[70] *Id.*

[71] City of Orlando, Orlando Easterly Wetlands Reclamation Project: From Experiment to Success (undated) at 4, www .orlando.gov/files/sharedassets/public/departments/parks-amp-rec/orlando-wetlands-park/Orlando   wetlandstechincal-booklet_final.pdf.

[72] Mark Sees, *Orlando Easterly Wetlands City Academy Presentation* (undated), www.cityoforlando.net/ wetlands/wp-content/uploads/sites/59/2014/04/Wetlands-City-Academy.pdf.

[73] *See e.g.*, Florida Endangered and Threatened Species Act, F. S. A. § 379.2291 et seq. (2019); Endangered Species Act, 16 U. S. C. § 1531 et seq. (2019 supp.).

[74] Sees *supra* note 54 at 24.

[75] *Id.* at 22.

[76] EPA, Office of Water, Orlando, FL - Wetland Treatment Systems: A Case History supra note 54.

[77] *Id.*

[78] *Id.*

[79] *Id.*

The change from a cow pasture to the wetlands yielded the many benefits listed above, including the fact that the treated effluent leaves no residual waste – i.e., the solids and other byproducts that must be transported to a landfill from a non-wetland effluent treatment facility.[80] Moreover, since wetlands are known to be some of the most biologically diverse and productive natural ecosystems in the world, their reconstructed siblings offer a similar dynamic, a biological ecological network that is aesthetically pleasing and adds to the natural environment and to the broader landscape. In contrast, the standard concrete treatment plants are neither aesthetically pleasing nor add to the environment.

ARE RECONSTRUCTED COMMONS A COMMON POOL RESOURCE?

Having established the benefits of two reconstructed commons, parks, greenspaces and other natural environments, I will now analyze what type of resource they are. We know that a CPR is one that is non excludable and rivalrous, or subtractable. An open commons or park – unless admission is charged, does not exclude anyone. But does your use of it limit or diminish my use or entry? Or is it like a streetlamp where my use does not exclude your use and my benefit does not diminish by your benefit – i.e., a public good?

I posit that when a small number of people use a commons or a park, it is akin to a public good. You use it in your way and I in another and we do not interfere with one another. But, when the Alexander or Orlando's Easterly become very crowded, which occurs daily after 6:00 p.m. and on the weekends, these sites become non-excludable but also rivalrous, or subtractable, making them a common-pool resource. Finally, the overuse of these two sites, which converts them into a CPR may lead to a tragedy of the commons problem, unless access is regulated.

CONCLUSION

We have seen how two communities have undone a "tragedy of commons." In the Alexander Stream's case, the rehabilitation of a polluted stream and in Orlando's case a new use and the revitalization of a pasture. The benefits accrued from the expansion of "living" and "thriving commons," including affording people a place for leisure and healthy activities, increases social capital. It also expands the natural environment, incorporating trees, plants and new homes for an array of animals in the urban core. This chapter also demonstrates that as the world witnesses more and more construction, thereby shrinking open spaces, particularly within urban areas, scientists and government agencies are now attempting to reclaim the many lost *commons* and to un-pollute the polluted ones. In addition, these efforts advance the interests of communities, individuals, social capital and biodiversity. The reclamation of the Alexander Stream and the creation of the Orlando Easterly Wetlands Reclamation Project provide proof positive that these efforts are bearing fruit. Hopefully, they will provide models that other localities will seek to duplicate.

---

[80] *Id.*

PART VII

Law, Legal Theory, and the Commons

21

Prior Appropriation as a Response to the Tragedy of the Commons

Robert Haskell Abrams[1]

INTRODUCTION

For many, Hardin's cows on the commons provide the most-remembered image of tragedy befalling the commons. Once predation, disease and other factors that limit the total population of cows on the common are eliminated, each herder is incentivized to "try to keep as many cattle as possible on the commons, [whereupon] the inherent logic of the commons remorselessly generates tragedy."[2] That same inherent logic is applicable to virtually all natural resource commons, not least of which are water bodies. Hardin offers water pollution as a second example of tragic overuse because the "rational man finds that his share of the cost of the wastes he discharges into the commons is less than the cost of purifying his wastes before releasing them ... [locking in] a system of 'fouling our own nest,' so long as we behave only as independent, rational, free-enterprisers."[3] Turning to food production, Hardin posits "private property, or something formally like it,"[4] as the antidote to the tragedy of the commons, but goes on to indicate that private property as applied to "air and waters ... that cannot readily be fenced,"[5] still "favors pollution." Here he indicates the need for coercive legal rules or effluent taxes, concluding, "[t]he law, always behind the times, requires elaborate stitching and fitting to adapt it to this newly perceived aspect of the commons."[6] This paper is concerned with the prior appropriation system used to allocate the use of water in the arid American West. Prior appropriation assigns a right to use water on the basis of the seniority in time of when the use was initiated. The scope of an appropriative water right is further defined by the characteristics of the use, including such things as the purpose of the use, the situs of the use, the duration of the use (often only during certain periods of the year), and the quantity of water that is withdrawn to effectuate the use. A form of privatization, prior appropriation solved a classic commons problem, frustration of established productive use of water by later-in-time users able to capture the water before it reaches the more senior-in-time users. Concurrently, prior appropriation planted the seed for a separate commons problem – destructive overuse of water.

---

[1] The author would like to thank all those who have read or commented on drafts of this article. The author also would like to thank Lauren Robertson, a member of the 2020 class at the College of Law for her research assistance with this article. All views expressed herein (and whatever errors there may be) are those of the author.

[2] Garrett Hardin, *Tragedy of the Commons*, 162 SCIENCE 1243, 1244 (1968).

[3] *Id.* at 1245.

[4] *Id.*

[5] *Id.*

[6] *Id.*

OF BANK ROBBING AND WATER USE IN ARID REGIONS

Hardin's discussion of bank robbing is squarely on point in explaining the initial need for the adoption of prior appropriation. Hardin observes that "the man who takes money from a bank acts as if the bank were a commons,"[7] an act whose prohibition meets with universal acceptance when coercive laws restrict the freedom of the robber. Under prior appropriation, rights to use water can be analogized to deposits made in a bank. The water user, or "depositor," relies on the rules governing the operation of the bank and the protection those rules provide against bank robbing. The need to protect established water users against being dispossessed by other users of the commons was the strongest impetus to the adoption of prior appropriation as the governing water law of the American West. Specifically, prior appropriation solves the bank robber problem by assigning enforceable rights in the water that are upheld against predation by later-in-time entrants, who otherwise would be free to treat the water resource as a commons.

Prior to westward expansion, the well-watered humid climate east of the Mississippi treated water rights very much as a commons open to all who owned riparian parcels. The riparian rights system resolved conflicts on a case-by-case basis by adjusting rights to allow all to make reasonable use in light of the correlative rights of others on the stream. It worked because there was enough water for all uses to continue simultaneously without undue harm to any one of them.

In the American West, the short supply of water called for a different rule. The genesis of prior appropriation is ascribed to the rules miners worked out for themselves in the mining camps of the California Gold Rush.[8] Riparianism was of no avail because under that system the right to share in the use of the water rested on owning lands underlying or abutting the stream and the miners were trespassers on the public domain, not riparian owners. As had been done with staking claims to certain areas, the miners adopted a rule of priority to allocate the right to use the water.

Beyond the mining camps, water scarcity conditions in the American West required a far more generalized application of legal principles to protect security of right in the use of the common pool water resource. Unlike the well-watered East, where crops in most locales could be grown using rainfall alone, and where domestic needs were met from nearby streams, shallow groundwater aquifers, or cisterns, large expanses of the West lacked water supplies. As with Hardin's grazing cows, with too many entrants, no single user could reliably secure enough water to support their water-dependent activities without legal protection placing the entire economic system at risk of collapse. To prevent the West from remaining barren except along the banks of its widely separated streams and rivers, the right to use water had to be divorced from ownership of riparian parcels and, due to shortage, the commons had to be privatized. Prior appropriation separated the right to use water from ownership of riparian land and set up a system of legally protected water rights. The adaptation of water law and the concomitant need to dig canals across intervening lands took hold:

> In a dry and thirsty land it is necessary to divert the waters of streams from their natural channels, in order to obtain the fruits of the soil, and this necessity is so universal and imperious that it claims recognition of the law. The value and usefulness of agricultural lands, in this territory, depend upon the supply of water for irrigation, and this can only be obtained by constructing artificial channels through which it may flow over adjacent lands.[9]

---

[7] *Id.*
[8] *See, e.g.,* A. Dan Tarlock, *Law of Water Rights and Resources* § 5.3 (2018).
[9] Yunker v. Nichols, 1 Colo. 551, 553–54. (1872).

OVERUSE: THE COMMONS TRAGEDY WROUGHT BY PRIOR APPROPRIATION

The greatest failing of the prior appropriation doctrine has been its inability to foresee and forestall a second central commons problem – destructive overutilization of the commons by those holding privatized rights to use the resource. As a comparison, the other principal water law system in the United States, the riparian rights doctrine, limits all having water rights to uses that are reasonable under the totality of circumstances, a limitation that simultaneously protects the resource base and the users. Under classic prior appropriation doctrine, the impact of new uses on the resource base itself is not germane, the principal constraint on the ability to commence a new use is the availability of unappropriated water. Even worse, as noted below, prior appropriation creates considerable incentives promoting overuse.

This facet of the commons problem is canvassed by Hardin in his pollution discussion. Prior appropriation creates several strong incentives for rapid development of water-dependent and excessive uses. First, just like the near-costless disposal option available to a polluter, the absence of any fee for withdrawing water leaves no incentive to moderate water use. Second, prior appropriation encourages both maximization of the amount of the free good used and over-rapid resource utilization because the extent of the water right is measured by the amount of water taken and its security is determined by its priority in time. Third, once initiated, the water right is essentially a free good to the water user and the use right is perpetual so long as it is continued. This "use it or lose it" aspect of prior appropriation ensures that uses persist even if their benefit is *de minimis*.[10]

The architects of prior appropriation were not blind to these incentives, nor were they unaware that excessive use by earlier-in-time entrants erected a barrier to entry of all later-in-time entrants. Thus, prior appropriation doctrine has always had checks intended to limit the amount of water rights. The primary ones are that the water must be put to a beneficial use, the water must be withdrawn from the stream to appropriate it, and the water must be used in a non-wasteful manner. Hardin might characterize these requirements as either forms of coercive law to temper behavior, or as part of the law's "elaborate stitching and fitting" that is needed to prevent the tragedy of the commons from occurring. Regardless, the evidentiary record demonstrates the failure of the prior appropriation doctrine in curbing inequitable entitlements and overuse of water despite having doctrinal elements that, in theory, might limit those adverse outcomes.

Historically, the beneficial use requirement set a very low bar. The prototypical example of a non beneficial use is using water to drown gophers. This aspect of the law did little more than mimic reality – no one would invest scarce resources to appropriate water if the project was not providing some form of benefit to the user. The real thrust of the beneficial use requirement, strongly reinforced by the diversion requirement, was its role in preventing speculation.[11] A would-be appropriator could not obtain a water right with a current priority date without having a present use for the water and taking physical action to divert the water to consummate that use. In a frontier society lacking mechanized earth moving equipment and little available capital, the diversion requirement was the greater obstacle to speculation. Most early diversions of water were initiated by individuals or small groups that dug canals by hand

---

[10] To avoid loss of the value of having a more senior water right due to non use, even marginal uses are maintained.

[11] Speculation refers to the practice of obtaining a water right with no significant value in its present use with the intent to later sell the water right when the competition for water has greatly increased the value of the water right due to its seniority.

with shovels, typically for use in farming or to support settlement.[12] Although the scope of water diversion projects grew over time, the difficulty of diverting and controlling water remained a check on speculation.

The clash between the self-interested efforts of early appropriators to obtain large appropriative rights in a least cosy manner and the societal benefit of limiting the amounts of water made subject to the early appropriations was largely won by the water users. To best appreciate that dynamic, they treat development of a basin's water resources as having an early and a more contemporary stage. In the early stage, two conditions predominated. Resources such as labor, capital, and materials like cement that would have to be "imported" from the East were not readily available to most water users, meaning that they couldn't implement their uses in a manner that avoided more water intensive diversion and irrigation methods. Additionally, in the early stages of development, there were so few water users that water had not become so scarce as to prevent new entry and development. Recalling Hardin's cows, in this stage of limited development there was no overuse of the commons, so devoting extra resources to limit grazing would have been counterproductive. The practices of the earlier period became a baseline. The then-current water users, all of whom were having their water rights fully satisfied, had no incentive to complain about the beneficiality or wastefully inefficient practices of the era. Indeed, they also were operating in a similarly inefficient manner. Those water use practices became enshrined as the norm despite their inefficiency when measured against efficiencies obtained using what would later become readily affordable technologies.

The acceptance of inefficient practices has functioned to frustrate almost entirely using the anti-waste component of prior appropriation to revisit and reduce older water rights. Courts hearing challenges to irrigation methods as wasteful look to the prevailing community practice. Finding many irrigators are employing the older methods, courts routinely uphold those practices as non-wasteful.[13] Only a single reported case, State Department of Ecology v. Grimes,[14] required a reduction in the amount of an appropriation based on a finding of waste. In that case, Grimes sought to continue diversions on the same basis as had been in place for almost a century. Relying on a state agency finding that a 50% reduction in the diversion rate from Grimes's historic methods could deliver the same amount of irrigation water using affordable newer technology, the court reduced the appropriative right to one calculated using newer technology. Despite its potentially vital role in reducing wasteful use, the Grimes precedent is rarely cited, and never in support of a similar holding on the issue of waste. Less direct modern inroads on waste have been made, most often taking the form of statutory conservation incentives, such as making a portion of the water saved by efficiency improvement available for additional use or transfer to others.[15]

In the modern era, competition for water in most basins of the West has increased to the point where there is no longer enough water to meet all demands for its use on a secure basis. This raises the obvious question of how new entrants obtain water. In some basins, there still may be unappropriated water that is available in wet years. As to that water, new appropriations can be granted, but they are not "secure" in the sense that they cannot be relied upon to provide water in dryer years. Many water users, however, need more secure water rights and obtain them by

[12] See generally, BARTON H. THOMPSON, JR. ET AL., LEGAL CONTROL OF WATER RESOURCES 769–77 (6th ed. 2018). For a modern example of the antipathy to speculation in prior appropriation, see, e.g., High Plains A & M, LLC v. Southeast Colo. Water Conservancy Dist., 120 P.3d 710, 717–18 (Colo. 2005).
[13] Tulare Irr Dist. v Lindsay Strathmore Irr Dist., 3 Cal.2d 489, 45 P.2d 972 (1935).
[14] 121 Wash.2d 459, 852 P.2d 1044 (1993).
[15] See, e.g., MONT. CODE §85-2-101(21). CAL. WATER CODE §1011.

procuring the transfer of sufficiently senior rights. Appropriative water rights are a form of property and, subject to important caveats, are transferrable. Typical water rights purchasers are growing municipalities, which cannot tolerate having years in which there is not sufficient water supply for their citizenry, or investment-intensive activities that require water for their operations. For these uses, the water is far more valuable than in agricultural use, creating the needed price differential to support water markets. Looking West-wide in 2020, the transfer device has, in regard to cities and high value industrial and commercial uses, functioned to satisfy the region's water needs. The principal impact of transfers has been retirement of less valuable agricultural lands that would otherwise have remained in production. The more concerning impact in some cases is the weakening of the overall stability of the farming community as the number of farms and jobs decreases.

What complicates such transfers is the interdependence of water rights. Each use begins from a particular point of diversion and most uses return a considerable portion of the water they divert to the stream from which it is taken or to an aquifer from which the water can be recovered. To prevent transfer from displacing the water rights of those dependent on the returned water for their uses, prior appropriation has adopted a "no injury" rule. This rule requires a transferor to prove that the transfer will not interfere with the legal rights of other water users, including return flow-dependent junior-in-time users. The no-harm rule adds considerably to the transaction costs, enough so that small scale transfers having third-party effects often are not economically feasible.

Even with transfers to facilitate new high value uses, just as Hardin's cows eventually will exhaust their commons, at some point the tragedy of the water commons begins when so much water is being withdrawn that the streams are exhausted for significant periods of time. In an increasing number of areas of the West, regional growth is already significantly constrained by lack of water. Westwide, two aspects of climate change predicted for the region will accelerate the risk of stream dewatering. The region is predicted to be drier, which puts more stream systems at ecological risk. More acutely for prior appropriation, increased climate variability in the form of increased depth and frequency of droughts inexorably will mean that in low flow years, the water uses of existing seniors often will exhaust the streams, and those streams will be tragically dewatered.[16] This will include many streams that in most years had water remaining under the previous norms. As Hardin suggested for pollution, the law needs to add coercive dimensions that constrict freedom of use of the water commons. Especially in urban areas, that evolution is already underway with aggressive conservation requirements such as xerophytic landscaping, low flow plumbing fixtures, and use of gray water and non-fully reclaimed waste-water for landscape irrigation. More broad-gauged efficiency standards and withdrawal fees to incentivize conservation by other types of water users have yet to find expression in the law.

Here again, Hardin's article is prescient. State water laws in prior appropriation states have engaged in a "behind the times" "elaborate stitching and fitting" to address dewatering as a commons problem. Roughly coterminous with Earth Day in 1970, prior appropriation states began to find ways to introduce protections of living streams in their law. Much like the anti-waste requirement, these efforts have not been very effective. The most direct way to use prior appropriation to protect instream flows is to allow appropriations for instream use to protect fish, wildlife, recreation, and so on. Facially, most western states now statutorily allow one or another

---

[16] Even in the face of shortages, there are still incentives to make junior appropriations in wet years, as that water may be cheaper to obtain than other sources, such as short-term transfers or pumped groundwater (due to the energy cost of pumping). This incentive "remorselessly generates tragedy"

state agency to appropriate instream flows.[17] The use of these powers has proved more complicated and the states' commitments under them somewhat inconstant. First, allowing instream
flow protection abandons the diversion requirement as an element of appropriations. In an early
leading case, *Idaho Department of Parks v. Idaho Department of Water Administration,*[18] the
Idaho Supreme Court permitted a statutorily designated state agency to secure appropriative
rights for an instream flow. A careful reading of the justices' opinions, however, makes it very
clear that the majority of the court was not in support of protecting the seniority of the instream
appropriation against later-in-time appropriations for other uses in the case of water shortages.
Similarly, the Colorado Supreme Court upheld statutory authorizations to state agencies to
make instream appropriations against challenges to their non diversionary nature.[19] When a later
decision did not allow the state agency to renounce the appropriation when the water was
needed for snowmaking to support a major ski resort,[20] the legislature intervened and reduced
the instream flow appropriation.[21] Oregon, in its effort to encourage conservation by its users,
awards the users the bulk of the saved water and dedicates the remainder to instream flow.[22]

   The second way in which prior appropriation doctrine, at least facially, gives recognition to
the ecological importance of riparian environments is by the increasing enactment of public
interest standards that must be satisfied before the state water agency will grant new appropriative
rights or allow changes to existing rights (transfers). These laws define the public interest
broadly,[23] usually in the form of statutes that list several factors (without a hierarchy) for the
state agency to consider in adjudicating water rights applications.[24] Environmental considerations, including the harms of dewatering and the protection of riparian ecosystems, are deemed
to be part of the public interest.

   As is the case with other protections of instream flows that have been grafted onto prior
appropriation, public interest laws seem to offer nine parts myth and one part coconut oil when
it comes to avoiding dewatering. There are no decided cases directly on point. The leading case
on the subject, *Shokal v. Dunn,*[25] arose in Idaho, which has both a public interest laundry list
statute[26] and a specific statute identifying streamflow as a beneficial use in the public interest.[27]
In *Shokal,* the appropriation being sought would have caused an 80% reduction in streamflow.
Despite referencing the statutory protection of instream flows as part of the public interest, the
public interest analysis considered only the issue of whether the remaining flow was sufficient to
dilute the water user's pollution from its aquaculture activities. The Idaho Supreme Court
rebuked the lower court for "failing to account for ... the public's legitimate interests in the

---

[17] See, BARTON H. THOMPSON, JR. ET AL., LEGAL CONTROL OF WATER RESOURCES 221 (6th ed. 2018).
[18] Idaho Dep't. of Parks v. Idaho Dep't. of Water Administration, 96 Idaho 440, 530 P.2d 924 (1974). *See also,* COLO. REV.
    STAT.§37-92-102(3)(b) (expressly allowing later-in-time economic use to see abrogation of instream flow appropriation).
[19] See, e.g., Colorado River Water Conservation Bd v. Upper Gunnison River Water Conservation Dist., 109 P.3d 585
    (Colo. 2005) discussing history of COLO. REV. STAT.§§37-92-102 & 103.
[20] Aspen Wilderness Workshop, Inc. v. Colorado Water Conservation Bd., 901 P.2d 1251 (Colo. 1995).
[21] COLO. REV. STAT.§37-92-102(3)(b) & (4)(a).
[22] *See,* OR. REV. STAT. §§ 537.455 to 537.500.
[23] *See* TARLOCK, *supra* note 10 at § 5.52. Professor Tarlock lists 14 states that have public interest statutes
    affecting appropriations.
[24] *See, e.g.,* N.D. CENT. CODE ANN. § 61–04–06(4) (West 2018).
[25] 707 P.2d 441 (Idaho 1985); *see also* Hardy v. Higginson, 849 P.2d 946 (Idaho 1993). A third case, *Collins Bros. v. Dunn
    (In re Permit No. 47-7680),* 759 P.2d 891, 898 (Idaho 1988), applied the public interest standard to geothermally
    valuable groundwater, upholding denial of a permit for use of the water that did not take advantage of its
    energy content.
[26] IDAHO CODE ANN. § 42–203A(5)(e) (West 2018).
[27] IDAHO CODE ANN. § 42–1501 (West 2018).

stream environment, wildlife, aesthetics, recreation, and alternative uses"[28] but nonetheless found that allowing the appropriation adequately protected the public interest because the lower flow "will not allow Billingsley Creek to become a nuisance or a health hazard."[29] The very low bar set for protection of the public interest – avoiding an affirmative nuisance or a threat to public health, something the more general law would forbid – does nothing to uphold the public interest in streamflow.[30]

TAKING THE DIRECT APPROACH: LEGISLATING AND ENFORCING MINIMUM FLOWS AND LEVELS

To date, the worst effects of overuse are limited to the seasonal dewatering of many stream stretches in the western United States. As water availability and reliability in that region decrease with the impacts of climate change, prior appropriation law is likely to cause far more extensive stream dewatering with the attendant loss of vital riparian habitat and ecosystem services. There are some signs that values are changing, however. In the past few decades, subtle signals evince recognition that prior appropriation's older way of thinking – any water left in a stream is wasted – has outlived its time.[31] Efforts to bend prior appropriation doctrine to meet the challenge of the current and coming water scarcity scenarios have been insufficient. The waste doctrine remains in desuetude and the public interest doctrine is undermined by its obligation to consider economic development along with environmental consequences. The value of the beneficial use requirement in this context has proved so ineffectual as to be ridiculed. Professor Eric Freyfogle states: "Beneficial use, as it stands today, is an affront to attentive citizens who know stupidity when they see it; who know, for instance, that no public benefit arises when a river is fully drained so that its waters might flow luxuriously through unlined, open ditches onto desert soil to grow surplus cotton and pollute the water severely."[32]

What is left as a solution to the dewatering problem is to take an approach that confronts the problem directly rather than through further tinkering with prior appropriation law. Since the problem is insufficient water in streams to support ecologically important functions, the coercive response that Hardin likely would endorse is legislated temperance. Employ science to ascertain how much water is required to have an ecologically sound water resource complex and prescribe maintenance of that state of affairs as a legal requirement. The means to do just that are already present in numerous states in the form of laws directing state agencies to prescribe minimum flows and levels (MFLs). Absent in many of those states, however, is the political, administrative, and judicial will to implement this process and, once implemented, to rigorously enforce the scientifically based limits that restrict off stream water use. At present, only one state,

---

[28] *See* Shokal v. Dunn, 707 P.2d at 450–51.

[29] *Id.* Health was a concern due to anticipated pollution from the fish farm water use which might result in water quality poor enough to pose a hazard.

[30] TARLOCK, *supra* note 10 at §§ 5.52–5.59. In the cited sections, the Tarlock treatise describes many cases decided under state public interest laws. Tellingly, none of them show the public interest standard being used to prevent stream dewatering due to overappropriation.

[31] *See, e.g.,* Pagosa Area Water and Sanitation Dist. v. Trout Unlimited, 170 P.3d 307, 313–14 (Colo. 2007) (, "[M]aximum utilization does not mean that every ounce of Colorado's natural stream water ought to be appropriated; optimum use can be achieved only through proper regard for all significant factors, including environmental and economic concerns.").

[32] Eric Freyfogle, *Water Rights and the Common Wealth*, 26 ENVTL. L. 27, 42 (1996).

Washington, has assiduously erected MFLs and thereafter had its courts rigorously interpret and enforce the streamflow protective requirements.[33]

The underutilization of MFLs in other states is not surprising. If MFLs are put in place before streams are critically dewatered, the MFLs become a limit to growth which is politically unpopular. If MFLs are set after the flows and levels are depleted beyond ecologically sound levels, the MFLs not only limit growth, they require affirmative steps to recapture water from current users in all but unusually wet years. If the recapture is done via purchase, it is expensive and competes with the high costs associated with water transfers needed to support new economic and population growth activities. If the recapture is done by regulation alone, it imposes restrictions on economic growth and frustrates water users, who often claim that this is an unconstitutional taking of their property. Here, too, Hardin seems to have foreseen this response by rights holders: "Every new enclosure of the commons involves the infringement of somebody's personal liberty . . . Infringements made in the distant past are accepted because no contemporary complains of a loss. It is the newly proposed infringements that we vigorously oppose; cries of 'rights' and ' freedom' fill the air."[34]

CONCLUSION

Prior appropriation law averted the bank robber free-for-all tragedy of the commons by privatizing the rights to use the water. Simultaneously, the basic doctrine of prior appropriation, despite some potential checks on over-rapid and excessive water use, carried the seeds of a more familiar tragedy of the commons problem: destructive overuse. At the extreme, under prior appropriation streams are becoming dewatered for periods of the year and the lack of water is wreaking havoc with their riparian ecosystems.

In defense of prior appropriation, it is well to point out that the American West has prospered greatly in the time since its Anglo settlement began in earnest in the mid-nineteenth century. More recently, the cost discipline imposed by the need to rely on market transfers to supply new uses and growing populations ensure that the region's water resources are increasingly being used more efficiently. To date, the more dire ecological effects of dewatering have not been so great as to cause widespread regional disruption. Thus, in sum, prior appropriation has had a very productive 170-year run in the American West. At the same time, however, in the face of climate change induced reductions in regional water supply, the consequences of tragic overuse pose a substantial threat to regional well-being.

Protections against the threat of dewatering could have been institutionalized into prior appropriation, but those doctrinal opportunities were never realized. A direct complementary legal regime, instituting and enforcing MFLs could avert the impending tragedy of the commons caused by the prior appropriation regime. What is required to take that legal step is a change in attitude and morality in regard to the meaning and content of water *rights*. The current holders of appropriative rights almost certainly will see those rights diminished as part of the implementation of MFLs or other protections of ecosystems. Even in this realm, Hardin's short article has great explanatory power. It is not that the diversions and use of the appropriators were a vice or in some sense contrary to the common weal. Rather, the change in context

---

[33] A series of cases decided by the Washington Supreme Court have set the state on a path that enforces protection of MFLs. The leading cases are, Postema v. Pollution Control Bd., 11 P.3d 726, 735 (Wash. 2000), Swinomish Tribal Cnty. v. Wash. St. Dep't of Ecology, 311 P.3d 6 (Wash. 2013); Foster v. Wash. St. Dep't of Ecology, 362 P.3d 959 (Wash. 2015), and Whatcom Cnty. v. Hirst, 381 P.3d 1 (Wash. 2016).

[34] Hardin, *supra* note 2, at 1248.

wrought by increased congestion of the commons and the diminished water supply that will accompany climate change make continuation of the status quo untenable. As Hardin put it: *"the morality of an act is a function of the state of the system at the time it is performed."*[35] The state of the system in the American West no longer resembles that of the nineteenth century in which prior appropriation was adopted.

---

[35] Hardin, *supra* note 2, at 1245. Emphasis in the original.

22

Using the Public Trust Doctrine to Manage Property on the Moon

*Hope M. Babcock**

The race to develop outer space is on. Near-space is rapidly filling up with public and private satellites, causing electromagnetic interference and dangerous debris from collisions and earlier launches.[1] The lack of regulation of private commercial development of outer space will allow these near space problems to be exported further into the galaxy. Without a governing authority or rules controlling entry or limiting its plunder, outer space could turn into the "wild west" of the twenty-first century.[2]

Space treaties executed in the 1960s do not offer a regulatory framework.[3] Private companies support privatizing outer space[4] and oppose any management scenario that would enable less developed countries to free-ride on their investments.[5] But establishing a system of private property–based rules would transport earth's current division between rich and poor nations into outer space, potentially causing destabilizing hostilities – the exact consequences that the early drafters of the space treaties hoped to avoid.[6]

Property owned in common offers an alternative approach for managing outer space, one more closely aligned with the treaties' animating principles. Elinor Ostrom wrote that commons property regimes allow the equitable use of commons' resources, while preventing their destruction or hostile disputes over entitlements to them.[7] She identified options for commons management that are neither exclusively public nor exclusively private. In her work, she identifies groups of users who cooperated to create and enforce rules for using and managing

---

[1] *This chapter, which is derived from her article, *The Public Trust Doctrine, Outer Space, and the Global Commons: Time to Call Home ET*, 69 Syr. L. Rev. 191 (2019), is published with permission of the editors of the Syracuse Law Review.

    Ezra J. Reinstein, *Owning Outer Space*, 20 Nw. J. Int'l L. & Bus. 59, 64 (1999). The space age started in 1957 with the Soviet launch of Sputnik I, followed shortly by the United States' Explorer I. Jared B. Taylor, Note, *Tragedy of the Space Commons: A Market Mechanism Solution to the Space Debris Problem*, 50 Colum. J. Transnat'l L. 253, 258 (2011). Today, over 115 countries own or share ownership of an orbiting satellite, and over 950 operational satellites circle the earth. *Id.* at 256.

[2] *See* Reinstein, *Owning Outer Space*, *supra* note 1, at 72 ("Any legal regime should guard against inefficient exploitation, waste, and environmental despoliation. Furthermore, space should not become the next Wild West. Destruction and sabotage must be discouraged.").

[3] *Id.* at 69.

[4] *See id.* at 72.

[5] *See id.* at 74.

[6] Carol R. Buxton, *Property in Outer Space: The Common Heritage of Mankind Principle vs. the "First in Time, First in Right" Rule of Property Law*, 69 J. Air L. & Com. 689, 700 (2004).

[7] Elinor Ostrom, *Institutional Arrangements for Resolving the Commons Dilemma: Some Contending Approaches*, in The Question of the Commons, *supra* note 240, at 250–65.

natural resources like grazing lands, fisheries, and irrigation waters, using "rich mixtures of public and private instrumentalities."[8] But, a commons approach works best where common pool resources are small, which space is decidedly not.[9]

A user-managed commons approach, like Ostrom advocates, risks allowing the resource to be over-used or inequitably distributed. Application of the common law public trust doctrine may lessen those risks. But, since the doctrine has been used to thwart growth, it may not stimulate space development. Supplementing the doctrine with private property management tools, like tradable development rights, as this chapter suggests, might provide a workable property management regime in outer space. A mix of private property tools with a state-based public trust approach is a solution that Ostrom might well have envisioned.

THE CURRENT SITUATION

There are untapped reserves of great wealth in space. The moon's helium-3 resources could meet the world's energy needs through fusion reactors.[10] Asteroids are rich in materials that are important for the development of electronics.[11] Exploiting these materials in space would avoid or reduce significantly the harmful environmental and community disrupting effects of terrestrial extraction.[12]

This potential wealth has created interest among private businesses. Several billionaires have invested in a company called Planetary Resources, which is developing technology to mine a near- Earth asteroid and bring those materials back to Earth.[13] Another privately financed company, Deep Space Industries (DSI), is designing a spacecraft to collect and transport outer space resources back to earth and creating the technology to manufacture finished products in space.[14] Microsoft billionaire Naveen Jain, in 2011, created Moon Express, to mine platinum and titanium on the Moon.[15] In that same year, Shackleton Energy Company began to raise money to mine the Shackleton Crater on the Moon for fuels to enable expeditions even deeper into space.[16]

In 2012, Space X, a private company, launched the first official commercial flight to the International Space Station.[17] Since then, SpaceX has sent six missions to the Space Station, while other private companies are developing the capacity to take passengers on quick jaunts into outer space.[18] Denis Hope, a private speculator, has sold 3,500 properties on the moon.[19] Although ignored by the international community, the proliferation of copycat companies

---

[8] *See* M. Alexander Pearl, *The Tragedy of the Vital Commons*, 45 ENVTL. L. 1021, 1061 (2015).

[9] *Id.*

[10] Sarah Coffey, Note, *Establishing a Legal Framework for Property Rights to Natural Resources in Outer Space*, 41 Case W. Res. J. Int'l L. 119, 120 (2009).

[11] Andrew R. Brehm, Note, *Private Property in Outer Space: Establishing a Foundation for Future Exploration*, 33 WIS. INT'L L.J. 353, 355 (2015).

[12] Kevin MacWhorter, *Sustainable Mining: Incentivizing Asteroid Mining in the Name of Environmentalism*, 40 Wm. & Mary Envtl. L. & Pol'y Rev. 645, 647–48 (2016).

[13] MacWhorter, *Sustainable Mining*, *supra* note 12, at 650–51.

[14] *Id.*

[15] Brehm, Note, *Private Property in Outer Space*, *supra* note 11, at 355.

[16] *Id.*

[17] Brian Abrams, *First Contact: Establishing Jurisdiction Over Activities in Outer Space*, 42 Ga. J. Int'l & Comp. L. 797, 799 (2014).

[18] *Missions*, SPACEX, www.spacex.com/missions (last visited Mar. 6, 2019).

[19] Davin Widgerow, Comment, *Boldly Going Where No Realtor Has Gone Before: The Law of Outer Space and a Proposal for a New Interplanetary Property Law System*, 28 Wis. Int'l L.J. 490, 501–2 (2011).

around the world selling lunar realty symbolizes the persistent enthusiasm that space ownership holds for thousands of people.

All this activity in space has potential environmental costs, like space debris, which can remain in orbit for thousands of years and could make space useless or dangerous, if not removed.[20] Once on the surface of any celestial body, humans may spill fuel and leave behind human waste and trash. These are classic tragedies of the commons, problems, externalities of otherwise productive activities, which trigger the need for some solution.

LEGAL FRAMEWORK FOR SPACE DEVELOPMENT

The applicable legal framework consists of two principal international treaties – the 1967 Outer Space Treaty[21] (OST) and the 1979 Moon and Other Celestial Bodies Treaty[22] (Moon Treaty). One hundred and nine countries have adopted the OST, including the United States and the former Soviet Union.[23] The Treaty's broad acceptance "has given it the character of binding international law even on those countries who have not ratified it."[24] Only thirteen countries have adopted the Moon Treaty, making it effective only in those countries.[25] The debate over whether property in outer space should be private or commonly owned occurs in the context of these treaties.[26]

The Outer Space Treaty declares that:

> outer space is *free for exploration and use by all states*, that the moon and other celestial bodies shall be *used exclusively for peaceful purposes*, that *outer space is not subject to national appropriation* by claims of sovereignty, and that the *exploration and use of outer space shall be carried out for the benefit and interest of all countries and shall be the province of all mankind*.[27]

The treaty's roots are in the post –Cold War desire to prevent the militarization of outer space.[28] However, the OST was basically a diplomatic stopgap prepared in haste so that the first landing on the moon did not ignite a new theater in the Cold War. The drafters did not envision

---

[20] Emily M. Nevala, Comment, *Waste in Space: Remediating Space Debris through the Doctrine of Abandonment and the Law of Capture*, 66 Am. U.L. Rev. 1495, 1498 (2017). Paint chips can damage functioning satellites. Taylor, *Tragedy of the Space Commons, supra* note 1, at 262.

[21] Treaty on Principles Governing the Activities of States in the Exploration and Use of Outer Space, Including the Moon and Other Celestial Bodies, *opened for signature* Jan. 27, 1967, 18 U.S.T. 2410, 610 U.N.T.S. 205.

[22] Agreement Governing the Activities of States on the Moon and Other Celestial Bodies, *opened for signature* Dec. 18, 1979, 1363 U.N.T.S. 3.

[23] The OST came into force upon ratification by five countries. OST Art. XIV, para 3. https://oxfordre.com/planetaryscience/view/10.1093/acrefore/9780190647926.001.0001/acrefore-9780190647926-e-43. Signing ceremonies were then held in Moscow, London, and Washington, D.C. on January 27, 1967, and the Treaty entered into force for all signatory countries later that year, on October 10, 1967. As of June 2017, 105 countries had ratified the Treaty. https://oxfordre.com/planetaryscience/view/10.1093/acrefore/9780190647926.001.0001/acrefore-9780190647926-e-43. Nearly two dozen countries have signed it, but not yet completed the ratification process. wikipedia.org/wiki/Outer_Space_Treaty.

[24] Reinstein, *Owning Outer Space, supra* note 1, at 66.

[25] Coffey, Note, *Establishing a Legal Framework for Property Rights to Natural Resources in Outer Space, supra* note 10, at 127.

[26] Other outer space treaties include Convention on the International Liability for Damage Caused by Space Objects, *opened for signature* Mar. 29, 1972, 24 U.S.T. 2389, 961 U.N.T.S. 187; Agreement on the Rescue of Astronauts, the Return of Astronauts and the Return of Objects Launched into Outer Space, *opened for signature* Apr. 22, 1968, 19 U.S.T. 7570, 672 U.N.T.S. 119.

[27] *Id.* (citing Outer Space Treaty, *supra* note 119, arts. I–II) (emphasis added).

[28] Brehm, *Private Property in Outer Space, supra* note 11, at 357.

the rise of private space flight and the push by private companies to engage in commercial activities in outer space, or the legal and equitable problems these would create. "Concerns over space imperialism were the main impetus for the central provision of the OST," the principle of "nonappropriation of space by Nation-States."[29] This principle makes any claim exclusive jurisdiction over any part of outer space impermissible under international law.[30]

The Moon Treaty reiterates the OST's designation of space for the exploration and use of all nations and extends the ban against physical appropriation of celestial bodies to non governmental entities.[31] The Moon Treaty elevates the right to explore and use the Moon for scientific benefit above private property rights and declares the Moon to be part of *the common heritage of all mankind*.[32] However, the failure of the United States and Russia to ratify the Moon Treaty and the limited number of signatories severely limits its "practical" effect.[33]

Application of the Moon Treaty's declaration that "the moon and its natural resources are the *common heritage of mankind* could restrict countries to managing resources in designated international zones governed by international law.[34] Other clauses require the equitable apportionment of the benefits from exploitation of the moon, including to non-spacefaring countries, and the protection and preservation of these resources to *benefit all mankind*.[35]

The phrase *province of all mankind* in the OST and the phrase *common heritage of mankind* in the Moon Treaty are controversial and subject to conflicting interpretations. Non spacefaring and less developed countries favor an interpretation that creates "common property" under "common management," with exploited resources distributed *equally* to all nations, regardless of which nation actually funds the effort. Developed countries resist that interpretation, considering it unfair since they spent the time and money developing the technology that enables the harvesting of resources and funded the expeditions to gather them, while non developed nations have contributed little or nothing to the effort.[36]

PRIVATE OWNERSHIP OF PLANETARY RESOURCES

Having a private property regime in outer space might reduce wasteful use of space resources; while allowing property owners to transfer celestial property, adds to existing incentives to develop them. Private property would enable colonization of celestial bodies, like the Moon, and could inspire the commercial confidence necessary to attract the enormous investments needed for tourism, settlement, and mining. Without the right to gain the proceeds from the sale of space resources, companies may be unwilling to undertake the risks implicit in all space

---

[29] Elliott Reavan, Comment, *The United States Commercial Space Launch Competitiveness Act: The Creation of Private Space Property Rights and the Omission of the Right to Freedom from Harmful Interference*, 94 WASH. U.L. REV. 238, 243 (2016).

[30] Johnson, *Limits on the Giant Leap for Mankind*, *supra* note 33, at 1501.

[31] Moon Treaty, *supra* note22, art. 11 ("neither the surface nor the subsurface of the [m]oon, nor any part thereof or natural resources in place, shall become property of any State, international intergovernmental or non-governmental organization, national organization or non-governmental entity or of any natural person.").

[32] Mac Whorter, *Sustainable Mining*, *supra* note 12, at 664.

[33] David Johnson, Comment, *Limits on the Giant Leap for Mankind: Legal Ambiguities of Extraterrestrial Resource Extraction*, 26 Am. U. Int'l L. Rev. 1477, 1497–98 (2011) (Limited state practice under the Treaty prevents considering the "common heritage doctrine" embodied in it an enforceable legal custom).

[34] Buxton, *Property in Outer Space*, *supra* note 6, at 691–92.

[35] *See* Moon Treaty, *supra* note 22, art. 11.

[36] *See generally* Buxton, *Property in Outer Space*, *supra* note 6, at 692–93 (for additional development of these arguments).

travel. The lack of a stable private property regime in outer space also means that space settlements will not be able to claim sufficient land to sell profitably and thus survive.

Private property exacerbates income disparities and economic tensions among individuals. The lack of static or physical boundaries makes it difficult to define and defend boundaries in outer space. But, any recognition of private property claims would violate both the OST and Moon treaties' ban on the appropriation of space resources. And allowing private ownership of space resources disregards the concerns of developing nations, who would be quickly priced out of the market – running afoul of the OST's hortatory language that outer space and its resources shall be the *province of all mankind*.

A private property regime might encourage application of first possession rules, vesting rights in the first possessor.[37] Applying the rules to commercial enterprises, without a means for establishing property boundaries, could result in disputes among competing property owners.[38] These could trigger a race for property in outer space.[39] If the disputants are nations, the result might be war. This "right of first grab"[40] could transfer current disparities in global wealth distribution on Earth to space. At the point at which non spacefaring countries develop the technical capability and capital to fund any meaningful initiatives, the most accessible and valuable resources will have been locked up by the rich.

There are various ways around the ban against private property in space, such as creating less than full fee ownership property regimes, like defeasible fees, that limit the property owner's right to alienate their property. Leases, licenses, easements, and covenants are other types of reversionary interests that might work in outer space without violating international laws. Since less than a full fee interest is conveyed, the conveyance may not be permanent and may be heavily restricted.[41] But, each situation is predicated on some entity initially owning or holding the property in question, which would violate the terms of international space law unless the entity was some international institution. These can be costly to establish and maintain.

The idea of extending terrestrial property law to outer space is also flawed because it allows powerful countries to control activities in outer space through their domestic laws and greater resources, thus potentially extending disparities between have and have-not nations into the space age.[42] This idea risks violation of the OST's *province of all mankind* principle because developing nations may not be able to compete under the rules of more powerful countries. Thus, while establishing a private property regime in outer space might encourage development of celestial resources, it is hard to design a way around the ban against appropriating property and establish a system that is both workable and protects the interests of less developed countries.

COMMON OWNERSHIP OF PLANETARY RESOURCES

An alternative approach is managing outer space as a *commons*. The claim that something is a commons fits comfortably with the idea that outer space is the "province of all mankind." Early space treaties viewed space as a commons, beyond the possession and control of any country or

[37] Application off the doctrine of first possession would enable a country to claim any territory it discovered and open it just to its own citizens or to the entire international community. Abrams, *First Contact*, *supra* note 17, at 811.
[38] *Id.* at 810–11
[39] Reinstein, *Owning Outer Space*, *supra* note 1, at 84–85.
[40] *Id.* at 64.
[41] *See* Babcock, *The Public Trust Doctrine, Outer Space, and the Global Commons: Time to Call Home ET*, 69 Syr. L. Rev. 191, 247–57 (2019) (for a more robust discussion of these different forms of ownership).
[42] *See generally* Reinstein, *Owning Outer Space* (arguing against extending the rule of first possession and the concept of private property law into outer space), *supra* note 1.

individual.[43] There are useful commonalities between outer space and terrestrial commons, like the oceans and Antarctica, that function as international areas in which no individual nation has a sovereign claim.

But, the impulse of commons' users to pursue their self-interests must be restrained, lest common resources be harmed or exhausted.[44] The problem of incompatible commons' uses, which can lead to rivalry,[45] may be particularly true in outer space, where its openness and the potential wealth of its resources is already attracting users with competing ideas about how these resources should be exploited. Too many entities vying for the same space resources could lead to accidents and serious conflict – conditions the space treaties are intended to avoid.

"Informal governance" can "privatize" common pool resources, like the "'lobster gangs' chronicled by James Acheson."[46] Ostrom writes about how well-defined and self-governing communities can protect valuable common pool resources from over-consumption or damage."[47] She promotes "a range of management techniques specific to that community in order to redirect the march towards total exhaustion."[48] But, none of these approaches appears appropriate for circumstances in outer space where small groups, like Acheson's lobster gangs or Ostrom's well-defined communities, are unlikely to form around large scale common pool resources or where communication among entities will be intermittent making any sharing of informal management approaches unlikely.[49]

Since there is no right to exclude any member from a commons, a user of common pool resources has no incentive to preserve them because if she refrains, her co-users will not.[50] The result is an "open access resource vulnerable to the tragic conditions of rivalry, overexploitation, and degradation,"[51] as discussed above. Any user of communal property, who desired to manage the commons sub optimally to preserve it for future generations, would face the potentially

---

[43] Taylor, *Tragedy of the Space Commons*, *supra* note 1, at 259–60.

[44] Garett Hardin, *The Tragedy of the Commons*, 162 Science 1243–48 (Dec. 13, 1968).

[45] Sheila R. Foster & Christian Iaione, *The City as Commons*, 34 Yale L. & Pol'y Rev. 281, 298 (2016).

[46] James M. Acheson, *The Lobster Fiefs Revisited: Economic and Ecological Effects of Territoriality in the Maine Lobster Industry*, in THE QUESTION OF THE COMMONS: CULTURE AND ECOLOGY OF COMMUNAL RESOURCES (eds. McCay & Acheson, Univ. AZ Press 1990) 37–65 (discussing private property's emergence in the Maine lobster fishing industry and avoidance of Hardin's tragedy of the commons).

[47] Zachary C. M. Arnold, *Against the Tide: Connecticut Oystering, Hybrid Property, and the Survival of the Commons*, Note, 124 YALE L.J. 1206, 1215 (2015) (Elinor Ostrom argues that the community enjoying access to the commons must be well defined and self-governed to enable it to define rights, exclude outsiders, and monitor and discipline insiders). *See also* Elinor Ostrom, Institutional Arrangements for Resolving the Commons Dilemma: Some Contending Approaches, in THE QUESTION OF THE COMMONS: CULTURE AND ECOLOGY OF COMMUNAL RESOURCES (eds. McCay & Acheson, Univ. AZ Press 1990) 250–65 (using two case studies to examine the validity of theoretical statements about the commons); Pammela Quinn Saunders, *A Sea Change off the Coast of Maine; Common Pool Resources as Cultural Property*, 60 EMORY L. REV. 1323, 1369 (2011) ("research by social scientists concludes that, under the right conditions, groups can cooperate and self-regulate to sustainably manage CPRs under their control.").

[48] Pearl, *The Tragedy of the Vital Commons*, *supra* note 8, at 1047. *See also* Foster & Iaione, *The City as Commons*, *supra* note 45, at 289 ("Hardin famously postulated that threats of degradation and destruction of the commons give rise to either a system of centralized public regulation or the imposition of private property rights in order to avoid the 'tragedy.' Ostrom's groundbreaking work, on the other hand, demonstrated that there are options for commons management that are neither exclusively public nor exclusively private. Ostrom identified groups of users who were able to cooperate to create and enforce rules for using and managing natural resources – such as grazing land, fisheries, forests and irrigation waters – using "rich mixtures of public and private instrumentalities.").

[49] Foster & Iaione, *The City as Commons*, *supra* note 45, at 325 (commenting that "Ostrom's study focused on small-scale resources affecting a relatively small number of persons (50–15,000) who are heavily dependent on the resource for economic returns").

[50] *See* Pearl, *The Tragedy of the Vital Commons*, *supra* note 8, at 1053 ("The absence of the right to exclude is what allows the tragedy of the 'privatized commons' to exist.").

[51] *Id.*, *supra* note 50, at 287.

insurmountable transaction cost of having to negotiate with members of the community who wanted to use it now.[52] Exiting a commons for any reason, even when group action causes individual harm, is hard.[53] Therefore, approaches based on private property and commons theory are both flawed and could create implementation problems in outer space.

PROPERTY MANAGEMENT APPROACHES THAT MIGHT WORK IN EITHER OWNERSHIP REGIME

There are various ways to manage property in outer space, which might work in a private or common property regime. However, any approach would have to allow the profitable development of outer space equitably and sustainably, as well as be efficient, fair, cost effective, and easy to implement and enforce. Above all, it must not run afoul of international law.

One idea is to establish *economic development zones*. Under this approach, international organizations would allocate areas on celestial bodies to various countries for the construction of structures, from which exclusive economic zones would radiate.[54] Alternatively, an international organization might divide celestial bodies into shares for each country to exploit. Separating incompatible land uses in outer space might avoid negative spillovers from the co-location of conflicting uses,[55] and could be used to exclude entities which might over-consume a common resource, leaving other users worse off. This latter feature of the proposal, however, conflicts with the OST's free exploration and use principles.[56]

The proposal also requires an international institution to administer the system, which would be expensive to create and maintain.[57] Spending money to create a new administrative authority, which might otherwise have helped poorer countries develop the capacity to participate in outer space. Additionally, it would be technically difficult to monitor and enforce what happens within these distant zones. And, depending on the perceived "fairness" of the zones and the allocation process, the proposal could lead to "discord" among various countries, straining any civility norms previously established among spacefaring nations.

Having a *lottery or an auction* of "ownership rights," or establishing a system of *tradable credits* might lessen the equity and technical problems with the economic zone management proposal. While an auction theoretically would open up the market in development rights to non space-faring nations, in practice, only the wealthy nations would be able to effectively bid on and secure those rights.[58] However, the idea of tradable credits might work.[59]

Under an outer space trading system, participant nations, regardless of their space faring capacity, would be allotted a fixed number of resource development credits, allowing the credit holder to extract a certain tonnage of materials or develop a fixed amount of celestial surface, during a specified time period.[60] The credits could apply to the amount of the resource a

---

[52] Pearl, *The Tragedy of the Vital Commons, supra* note 8, at 1029.

[53] *Id.* at 1035–36.

[54] Stephen DiMaria, Note, *Starships and Enterprise: Private Spaceflight Companies' Property Rights and the U.S. Commercial Space Launch Competitiveness Act*, 90 St. John's L. Rev., 415, 435 (2016).

[55] Foster & Iaione, *The City as Commons, supra* note 45, at 311–12.

[56] DiMaria, *Starships and Enterprise, supra* note 54, at 437.

[57] Coffey, *Establishing a Legal Framework for Property Rights to Natural Resources in Outer Space, supra* note 10, at 136.

[58] *See* Reinstein *Owning Outer Space, supra* note 1, at 92 (suggesting auctions might offer a "middle ground between laissez faire privatization of space development and a belief that space is the equal birthright of all humanity").

[59] *See* Taylor, *Tragedy of the Space Commons, supra* note 1, at 279 (concluding tradable allowances offer the "most promising solution to the tragedy of the space commons" because they can be more cost-effective, can generate more innovation, and might enable greater global participation than the other potential resource management strategies).

[60] Coffey, *Establishing a Legal Framework for Property Rights to Natural Resources in Outer Space, supra* note 10, at 138.

participant was allowed to extract, regardless of location, or could be tied to a particular area of a celestial body. Participants could buy credits from and sell them to other participants.[61] The proposal would allow developing nations to benefit from space exploration and exploitation, and participants would run the market reducing the need for an administering international agency.

Even though market participants would run the market, an international institution will be needed to allocate tradable credits and devise an allocation methodology that assures non-space-faring nations receive some benefit. International oversight also will be needed to ensure that nations do not exceed their allotted credits. And tradable credits would need to be anchored by some form of authorization, like a permit, creating another need for a central administrative body.

While the idea of tradable development credits is consistent with international law, could assure equitable distribution of the benefits of space development, and provide sufficient incentives for development of these resources, the approach may be too administratively encumbered.

The public trust doctrine offers another approach for managing an open access commons.[62] Under this doctrine, the sovereign holds certain common properties in trust in perpetuity for the free and unimpeded use of the general public. The public's right of access to and use of trust resources is never lost, and neither the government nor private individuals can alienate or otherwise adversely affect those resources unless for a comparable public purpose. Showing its adaptability, supporters of the doctrine are currently arguing in court that it applies to the atmosphere.[63]

The doctrine places on governments an affirmative, ongoing duty to safeguard the perpetual preservation of trust resources for the benefit of the general public, limiting the sovereign's power on behalf of both present and future entities. It directs the government not to manage them for private gain and applies to private as well as public resources. Uses of trust resources that are inconsistent with the doctrine can be rescinded. The doctrine effectively places a permanent easement over trust resources that burdens their ownership with an overriding public interest in their preservation. Thus, the public trust doctrine protects the "people's common heritage,"[64] just as the Moon Treaty protects outer space as part of the common heritage of mankind.

A doctrine that imposes an enforceable perpetual duty on the sovereign to preserve trust resources, prevents their alienation for private benefit, and assures public access to them seems a particularly apt property management tool in outer space. The fact that public access to trust resources is so central to the doctrine[65] is consistent with international space law's open access principles. It avoids the problems of alienation and exclusion associated with private property management approaches and does not require the creation of a new administrative authority, as anyone can invoke the doctrine. Of all the management approaches discussed, the public trust doctrine seems the most suited to managing property in outer space.

---

[61] The acid rain program in the Clean Air Act is a model for this approach. *See* 42 U.S.C. §§ 7651a–7651o (2012).

[62] *See generally* Babcock *Time to call Home ET, supra* note 41 at 1066–69 (discussing key elements of the public trust doctrine).

[63] *See generally* Michael C. Blumm & Mary Christina Wood, *"No Ordinary Lawsuit"*; *Climate Change Due Process, and the Public Trust Doctrine*, 67 Am. Univ. L. Rev. 1 (2017).

[64] *Nat'l Audubon Soc'y v. Superior Court of Alpine County (Mono Lake Case)*, 658 P.2d 709, 724 (Cal. 1983) ("The public trust is more than an affirmation of state power to use public property for public purposes. It is an affirmation of the duty of the state to protect the people's common heritage[,]... surrendering that right ... only in rare cases when the abandonment of that right is consistent with the purpose of the trust.").

[65] *See Ill. Cent. R.R. Co. v. Illinois*, 146 U.S. 387, 433 (1892) (Since "absolute private dominion over property impressed with the public trust" interferes with public access, it can never be granted unless it is in the public interest to do so.).

However, the doctrine provides no incentives for development of trust resources.[66] Its traditional use has been to curtail development, making it potentially a counter productive solution to the beneficial development of outer space. Allowing limited use of private property management approaches, like tradable development credits, might buffer that effect – a form of overlapping hybridity[67] between one type of property, a commons, and a management regime from another, private property, enabled by application of the public trust doctrine. This approach might allow development of outer space, while assuring that it will not just be profitable for a few; rather, space's development will be sustainable and equitable, ideally for all.

CONCLUSION

Guided by the insights of Elinor Ostrom, this chapter proposes that viewing outer space as a commons will lead to a durable, equitable management regime where the wealthy are neither able to accumulate nor control the resources that space has to offer nor over exploit them. Using the public trust doctrine, supplemented by tradable development credits, as the preferred management approach will help assure that result and allow the development of space for the "benefit of all mankind."

[66] *See* Hope M. Babcock, *Using the Federal Public Trust Doctrine to Fill Gaps in the Legal Systems Protecting Migrating Wildlife from the Effects of Climate Change*, 95 NEB. L. REV. 649, 697–700 (2017) (discussing ways to modify the doctrine to reduce controversy associated with its application, none of which has direct relevance to the challenge of creating incentives for resource development. But, to the extent the proposals limit the use of the doctrine by tethering it to public lands, releasing lands from its strictures to the extent those lands no longer need to be protected by the doctrine because some other form of protection is available or because the land has dropped out of commons ownership, or the entities covered by the doctrines application have agreed to take protective steps that eliminate some of the problems associate with the doctrine, like externalities, making continued application of the doctrine unnecessary, then the ideas set forth in the referenced article might have some utility).

[67] For a closer look at the concept of hybridity, *see* Babcock, *Time to Call Home ET*, *supra* note 41, at 243.

23

A Biotechnology "Regulatory Commons" Problem

David M. Forman

Elinor Ostrom's *Governing The Commons* "continues to have a broad appeal in the legal academy" particularly in the areas of property theory, natural resource/environmental law, and intellectual property.[1] This chapter interrogates legal scholar William Buzbee's suggestion that Ostrom neglected a pervasive "regulatory commons" problem: jurisdictional mismatch and overlap in fragmented legal regimes that provide strong incentives for regulatory inaction.[2] The common resources exposed to dysfunction and underutilization in such regimes are *regulatory opportunities* to address social ills at federal, state and local levels.[3]

Focused upon reconciling his regulatory commons inaction theory with prominent over-regulation hypotheses, Buzbee dismisses examples of greater local rather than federal government protection.[4] Although Buzbee concedes that preserving local authority can help avoid regulatory failure in an *ideal* world, his subsequent writings reference Ostrom just once: calling Ostrom the most optimistic counter to his skepticism about achieving intergenerational equity given individual and political economic tendencies.[5] By comparison, other legal scholars explicitly rely upon Ostrom for: more precautionary approaches to natural resources management that incorporate recreational, ecological and spiritually motivated value systems;[6] reduction of barriers prohibiting local governments from sustainably managing natural resources;[7] and, shifting to decentralized, multi-modal, networked forms of

---

[1] Carol M. Rose, "Ostrom and the Lawyers: The Impact of Governing the Commons on the American Legal Academy," *International Journal of Commons* 5 (2011): 28, 29n1, 32.

[2] William W. Buzbee, "Regulatory Commons: A Theory of Regulatory Gaps," *Iowa Law Review* 89 (2003): 6nn6–7, 17n52 (citing Elinor Ostrom, *Governing the Commons: The Evolution of Institutions for Collective Action* (New York: Cambridge Univ. Press, 1990): 215–16).

[3] Ibid., 5, 22.

[4] Ibid., 4, 37–48; William W. Buzbee, "The Regulatory Fragmentation Continuum, Westway and the Challenges of Regional Growth," *Journal of Law and Policy* 21 (2005): 352n65–66; William W. Buzbee, "Contextual Environmental Federalism," *New York University Environmental Law Journal* 14 (2005): 110–11.

[5] Buzbee, "Regulatory Commons," 64; William W. Buzbee, "Preemption Hard Look Review, Regulatory Interaction, and the Quest for Stewardship and Intergenerational Equity," *George Washington Law Review* 77 (2009): 1533n35.

[6] Robin Kundis Craig, "Trickster Law: Promoting Resilience and Adaptive Governance by Allowing Other Perspectives on Natural Resource Management," *Arizona Journal of Environmental Law & Policy* 9 (2019); ibid., 140n1 (citing Thomas Dietz, Elinor Ostrom and Paul C. Stern, "The Struggle to Govern the Commons," *Science* 302, issue 5652 (2003): 1907–8).

[7] Jonathan Rosenbloom, "Local Governments and Global Commons," *Brigham Young University Law Review* 2014; ibid., 1502n44 (quoting Dietz et al.).

governance.[8] This chapter joins the fray by exploring Hawai'i's ongoing efforts to address a biotechnology regulatory commons problem.

CRITICALLY ANALYZING THE BIOTECHNOLOGY REGULATORY COMMONS

Buzbee's regulatory commons scholarship briefly references bioengineered foods and plant genetic resources.[9] US regulation of genetically engineered ("GE") seed and/or genetically modified organisms ("GMO") is based on assumptions that such crops are "substantially equivalent" to conventional crops; accordingly, restrictions may only be imposed if regulators prove GE/GMO crops are unsafe – even though the regulatory assumptions are scientifically indefensible.[10] Meanwhile, states may review GE/GMO field test permit applications and assert "special need"[11] to protect local interests, but that power is hampered by budgetary constraints and redaction of confidential business information.[12]

Conceding that regulation primarily serves the regulated,[13] Buzbee warns about "rare" but pervasive regulatory underkill risks when more protective local actions (including citizen enforcement) are preempted – or trumped – by higher levels of government.[14] Under "preemption" doctrine, laws passed by higher authorities expressly or implicitly displace conflicting laws passed by lower authorities. *Federal* preemption is rooted in the US Constitution's supremacy clause (Article VI),[15] while *state* preemption limits Tenth Amendment "police powers" (and other reserved authority) otherwise delegable to local governments.[16]

To avoid regulatory underkill, Buzbee stresses: rigorous contextual analysis;[17] avoiding simplistic views about regulatory fragmentation;[18] skepticism about government, while retaining different roles;[19] along with open, transparent and deliberative action by regulators.[20] Accordingly, this chapter applies "contextual legal analysis" to judicial opinions invalidating three distinct Hawai'i ordinances. Contextual legal analysis[21] acknowledges the failure of legal formalism[22] to fully

[8] Tracey M. Roberts,"Innovations in Governance: A Functional Typology of Private Governance Institutions," *Duke Environmental Law & Policy Forum* 22 (2011): 134n299 (citing Elinor Ostrom, "A Diagnostic Approach for Going Beyond Panaceas," *Proceedings of the National Academy of Sciences* 104 (2007): 15,181).

[9] Buzbee, "Regulatory Commons," 9n9; Buzbee, "Contextual Environmental Federalism," 126; Buzbee, "Regulatory Fragmentation," 341n47.

[10] David M. Forman, "Marooned in the Doldrums While Ignoring Indigenous Ecological Knowledge: Attempting to Regulate Pesticide Use in Hawai'i," in *Legal Actions for Future Generations*, eds. Emilie Gaillard & David M. Forman (Brussels: Peter Lang, 2020): 268–73.

[11] Ibid., 274n54.

[12] Ibid., 273–75.

[13] Buzbee, "Contextual Environmental Federalism," 125–27.

[14] Ibid., 126–29.

[15] Stephen A. Gardbaum, "The Nature of Preemption," *Cornell Law Review* 79 (1994): 769.

[16] *See, e.g.,* Hawai'i Revised Statutes ("HRS") § 46-1.5(13).

[17] Buzbee, "Contextual Environmental Federalism," 129.

[18] Buzbee, "Regulatory Fragmentation," 363.

[19] Buzbee, "Asymmetrical Regulation," 169.

[20] Buzbee, "Preemption," 1580.

[21] D. Kapua'ala Sproat, "*Wai* through *Kānāwai*: Water for Hawai'i's Streams and Justice for Hawaiian Communities," *Marquette Law Review* 95 (2011): 154–72; D. Kapua'ala Sproat, "Where Justice Flows Like Water: The Moon Court's Role in Illuminating Hawai'i Water Law," *University of Hawai'i Law Review* 33 (2011): 547nn75–77.

[22] "Legal formalism" contends that non-legal reasoning is irrelevant, because law is rationally determinate, judging is mechanical, and legal reasoning is autonomous — leading to unique outcomes. Sproat, "*Wai* through *Kānāwai*," 134n31, 154.

consider social factors that impede judicial ability to render just decisions and public understanding of how law shapes society, thus hindering restorative justice.[23]

Despite Buzbee's assurances about rare displacement of protective local action, the US Court of Appeals for the Ninth Circuit ("Ninth Circuit") applied preemption doctrine to three local Hawaiʻi ordinances targeting perceived GE/GMO crop-related harms.[24] These court rulings facilitate a regulatory commons tragedy by enforcing limitations on municipal power rooted in an ideology that prevents local governments from performing functions supposedly better left to market forces or Hobbesian regulation.[25] As a result, private enterprise continues to be privileged by a centralized management scheme full of federal and state gaps.[26]

LEGAL FORMALISM FAVORS PRIVATE INDUSTRY

Syngenta Seeds I briefly summarizes Kauaʻi County Ordinance 960, which required commercial farmers to: maintain buffer zones with certain surrounding properties when applying pesticides to crops; provide pre- and post-application notices; and, file annual reports disclosing GE crop cultivation. Citing Hawaiʻi Revised Statutes ("HRS") § 46–1.5(13)'s prohibition on counties enacting ordinances to protect health, life or property inconsistent with state statutory schemes, the Ninth Circuit concluded that Hawaiʻi's Pesticides Law (HRS chapter 149A) comprehensively regulates pesticides with implicit intent to preempt local pesticide regulation like Ordinance 960's general crop reporting provisions. Similarly, the unpublished[27] *Syngenta Seeds II* opinion held the ordinance's GMO reporting requirement implicitly preempted by other state laws: HRS chapters 141 (the state Department of Agriculture ("HDOA") enabling act), 150 (Seed Law), 150A (Plant Quarantine Law), 152 (Noxious Weed Control), and 194 (Invasive Species Council).

Another unpublished Ninth Circuit decision, *Hawaiʻi Papaya Industry*, explains that Hawaiʻi County Ordinance 13-121 grandfathered existing GE/GMOs from its ban on open air testing and open air cultivation, propagation, or development of such crops/plants. The ordinance sought to prevent GE to non-GE plant pollination and preserve the island's vulnerable ecosystem, while promoting the cultural heritage of indigenous agricultural practices. Noting substantial similarities with *Atay* (below) and the *Syngenta Seeds* cases, the court invalidated Ordinance 13-121 based on express federal and implied state law preemption principles.

In *Atay*, the Ninth Circuit describes a Maui County ordinance as "banning" cultivation and testing of GE plants rather than a "Temporary Moratorium," because amendment or repeal would require: an Environmental and Public Health Impacts Study ("EPHIS"); public hearing; *and* a two-thirds County Council vote establishing significant benefit without significant harm. The ordinance sought to protect vulnerable ecosystems and indigenous cultural heritage (as well as organic and non-GE farmers) from transgenic contamination and pesticides. In addition to

---

[23] Ibid., 155.

[24] Atay v. County of Maui, 842 F.3d 688 (9th Cir. 2016); Syngenta Seeds, Inc. v. County of [Kauaʻi] (*Syngenta Seeds I*), 842 F.3d 669 (9th Cir. 2016); Hawaiʻi Papaya Indus. Ass'n v. County of [Hawaiʻi] (*Hawaiʻi Papaya Industry*), 666 F. App'x 631 (9th Cir. 2016); Syngenta Seeds, Inc. v. County of [Kauaʻi] (*Syngenta Seeds II*), 664 F. App'x 669 (9th Cir. 2016).

[25] *Compare* S. Candice Hoke, "Preemption Pathologies and Civic Republican Values," *Boston University Law Review* 71 (1991): 685, 696n43, *with* Blake Hudson and Jonathan Rosenbloom," Uncommon Approaches to Commons Problems: Nested Governance Commons and Climate Change," *Hastings Law Journal* 64 (2013): 1285-86nn19–28.

[26] Forman, "Marooned," 266n20, 268–75; Heather Hosmer, "Outgrowing Agency Oversight: Genetically Modified Crops and the Regulatory Commons Theory," *The Georgetown International Environmental Law Review* 25 (2013).

[27] Unpublished rulings only bind the parties, but may be cited for persuasive value by others.

civil penalties and criminal liability, the ordinance authorized entry onto private property, removal of GE organisms at the violator's expense, and citizen enforcement.

For non-commercialized plants, the Ninth Circuit concluded that strict inspection and reporting requirements under the federal Plant Protection Act expressly preempted the ordinance. A comprehensive state statutory scheme impliedly preempted commercialized plants no longer regulated under federal law. Relying on *Syngenta Seeds I*, the Ninth Circuit upheld the lower court's refusal to: return the case to state court; allow discovery of information concerning the scope of GE regulations; or, ask the Hawai'i Supreme Court to decide the implied state law preemption question.

CONTEXTUAL LEGAL ANALYSIS EXPOSES RESTORATIVE JUSTICE FAILURES

The three county ordinances were not "one-size-fits-all approaches, but rather exercises in independent local governance."[28]

Absent any GE/GMO seed company presence on the island, Hawai'i County's May 2013 bill preceded the Kaua'i (June) and Maui (November) proposals. Following an industry-devastating Papaya Ringspot Virus outbreak: Hawai'i County GE/GMO field trials began in 1992; government-approved plantings commenced in 1998; and GE/GMO papaya eventually covered 75% of commercial papaya plantings. In 2008, the Hawai'i County Council overrode a mayoral veto and prohibited GE/GMO taro and coffee.[29] 2012 protests targeted a dairy farm growing GE/GMO corn for its cows; additional community concerns included county workers' allegedly indiscriminate off-label spraying of restricted use pesticides. During the four-year period before adopting Hawai'i County Ordinance 13-121 in mid-November 2013 (with mayoral support), acres of GE/GMO papaya trees were vandalized three separate times.

Hawai'i County Ordinance 13-121 banned GE/GMO crops and plants with exceptions for (i) existing operations that paid a nominal fee to register their locations, and (ii) emergencies involving non-GE/GMO crops harmed by plant pestilence. Initial legislative findings cite Hawai'i Constitution Article XI, §§ 1 and 9 (discussed below) as authority for protecting public and private property along with surface waters, vulnerable watersheds, and the Island's coastal waters. The ordinance's express purposes included: protecting non-genetically modified crops and plants from cross pollination, promoting the cultural heritage of indigenous agricultural practices, and preventing the transfer or uncontrolled spread of GE organisms.

Enacted over mayoral veto three days before the Hawai'i County ordinance,[30] Kaua'i County Ordinance 960 affected more than half the state's total acreage of GE/GMO seed crops. Proponents relied in part on pesticide use documented from lawsuits filed against Pioneer Hi-Bred ("Pioneer") on behalf of 150 Kaua'i residents, led by *kalo* (taro) farmer John A'ana, and a parallel case involving 17 additional plaintiffs. The company removed the *Aana* [sic]/*Casey* lawsuits from state to federal court under the so-called Class Action Fairness Act.[31] This euphemistically titled legislation employs neutral efficiency language while sharply

---

[28] James Pollack, "Case Comment: *Atay v. County of Maui*," *Harvard Environmental Law Review* 42 (2018): 314.

[29] Hawai'i County Code §§ 14-90 to -95 (2008).

[30] GaryHooser's Blog, "An almost complete history of Bill No. 2491" (Oct. 24, 2015); Kevin Tongg, "Poisons in Our Communities: Environmental Justice's Role in Regulating Hawai'i's Biotechnology Industry," *University of Hawai'i Law Review* 40 (2018): 169–70nn136–40.

[31] 2012 WL 3542503 (D. Haw. July 24, 2012), *aff'd*, 2013 WL 1817264 (D. Haw. Apr. 26, 2013).

constricting court access and development of legal claims to the detriment of less powerful social groups.[32]

The federal magistrate judge[33] assigned to handle the *Aana/Casey* cases – and all three lawsuits challenging the county ordinances – narrowly interpreted state negligence law in dismissing multiple claims. For example, the magistrate concluded that Hawai'i's Pesticides Law (HRS chapter 149A) and Air Pollution Control Act (HRS chapter 342B) do not provide for citizen enforcement, even though Hawai'i law clearly provides that laws relating to environmental quality define a self-executing[34] constitutional right to a clean and healthful environment.[35]

The magistrate also prohibited evidence or argument regarding health and environmental effects of Pioneer's pesticide use,[36] explaining that such testimony would exponentially increase trial length and complexity while likely causing jury confusion.[37] In September 2013, a broad coalition of supporters organized the largest march in Kaua'i history – dubbed the "Mana March" (*mana* meaning spiritual energy and healing power) – a month after the magistrate's dismissal order.[38] As adopted in mid-November, Ordinance 960's initial legislative finding acknowledged rights of future generations and constitutional public trust obligations. The ordinance neither banned GE/GMO seed operations, nor imposed a temporary moratorium. Instead, it required Mandatory Disclosure of Restricted Use Pesticides ("RUPs") and GMOs, Pesticide Buffer Zones, and an EPHIS (along with penalties for non-compliance) utilizing a community-based Joint Fact[-]Finding Group ("JFFG").

The so-called Maui Ordinance was never formally codified. A late-November 2013 bill proposed buffer zones, mandatory disclosure of pesticide use and GMOs, along with a "Temporary Moratorium." Following the bill's defeat, proponent SHAKA Movement (Sustainable Hawaiian Agriculture for Keiki and ʻĀina – respectively, "child" and "land that feeds") organized a major rally supporting the county's first citizens' initiative. An effort by seed companies to strike the question from the November 2014 ballot failed,[39] and the initiative passed by a margin of 1,007 votes (50% for, 48% against) notwithstanding a record-setting $7.9 million campaign funded primarily by Monsanto (later acquired by Bayer in 2018) against what the company described as a "ban on farming."

---

[32] Eric K. Yamamoto, "Critical Procedure: ADR and the Justices' 'Second Wave' Constriction of Court Access and Claim Development," *Southern Methodist University Law Review* 70 (2017): 776.

[33] Based on recommendations from a citizens' merit screening committee, magistrates are appointed by majority vote of active district court judges – who are, themselves, nominated by the president then confirmed by the United States Senate.

[34] Constitutional provisions are "self-executing" absent any indication that supplemental legislation was intended to make them operative.

[35] In re Application of Maui Elec. Co., 408 P.3d 1 (Haw. 2017) (citing Haw. Const. art. XI, § 9); County of Hawai'i v. Ala Loop Homeowners, 235 P.3d 1103 (Haw. 2010); Haw. Const. art XVI, § 16 (providing that constitutional provisions "shall be self-executing to the fullest extent that their respective natures permit").

[36] *Aana/Casey*, 2014 WL 4244221 (D. Haw. Aug. 26, 2014), *reconsideration denied*, 2014 WL 5528373 (D. Haw. Oct. 31, 2014). One day earlier, the magistrate barred Kaua'i Ordinance 960 from taking effect citing implied state preemption. *Syngenta Seeds*, 2014 WL 4216022 (D. Haw. Aug. 25, 2014).

[37] Fifteen bellwether plaintiffs eventually obtained a $500,000+ jury verdict against Pioneer. *Aana/Casey*, Doc. No. 1088 (D. Haw. May 8, 2015). Most of the remaining 100-plus plaintiffs settled for a confidential amount. Email from attorney Kyle Smith to author (May 18, 2018).

[38] Le'a Malia Kanehe, "Indigenous Cultural Property," in *Native Hawaiian Law: A Treatise*, Melody MacKenzie, et al., eds. (Honolulu, Kamehameha Publishing, 2015): 1066n483; ibid., 1058–1060 (discussing prior cultural opposition to GE taro).

[39] Transcript of Proceedings, Taal v. Mateo, Civ. No. 14-1-0506(1) (Haw. 2d Cir. Sep. 15, 2014).

Interestingly, the state's first GE/GMO seed nurseries arrived in Moloka'i (Maui County) in 1966.[40] Following cultural protests involving GE/GMO taro in the early 2000's,[41] well-known Native Hawaiian activist Walter Ritte organized another protest lamenting lack of regulatory transparency and community participation. Ritte later verbally attacked the island's largest employer (Monsanto) for its adverse impact on the environment compared with Moloka'i's history of self-sufficiency. Perhaps a millennium ago, the traditional Native Hawaiian *Moku* (District or Region) system of localized biocultural resource management originated on Moloka'i – and recently reemerged.[42] The *Moku* system's sophistication far exceeds both the environmental impact assessment process, and Ostrom's design principles for managing commons resources.[43] Since 2012, a newly formed 'Aha Moku [District Council] Advisory Committee ("AMAC") has proactively collaborated with state, county and federal agencies on public trust resource management.[44] AMAC recognizes itself as a "global leader in the integration of Indigenous resource management models into modern legal and regulatory structures."[45]

This innovative *Moku* approach furthers reconciliation and restorative justice principles enshrined in voter-ratified 1978 Hawai'i constitutional amendments.[46]

RESTORATIVE JUSTICE UNDER THE HAWAI'I CONSTITUTION

In greater detail than my previous publications,[47] this chapter probes a missed opportunity to evaluate biotechnology regulation under the Hawai'i Constitution's normative public trust framework:

> "For the benefit of present and future generations, the State *and its political subdivisions* shall conserve and protect Hawaii's natural beauty and all natural resources, including land, water, air, minerals and energy sources, and shall promote the development and utilization of these resources in a manner consistent with their conservation and in furtherance of the self-sufficiency of the State.
>
> *All public natural resources are held in trust* by the State for the benefit of the people."[48]

Hawai'i Supreme Court rulings sandwiched around this 1978 amendment declared that public trust obligations governing water survived the Hawaiian Kingdom's mid-nineteenth-century establishment of private property interests.[49]

---

[40] Paul Brewbaker, Ph.D., *Fifty Years of Seed in the Fiftieth State: An Economic Report of the Hawaii Crop Improvement Association* (Aug. 2016): 15, 20.

[41] Le'a Malia Kanehe, "Indigenous Cultural Property," in *Native Hawaiian Law: A Treatise*, Melody MacKenzie, et al., eds. (Honolulu: Kamehameha Publishing, 2015): 1058. The County subsequently enacted an ordinance making it unlawful to test, propagate, cultivate, raise, plant, grow, introduce, or release GE taro. Maui County Code § 20-38-030 (2009).

[42] Kawika M. Winter, et al., "The *Moku* System: Managing Biocultural Resources for Abundance within Socio-Ecological Regions in Hawai'i," *Sustainability* (Oct. 2018); Trevor N. Tamashiro, "Moloka'i: Resurrecting 'Aha Moku on the 'Last Hawaiian Island,'" *Asian-Pacific Law & Policy Journal* 12:1 (2011): 297n18.

[43] David M. Forman, "Applying Indigenous Ecological Knowledge for the Protection of Environmental Commons: Case Studies from Hawai'i for the Benefit of 'Island Earth'," *University of Hawai'i Law Review* 41 (2019): 327–30nn83–91; Wayne H. Tanaka, "Ho'ohana aku, Ho'ōla aku: First Steps to Averting the Tragedy of the Commons in Hawai'i's Nearshore Fisheries," *Asian-Pacific Law & Policy Journal* 10:1 (2008):267–89 (applying Elinor Ostrom, "The Rudiments of a Theory of the Origins, Survival, and Performance of Common-Property Institutions," in Daniel W. Bromley ed., *Making the Commons Work* (1992): 304–14).

[44] HRS § 171-4.5(d); Forman, "IEK," 325-27nn79–80.

[45] Forman, "IEK," 330; [AMAC] Rules § 2-1(d) (Oct. 2016).

[46] Sproat, "*Wai* through *Kānāwai*," 131n16 & 147-48nn96–97.

[47] Forman, "Marooned," 261–84; Forman, "IEK," 300–52.

[48] Haw. Const. art. XI, § 1 (1978) (emphases added).

[49] McBryde Sugar Co. v. Robinson, 504 P.2d 1330 (1973); Robinson v. Ariyoshi, 658 P.2d 287 (1982) (describing Hawai'i's public trust doctrine as "much more than a restatement of police powers").

Before sugar barons diverted this common resource for private use, *kānāwai* (early laws that evolved around management/use of fresh water) reflected the vital role *wai* (fresh water) played in traditional *Kānaka ʻŌiwi* (Native Hawaiian, or *Kānaka Maoli*) society.[50] Hawaiians revered water as: literal and figurative life-giver; manifestation of a principal *akua* (god, ancestor); and, resource managed for the community's benefit rather than commodity reducible to physical ownership.[51] The staple crop *kalo* (taro, *colocasia esculenta*) likewise symbolizes Hawaiians' elder brother in a reciprocal relationship that obligates people to care for all cultural and natural resources, including the land that feeds them.[52] Sufficient cool water flow prevented taro diseases, while supporting reproduction of native stream species as alternative food sources. Fertile coastline runoff also created ideal environments for nearly 500 *loko iʻa* (fishponds).[53] However, many streams dried up after sugar plantations constructed massive ditch systems transporting water from wet, windward (mostly Native Hawaiian) communities to arid central and leeward plains – exemplifying "decisions and practices [that] increasingly reflected Western notions of *ownership* as opposed to *management*."[54]

Turn-of-the-century water rights decision *In re Water Use Permit Application* (*Waiāhole*) explained that public trust principles require global, long-term planning and decision-making that compromises public rights pursuant only to decisions made with openness, diligence, and foresight.[55] Public trust principles require application of the precautionary principle, meaning that lack of firm scientific proof should not prevent the government from adopting reasonable measures designed to further the public interest. Enactment of the State Water Code's comprehensive regulatory scheme did not trump these constitutional obligations.

In 2006, *Kelly* v. *1250 Oceanside Partners* likewise rejected arguments that county public trust obligations were trumped by laws vesting land management authority in the state, combined with unexercised legislative power to transfer public lands to counties for public uses or purposes.[56] Elaborating upon the self-executing constitutional provision, HRS § 180C-2 authorized counties to cooperate with state and federal agencies to enact ordinances meeting – or exceeding – minimum standards for controlling soil erosion and sediment. However, the *Kelly* plaintiffs failed to prove governmental breach of trust when they relied solely on a state agency–issued Notice and Finding of Violation regarding construction-related storm water pollution.

In 2014, *Kauai Springs, Inc.* v. *Planning Commission of Kauaʻi* (*Kauai Springs*) reaffirmed the affirmative constitutional "duty and authority of the state *and its political subdivisions* … independent of statutory duties and authorities created by the legislature."[57] Two subsequent rulings also warrant mention: first, the "plain language" of Hawaiʻi's Constitution indisputably applies public trust obligations to *all* public natural resources, including land;[58] second, the fiduciary duty to reasonably protect and preserve trust property includes the obligation to reasonably monitor and inspect property leased to a third party.[59]

---

[50] Sproat, "*Wai* through *Kānāwai*," 139–42.

[51] Ibid., 127-28n4, 141.

[52] Ibid., 527; Forman, "IEK," 333–34, 350.

[53] Joseph M. Farber, *Ancient Hawaiian Fishponds: Can Restoration Succeed on Molokaʻi?* (California: Neptune House Publications, 1997): 6, 8.

[54] D. Kapuʻala Sproat, "From *Wai* to *Kānāwai*: Water Law in Hawaiʻi," in MacKenzie, *Native Hawaiian Treatise*, 532–34n67.

[55] 9 P.3d 409 (Haw. 2000).

[56] 140 P.3d 985 (Haw. 2006).

[57] 324 P.3d 951 (Haw. 2014).

[58] In re Conservation District Use Application (CDUA) HA-3568 (*Mauna Kea II*), 431 P.3d 752 (Haw. 2018).

[59] Ching v. Case, 449 P.3d 1146 (Haw. 2019).

By ignoring Article XI, § 1, federal judges transformed efforts to implement these constitutional obligations into a public message that reinforces the prevailing regulatory narrative of "substantial equivalence" while rewriting history and silencing indigenous voices.[60]

KAUAʻI COUNTY CONTEXT

Although Monsanto (now Bayer) does not operate on Kauaʻi, the other four major GE/GMO seed companies sued the county in federal court on January 10, 2014. After correctly rejecting the seed companies' reliance on a constitutional declaration that agriculture is a matter of statewide concern,[61] the magistrate decided that counties (as state creations) may only exercise powers conferred through general laws[62] – failing to acknowledge Article XI, § 1's self-executing nature,[63] and its *express* reference to "political subdivisions" (counties).[64] (Despite the adverse ruling, Kauaʻi's mayor and the HDOA chairperson convened a JFFG consistent with collaborative rulemaking authority extended by the ordinance and HRS § 149A-35.[65])

Setting off a domino effect by mischaracterizing county authority in Hawaiʻi,[66] the magistrate gave no explanation for refusing to seek a Hawaiʻi Supreme Court ruling on the determinative state law question[67] – despite having rejected the seed companies' federal preemption claims.[68] The magistrate's conclusion that state law preempts Ordinance 960 relies upon an ideology favoring private enterprise,[69] while ignoring centuries of prior local rule: before King Kamehameha unified the Hawaiian Islands (1810); continuing thereafter; as well as during the fifty- plus-year period between Maui County's establishment by the Territory of Hawaii (1905); and, Hawaiʻi statehood (1959).[70] Oral histories indicate the *Moku* system of localized biocultural resource management flourished in Hawaiʻi for about a millennium:[71] "Hawaiians often assert that management of resources under the Euro-American paradigm involves formal centralized control of resources and habitats and thus less sensitivity to local biophysical dynamics, less

[60] Troy J.H. Andrade, "(Re)Righting History: Deconstructing the Court's Narrative of Hawaiʻi's Past," *University of Hawaiʻi Law Review* 39 (2017): 631–32, 657n166.
[61] Haw. Const. art. XI, § 3 (1978).
[62] *Compare* Jon D. Russell & Aaron Bostrom, "Federalism, Dillon Rule and Home Rule" (American City County Exchange, Jan. 2016): 6 (noting the Hawaiʻi Constitution provides for *self-executing* Home Rule).
[63] *Compare* Save Sunset Beach Coal. v. City & County of Honolulu, 78 P.3d 1 (Haw. 2003) (concluding the constitution's agricultural lands provisions are *not* self-executing).
[64] Absolute state legislative control over a municipality's governmental functions applies *absent* specific, contrary constitutional limitations. Koike v. Board of Water Supply, 342 P.2d 835 (Haw. 1960); McKenzie v. Wilson, 31 Haw. 216 (1930).
[65] Peter S. Adler, Ph.D., Pesticide Use by Large Agribusinesses on Kauai: Findings and Recommendations of the [JFFG] (May 25, 2016), available at www.accord3.com/crops-and-pesticides-on-kauai/.
[66] Professor David Callies contends that Hawaiʻi has extremely weak home rule. *See* Jacob Garner & Ian Wesley-Smith, "State Preemption of Local GMO Regulation: An Analysis of Syngenta Seeds, Inc. v. County of Kauai," *Urban Lawyer* 47, no. 2 (2015): 291–92n128. However, this analysis ignores self-executing county public trust obligations recognized in *Waiāhole, Kelly* and *Kauai Springs*. *Cf. Mauna Kea II.*
[67] Hawaiʻi Rules of Appellate Procedure 13(a) authorizes such requests for "certification" absent clear controlling precedent.
[68] *Cf.* Carnegie-Mellon University v. Cohill, 484 U.S. 343 (1988) (observing that "judicial economy, convenience, fairness, and comity … point toward declining to exercise jurisdiction over the remaining state-law claims" when federal law claims are eliminated before trial).
[69] Pollack, "Atay," 317n91.
[70] Ibid., 316–17n88.
[71] Forman, "IEK," 323–30.

appreciation for the needs and interests of the indigenous human populations, and less capacity for enforcing rules and regulations at the local level."[72]

On appeal, a coalition of nonprofits led by *Ka Makani Ho'opono* ("wind that makes right" – representing Kaua'i residents living next to GE/GMO fields) argued courts must be particularly cautious about invalidating ordinances on preemption grounds when constitutional duties to county residents are implicated.[73] Unpersuaded that Hawai'i counties have any inherent (or reserved) constitutional authority, the Ninth Circuit focused instead on two court rulings predating the November 1978 public trust provision – *Hawaii Govt. Employees' Ass'n v. Maui* (*HGEA v. Maui*),[74] and *In re Application of Anamizu*.[75] Calling Article XI, § 1 "irrelevant,"[76] the Ninth Circuit reiterated the magistrate's erroneous conclusion that counties may only exercise powers expressly granted by the State, and upheld his refusal to certify the state law question.[77] Ignoring *Ka Makani Ho'opono*'s citations to *Waiāhole* and *Kelly*,[78] along with Kaua'i County's reliance on *Kauai Springs*,[79] the Ninth Circuit disregarded the self-executing nature of county public trust obligations, which do not lie dormant awaiting express grants of legislative power by the state.

HAWAI'I COUNTY CONTEXT

In March 2014, two papaya farmers obtained a state court order staying the deadline for existing operations to pay an annual $100 registration fee and disclose their locations.[80] Industry groups later challenged Hawai'i County Ordinance 13-121 in federal court.[81] Relying on his earlier *Syngenta Seeds* opinion, the magistrate: found the ordinance preempted[82]; refused certification to the Hawai'i Supreme Court; and, denied the County's request to gather additional information to support its reliance on *Kelly* and *Waiāhole*.[83]

Glossing over obvious contextual distinctions, *Hawai'i Papaya Industry* suggests on appeal that *Atay* involved "substantially similar" facts. Two Ninth Circuit footnotes likewise dismiss fundamental state constitutional questions: first, rejecting the county's certification request because of Hawai'i's purportedly "well-defined" implied state preemption analysis; and, finally, relying on *HGEA v. Maui* and *Anamizu* to conclude that Article XI, § 1 does not alter the analysis absent legislation expressly granting counties power to enact relevant ordinances. Once again, these conclusions ignore the constitutional provision's self-executing nature and its pre-existing status as background principle of Hawai'i law (reflecting centuries of localized natural resource management experience).

---

[72] Ibid., 335n75.
[73] Opening Brief, 2015 WL 8004262 (citing Robinson Township v. Pennsylvania, 83 A.3d 901 (Pa. 2013): "constitutional commands ... cannot be abrogated by statute"); Reply Brief, 2015 WL 2265299.
[74] 576 P.2d 1029 (Haw. [Mar. 22,] 1978).
[75] 481 P.2d 116 (Haw. 1971)).
[76] *Compare* Forman, "Indigenous Knowledge," 334-46nn107–46 (discussing *nine* post-1978 decisions concerning state or county public trust obligations); ibid., 316n48 (discussing *Robinson Township*).
[77] Hawai'i Rules of Appellate Procedure 13(a) authorizes federal courts to certify determinative questions about Hawai'i law absent clear controlling precedent.
[78] Opening Brief, 2015 WL 8004262; Reply Brief, 2015 WL 2265299.
[79] Reply Brief, 2015 WL 2193643.
[80] John Doe v. County of Hawai'i, Civ. No. 14-1-0094 (Haw. 3rd Cir. Mar. 7, 2014).
[81] Hawai'i Floriculture and Nursery Ass'n v. County of [Hawai'i], 2014 WL 2587282 (D. Haw. filed June 9, 2014).
[82] 2014 WL 6685817 (D. Haw. Nov. 26, 2014).
[83] Defendant-Appellants' Principal Brief, 2015 WL 8004268.

MAUI COUNTY CONTEXT

A week after the November 2014 election, the SHAKA Movement joined councilmember (and indigenous farmer) Alika Atay's state court lawsuit seeking timely implementation of the Maui Ordinance.[84] The next day, an industrial group including two GE/GMO seed companies filed *Robert Ito Farm, Inc. v. County of Maui (Ito Farm)* asking the federal court to block the ordinance. Four days later, Maui County agreed not to implement the ordinance – after repeatedly declining to defend it.[85] Dow Agrosciences removed *Atay* to federal court; then, the magistrate refused to conduct a hearing before deciding against sending *Atay* back to state court – despite the SHAKA Movement withholding consent to the magistrate's continued involvement.[86]

Ignoring this discrepancy, the succeeding judge affirmed the magistrate's decision to keep *Atay* in federal court based on federal preemption questions. Rejecting the SHAKA Movement's attempt to gather additional documentation undermining the preemption argument, the judge explained that oversight of specific industry operations or their health and environmental impacts is not relevant[87] – i.e., proof of regulatory gaps would not prevent preemption of the Maui Ordinance. Despite the SHAKA Movement's legal citations,[88] *Ito Farm* and *Atay* do not even mention the Hawai'i Constitution's public trust provision when declining to certify the novel implied state preemption question.

The Ninth Circuit's unsupported characterization of the temporary moratorium as a "ban" conflicts with available precedent.[89] In any event, the appellate court turned a blind eye to the SHAKA Movement's reliance on *Kauai Springs*.[90] Consequently,

> *Atay* constrains local power to mitigate risk and places biodiversity and native plants at the whims of . . . the free market, which will determine whether and where GE research is conducted . . . . *Atay* allows corporations that may have sway over state and federal authorities to dictate the risk experienced by Maui County residents, all on an island scarred by a history of environmental damage.[91]

Preemption thus "dampens legitimate and responsive local democratic activity, privileges the private corporation over the public corporation, and privatizes control over the lived environment."[92]

NEXT STEPS

The *Atay, Syngenta Seeds, and Hawai'i Papaya Industry* preemption rulings silenced indigenous and other community voices by transforming efforts to implement constitutional public trust

[84] Atay v. County of Maui, No. 14-1-0638 (Haw. 2d Cir. Nov. 12, 2014).
[85] 2014 WL 7148741 (D. Haw. Dec. 15, 2014); 2015 WL 1279422 (D. Haw. Mar. 19, 2015) (extending injunction).
[86] 2015 WL 134070 (D. Haw. Jan. 9, 2015) (discussing 28 U.S.C. § 636(c)'s consent requirement).
[87] 111 F. Supp. 3d 1088 (D. Haw. June 30, 2015).
[88] Objections to the Findings and Recommendation to Deny Plaintiffs' Motion to Remand, Atay v. County of Maui, Civ. No. 14-00582 SOM-BMK (D. Haw. Mar. 7, 2015).
[89] *Compare* Tahoe-Sierra Preservation Council, Inc. v. Tahoe Regional Planning Agency, 216 F.3d 764 (9th Cir. 2000) (distinguishing permanent development bans from temporary moratoria, which expire after meeting certain conditions precedent), *aff'd*, 535 U.S. 302 (2008); Department of Transportation v. Public Citizen, 541 U.S. 752 (2004) (discussing congressional moratorium lifted by the President after *twenty* years).
[90] Appellants' Opening Brief; Appellants' Reply Brief.
[91] Pollack, "Atay," 308.
[92] Ibid., 307, 318.

obligations into a public message that reinforces a narrative of "substantial equivalence" favoring GE/GMO seed companies. Economic development absent precautions for present and future generations facilitates a regulatory commons problem: unnecessary evisceration of local authority producing strong incentives for governmental inaction. By comparison, restorative justice principles enshrined in the Hawai'i Constitution reflect the grassroots approach championed by Nobel Prize–winning economist Elinor Ostrom.[93]

In the wake of these preemption decisions, Ostrom-like networked forms of governance achieved some limited successes through: federal enforcement,[94] state legislation,[95] state administrative action,[96] and private litigation.[97] Legislation specifically authorizing counties to adopt relevant ordinances could, theoretically, address remaining state GE/GMO regulatory gaps. Alternatively, administrative rulemaking petitions could be filed with Hawai'i's agricultural and health departments.[98] For example, proposals to: adopt rules requiring environmental and public health risk assessments; establish standards governing plant-incorporated protectants for National Pollutant Discharge Elimination System general permits; and/or mandate consultation with the 'Aha Moku Advisory Council consistent with the United Nations Declaration on the Rights of Indigenous Peoples.[99] Rulemaking approaches arguably would be more open, transparent and deliberative than other options.

If the agencies exercise the kind of "rational thinking" that perpetuates ongoing regulatory commons problems – i.e., rejecting "irrational" actions that might adversely impact economic development opportunities[100] (by failing to timely act on the petitions, formally declining to institute rulemaking proceedings, or commencing the rulemaking process but failing to adopt necessary provisions) – challenges can be pursued as pure state law matters in state court.[101] If the agencies instead promulgate gap-filling regulations over GE/GMO industry objections, the appropriate forum for legal challenges is also state court.[102] Either way, Hawai'i courts will not be bound by erroneous Ninth Circuit predictions about unique state constitutional provisions.[103]

[93] Dietz, "The Struggle," 1907-08; Ostrom, "A Diagnostic Approach," 15,181; Elinor Ostrom,"Polycentric Systems for Coping with Collective Action and Global Environmental Change," *Global Environmental Change* 20 (2010): 552.
[94] Press Release, U.S. Dept. of Justice, "Monsanto Agrees to Plead Guilty to Illegally Spraying Banned Pesticide at Maui Facility," November 21, 2019 (describing $10.2 million deferred prosecution agreement).
[95] Act 45 (2018) amended chapter 149A by adding: a Pesticide Reporting and Regulation Program; buffer zones around schools; a ban on permits authorizing use/application of pesticides containing active chlorpyrifos after December 31, 2022; and, a required pesticide drift monitoring study.
[96] In June 2019, the Hawai'i Department of Education ("DOE") banned herbicide use on public school grounds. Gary Hooser, "A Twofer – DOE bans herbicides and GMO acreage plummets," *The Garden Island*, July 3, 2019.
[97] "Maui Lawsuit Alleges Birth Defects Caused by Monsanto's 'Reckless Use of Pesticides'," *Maui News*, October 25, 2019; Stewart Yerton, "Monsanto Could Soon Be Facing Dozens of Lawsuits in Hawaii Over Pesticide," *Civil Beat*, Aug. 29, 2019.
[98] *See* HRS §§ 91-3, -6; Haw. Admin. R. §§ 4-1-23, 11-1-51.
[99] AMAC Rules §§ 2-3(c).
[100] Hudson & Rosenbloom, "Uncommon Approaches," 1292-93.
[101] *Cf.* Green Party of Hawai'i v. Nago, 378 P.3d 944 (Haw. 2006) ("if the agency refuses, then the petitioning person would have an action in circuit court").
[102] *Id.* (citing HRS § 91-7).
[103] The United States Constitution acknowledges and preserves state judicial autonomy and independence. Erie Railroad Co. v. Tompkins, 304 U.S. 64 (1938).

24

Can Affirmative Action Offer a Lesson in Fighting Enclosure?

Sheldon Bernard Lyke

This chapter explores the parameters of using anticommons property arrangements (i.e., gridlock) as a tool for protecting the commons. Michael Heller has written about the anticommons, which is a kind of property arrangement where multiple parties can exclude others from using a property. The anticommons can produce gridlock and lead to inefficiencies in land use. Abraham Bell and Gideon Parchomosky observed that the anticommons and its accompanying gridlock could function to preserve common pool resources. Bell and Parchomovsky argued that a strategy that incorporates the anticommons and gives nearby landowners formal veto rights over land development (i.e., negative easements) could safeguard a commons (e.g., public parks). In summary, they argue that gridlock – the introduction of multiple negative easement holders into the commons – will introduce inefficiencies in the development of commons lands and lead to conservation.

This project explores the parameters of the anticommons concept as it relates to conserving the commons. When creating gridlock (i.e., creating an anticommons or assigning rights to exclude) for commons conservations, it is necessary to consider the interests of the parties to who you will assign rights and how they best align to saving the commons. Without this consideration, the risk exists that the interests of the anticommons members align with developers, and no member utilizes their right to exclude.

If gridlock is to function as a conservation tool, this chapter argues that member parties must have diverse interests so that at least one member will have interests that do not align with developers so that members will exercise their right to exclude. This property theory argument was developed based on an unusual case study observing the management of a race-based affirmative action scholarship program. Although intangible, there is a shared property – educational racial diversity – that comprises a managed commons.[1] In the educational diversity commons, the commons members – universities, private charities, and admitted students can use, access, and benefit from diversity. Examining affirmative action from the perspective of the commons allows one to identify precisely why claims of reverse discrimination are so troubling. Individuals who sue to abolish considerations of race serve as agents of enclosure and their actions to end affirmative action programs destroy the diversity commons.

A commons requires management to protect it from depletion, overuse, attack, or enclosure. The management of the educational diversity commons has mostly fallen to universities who admit diverse students into elite institutions, and – along with the assistance of private

---

[1] Sheldon Bernard Lyke, "Diversity as Commons," *Tulane Law Review* 88, No. 2 (2013): 317.

charities – fund student attendance. I argue that universities and private charities hold anticommons rights of exclusion concerning which "development" plans (i.e., legal strategies) they will use in defending educational diversity.

This specific case study examines the Mellon Foundation and its restructuring of a race-based graduate student scholarship pipeline program currently known as the Mellon Mays Undergraduate Fellowship (MMUF). In 2003, the Mellon Foundation changed the pipeline program from a race-exclusive program (i.e., only Blacks and Latinos could apply for admission), to a race-conscious program (i.e., any race can apply) where Blacks and Latinos are preferred), in response to the Supreme Court's affirmative action decisions in *Gratz* v. *Bolinger*[2] and *Grutter* v. *Bolinger*.[3]

I argue that when universities and private charities fight anti-affirmative action litigation, they are exercising their anticommons veto rights. They are vetoing the "development" of the diversity commons and "conserving" diversity and the use of race as a factor in admissions. Universities and private charities do not exercise their anticommons veto rights, however, when they limit their defense of affirmative action by either: (1) refusing to defend against anti-affirmative action attacks or (2) restricting the available litigation defense arguments available to protect against anti-affirmative action attacks. When universities and private charities limit their defenses of affirmative action, they act in a self-interested nature. They suppress other "conservation" strategies and legal arguments (e.g., equality and desegregation justifications for affirmative action) that minority applicants and students could implement.

Ultimately, this chapter relies on the diversity commons example as a lesson that a commons is better served if there is an accompanying anticommons with a membership that has varied interests. For instance, if minority students that were in favor of affirmative action policies were anticommons members, they would have standing to defend affirmative action litigation. These minority students could advance legal arguments that overlap but are different from those used by colleges. One argument that students would likely use is that affirmative action is a necessary tool for equality because it offsets the discrimination in admissions standards that utilize racially biased measures like standardized tests.[4]

This chapter first provides a brief discussion of the anticommons. Next, I present a case study of the MMUF program and examine why an anticommons framework was not successful in stopping the Mellon Foundations policy shift in allowing White students to enter the minority pipeline program. Finally, I end with a discussion of the lessons that the case study presents concerning the anticommons.

UNDERSTANDING THE ANTICOMMONS AND GRIDLOCK

Over the past three decades, scholarship has emerged introducing the anticommons.[5] Coined by Frank Michelman,[6] the anticommons property concept was originally a thought experiment reifying the abstract qualities that Michelman perceived antipodal to a commons.[7]

---

[2] Gratz v. Bollinger, 539 U.S. 244 (2003).
[3] Grutter v. Bollinger, 539 U.S. 306 (2003).
[4] This argument was made by the student-intervenors in *Grutter*. *See* Brief of Respondents Kimberly James, et al., Grutter v. Bollinger, 539 U.S. 306 (2003) (No. 02–241).
[5] See e.g., Frank I. Michelman, "Ethics, Economics and the Law of Property," in *Nomos* 24 3 (1982) and Michael A. Heller, "The Tragedy of the Anticommons: Property in the Transition from Marx to Markets," *Harvard Law Review* 111 (1998): 621, 667.
[6] *See* Michelman, *supra* note 5.
[7] *Id.* See Heller, *supra* note 5 at 667 (1998).

Property held in a commons is subject to few rights to exclude commons members. Scholars of the anticommons reason that the anticommons is the "mirror image of commons property" where multiple owners hold rights to exclude others from using a scarce resource.[8] The concept received little attention until 1998 when Michael A. Heller discussed the tragedy of the anticommons where a resource faces the risk of underuse because too many owners hold rights of exclusion.[9]

Shortly following Heller's work, Abraham Bell and Gideon Parchomovsky observed that elements of the anticommons could serve as a conservation tool that only allows socially desirable development on commons lands.[10][11] Using famous examples of Central Park in New York City, and Grant Park in Chicago, Bell and Parchomovsky questioned how parks that sit on valuable ground avoid succumbing to the economic and political pressures of potentially enormous lucrative development and commercial gain.[12] They argued that those luxury private property holders with property appurtenant to the parks held a unique interest in those green spaces because their proximity added value to their real estate.[13] Out of self-interest, these adjacent property owners acted as "public guardians" for the parks, and held a nonpossessory interest in their maintenance and continued existence.[14] Using political pressure, these neighbors protect their nonpossessory interest in the park in favor of conservation by blocking development that is harmful to their interests.[15]

Bell and Parchomovsky argued that an anticommons gridlock blocked undesirable development. Bell and Parchomovsky discussed this gridlock as political de facto negative easements and named it by coining the term "antiproperty." They argued that if formalized and granted to a large number of private actors (specifically private actors who held property appurtenant to the commons), these negative easements "in the hands of the neighbors are likely to produce a regime in which it is practically impossible for unwanted development to threaten the conservation of the defended property."[16]

In some ways, the antiproperty concept is Bell and Parchomovsky's attempt to import the benefits of the tragedy of the anticommons (underuse) into the commons arena to avoid the often misunderstood tragedy of the commons (overuse and exploitation).[17] Heller acknowledged that the anticommons is not necessarily tragic, specifically when it can create value.[18] In his work, Heller used a development conservation example similar to Bell and Parchomovsky, where homeowners in a residential subdivision held a restrictive covenant and exercised veto

---

[8] See Heller, *supra* note 5 at 622.
[9] *Id.*
[10] Abraham Bell and Gideon Parchomovsky, "Of Property and Antiproperty," *Michigan Law Review* 102 (2003): 1.
[11] *Id.*
[12] *Id.* at 4.
[13] *Id.* at 5.
[14] *Id.*
[15] *Id.*
[16] *Id.* at 6. The formalization of the antiproperty rights would give private landowners an additional site (i.e., the courts) to fight for conservation.
[17] Garrett Hardin, "The Tragedy of the Commons," *Science* 162 (1968): 1243. I write that the tragedy of the commons is often misunderstood because a number of scholars have pointed out the problems with Hardin's work, specifically that the property that Hardin described in his seminal work was not a commons, but an open access resource that lacked ownership. *See e.g.*, Elinor Ostrom. *Governing the Commons: The Evolution of Institutions for Collective Action* (Cambridge University Press, 1990). In addition, scholars have often stated that common ownership norms can serve to manage a commons efficiently without the need of privatization to avoid overconsumption and exploitation. *See e.g.*, Susan Jane Buck Cox, "No Tragedy on the Commons," *Environmental Ethics* 7 (1985): 49.
[18] Heller, *supra* note 5 at 673–76.

rights over development in their community.[19] The result of Bell and Parchomovsky's public park antiproperty normative prescription is to have a public park simultaneously function as both a commons – shared use subject to few exclusions – and an anticommons.

A CASE STUDY OF A RACIAL DIVERSITY COMMONS

The MMUF program is an example of an educational and racial diversity commons. One mechanism that this case study uncovers is the role of charities and universities and their refusal to exercise anticommons exclusion rights in contesting the transformation and gradual destruction of race-exclusive scholarships.

THE TRANSFORMATION FROM MINORITY TO MAYS

In June 2004, a group of Black, Native American, and Latino graduate students from around the country sat down in a cramped St. Louis room to discuss a name change. They were emotional. While expressions of their feelings were diverse and ranged from anger and disdain, to calm, measured cunning – every student was charged with passion about a disappointing transformation in an organization with which they shared a deep personal connection. The emotional students were attending a conference as members of the Mellon Minority Undergraduate Fellowship program, a pipeline program instituted by the Mellon Foundation, whose goal was to increase the number of highly qualified, severely underrepresented minority candidates for PhDs within the arts and sciences.[20]

In October 2003, Lydia English, Mellon Foundation program officer for MMUF, sent a letter to the Mellon fellows regarding a policy change in response to the Supreme Court of the United States landmark affirmative action rulings in *Gratz* v. *Bollinger*[21] and *Grutter* v. *Bollinger*[22] (hereinafter the "Michigan Affirmative Action" cases). In the letter, she stated that the MMUF program would be changing its name from the Mellon Minority Undergraduate Fellowship to the Mellon Mays Undergraduate Fellowship.[23] Also, the program would broaden its mission statement and end its race exclusive selection process. MMUF would no longer require an applicant to be a member of a disadvantaged minority group and would begin allowing non-minority students to apply for the fellowship.[24] When MMUF graduate students learned about the policy change, they were overwhelmingly frustrated. The June 2004 conference was the first time Mellon fellows had an opportunity to meet since receiving the English letter, and the climate was tense.

The 2004 Mellon Conference was held at Washington University. The conference usually ended with a final late Sunday morning session. This last session was a firestorm of Mellon fellows voicing their concerns and frustrations about MMUF's decision to admit white students. Fellows questioned why they were not informed before the Mellon Foundation decided to

---

[19] *Id.* at 674–75.
[20] See Andrew W. Mellon Foundation, 2003 *Annual Report: Presidents Report*, https://mellon.org/about/annual-reports/2003-presidents-report/.
[21] See *Gratz, supra* note 2.
[22] See *Grutter, supra* note 3.
[23] The program changed its name to Mellon Mays Undergraduate Fellowship both to keep the MMUF acronym unchanged, but also to honor Dr. Benjamin E. Mays, former president of Morehouse College. See Andrew W. Mellon Foundation, *supra* note 20.
[24] See Andrew W. Mellon Foundation, 2003 *Annual Report: Presidents Report*, https://mellon.org/about/annual-reports/2003-presidents-report/.

include non-minority students. Students were worried about the effect that having white students would have on what had become a safe space for disadvantaged people and whether their white presence would stifle conversation. Some students thought that the Mellon Foundation was ceding too much ground and that this was a step backward concerning civil rights. Other students refused to be acknowledged as Mellon Mays fellows and stressed that the second "M" in MMUF would continue to stand for "minority" in their eyes.

After the last session, fellows organized an MMUF Research Committee to compile data on the MMUF program's history, contextualize the legal context of the MMUF policy, collect personal statements from fellows and generate working documents that assessed the general social moment. What the students did not know at the time was that no changes were going to result from their efforts. Very few students understood that the actions that the Mellon Foundation took were made in the context of a larger debate on affirmative action and the use of race in selection procedures in higher education. In autumn 2003, the Mellon Foundation convened a "well attended meeting" where college and university presidents, officers and general counsels met with the Mellon Foundation's general Counsel, along with Paul Smith and other attorneys from Jenner Block's Washington, DC, office.[25]

THE UNIVERSITY AS LUXURY CONDO OWNER?
APPLYING THE ANTICOMMONS FRAMEWORK

Educational diversity and the MMUF case study can both be described using an anticommons framework. Bell and Parchomosky discuss private owners who are appurtenant to green spaces like Central Park, who hold de facto exclusionary rights to veto development. Just as Central Park is formally owned by the public as a commons and is "surrounded by luxury properties whose owners enjoy the amenities and views of the adjacent park," diversity is also a commons that largely benefits students, but is surrounded by privileged institutions (i.e., colleges/universities and private charities) that also benefit.[26] Like luxury condo owners to parks, these institutions are "adjacent" to diversity.[27] Universities enjoy the amenities and benefits of diversity and possess a de facto quasi property interest of value that provides an incentive for them to protect diversity – even though other individuals with slightly different interests also benefit from it. Universities' self-interest transforms these institutions into the public guardians of affirmative action.[28] They have offered defenses in favor of affirmative action as defendants in litigation.

The antiproperty framework applies to the Mellon Foundation because the foundation's interests – as expressed in its mission statement – overlaps with universities' interest in protecting diversity. The original mission of the Mellon Foundation is "to help remedy the serious shortage of faculty of color in higher education."[29] When implementing the MMUF program, the

---

[25] See Andrew W. Mellon Foundation, *supra* note 20.

[26] Bell and Parchomovsky, *supra* note 10 at 4.

[27] Spatial analogies are difficult to attach when discussing proximity of the university/private charity to an intangible educational diversity commons. One might argue that the university is not like the condo owner adjacent to the public park, because the university is not adjacent to the diversity commons, but resides within the commons. This distinction is valid, but potentially irrelevant for the overall argument presented in this Article. Bell and Parchomovsky acknowledge that their analysis of antiproperty applied with equal force to both green space in parks and the preservation of historic districts. They note that historic districts differ insofar as there may be persons with private property interests within the zone of the protected space. That is, while ordinarily there will be no private property interests in a city park, for example, there will be numerous private property owners with stakes in a neighborhood with historically significant architecture. *Id.* at fn 7.

[28] *See* Bell and Parchomovsky, *supra* note 10, at 4.

[29] "History|MMUF," MMUF, www.mmuf.org/about/history, accessed August 1, 2020.

Mellon Foundation articulated this mission more precisely and stated that the program had both immediate and longer-term objectives.[30] First, the foundation's short term objective was "to increase the number of highly qualified candidates for PhDs in core fields within the arts and sciences who come from minority groups that are seriously underrepresented in these fields (African-Americans, Hispanic Americans, and Native Americans)."[31] The second, longer-term objective was "to increase diversity of faculties at colleges and universities throughout the country to bring a wider range of experiences and perspectives to teaching and scholarly discussion. By providing increased opportunities for all students to work with minority professionals, diversity serves the related goals of structuring a campus environment more conducive to improved racial and ethnic relations and of providing role models for all youth."[32]

The interests of the MMUF program and its fellows, however, are not synonymous. Their interest divergence is seen most clearly in their respective responses to the Michigan affirmative action cases. Minority graduate students viewed an uncontested change in the fellowship's selection policy as negatively affecting their potential gains in professionalization. They would no longer have an all-minority safe space to discuss candidly the issues of ethnic and racial discrimination that solely plague minority graduate students. Mellon fellows also expressed that the admission of non-minority students into the MMUF program decreased the number of future minority students into the professoriate pipeline.

The Mellon Foundation's interests, however, were not inhibited by the policy change. For example, concurrent with its mission to remedy the shortage of minority faculty, the Mellon Foundation had a self-interested objective to produce quantifiable results that the organization can report and publicize. This is present in its reports and assessments of its practices.[33]

An organization focused on results might not have a problem with a transformation that only modified those goals. The MMUF could still work with universities to remedy race; all they had to do was make modifications in their mission statement and their selection processes. They could continue to appear to fulfill their mission because the foundation would be able to produce statistics that showed that they were effective at increasing the number of Black and Latino graduate students in the PhD pipeline. Therefore, they could present evidence that they were remedying "the serious shortage of faculty of color in higher education" in their original mission statement.

Universities and private charities do not make arguments that defend the use of race-conscious decision making in higher education without relying on the diversity rationale. The cost of advancing non-diversity defenses might be too high for these institutions, as it might highlight their discriminatory practices and maintenance of social inequality. In the case of the MMUF program, the Mellon Foundation may have made a conscious choice that it was more sound to alter its mission than to face losing partnerships with universities that were risk-averse to litigation.

---

[30] See Andrew W. Mellon Foundation, *supra* note 20

[31] *Id.*

[32] *Id.*

[33] One can witness this quantification in one of the earliest assessments of the MMUF program. In its 1993 Annual Report, the Mellon Foundation stated that as of the fall of 1993, 537 undergraduates were admitted to the MMUF program, of which 262 received bachelor degrees. Thirty-four percent of the fellows who received bachelor degrees entered PhD programs in Mellon designated fields. Additionally, this report briefly provided qualitative narrative profiles of four fellows. Even these more qualitative narrative data detail objective accounts of the accomplishments of these fellows and how the MMUF program assisted these four minority students in choosing graduate programs and developing research skills. See Andrew W. Mellon Foundation, *1993 Annual Report*, https://mellon.org/about/annual-reports/annual-reports-1988-1996/.

CONCLUSION: LESSONS LEARNED FROM AFFIRMATIVE ACTION

One might argue that the Mellon Foundation is not an excellent example of the anticommons concept at work. Bell and Parchomovsky say that for the antiproperty veto to work, it must be available to a large number of private actors. Bell and Parchomovsky likely call for many private actors because they assume that the larger the number of actors, the more varied their interests. One might argue that there were not enough private actors in the case of the MMUF case study. A response in the form of a corollary question is: If a large group of private owners have similar interests, does the size of the group matter?

The MMUF example might reveal that instead of solely focusing on the sheer number of private members, maybe property theorists need to think about why many private actors are required to stimulate underuse. A large number of anticommons members with disparate interests are desired so that at least one of those actor's interests overlaps with saving the commons. Therefore, a large population of private actors is not necessary. The size of the anticommons can be small if there are enough members whose interests somehow overlap with conserving the commons at issue.

How do we identify anticommons members with interests that can conserve the commons? Bell and Parchomovsky argue to assign formal antiproperty veto rights to landowners who are proximate to the commons because they already hold de facto veto rights due to their engagement with the political process. Proximate owners, however, are not the only ones who lobby political institutions to save commons land. Bell and Parchomovsky rely on examples – where nearby residents (e.g., owners and non-owner renters), along with community organizations, use politics to preserve property of public importance.[34]

If Bell and Parchomovsky's goal is to formalize de facto conservation methods that are already in place, then it would be helpful to have a better empirical picture of the interested parties. Proximate users of nearby commons (i.e., renters) and interested organizations work to veto park development. Following Bell and Parchomovsky's logic, antiproperty rights could also be given to those non-owners who have an interest in the success of the greenspaces and who have exercised de facto rights.

The MMUF program case study provides further support for including proximate users in the anticommons and assigning them rights to veto development. If universities and private charities are the proximate owners in the diversity commons, then minority students are the proximate users (i.e., "renters"). While publicly funded universities have held antiproperty veto rights over the development of the diversity commons, how would the scenario differ if other members of the commons were assigned antiproperty veto rights? Could the commons be better protected if other members (i.e., minority students) who held different interests and uses for diversity were able to advocate for its conservation? Facilitating minority students' ability to utilize affirmative action defense strategies could result in more complete defenses of affirmative action in litigation, and the subsequent protection of educational racial diversity as a resource.

How do minority students already exercise their de facto veto rights in affirmative action contests? The most obvious method is via litigation. Students can intervene.[35] In *Grutter*, a

---

[34] Bell and Parchomovsky, *supra* note 10 at 24, see text accompanying notes 99–102.

[35] Joanne Villanueva tells the history behind the students who sought intervention in two supreme court affirmative action cases: *Grutter* and *Bakke v. Regents of California*. The students in *Bakke* were unsuccessful. Initially the trial court denied the students' motion to intervene in *Grutter*. The students challenged the trial court's opinion in United States Court of Appeals for the Sixth Circuit, and the Sixth Circuit eventually granted them intervenor status. Joanne Villanueva, "The Power of Procedure: The Critical Role of Minority Intervention in the Wake of Ricci v. DeStefano," 99 *California Law Review* 1083, 1088–96.

group of forty-one individually named students, along with three coalitions – the Coalition To Defend Affirmative Action, Integration, and Immigrant Rights and Fight for Equality by Any Means Necessary (BAMN); United for Equality and Affirmative Action Legal Defense Fund (UEAALDF); and Law Students for Affirmative Action – intervened in the district court trial.[36] The student intervenors defended the University of Michigan Law School's affirmative action plan arguing that Grutter's claim of reverse discrimination should fail because it rested on the false premise that, aside from affirmative action, the university's assessments of merit (i.e., the use of the LSAT) were race-neutral.[37] Instead of focusing solely on the diversity rationale to support affirmative action, the student intervenors supplemented it with arguments for integration and equality. In support of their arguments, the intervenors called fifteen witnesses.[38] They presented a majority of the trial evidence to highlight the history of racial inequality in the United States, the racial bias of the LSAT, the hostile environments that depress minority students' undergraduate GPA, and the poor performance (i.e., predictive validity) of measures like the LSAT, undergraduate GPA, and law school grades in predicting success after law school graduation.[39]

Instead of formalizing negative easement rights to appurtenant property owners, governments could allow private third parties to have property rights in conservation easements or covenants.[40] If the goal is to conserve the commons, there does not seem to be a reason to limit private-party rights to proximate landowners. A better system might be to either provide rights of exclusion to anyone that has use rights to a commons. Providing rights of exclusion to all commons members would create a commons that simultaneously functions as an anticommons. In this scenario, members have both a right to use the resource, but also have the exclusionary right to veto development efforts. Creating a veto right for all commons members might be the best way to get a variety of interests where at least one commons member will exercise their right to halt development.

[36] *See* Brief of Respondents Kimberly James, et al., *supra* note 36.
[37] *Id.* at 40–46.
[38] *Id.* at 1.
[39] *See* Villanueva, *supra* note 35, at 1101–2.
[40] *See* Carole Necole Brown, "A Time to Preserve: A Call for Formal Private-Party Rights in Perpetual Conservation Easements," *Georgia Law Review* 40 (2005): 85.

PART VIII

Technology, the Internet, and the Future of Commons Governance

25

Can Technological Change Weaken the Robustness of Common-Property Regimes?

Maija Halonen-Akatwijuka and Evagelos Pafilis

Ostrom challenged Hardin's "tragedy of the commons" argument through numerous field studies of successful common-property regimes, such as irrigation systems in the Philippines and Spain and common lands in Switzerland and Japan.[1] While many of these common-property regimes have been robust for hundreds of years, a question arises whether such commons can continue to exist in the face of rapid technological progress. This is the question we address in this chapter, focusing on the provision of common-pool resources (CPRs), for which it is hard to exclude users. We find that major technological improvement, such as replacing a primitive irrigation system with modern technologies, risks compromising cooperation because the temptation to freeride on other farmers' maintenance activities is increased. However, a minor technological improvement within an existing irrigation system, such as strengthening water diversion devices, does not harm incentives to cooperate. Our analysis implies that the characteristics of the resource and the technologies used both have an important effect on whether a common-property regime can be successful.

Ostrom referred to the theory of repeated games in explaining how the tragedy of the commons can be avoided. Using insights from repeated games, she argued that cooperation among individuals can be achieved if the benefits of future cooperation outweigh the one-off gain from over-appropriating the resource or under-providing to its maintenance and improvement. Cooperation is more likely if the individuals are patient so that they place a significant value on the benefits of future cooperation.[2] She further argued that this condition is satisfied in a traditional community managing a CPR, as individuals live side by side and expect their children and grandchildren to inherit their land.[3] However, she also criticized the theory of repeated games for employing trigger strategies, which punish infractions with a permanent breakdown of cooperation, as she concluded they are rarely observed in actual field studies.[4] Instead, Ostrom found that punishment often took the form of fines that the offender is required to pay to the community. In this chapter, we take the repeated games approach to CPRs, but we include such fines in our analysis.

---

[1] Elinor Ostrom, *Governing the Commons: The Evolution of Institutions for Collective Actions* (Cambridge University Press, 1990); Garett Hardin, "Tragedy of the Commons," *Science* 162 (1968): 1243–8.

[2] For more details on how Ostrom utilized game theory in her research see Elinor Ostrom, Roy Gardner and James Walker, *Rules, Games, and Common-Pool Resources* (University of Michigan Press, 1994).

[3] Ostrom, *Governing the Commons*, 88.

[4] Ostrom, *Governing the Commons*, 98.

Our focus is on analyzing the effect of technological change on the incentives to cooperate. In order to address this question, we examine a CPR, such as an irrigation system, owned and managed by a group of farmers. The irrigation system requires maintenance. The farmers can also invest in expanding and improving the irrigation system. If the farmers interacted only once, for example, they would choose investments that maximize their own payoffs, not taking into account that the other farmers also benefit from the improvements. Such behavior would result in a poorly maintained irrigation system, which, in effect, is a type of "tragedy of the commons." However, in reality, the farmers interact repeatedly, which may enable them to cooperate and manage the irrigation system well. If the farmers are patient enough, the temptation to freeride on others' investments will be deterred by the prospect of a future fine.

Consider then a technological change that makes the farmers' investments more effective in improving the irrigation system. How will it affect their incentives to cooperate? We find that a more effective technology increases the farmers' cooperative investments and, therefore, makes it more tempting to freeride on other farmers' higher investments. At the same time, the increased value of future cooperation makes fines more effective in disciplining the farmers. These factors have opposing effects on the incentives to cooperate. We find that the overall effect depends on the type of technological change. A major technological improvement, such as replacing a primitive irrigation system by a modern technology, hinders cooperation because the dominant effect is the increased temptation to freeride. However, a minor technological improvement within an existing irrigation system, such as strengthening water diversion devices, increases the temptation and its consequences proportionately, so that there is no effect on overall incentives to cooperate.

These results imply that the technologies used, as well as the characteristics of the resource, play an important role in determining whether a common-property regime can be successful. Our analysis differs from Ostrom's (largely endogenous) design principles, which were identified by comparing successful and unsuccessful CPRs. Our results suggest that applying these design principles may not be effective unless the resource *and* the technology used have the characteristics that support cooperation under a common-property regime.

In repeated interaction, the farmers can cooperate if they are patient enough. A major technological improvement increases the patience requirement. Therefore, more effective technology that could potentially improve the farmers' livelihoods may lead to a breakdown of cooperation and worse outcome. However, if the farmers are very patient and initially well above the patience requirement for cooperation, they can continue cooperation even after major technological improvement and benefit from increased payoffs. Alternatively, if the technological improvement is minor, it does not harm cooperation and the farmers' payoffs increase due to better technology. Therefore, it is possible that a CPR can be managed well for a long period of time during technological change, but when the patience requirement finally increases sufficiently, further technological improvement breaks down cooperation leading to deterioration of the CPR.

There is an extensive literature analyzing appropriation of renewable CPRs, such as fisheries and forests. According to Benhabib and Radner, a CPR can be appropriated sustainably – and the tragedy of the commons can be avoided – if the individuals are patient enough and the stock of the CPR is high enough.[5] Copeland and Taylor show that improvement in the harvesting technology initially leads to a transition from open access to active management of the CPR.

---

[5] Jess Benhabib and Roy Radner, "Joint Exploitation of a Productive Asset," *Economic Theory* 2, no. 2 (1992): 155–190.

However, further technological change undermines sustainable management of the resource.[6] We differ from this literature by focusing on provision rather than appropriation of the CPR. While it is intuitive that more effective appropriation technology can exacerbate the over-appropriation problem, it is less obvious that more effective provision technology might increase the *under*-provision problem.

We build on our earlier work where we also focus on provision, but compare incentives to cooperate under common-property regime to other ownership structures, such as government or private ownership.[7]

The literature has extensively examined the role of group size and heterogeneity in the management of CPRs, while the effect of technology has received less attention.[8] Several empirical studies, however, show that replacing primitive irrigation systems with modern technologies reduces agricultural productivity.[9] In these cases, technological change was accompanied with a move from a farmer-managed regime to a government-run regime. As such, the reduced productivity was attributed to the change in governance arrangement rather than technology. In our analysis a major technological change alone can reduce productivity by breaking down cooperation.

In related work, Harstad, Lancia and Russo show that technological investments can be geared to improving incentives to cooperate in an environmental treaty.[10] They find that over-investment in green technologies and under-investment in brown technologies can reduce the temptation to defect from agreed emission levels.[11]

INCENTIVES TO COOPERATE AND TECHNOLOGICAL CHANGE

The Model. Consider a CPR, such as an irrigation system, owned and managed by farmers. For simplicity, let us assume that there are only two farmers. Farmer h (high-valuation farmer) has a higher valuation for the irrigation system than farmer l (low-valuation farmer) because he has more land to irrigate. The farmers make investments, y_h and y_l, respectively, in improvement, expansion and maintenance of the irrigation system. The value of the irrigation system depends on the investments and is given by $v = \left[(y_h)^\alpha + (y_l)^\alpha \right]$, where $\alpha \leq 1$. Parameter α plays a key role is our analysis. It measures how responsive the value of the irrigation system is to farmers' investments. If the farmers increase their investments by 1 percent, the value of the irrigation

[6] Brian R. Copeland and Scott M. Taylor, "Trade, Tragedy, and the Commons," *American Economic Review* 99, no. 3 (2009): 725–49.

[7] Maija Halonen-Akatwijuka and Evagelos Pafilis, "Common Ownership of Public Goods," *Journal of Economic Behavior and Organization* 180 (2020): 555–578.

[8] Jeff Dayton-Johnson, "Small-Holders and Water Resources: A Review Essay on the Economics of Locally-Managed Irrigation," *Oxford Development Studies* 31, no. 3 (2003): 315–39; Amy R. Poteete and Elinor Ostrom, "Heterogeneity, Group Size and Collective Action: The Role of Institutions in Forest Management," *Development and Change* 35, no. 3 (2004): 435–61; Lore M. Ruttan, "Economic Heterogeneity and the Commons: Effects on Collective Action and Collective Goods Provisioning," *World Development* 36, no. 5 (2008): 969–85.

[9] Elinor Ostrom and Roy Gardner, "Coping with Asymmetries in the Commons: Self-Governing Irrigation Systems Can Work," *Journal of Economic Perspectives* 7, no. 4 (1993): 93–112; Elinor Ostrom, Wai Fung Lam and Myungsuk Lee, "The Performance of Self-Governing Irrigation Systems in Nepal," *Human Systems Management* 13 (1994): 197–207; Wai Fung Lam, "Improving the Performance of Small-Scale Irrigation Systems: The Effects of Technological Investments and Governance Structure on Irrigation Performance in Nepal," *World Development* 24, no. 8 (1996): 1301–15.

[10] Bård Harstad, Francesco Lancia and Alessia Russo, "Compliance Technology and Self-Enforcing Agreements," *Journal of the European Economic Association* 17, no. 1 (2017): 1–29.

[11] Brown technology is for example a drilling technology that is complementary to fossil fuel consumption, while renewable energy is an example of a green technology.

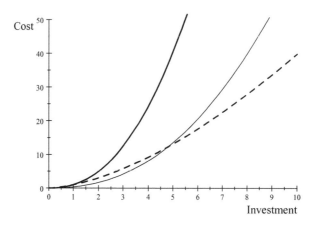

FIGURE 25.1 Major and minor technological improvements

system increases by α per-cent. A technological improvement can increase α so that the farmers' investments become more effective in increasing the value of the irrigation system.

The investments are costly to the farmers in terms of effort, time and materials. Investment costs for farmer h and l are given by $c_h = \sigma(y_h)^\beta$ and $c_l = \sigma(y_l)^\beta$, where $\beta \geq 1$.[12] A technological improvement will reduce the investment costs. Figure 25.1 displays two types of technological changes. A *major technological improvement* changes the shape of the cost function and shifts costs downward from the solid to the broken line. A reduction in β has such effect on the cost function. Replacing a primitive irrigation system by a completely modern system is an example of a major technological improvement.

A *minor technological improvement* does not change the shape of the cost function but will shift costs downward proportionately. This is displayed in Figure 25.1 by moving the cost function from the solid to the thin line. Lower value of σ has such effect on the investment costs. Strengthening water diversion devices within an existing irrigation system and providing simple canal lining are examples of minor technological improvements.

Whether technological change is major or minor affects also how the value of the irrigation system depends on farmers' investments. A major technological improvement can make the value of the irrigation system more responsive to investments (higher α) or the costs less responsive to investments (lower β). It turns out that the results depend on the ratio α/β. A minor technological improvement could have a proportionate effect also on the value of the irrigation system, but for simplicity we examine its effect only on costs.[13]

Our main interest is in how technological improvement affects farmers' incentives to cooperate. Are the farmers able to manage the irrigation system well or will they attempt to freeride on others' investments resulting in deterioration of the irrigation system? The results will depend on the type of technological change.

THE TRAGEDY OF THE COMMONS

When farmer h invests in the irrigation system, also farmer l benefits from the improved system. If farmer h were to take into account the benefit to both farmers, he would choose an

[12] We assume $\alpha/\beta < 1$.
[13] Minor technological improvement could also be measured by a multiplier on the value of the irrigation system. This would not change our results.

investment that maximizes the farmers' joint surplus. In determining his investment, farmer *h* would equate the marginal return of his investment to both farmers to its marginal cost. We call this the *cooperative investment*. Farmer *l*'s cooperative investment is determined in a similar manner.

Consider then a situation where the farmers interact only once. Farmer *h* chooses an investment level that maximizes his own payoff, not the farmers' joint surplus. Farmer *h* equates the marginal return to his investment, which is now lower than in the cooperative case as he is ignoring the benefit to the other farmer, to his marginal cost. As a result, his investment is lower than the cooperative investment. By the same logic, also farmer *l* underinvests and, accordingly, the irrigation system is not well maintained. The farmers are worse off than if they both made the cooperative investment. "The tragedy of the commons" in improvement of the irrigation system occurs because the farmers do not take into account the benefit of their investment to the other farmers.[14]

INCENTIVES TO COOPERATE IN A REPEATED GAME

In reality, the farmers are in an ongoing relationship and interact repeatedly. Such repeated interaction may enable the farmers to sustain cooperative investments because there can be a consequence for underinvestment in the future. Cooperation can be sustained if the farmers are patient so that they place sufficient weight on the future consequences of freeriding.

Cooperation can be achieved in a repeated game through the use of a trigger strategy.[15] The trigger strategy implies that a farmer cooperates as long as the other farmer cooperates, and any defection is punished by a permanent breakdown in cooperation. Suppose the game (inter-action) is infinitely repeated (or ends at a random date). In order to avoid a tragedy of the commons, the farmers want to have a meeting and agree to make cooperative investments. After the meeting, farmer *h* starts by making the cooperative investment in period 1. He then observes farmer *l*'s investment. If farmer *l* also made the cooperative investment, *h* continues with the cooperative investment in the next period and so on. However, if in any period farmer *l* underinvests and freerides on *h*'s cooperative investment, then according to the trigger strategy, the punishment starts from the next period: *h* will underinvest in all future periods. Then also farmer *l* will continue underinvesting. Any reneging from their agreement results in a complete breakdown of cooperation with both farmers underinvesting, resulting in a poorly maintained irrigation system reducing both farmers' payoffs.

Employing such trigger strategies can enable the farmers to sustain the higher cooperative investments if they are patient enough. In a repeated game, the farmer faces a trade-off between the immediate temptation to underinvest and free ride on the other farmer's coopera-tive investment and the future consequence of a breakdown of cooperation. Which effect dominates depends on how patient the farmer is. If he is patient enough, the farmer will place more weight on the future consequences than on the immediate temptation, and will make a cooperative investment.

While this reasoning works in theory, Ostrom argued that trigger strategies are not relevant for understanding real life CPRs because they are rarely observed in actual field studies. Instead,

---

[14] Hardin referred to the problem of over-appropriation by "the tragedy of the commons" (Hardin, "Tragedy of the Commons"). We use the term to describe under-provision of the CPR arising from a similar incentive problem.

[15] James W. Friedman, "A Non-Cooperative Equilibrium for Supergames," *Review of Economic Studies* 38, no. 1 (1971): 1–12.

Ostrom found that punishment often takes the form of fines that the offender is required to pay to the community. If a farmer is absent when the community gathers to work on the CPR, he will have to pay a fine to the community, unless an acceptable excuse is provided.[16] We take Ostrom's conclusion on board and introduce fines into the repeated game scenario.

When underinvestment can be punished by a fine, cooperation can continue, and the tragedy of the commons can potentially be avoided. Even if farmer l underinvests in one period, he can restore cooperation by paying a fine F to the community (or to farmer h in our model) in the next period. Then the farmer faces a trade-off between immediate temptation to freeride and the future consequence of paying the fine. If the farmer is patient enough, the future consequence outweighs the temptation and the farmer is better off by making the cooperative investment.

To enable us to examine the effect of technological change on the incentives for cooperation, we need to add detail to our analysis. Suppose that farmer l's payoff from cooperation is C and his payoff from defecting from the cooperative investment is D. The farmer can increase his payoff by $(D - C)$ if he freerides rather than makes the higher cooperative investment. $(D - C)$ measures the farmer's immediate *temptation* to freeride. The farmer compares the temptation to the consequence of free-riding: the fine he has to pay in the next period. This trade-off depends importantly on how patient the farmer is. Farmer's discount factor δ measures his patience. δ is today's value of $1 in the next period. Therefore, δ is large if the farmer is very patient.[17] If the farmer is very patient – and the fine is large enough – today's value of the fine, δF, outweighs the temptation, $(D - C)$, and farmer l is better off by cooperating. While an impatient farmer is more interested in increasing his immediate payoff: the temptation outweighs its consequences and the farmer is likely to free ride.

We also have to take into account that the farmers' agreement is informal and there is no formal institution to enforce the fine. This means that the defecting farmer has to be willing to pay the fine. What is the consequence of refusing to pay the fine? We assume that after underinvesting, if farmer l will not pay the fine, farmer h will also underinvest *for one period*, but not indefinitely as with a trigger strategy. This means that in the next period farmer l will not get another opportunity to freeride on h's cooperative investment but instead, will earn a punishment payoff. The punishment payoff is what the farmer would earn in a one-shot interaction (that is, the tragedy of the commons). After this punishment, farmer l is given another chance to pay the fine in the following period, after which cooperation can be restored.

We can then choose the level of the fine so that the future consequence of farmer h's underinvestment is enough deterrence to keep farmer l from defaulting on the fine. If farmer l pays the fine, cooperation is restored, and he starts earning C already in this period. Alternatively, if he does not pay the fine, also farmer h will underinvest (for one period) and farmer l will earn the punishment payoff P and defer paying the fine until the following period. If the farmer does not pay the fine, his payoff is reduced by $(C - P)$ every period until he pays the fine. The farmer is better off paying the fine as long as it is less costly than such payoff reduction. Therefore, $(C - P)$ measures the value of a cooperative relationship to farmer l. The higher is *the value of the relationship*, the higher fine farmer l is willing to pay to restore cooperation if he were to freeride. A high fine in turn can deter the farmer from freeriding in the first place. That is why high value of the relationship improves the incentives to cooperate.

---

[16] For example, in the villages of Japan the only acceptable excuses were illness, family tragedy or the absence of able-bodied adults. Margaret McKean, "The Japanese Experience with Scarcity: Management of Traditional Common Lands," *Environmental Review* 6, no. 2 (1982): 63–91.

[17] We assume that $\delta < 1$.

In the Appendix, we show that both farmers will make the cooperative investments if

$$\delta \geq \frac{T}{T+V} = \underline{\delta}.$$

T is the farmers' combined temptation to freeride and V is the farmers' combined value of the relationship. Together T and V determine $\underline{\delta}$, which is the minimum patience requirement for cooperation. If the farmers' discount factor δ is greater than the threshold $\underline{\delta}$, the farmers can overcome the potential tragedy of the commons and will make cooperative investments in the irrigation system. The equation shows that higher temptation increases $\underline{\delta}$ and hinders cooperation by making the patience requirement more difficult to satisfy. While higher value of the relationship decreases $\underline{\delta}$ and facilitates cooperation by relaxing the patience requirement.

Technological improvement and the incentives to cooperate

Our main interest is in how technological change affects the threshold $\underline{\delta}$ for cooperation. If technological change increases $\underline{\delta}$, cooperation is hindered because there is an increased patience requirement for the farmers. The threshold $\underline{\delta}$ depends on the ratio of the temptation to the value of the relationship. It is useful to first examine the effect of technological change on the temptation and the value of the relationship separately and then evaluate the overall effect on $\underline{\delta}$.

Let us first examine the effect of a major technological improvement on the value of the relationship (the difference between the cooperative payoffs and the punishment payoffs). Major technological improvement makes the value of the irrigation system more responsive to farmers' investments or the costs less responsive to investments. Therefore, the payoffs from cooperation increase but so do the punishment payoffs. However, since the cooperative investments are higher than the punishment investments, the payoffs from cooperation increase more than the punishment payoffs and the value of the relationship increases. A higher value of the relationship in turn has a positive effect on the incentives to cooperate by relaxing the patience requirement.

However, technological improvement also increases the temptation to freeride. Improved technology gives the farmers incentives to increase their investments. In particular, the cooperative investments increase making it more tempting to freeride on the other farmer's higher investment. Higher temptation has a negative effect on the incentives to cooperate by increasing the patience requirement.

Higher temptation hinders cooperation while higher value of the relationship facilitates cooperation and it is not immediately clear what the overall effect is on the incentives to cooperate. In the Appendix, we show how $\underline{\delta}$ depends on the major technological improvement measured by the ratio α/β. Higher α makes the farmers' investments more effective in increasing the value of the irrigation system, while lower β reduces the investment costs. According to simulations presented by the solid line in Figure 25.2, the effect of increased temptation is dominant and major technological improvement has a negative effect on the incentives to cooperate: patience requirement $\underline{\delta}$ is increased.

The broken line in Figure 25.2 presents a situation where the farmers have very different valuations for the irrigation system. In that case $\underline{\delta}$ is not smoothly increasing but even then, it is broadly increasing for a major technological improvement.[18]

---

[18] Furthermore, the range of α/β where higher α/β decreases $\underline{\delta}$ occurs only for $\alpha/\beta > 0.5$. In the next section we show that common-property regime is not the best way to govern the resource when $\alpha/\beta > 0.5$.

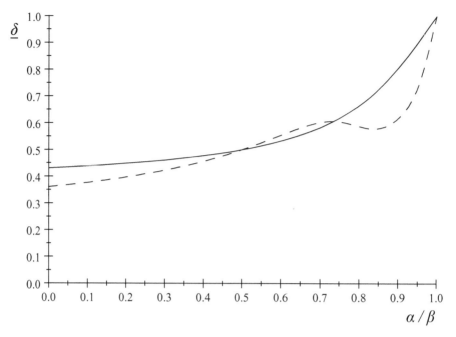

FIGURE 25.2 Incentives to cooperate for a major technological improvement

RESULT 1: MAJOR TECHNOLOGICAL IMPROVEMENT HINDERS COOPERATION

The dominant effect is that the farmers respond to a major technological improvement by increasing their cooperative investments. This makes it more tempting to freeride on the other farmer's cooperative investment. The increased temptation increases the threshold $\underline{\delta}$ and hinders cooperation.

Suppose that the farmers' discount factor is equal to 0.6. Initially, α/β is just below 0.7, so that, according to the solid line in Figure 25.2, $\underline{\delta}$ is just below 0.6 so that the farmers' patience requirement is satisfied. Then technological improvement increases α/β above 0.7. Higher α/β increases the farmers' cooperative payoffs so that the farmers would benefit from technological improvement if they were able to continue cooperation. However, higher α/β also increases $\underline{\delta}$ above 0.6 and cooperation breaks down because temptation to freeride has increased. This is why technological improvement can reduce the farmers' payoffs.

Alternatively, if α/β is initially very low, say 0.2, so that the farmers' discount factor is well above $\underline{\delta}$, the farmers can continue cooperation even after significant technological change occurs. This implies that it is possible that the irrigation system can be well managed for a long period of time during technological change, but when α/β finally reaches 0.7, further technological improvement breaks down cooperation resulting in a collapse in investments in the irrigation system.[19]

We turn our attention now to minor technological improvement, which is measured by lower σ. In the Appendix we show that $\underline{\delta}$ does not depend on σ. This gives our second result.

---

[19] Furthermore, the shape of $\underline{\delta}$ in Figure 25.2 shows that for low values of α/β technological change increases $\underline{\delta}$ marginally but eventually the increase is significant. This strengthens the argument that the irrigation system can be robust for a long time but when the threshold is reached, cooperation breaks down.

RESULT 2: MINOR TECHNOLOGICAL IMPROVEMENT HAS NO EFFECT ON THE INCENTIVES TO COOPERATE

Technological improvement that shifts costs downward proportionately increases the farmers' cooperative payoffs. But such technological improvement does not change the farmers' incentives to cooperate. So if the farmers were able to cooperate before the change, they can continue cooperation after the improvement and benefit from the increased cooperative payoffs.

Although minor technological improvement does not affect $\underline{\delta}$, it has an effect on the value of the relationship and the temptation to freeride. In fact, as with a major technological improvement, both the value of the relationship and the temptation increase but because the increase is proportionate their ratio remains constant and so does $\underline{\delta}$.

With this type of technological improvement, the degree of responsiveness of costs to investments (parameter β) remains constant, which explains why the changes are proportionate. Major technological improvement changes the degree of responsiveness (ratio α/β) itself, leading to different results.

ALTERNATIVE OWNERSHIP STRUCTURES

In the previous section we found that major technological improvement hinders cooperation under a common-property regime. Therefore, if α/β increases significantly, common-property regimes may cease to be optimal. (Minor technological improvement does not have such effect.) This is indeed what we find in our earlier work where we compare common-property regime to other ownership structures such as joint ownership and single ownership by farmer h or l.[20] Joint ownership is a shared structure where both farmers have a veto power, while single ownership can be interpreted as private or government ownership.

We find that the value of the relationship (the difference between cooperative payoffs and the punishment payoffs) is large under a common-property regime as compared to joint ownership or ownership by farmer h.[21] In the previous section we found that the high value of the relationship improves the incentives to cooperate. This strength of common-property regimes arises from the possibility of the tragedy of the commons. Defecting farmer has strong incentives to pay the required fine to avoid underinvestment by the other farmer at the level of the tragedy of the commons. Ownership by farmer h or joint ownership have less punishment power as they provide better incentives for investments *in the one-shot interaction*.

However, the weakness of a common-property regime is that the temptation to freeride is large. Temptation is larger under a common-property regime because farmer h can keep his high benefit from the CPR to himself, while under joint ownership or h-ownership the farmers have to bargain how to share the benefits. In the previous section we found that technological progress in terms of higher α/β has a greater effect on the temptation than on the value of the relationship under a common-property regime. Therefore increasing α/β eventually reduces the incentives to cooperate so much that it is better to switch to an ownership structure that minimizes the temptation to freeride: either ownership by agent h or joint ownership. We find that this switch is optimal when $\alpha/\beta > 0.5$. Higher α/β increases $\underline{\delta}$ even under agent h ownership and joint ownership, but less than under a

---

[20] Halonen-Akatwijuka and Pafilis, "Common Ownership of Public Goods".
[21] Ibid.

common-property regime. Therefore, the incentives to cooperate can be improved by switching away from a common-property regime.

While a common-property regime is no longer optimal when technological improvement has increased α/β above 0.5, a common-property regime provides the best incentives for cooperation for less effective technologies for which $\alpha/\beta < 0.5$. This condition can be satisfied either because of a low α or a high β. Low α implies that the value of the CPR is not very responsive to investments. This is consistent with a stylized fact of communal grazing lands in the Swiss Alps identified by Netting and discussed by Ostrom: the value of the communal grazing lands cannot be increased much due to altitude, a limited growing season and thin soil.[22] This is in contrast to privately owned arable lands in the mountain valleys, the yield of which can be increased by "irrigation, manuring, erosion control, crop rotation, and careful horticulture."[23]

Alternatively, the rationale for a common-property regime ($\alpha/\beta < 0.5$) can arise from high β. High β implies that higher investment increases costs significantly. Then a common-property regime can be optimal even when investments increase the value of the CPR significantly, contrary to the above stylized fact. This is the case with respect to the irrigation systems in Nepal and the Philippines studied by Ostrom and Yoder.[24] There, the ineffectiveness of the technology is driven by high maintenance costs. For example, in one of the Zanjera irrigation communities in the Philippines, the average annual contribution to maintenance was 37 days of work per person.[25] The major cost of maintenance arises from the time and effort taken away from cultivating privately owned fields. When maintenance activities are at such a high level, they can have a significant effect on the productivity of private cultivation. Therefore, the costs in terms of lost productivity of private cultivation are very responsive to increasing maintenance activities. According to our results, this is when common-property regime provides the best incentives for cooperation. Zanjera communities have indeed been successful in routinely mobilizing labor for maintenance of the irrigation system. A compliance rate of 94 percent was reported.[26]

OSTROM'S DESIGN PRINCIPLES

Our analysis implies that the exogenous characteristics of the particular resource and the technologies used are relevant to determining whether a common-property regime can be successful. Low α/β is favourable to common-property regime, while incentives to cooperate are weak and can be improved by changing the ownership structure when α/β is high.

We will now apply our results to Ostrom's design principles. Ostrom examined numerous field studies of successful and unsuccessful CPRs and identified the key principles that characterize the successful ones.[27] The design principles include well-defined boundaries, graduated

---

[22] Robert McC Netting, "What Alpine Peasants Have in Common: Observations on Communal Tenure in a Swiss Village," *Human Ecology* 4, no. 2 (1976): 135–46; Ostrom, *Governing the Commons*, 63.

[23] Netting, "What Alpine Peasants Have in Common," 143. Also, in the common lands in Japan, maintenance investments, such as the annual burning of the grasslands, have a limited impact on the yield. Margaret McKean, "The Japanese Experience with Scarcity: Management of Traditional Common Lands,"; Ostrom, *Governing the Commons*, 67.

[24] Ostrom, *Governing the Commons*, 82–88; Robert Yoder, *Organization and Management by Farmers in the Chhatis Mauja Irrigation System, Nepal*, (Colombo, Sri Lanka: IIMI, 1994).

[25] Walter E. Coward and Robert Y. Siy, "Structuring Collective Action: An Irrigation Federation in the Northern Philippines," *Philippine Sociological Review* 31 (1983): 3–17; Ostrom, *Governing the Commons*, 85-86.

[26] Ostrom, *Governing the Commons*, 86.

[27] Ostrom, *Governing the Commons*.

sanctions and low-cost conflict-resolution mechanisms, among others, all of which are largely endogenous. According to our results, applying these design principles may not be effective unless the characteristics of the resource and technology are such that a common-property regime provides good incentives for cooperation.

However, we show that the classical case studies of successful common-property regimes (where investments play a role) – irrigation systems in Nepal and the Philippines and common lands in Switzerland and Japan – have similar design principles and can also be characterized by ineffective technology.

OSTROM ON IRRIGATION TECHNOLOGIES

Ostrom was critical of the view that irrigation is simply an engineering problem; she focused on the importance of governance as well. Replacing primitive farmer-managed irrigation systems with modern technology and coupling it with management by a government agency is typically associated with a reduction in agricultural productivity.[28] Ostrom's explanation is that government agencies – unlike the farmers themselves – lack incentives to manage the irrigation system well.

However, it is also possible to improve technology without handing over the management to a government agency. Our results speak to this situation. In our analysis of an irrigation system owned and managed by farmers, major technological improvement alone may lead to a breakdown of cooperation among the farmers and, ultimately, the deterioration of the irrigation system itself. This is the case when the farmers' discount factor is initially close to the critical discount factor $\underline{\delta}$. In most of the cases covered by the empirical literature, major technological improvements have been accompanied by a move to a government-run regime and the change in ownership has been seen to be responsible for the poor performance of these irrigation systems. We argue that the nature of the technological improvement and its impact on the farmers' incentives to cooperate play a role in poor performance.

Alternatively, in our analysis technological change may lead to a genuine improvement without disrupting farmers' incentives to cooperate. This is the case with major technological improvement when the farmers' discount factor is well above $\underline{\delta}$. Furthermore, minor technological improvements within an existing irrigation system – such as strengthening water diversion devices, providing simple canal lining or training programs – can increase productivity without compromising cooperation.[29] Lam and Ostrom find that these minor technological changes improved water adequacy in farmer-managed irrigation systems.[30]

---

[28] Ostrom and Gardner, "Coping with Asymmetries in the Commons"; Ostrom, Lam and Lee, "The Performance of Self-Governing Irrigation Systems in Nepal"; Lam, "Improving the Performance of Small-Scale Irrigation Systems"; Elinor Ostrom, Joanna Burger, Christopher B. Field, Richard B. Norgaard and David Policansky, "Revisiting the Commons: Local Lessons, Global Challenges," *Science* 284 (5412) (1999): 278–282.

[29] Training programs have been offered e.g. in Nepal with the aim to "stimulate the transfer of experience from farmers in well-managed systems to those in poorly managed systems". Naresh Pradhan, *A Farmer to Farmer Exchange Training for Improved Irrigation Management Organized by DIHM's Irrigation Management Center* (Kathmandu, Nepal: Irrigation Management Project Memo, 1987), 1.

[30] Wai Fung Lam and Elinor Ostrom, "Analyzing the Dynamic Complexity of Development Interventions: Lessons from an Irrigation Experiment in Nepal," *Policy Sciences* 43 (2010): 1-25. Lam and Ostrom also show that the positive effect on technical efficiency was only short-term. See also Torsten R. Berg (2008). *Irrigation Management in Nepal's Dhaulagiri Zone: Institutional Responses to Social, Political and Economic Change* (PhD Thesis, Aalborg University, Department of History, International and Social Studies, 2008).

CONCLUSION

In this chapter, we examined the robustness of common-property regimes in the face of technological progress. Our focus has been on their provision. We show that technological change can potentially hinder cooperation. This is the case for major technological changes, such as switching from a primitive to a modern irrigation system. Such a change hinders incentives to cooperate by increasing the temptation to freeride on others' cooperative investments. While minor improvements within an existing irrigation system, such as introducing simple canal linings, leave incentives to cooperate unaffected. This is because both the temptation to deviate and its consequences increase proportionately leaving overall incentives for cooperation unchanged.

Our model can be helpful for understanding the long-term success of common-property regimes during times of technological progress. Even when technology changes are major, cooperation can be maintained if the community is patient and initially their discount factor is well above the critical level. However, when the threshold is reached, any further technological change can lead to a breakdown of cooperation and collapse in investments in the CPR.

Our analysis has focused on the provision of CPRs such as irrigation systems and common lands. More work emphasizing provision rather than appropriation of CPRs is needed. Some of the biggest challenges faced by humankind involve global CPRs, such as the earth's shared natural resources and outer space.[31] Such CPRs not only differ in terms of their characteristics but also pose different challenges and opportunities. The impact of technological change on such resources remains an interesting and critical question for future research.

---

[31] See, e.g., the chapters in this volume by Babcock and Burns.

Appendix

We first derive the cooperative investments, y_h^* and y_l^*. The farmers' joint surplus is equal to $S = (\theta_h + \theta_l)\left[(y_h)^\alpha + (y_l)^\alpha\right] - \sigma(y_h)^\beta - \sigma(y_l)^\beta$ where 'θ_i is the valuation parameter of farmer $i = h, l$ and '$\theta_h > \theta_l$'.

Maximizing the joint surplus with respect to investments gives

$$y_i^* = \left(\frac{\alpha(\theta_h + \theta_l)}{\sigma\beta}\right)^{\frac{1}{\beta-\alpha}} \quad \text{for} \quad i = h, l. \tag{A1}$$

In the one-shot game, each farmer maximizes his own payoff $P_i = \theta_i\left[(y_h)^\alpha + (y_l)^\alpha\right] - \sigma(y_i)^\beta$ and chooses investment given by

$$y_i^e = \left(\frac{\alpha\theta_i}{\sigma\beta}\right)^{\frac{1}{\beta-\alpha}} \quad \text{for} \quad i = h, l. \tag{A2}$$

In the repeated game, the combined incentive constraint for both farmers to make the cooperative investments is given by[32]

$$\delta(F_h + F_l) \geq (D_h + D_l) - (C_h + C_l), \tag{A3}$$

where F_i is the fine, D_i is the defection payoff and C_i is the cooperative payoff of farmer $i = h, l$. The combined incentive constraint for both farmers to be willing to pay the fine is given by

$$(F_h + F_l) \leq \frac{1}{1-\delta}\left[(C_h + C_l) - (P_h + P_l)\right] \tag{A4}$$

where P_i is the punishment payoff of farmer $i = h, l$. Substituting the maximal fines to equation (A3) and simplifying, we obtain

$$\delta \geq \frac{T}{T+V} = \underline{\delta}. \tag{A5}$$

where $T = (D_h + D_l) - (C_h + C_l)$ is the farmers' combined temptation to freeride and $V = (C_h + C_l) - (P_h + P_l)$ is the combined value of the relationship.

---

[32] If the discounted value of the fines outweigh the combined temptation to freeride, the farmers can find a suitable monetary transfer (if necessary) to satisfy each farmer's individual incentive constraint. See Halonen-Akatwijuka and Pafilis, "Common Ownership of Public Goods."

The explicit form of T is given by

$$T = \left[\theta_h\left((y_h^e)^\alpha + (y_l^*)^\alpha\right) - \sigma(y_h^e)^\beta\right] + \left[\theta_l\left((y_l^e)^\alpha + (y_h^*)^\alpha\right) - \sigma(y_l^e)^\beta\right]$$

$$- \left[(\theta_h + \theta_l)\left((y_h^*)^\alpha + (y_l^*)^\alpha\right) - \sigma(y_h^*)^\beta - \sigma(y_l^*)^\beta\right].$$

While $T + V$ is given by

$$T + V = (D_h + D_l) - (P_h + P_l)$$

$$= \left[\theta_h\left((y_h^e)^\alpha + (y_l^*)^\alpha\right) - \sigma(y_h^e)^\beta\right] + \left[\theta_l\left((y_h^*)^\alpha + (y_l^e)^\alpha\right) - \sigma(y_l^e)^\beta\right]$$

$$- \left[\theta_h\left((y_h^e)^\alpha + (y_l^e)^\alpha\right) - \sigma(y_h^e)^\beta\right] - \left[\theta_l\left((y_h^e)^\alpha + (y_l^e)^\alpha\right) - \sigma(y_l^e)^\beta\right]$$

$$= \theta_h\left[(y_l^*)^\alpha - (y_l^e)^\alpha\right] + \theta_l\left[(y_h^*)^\alpha - (y_h^e)^\alpha\right].$$

Finally, we solve for the threshold $\underline{\delta} = \frac{T}{T+V}$. We substitute the investments from (A1) and (A2) in T and $T + V$ and simplify, obtaining

$$\delta = \frac{\left[1 + \left(\frac{\theta_h}{\theta_l}\right)^{\frac{1}{1-\alpha/\beta}}\right]\left(1 - \frac{\alpha}{\beta}\right) - \left(\frac{\theta_h}{\theta_l} + 1\right)^{\frac{1}{1-\alpha/\beta}}\left(1 - \frac{2\alpha}{\beta}\right)}{\frac{\theta_h}{\theta_l}\left[\left(\frac{\theta_h}{\theta_l} + 1\right)^{\frac{\alpha/\beta}{1-\alpha/\beta}} - 1\right] + \left[\left(\frac{\theta_h}{\theta_l} + 1\right)^{\frac{\alpha/\beta}{1-\alpha/\beta}} - \left(\frac{\theta_h}{\theta_l}\right)^{\frac{\alpha/\beta}{1-\alpha/\beta}}\right]}.$$

26

Internet Governance in the Digital Cold War

Scott J. Shackelford and Angie Raymond

The global trade in data is nothing new, as many commentators including George Washington University professor Susan Aaronson have argued, noting: "As long as humans have traded, they have traded data about the world they encountered."[1] However, for most of the history of trade liberalization following WWII, the focus has been on lowering barriers to the free flow of products across national boundaries. This multilateral, decades-long effort has led to an array of economic success stories, with tariffs being reduced "from an average of 40 percent in 1948 to 4 percent" by 2007, leading to clear and largely positive results: "countries that are more open to trade grow faster than those that are relatively closed."[2] Yet, while this increasingly liberalized, global trade regime has helped some narrow some divides particularly in Asia,[3] it has also exacerbated others leading to higher inequality with displaced workers being unable to find new opportunities at the rates needed.[4] This trend, and the resulting backlash against globalization that has, in turn, helped fuel the rise of populist movements in the United States and elsewhere, leading now to a drive toward protectionism from some politicians even as support for free trade generally remains high including in the United States.[5]

The drive to liberalize services has become a priority as it has become an increasingly vital component of the global economy, accounting for $752 billion in U.S. exports in 2016.[6] The lifeblood of a services-based economy is, of course, intellectual property, as may be seen by the shift in the S&P 500 with 'intangible assets' "not captured on the balance sheet" accounting for 84 percent of its value by 2019, a reversal in this proportion from decades prior.[7] This means that the protection of intellectual property, including enhanced cybersecurity, has taken an

---

[1] See Susan Ariel Aaronson, *Data Governance in a Digital Age: Who Makes the Rules for the Information Trade?*, Fin. Post (May 23, 2018).

[2] Daniel J. Ikenson, *Is Trade Liberalization a Product of Domestic or International Processes? Lessons from Doha*, Cato Inst. (June 4, 2007).

[3] See Jeffrey Frankel, *Do Globalisation and World Trade Fuel Inequality?* Guardian (Jan. 2, 2018).

[4] See Jennifer Mason & Mireya Solis, *Globalization on the Cheap: Why the U.S. Lost Its Way on Trade*, Brookings Inst. (Aug. 28, 2017).

[5] Pushan Dutt & Devanshish Mitra, *The Paradox of Protectionist Populism*, INSEAD Blog (Apr. 17, 2018).

[6] See Rachel F. Fefer, *U.S. Trade in Services: Trends and Policy Issues*, Cong. Res. Serv. R43291, at i (Jan. 26, 2016),

[7] James Mitchell, *Intangible Assets Account for 84% of S&P 500, Says Researcher*, Investor Daily (Apr. 30, 2019).

increasingly central place in trade negotiations.[8] Indeed, it has become integral to the ongoing – as of this writing – U.S.-China trade dispute.[9]

The issue has taken on added urgency with the rollout of 5G connectivity, which promises "[h]igher maximum speeds[,] "[l]ower latency[,]" and [c]onnecting more devices in unison."[10] This technology is of paramount importance to both the United States and China given that it promises to power the next wave of the Internet of Things (IoT), which heralds a hyper-connected future.[11] Recent estimates for 2020–2021 range from about 9–25 billion connected devices, though more dated estimates for 2020 have been as high as 75 billion.[12] Regardless of the number, the salient point is that the stakeholder that gets to write the standards and build the hardware underlying 5G systems will have an outsized impact on the future shape and evolution of this Internet of Everything.[13] Already, for example, Huawei technology is powering 5G infrastructure across some sixty-five nations, with even some close U.S. allies such as the United Kingdom considering its adoption. Yet a binary conceptualization of whether to adopt Western or Chinese technology in rolling out 5G masks the larger debate underway about data governance in an (increasingly multipolar) Information Age.

This chapter frames governance using the literature developed by the Ostroms and their collaborators including polycentricity to discuss these issues and what they portend for the future of data governance. We argue that this literature includes useful lessons on the importance of building trust through communication, and the requirements for successful self-organization that are vital to navigating current tensions so as to help ensure that they do not lead to a true Digital Cold War.[14] The chapter is structured as follows: Part 1 offers a short history of Internet governance, which is informed by the discussion of the relevant commons literature in Part 2; Part 3 then dives into the 5G debate before concluding with an exploration of Huawei and trends in IoT governance in Part 4 and what all this means for cyber peace in Part 5.

AN INTRODUCTION TO INTERNET GOVERNANCE

There are many possible starting points to the story of cyberspace. One could begin by discussing the coinage of the term by sci-fi author William Gibson in his novel *Neuromancer* in 1984, in which he described "a consensual hallucination experienced daily by billions."[15] Or even earlier in 1969 with the first message sent via ARPANET: "lo," which was supposed to be "login" but the system crashed before the rest of the message could be sent.[16] Indeed, it is possible to go back even further, even to the 1940s when "cybernetics" ("the study of communication and control

---

[8] See, e.g., Scott J. Shackelford et al., *Using BITs to Protect Bytes: Promoting Cyber Peace and Safeguarding Trade Secrets through Bilateral Investment Treaties*, 52 Am. Bus. L.J. 1 (2015)
[9] See Lingling Wei & Bob Davis, *U.S. Trade Negotiators Take Aim at China's Cybersecurity Law*, Wall St. J. (Mar. 29, 2019).
[10] Omar Sohail, *What Is 5G Connectivity? Here Is Everything You Want to Know about the Next Wireless Networking Standard*, Wccftech (Apr. 21, 2018).
[11] See Scott J. Shackelford et al., *When Toasters Attack: Enhancing the 'Security of Things' through Polycentric Governance*, 2017 Univ. Ill. L. Rev. 415 (2017).
[12] Bruce Schneier, Click Here to Kill Everybody: Security and Survival in a Hyper-Connected World 5 (W.W. Norton, 2018).
[13] See Scott J. Shackelford, The Internet of Things: What Everyone Needs to Know (Oxford Univ. Press, 2020).
[14] See Eric Lutz, *Trump's Cold War with China could Literally Break the Internet*, Vanity Fair (May 22, 2019).
[15] William Gibson, *Neuromancer* 52 (Ace, 1984).
[16] Mike McDowall, *How a Simple 'Hello' Became the First Message Sent via the Internet*, PBS (Feb. 9, 2015).

systems in living beings and machines") was all the rage.[17] For our purposes, though, we are mostly concerned with the modern history of Internet governance to provide a frame for trends in data governance.

The history of Internet governance may be broken down into phases, which loosely correlate to the evolution of the Web itself from Web 1.0 to Web 3.0.[18] Phase One extended from the creation of ARPANET in the late 1960s up through the release of the Transmission Control Protocol/Internet Protocol (TCP/IP) in 1983, which enabled the scaling and eventual creation of "the" Internet.[19] Then, from 1983 to 1998, a second phase may be defined in which informal, bottom-up governance featuring grassroots organizations such as the Internet Engineering Task Force (IETF) discussed further below was the norm and state control largely the exception. This may be seen by John Perry Barlow's famous maxim in his *Declaration of the Independence of Cyberspace*, "Governments of the Industrial World, you weary giants of flesh and steel ... [,] [y]ou have no sovereignty where we gather."[20]

Starting in 1998, though, and following the emergence of cyberspace as a vital commercial domain in which national security interests were beginning to mount, the U.S. government began to exert more direct control over Internet governance through the creation of the Internet Corporation for Assigned Names and Numbers (ICANN).[21] This non-profit corporation based in California was, and remains, responsible for the *global* Domain Name System, under contract from the U.S. Department of Commerce. Thus, this third phase of Internet governance was marked by the emergence of hybrid governance structures in cyberspace. This system prevailed – though with growing resistance on the part of some nations as the globalization of cyberspace continued – through the early 2010s. The Snowden revelations, and the resulting diplomatic rows that it helped touch off, caused an increasing number of states to question the prevailing multi-stakeholder governance status of cyberspace.[22] Although ICANN – which cut its official ties with the U.S. government in 2016[23] – the Obama administration, and its allies, were able to maintain this governance structure, this emerging fourth phase of Internet governance is one in which state-centric, multilateral views of cyberspace backed up by national security concerns appear resurgent.[24] For example, widely varying estimates for the cost of these attacks range from $275 billion to $22.5 trillion,[25] with U.S. government entities regularly warning that the danger from cyber attacks now "exceed the danger of physical attacks."[26] Such an evolution underscores the increasingly polycentric nature of cyberspace, which makes the Ostroms work – and the Bloomington School in particular – relevant in understanding the policy implications explored below.

[17] *What Is the Origin of 'Cyber'?*, Oxford Dictionaries.
[18] See Scott J. Shackelford et al., *Back to the Future of Internet Governance?*, Georgetown J. Int'l Aff. 83 (2015); Charles Silver, *What Is Web 3.0?*, Forbes (Jan. 6, 2020).
[19] See Nat'l Sci. Found., Science and Engineering Indicators 8–6 (1998).
[20] Christopher Shea, *Sovereignty in Cyberspace*, Boston Globe (Jan. 15, 2006).
[21] *See Internet Governance Routing It Right*, Economist (Dec. 2, 2010).
[22] *See, e.g.*, Matthew Shears, *Snowden and the Politics of Internet Governance*, Ctr. Democracy & Tech. (Feb. 21, 2014).
[23] *See Stewardship of IANA Functions Transitions to Global Internet Community as Contract with U.S. Government Ends*, ICANN (Oct. 1, 2016).
[24] *See, e.g.*, Justin Sherman, *Russia's Tightening Control of Cyberspace Within Its Borders*, Just Sec. (Dec. 24, 2018).
[25] Schneier, *supra* note 12, at 103.
[26] Derek Hawkins, *The Cybersecurity 202: Pence Takes Tough Tone on Russia in First Cybersecurity Speech*, Wash. Post (Aug. 1, 2018).

RELEVANCE TO COMMONS LITERATURE

The commons literature generally, and the Ostroms' work in particular, contain numerous implications and insights as applied to data governance. This section begins with a brief look at polycentricity generally. Other works have already focused on the Ostrom Design Principles and the more recent Governing Knowledge Commons (GKC) Framework in particular, which builds from the Institutional Analysis and Development Framework, as applied to cybersecurity in particular.[27]

The concept of polycentric governance is multi-faceted and enjoys a long, and storied – if perhaps still somewhat enigmatic – history. Although a variety of scholars including Professors Michael Polanyi and Lon Fuller deserve credit for creating the field,[28] Vincent and Elinor Ostrom did much to jumpstart popular interest and to provide it with empirical depth.[29] Overall, the concept denotes "a complex form of governance with multiple centers of decision making, each of which operates with some degree of autonomy."[30] Vincent Ostrom famously defined it as: "A pattern of organisation where many independent elements are capable of mutual adjustment for ordering their relationships with one another within a general system of rules."[31] Being nested at multiple jurisdictional levels – both public and private – means that polycentric systems "may be capable of striking a balance between centralized and fully decentralized or community-based governance."[32] However, the success of polycentric systems is not foreordained; healthcare and energy are cases in point.[33] Success likely requires functionality, which may be defined as systems that are: (i) "better able to adapt when faced with social and environmental change"; (ii) "provide good institutional fit for complex ... systems; and (iii) "mitigate the risk of institutional failure and resource losses ... ."[34] Although there are no panaceas, as Elinor Ostrom famously remarked, studies have demonstrated that "polycentric governance systems may be more likely than monocentric or centralized governance to exhibit enhanced adaptive capacity and therewith lead to better environmental and social outcomes."[35]

The Internet governance ecosystem has been described as "polycentric" given that it is comprised of a regime complex of stakeholders including businesses, non-profit corporations, governments, civil society groups, academics, and multilateral treaties.[36] Despite the growing prevalence of web filtering and state-sponsored cyber attacks, to date the Internet has been resilient in its multi-stakeholder approach to polycentric governance. Efforts have been made to determine to what extent the literature on polycentric governance generally, as well as the GKC, IAD, and SES frameworks may be useful in building resilience in Internet governance, such as

---

[27] *See, e.g., Governing Knowledge Commons*, in GOVERNING KNOWLEDGE COMMONS 1, 16 (Brett M. Frischmann, Michael J. Madison, & Katherine J. Strandburg eds., Oxford Univ. Press, 2014).

[28] See Paul D. Aligica & Vlad Tarko, *Polycentricity: From Polanyi to Ostrom, and Beyond*, 25 GOVERNANCE 237, 245 (2012).

[29] *See* Keith Carlisle & Rebecca L. Gruby, *Polycentric Systems of Governance: A Theoretical Model for the Commons*, POL'Y STUD. J. (2017).

[30] *Id.*

[31] Vincent Ostrom, *Polycentricity* 21 (Am. Pol. Sci. Ass'n, Working Paper No. W72–2, 1972).

[32] Carlisle & Gruby, *supra* note 29.

[33] *See, e.g.,* Emilia Melville, *Persistent Problems of Polycentric Governance as a Tool for Improving UK Energy System Governance*, INT'L ASSOC. COMMONS (2017).

[34] Carlisle & Gruby, *supra* note 29.

[35] *Id.*

[36] *See* Joseph S. Nye, Jr., *The Regime Complex for Managing Global Cyber Activities*, GLOBAL COMM'N ON INTERNET GOVERNANCE 8 (Chatham House, 2014).

by producing better outcomes including enhanced cybersecurity and even cyber peace.[37] What follows is an attempt to apply these insights more specifically to the fields of Internet and data governance in the context of the 5G debate.

5G & DIGITAL FRAGMENTATION

Despite overall growth in global trade and services as was noted in the introduction, digital fragmentation has been steadily increasing since 2009 with the introduction of 5G adding to the dilemma. Digital fragmentation involves "increasing obstructions to the flows of data, IT products, IT services and IT talent" that jeopardize "the journey toward global digital business models."[38] A recent Accenture report, for example, notes that the number and variety of protectionist policies have soared since 2011 thanks in part to populist pushback against globalization.[39] These national regulations include efforts to control data, such as through localization requirements, or mandating backdoors in encryption as in the case of Australia.[40] Taken to an extreme, such fragmentation can lead to a so-called Splitnernet, [41] in which cyberspace may be conceptualized as less of a global networked commons, and more of a series of digital walled gardens tended to by nations practicing cyber sovereignty.

The global race for 5G, as with previous efforts to rapidly scale new communications tech seen throughout the history of Internet governance described above, is now threatening to deepen these new digital divides into chasms.[42] Unlike prior generations, 5G is uniquely important because it "brings three new aspects to the table: greater speed (to move more data), lower latency (to be more responsive), and the ability to connect a lot more devices at once (for sensors and smart devices)."[43] Put simply, it is disruptive, and likely transformative. As a result, the stakes are high for both the public and private sectors. As Accenture notes, the "business implications are tangible"[44] including "rising IT costs"[45] and "increasing operational complexity"[46] that cause "digital capabilities to be impacted"[47] and businesses to "rethink strategic and operational plans."[48] Indeed, there is some evidence that the implications were perceived to be significant enough that some groups within China lobbied its government to at least partially support the multi-stakeholder status quo that marked the third phase of Internet governance described above. With the change in U.S. administrations, coupled with an increasingly centralized Chinese political apparatus, that hesitation may now be abating.[49]

---

[37] See SCOTT J. SHACKELFORD, MANAGING CYBER ATTACKS IN INTERNATIONAL LAW, BUSINESS, AND RELATIONS: IN SEARCH OF CYBER PEACE (Cambridge Univ. Press, 2014) [hereinafter SHACKELFORD, MANAGING CYBER ATTACKS].

[38] Accenture, *Digital Fragmentation: Adapt to Succeed in a Fragmented World* (2017), www.accenture.com/_acnmedia/pdf-60/accenture-digital-fragmentation-interactive-pov.pdf [hereinafter *Digital Fragmentation*].

[39] *Id.* at 2.

[40] *Id.*

[41] Jeff John Roberts, *The Splinternet Is Growing*, FORTUNE (May 29, 2019).

[42] Classic digital divides involved the distinction between those (often developing) nations lacking Internet access and those enjoying it. The "new" digital divide is not between the haves and have-nots, but the open and the closed (e.g., between those nations practicing multi-stakeholder Internet governance with safeguards for various Internet freedoms, and those preferring closed systems of cyber sovereignty).

[43] Sascha Segan, *What Is 5G?*, PC MAG. (Aug. 28, 2019).

[44] *Digital Fragmentation*, supra note 38. Similar assessments have been released by multiple industry evaluators. See, e.g., Tom Bobrowski, *Digital Insurer*.

[45] *Digital Fragmentation*, supra note 38.

[46] *Id.*

[47] *Id.*

[48] *Id.*

[49] *See, e.g.*, Evan Osnos, *Making China Great Again*, NEW YORKER (Jan. 8, 2018).

Unfortunately, digital fragmentation – what has been called a "new digital divide"[50] – is increasing as trade tensions and geopolitics entered the equation. For example, in May 2019, the Trump administration issued an executive order declaring a "national economic emergency" intended to "empower the government to ban the technology and services of "foreign adversaries" deemed to pose "unacceptable risks" to national security."[51] And while the intention is laudable, many argue it is better thought of as a by-product of an escalating trade war.[52] The restrictions of market entry, coupled with the growing concerns surrounding the energy impacts associated with the deployment of 5G,[53] demonstrate the growth of political aspects of decision making that is impacting digital fragmentation that had previously been driven famously by "rough consensus and running code."[54]

ONE STANDARD TO RULE THEM ALL? HUAWEI AND BUILDING THE INTERNET OF EVERYTHING

The impacts of digital fragmentation – particularly impacts associated with restrictions on the deployment of global 5G – is likely to cause: (1) haphazard uptake of IoT devices, platforms, and services; (2) divergent architecture that could compromise the very idea of an Internet of Everything, and (3) stagnation in innovation and entrepreneurial activity in the tech industry. If these obstacles may be overcome, then "[f]ifth-generation networks … will lead to a bevy of technological breakthroughs, allowing self-driving cars to communicate with each other and doctors to conduct surgeries remotely."[55] Simply put, 5G is transformative, shaping the way in which societies function and communicate. But global debate underway about who gets to build out this tech and write the rules governing it, carries with it profound implications for the future of high-speed Internet access and, with it, will shape debates over human rights and even sustainable development.[56]

Consider the IETF, introduced in Part 1. This group is not focused on the Internet's *address* system but rather its *communications* system. In so doing, its operations are less obvious than an entity like ICANN, which has the authority to decide who gets to be awarded a Top-Level Domain (TLD).[57] As such, it has managed to avoid many of the controversies that have plagued other Internet governance bodies.[58] For example, the IETF is an open access community "of network designers, operators, vendors, and researchers concerned with the evolution of the Internet architecture" that helps coordinate interoperability in the Internet's

---

[50] See Scott J. Shackelford & Amanda N. Craig, *Beyond the New 'Digital Divide': Analyzing the Evolving Role of Governments in Internet Governance and Enhancing Cybersecurity*, 50 Stan. J. Int'l L. 119, 120 (2014).

[51] Lily Kuo & Sabrina Siddiqui, *Huawei Hits Back over Trump's National Emergency on Telecoms 'Threat,'* Guardian, (May 16, 2019).

[52] *See* Lily Kuo & Julian Borger, *US Ban on Huawei a 'Cynically Timed' Blow in Escalating Trade War, Says Firm*, Guardian, (May 201, 2019).

[53] *See* Dexter Johnson, *The 5G Dilemma: More Base Stations, More Antennas—Less Energy?*, IEEE Spectrum, (Oct. 3, 2018).

[54] *Mother of Consensus*, Economist (Mar. 3, 2016).

[55] Preston Lim, *If Canada Bans Huawei, Leaders Better Have a New Plan For 5G*, The Star.com, MSN Money (Sept. 24, 2019) www.msn.com/en-ca/money/topstories/if-canada-bans-huawei-leaders-better-have-a-new-plan-for-5g/ar-AAHJEni.

[56] *See, e.g.*, Scott J. Shackelford, Timothy L. Fort, & Danuvasin Charoen, *Sustainable Cybersecurity: Applying Lessons from the Green Movement to Managing Cyber Attacks*, 2016 Univ. Ill. L. Rev. 1995; Scott J. Shackelford, *Should Cybersecurity Be a Human Right? Exploring the 'Shared Responsibility' of Cyber Peace*, 55 Stan. J. Int'l L. 155 (2019).

[57] *See* Tobias Mahler, Generic Top-Level Domains: A Study of Transnational Private Regulation 3 (Edward Elgar, 2019).

[58] For more on this topic, see Chapter 1, in Shackelford, Managing Cyber Attacks, *supra* note 37.

communication system.[59] This is done through volunteers creating, updating, and publishing protocols for the global TCP/IP network and Internet standards, which are put out by informal working groups. In other words, this voluntary group "writes the code that defines the Internet's architecture."[60] That helps explain why China generally and Huawei in particular are increasingly interested in the IETF. For example, during the 2016 meeting "Cisco sent around 100 engineers, Google 50 and Huawei, a Chinese hardware maker, about 60."[61] Clearly, the IETF community is continuing to shape a variety of standards of core interest to leading public and private sector stakeholders.

Yet, the IETF risks "turning into more of a conventional standards body" due to this increased private sector and geopolitical interest there are still some safeguards in place. For example, any stakeholder would have to take over a supermajority of the IETF in order for it to get around its rules on consensus.[62] Moreover, due to the polycentric nature of Internet governance, capturing one forum such as the IETF – however influential – is insufficient to write the rules for 5G, to say nothing of dictating our hyper-connected future.[63] Indeed, myriad bodies, including the National Institute for Standards and Technology (NIST), remain influential as seen in its NIST Cybersecurity Framework and draft Privacy Framework, along with the efforts of states like California to define "reasonable" cybersecurity for IoT products and services.[64] As such, now is the time to consider the wider questions of long-term, sustainable, governance.

IMPLICATIONS & PROSPECTS FOR CYBER PEACE

The increasingly fragmented and polycentric nature of cyberspace brings to the fore core questions that have long vexed academics, practitioners, and policymakers alike. For example, consensus – even rough consensus – has been elusive as to whether or not cyberspace is, or should be considered, a "global networked commons" to which certain Internet freedoms should attach.[65] As is evident from the foregoing discussion, cyberspace may be better understood as a pseudo commons that is comprised of a network of polycentric "clubs," each contributing to Internet governance,[66] which in turn underscores the conceptualization of cyberspace as a "club good" that is "available to some, but not all."[67] Yet depending on the preferred lens, cyberspace is so multifaceted that it may be thought of as merely an extension

---

[59] *Glossary*, ICANN, www.icann.org/en/about/learning/glossary (last visited Oct. 3, 2019).

[60] Andrew W. Murray, THE REGULATION OF CYBERSPACE: CONTROL IN THE ONLINE ENVIRONMENT 91 (Routledge-Cavendish, 2006).

[61] *Mother of Consensus, supra* note 54.

[62] *See id.* ("Rather than having governments or companies haggle over changes to networking protocols or routing services, 'rough consensus and running code' is the rule. 'Not everyone has to agree. And no votes are counted,' explains Scott Bradner... If the difference between two options is merely cosmetic, the IETF generally goes ahead with the more popular one if dissenters do not number more than about 20–30% of the total, although there is no firm rule. That proportion shrinks to 5–10% when a more fundamental choice must be made.").

[63] For a sense on the large array of IoT regulations under consideration, see Edward Wood, *It's Time To Secure The Internet of Everything: Regulations Rise as the IoT Continues to Expand*, FORBES (Sept. 30, 2019).

[64] *See id.*

[65] Hillary Rodham Clinton, U.S. Sec'y of State, Remarks on Internet Freedom (Jan. 21, 2010), www.state.gov/secretary/rm/2010/01/135519.htm (emphasizing the need for behavioral norms and respect among states to encourage the free flow of information and protect against cyber attacks).

[66] See Mark Raymond, *Puncturing the Myth of the Internet as a Commons*, GEORGETOWN J. INT'L AFF. 57, 66 (2013).

[67] Joseph S. Nye, Jr., *The Regime Complex for Managing Global Cyber Activities* 3 (Global Comm'n on Internet Governance, Paper No. 1 2014), https://dash.harvard.edu/bitstream/handle/1/12308565/Nye-GlobalCommission.pdf.

of the state, a network of private goods (such as personal devices), or a virtual infrastructure.[68] At the highest-level, cyberspace may even be considered a quasi-common pool resource (CPR) regime given that it is difficult to exclude users due to the widespread availability of Internet access, and that such use "can create consequences for linked resource systems"[69] such as in the IoT context.

With the rise of digital barriers, cyberspace is being increasingly fragmented into a series of – in the most extreme scenario – digital walled gardens, though more likely polycentric public-private clubs. Such self-organized communities have the power to set their own boundary conditions and rules in use, and are becoming increasingly active in managing an array of cybersecurity challenges ranging such as an effort to hold nation-states accountable for cyber attacks targeting civilian critical infrastructure.[70] In order to manage common global collective action challenges such as cyber attacks in such a fragmented structure, it is necessary to consider findings from the literature on polycentric governance.

As Professor Fikret Berkes has stated, "[p]olycentric and multilayered institutions improve the fit between knowledge and action" by engaging numerous sectors and stakeholders at multiple scales.[71] Yet such networks can also be "inefficient"[72] and are susceptible to institutional fragmentation and gridlock caused by overlapping authority that must still "meet standards of coherence, effectiveness, [and] . . . sustainability."[73] A key finding with resonance to more authoritarian approaches to Internet governance from this literature is that "a single governmental unit" may be incapable of dealing with "global collective action problems" like climate change in part because free riders discourage "trust and reciprocity" between stakeholders.[74]

Another factor is the capacity for spontaneous self-correction in successful polycentric systems. In the words of Professor Elinor Ostrom: "[A] political system that has multiple centers of power at differing scales provides more opportunity for citizens and their officials to innovate and to intervene so as to correct maldistributions of authority and outcomes. Thus, polycentric systems are more likely than monocentric systems to provide incentives leading to self-organized, self-corrective institutional change."[75]

One key element of polycentricity is this spontaneity, which to Professor Vincent Ostrom, meant that "patterns of organization within a polycentric system will be self-generating or self-organizing" in the sense that "individuals acting at all levels will have the incentives to create or

---

[68] For more on this topic, see SCOTT J. SHACKELFORD, GOVERNING NEW FRONTIERS IN THE INFORMATION AGE: TOWARD CYBER PEACE (Cambridge Univ. Press, 2020).

[69] Tatyana Ruseva, James Farmer, & Michael Drescher, *Extending the Design Principles for Common-Pool Resource Governance to Conservation Easements on Private Lands*, at 3–4 (Ostrom Workshop Working Paper, 2017), https://ostromworkshop.indiana.edu/pdf/seriespapers/2017fall-colloq/farmer-paper.pdf.

[70] *See* Joseph Marks, *The Cybersecurity 202: U.S. to Try New Approach to Punish Hacking Nations: Working with Allies*, WASH. POST (Mar. 7, 2019).

[71] FIKRET BERKES, COASTS FOR PEOPLE: INTERDISCIPLINARY APPROACHES TO COASTAL AND MARINE RESOURCE MANAGEMENT 129 (Routledge, 2015).

[72] *Id.*

[73] Robert O. Keohane & David G. Victor, *The Regime Complex for Climate Change*, 9 PERSP. ON POL. 7, 15 (2011) (arguing that "the structural and interest diversity inherent in contemporary world politics tends to generate the formation of a regime complex rather than a comprehensive, integrated regime.").

[74] Elinor Ostrom, *A Polycentric Approach for Coping with Climate Change* 35 (World Bank Pol'y Research, Working Paper 5095, Oct. 2009), https://papers.ssrn.com/sol3/papers.cfm?abstract_id=1494833 (defining "polycentric" as "one where many elements are capable of making mutual adjustments for ordering their relationships with one another within a general system of rules where each element acts with independence of other elements"); see Keohane & Victor, supra note 73, at 9 (discussing the feasibility of managing diverse problems within the climate change context with diverse institutions).

[75] Aligica & Tarko, *supra* note 28, at 246.

institute appropriate patterns of ordered relationships."[76] What factors are most important to engender such spontaneous self-correction, and how important is the principle of nestedness to the ability of polycentric systems to be truly self-corrective at the scale of the resource? Free entry, and the incentivized enforcement of rules, which in turn are continually revised.[77] As such, the IETF is ideally suited to play a critical organizing role in helping to bridge this fractured Internet governance landscape given that: (1) anyone can join the organization, and (2) rules (e.g., Protocols) are continually revised. Unlike ICANN, IETF has survived and thrived for more than thirty years as a grassroots product created and managed by an interested, volunteer network. True, its rules are not enforced in a traditional sense, but the consensual governance structure has led to widespread uptake regardless. However, for the IETF to play this coordinating role effectively, it is imperative for the IETF to immunize itself from being taken over further by corporate and geopolitical interests. If it can, then it could become an important part of the Internet ecosystem contributing to cyber peace, defined as a system that "respects human rights, spreads Internet access along with best practices, and strengthens governance mechanisms by fostering multi-stakeholder collaboration."[78]

CONCLUSION

Although current trends toward greater protectionism, fragmentation, and isolationism, both online and offline, seem inevitable, they are also not foreordained. All political movements, including populist sentiments fueling the current conflicts in trade, services, and data, are arguably cyclic, and the global political economic system in place since World War II has proven to be remarkably durable and self-correcting despite numerous challenges. Still, if a more fragmented future – including a Digital Cold War – were to materialize, making use of polycentric clubs and coordinating institutions such as the IETF could help to build mechanisms for communication, which are essential to building trust. After all, as Elinor Ostrom famously remarked, at the end of the day "[t]rust is the most important resource."

---

[76] *Id.*
[77] *Id.*
[78] SHACKELFORD, MANAGING CYBER ATTACKS, *supra* note 37, at xxvi.

Index

Ingram Content Group UK Ltd.
Milton Keynes UK
UKHW031233140623
423415UK00027B/480